Governing China's Population

Governing China's Population

From Leninist to Neoliberal Biopolitics

SUSAN GREENHALGH

and

EDWIN A. WINCKLER

Stanford University Press
Stanford, California
2005

Stanford University Press
Stanford, California

© 2005 by the Board of Trustees of the Leland Stanford Junior University.
All rights reserved.

No part of this book may be reproduced or transmitted in any form or by any means, electronic or mechanical, including photocopying and recording, or in any information storage or retrieval system without the prior written permission of Stanford University Press.

Printed in the United States of America on acid-free, archival-quality paper

Published with the assistance of the Open Society Institute.

Library of Congress Cataloging-in-Publication Data
Greenhalgh, Susan.
    Governing China's population : from Leninist to neoliberal biopolitics / Susan Greenhalgh and Edwin A. Winckler.
        p.   cm.
    Includes bibliographical references and index.
    ISBN 0-8047-4879-9 (cloth : alk. paper)—ISBN 0-8047-4880-2 (pbk. : alk. paper)
        1. Birth control—Government policy—China—History—20th century.
2. China—Population policy—History—20th century.   3. China—Politics and government—1949–   I. Winckler, Edwin A.   II. Title.
HQ767.5.C6G74 2005
363.9′6′0951—dc22   2005010575

Typeset by G&S Book Services in 10.5/12.5 Bembo

Original Printing 2005

Last figure below indicates year of this printing:
14   13   12   11   10   09   08   07   06   05

*In good Chinese fashion
we dedicate this book to our parents*

Contents

List of Tables

Acknowledgments

OVER THE YEARS the authors have accumulated countless debts, only a portion of which we can acknowledge here. We have benefited greatly from the generous hospitality of agencies of the Chinese government in charge of population and birth work. Winckler thanks the National Population and Family Planning Commission for endorsing his late 2003 visit (particularly Ru Xiaomei for arranging it); the China Population Information and Research Center for hosting him on that visit (particularly Yu Xuejun, then executive director, and Xie Zhenming for their exceptional helpfulness, including personally escorting him to Heilongjiang and Qinghai, respectively); and provincial, local, and community birth planning officials in both provinces for enduring long weekend visits. He thanks too the many high former PRC birth planning officials who came out of retirement to share recollections and materials with him (Li Xiuzhen, Yu Wang, Liang Jimin, Wu Jingchun, and Jiang Yiman); and many high current PRC birth planning officials for making room for him in their busy schedules (particularly vice ministers Wang Guoqiang and Zhao Baige and department heads Zhang Hanxiang, Cui Li, and Chen Li).

Greenhalgh is indebted to the CPIRC for hosting her December 2003 research trip. Special thanks go to Yu Xuejun for arranging the trip; to Xie Zhenming, Liang Jimin, Li Bohua, Zhang Mincai, and Ma Yingtong for lengthy conversations about the history of policymaking; to Zhao Yongfu and Shi Zhuo for facilitating arrangements that made this trip so productive; and to Zhu Hong and Guo Weiming for help in accessing the library's outstanding collection of materials. During that trip and another one in 1999, many current and former high officials of the SFPC—including Yu Wang, Li Honggui, Zhang Erli, Chen Shengli, and Xiao Zhenyu—provided rare personal insight into the development of the birth policy and program. Since the mid-1980s Greenhalgh has met and talked with all three heads of the State Family Planning Commission—Wang Wei, Peng Peiyun, and Zhang

Weiqing. These discussions deepened our understanding of the opportunities and constraints the project of population governance has posed for the PRC regime. We are grateful to all of these individuals for frank discussion of sensitive issues in Chinese domestic and international political relations.

Population science in various guises has been fundamental to the making of post-Mao birth policy. Greenhalgh extends deepest thanks to professional colleagues in China who over twenty years have provided unique insight into the role of Chinese social and natural science in the making of China's population policy. She learned about social science of population from, among others, Liu Zheng, Wu Cangping, Lin Fude, Zha Ruichuan, and Qiao Xiaochun (People's University of China); Zhang Zhunyuan (Peking University); Tian Xueyuan and Zheng Zhenzhen (Chinese Academy of Social Sciences); Li Jingneng and Tan Lin (Nankai University); Gui Shixun (East China Normal University); Peng Xizhe (Fudan University); and Jiang Zhenghua and Zhu Chuzhu (Xi'an Jiaotong University). She learned about a very different, natural science of population from Song Jian (formerly of the Beijing Institute of Information and Control, later Minister-in-Charge of the State Science and Technology Commission, now retired) and Yu Jing-yuan (BIIC). She is particularly indebted to to Gu Baochang (CPIRC and other organizations) and Zeng Yi (Peking and Duke Universities), who have lent generously of their time on a great many occasions; to Liang Zhong-tang (formerly of the Shanxi Provincial Academy of Sciences, now Economic Research Institute, Shanxi Provincial Government), who took days out of his work schedule to share the history of his proposal for a two-child-with-spacing policy; and to sociologist Cai Wenmei (Peking University), whose descriptions over many years of the human costs of the one-child policy borne by rural women and girls made a profound impression

The Population Research Institute of Xi'an Jiaotaong University served as host and collaborator for Greenhalgh's 1988 and 1993 field research in rural Shaanxi. She is indebted to its then-director and deputy director, Jiang Zhenghua and Zhu Chuzhu, for making these productive collaborations possible; to Li Nan for many wonderful experiences in the field; to Li Shu-zhuo for discussions in later years; and to all those at the Institute who made her stay so enjoyable and productive. Winckler extends personal thanks to Zhu Chuzhu and Jiang Zhenghua for their hospitality when he visited the university in 1988 and for arranging site visits to Xianyang, Shaanxi and Huizhou, Anhui on that trip.

To the other PRC officials, specialists, and Chinese people who have given so generously of their hospitality, experiences, and insights during these trips and exchanges we extend deep thanks.

The authors gained extraordinary insight into the dynamics of policymaking in the late 1980s to early 1990s when they visited China in 1993 as part of a high-level mission of the United Nations Population Fund. The authors thank the Fund (particularly the formidable Nafis Sadik and the indomitable Sterling Scruggs) for including them on the mission; many Chinese officials and demographers for high-level discussions on that trip; and Peng Xizhe for arranging site visits to Taicang, Jiangsu and Fengyang, Anhui on that trip. UNFPA officials have provided important insights into Chinese population politics at other times as well. The authors are grateful to Prod Laquian who headed the UNFPA China program in the mid- to late 1980s, and Siri Tellier, who heads it today, for extended discussions of many matters of policy and politics. We have also benefited greatly from frank discussions with a succession of program officials at the Ford Foundation's Beijing office—Mary Ann Burriss, Joan Kaufman, and Eve Wen-Jing Lee.

Greenhalgh's interest in Chinese population affairs was greatly stimulated and shaped by conversations with colleagues at the New York-based Population Council, where she worked as research associate from 1984 to 1994. She extends the deepest personal thanks to Paul Demeny, for his enduring support of her many, sometimes unorthodox projects in China; to Geoffrey McNicoll and John Bongaarts for discussions of demography and other subjects; to Ethel Churchill for advice of many kinds; to Geoge Zeidenstein, for his general support of her work in China; and to many other colleagues in the Center for Policy Studies, Research Division, and International Projects Division for conversations about China's place in the population world.

Winckler learned much about the dynamics of reform in the 1990s and early 2000s from top PRC birth planning officials who participated in the 1998–2002 Advanced Leadership Program. We thank the Center for Health and Social Policy and Public Media Center for inviting both of us to participate in those exciting workshops. Special thanks go to Axel Mundigo for the initial invitation, Steve Isaacs and Elizabeth Dawson for the arrangements, and Herb Gunther for later support.

The Resource Information Center of the U.S. Immigration and Naturalization Service funded the project that originally inspired this book. Discussions with INS officers dealing with Chinese applicants for asylum due to persecution under the one-child policy enhanced our understanding of the human costs of that policy and of the way China's policies have played out in U.S. politics. We are grateful to the INS for these opportunities.

American colleagues have given generously of their time. Particular thanks go to G. William Skinner and David Bachman for very helpful reviews of the book manuscript, as well as for valuable exchanges over the years; and to Joan Kaufman (now Visiting Scholar, East Asia Legal Studies Program, Harvard University) for discussions over many years, especially of the reproductive health aspects of China's birth program. Greenhalgh is indebted to colleagues at the University of California, Irvine, for reading various chapters in draft (Tom Boellstorff, Bill Maurer, Mei Zhan) and for conversations about contemporary Chinese social and political developments (Dorie Solinger, Wang Feng). Winckler thanks colleagues in New York, particularly members of the Weatherhead East Asian Institute of Columbia University, and Paul Demeny and Judith Bruce at The Population Council; and in Washington D.C., particularly the Congressional-Executive Commission on China, and the U.S. Department of State. The reactions of colleagues to presentations given at Columbia University's Modern China Seminar; Harvard University's Fairbank Center for East Asian Research; the Harvard Center for Population and Development Studies; Duke University's Chinese Studies Center; Brown University's Anthropology Department; the University of California, Berkeley's Departments of Anthropology and Demography; the University of Washington's Chinese Studies Center; the Australian National University's Chinese Studies Center, and other centers have helped us sharpen our arguments. Winckler acknowledges, with gratitude, the assistance of librarians at Columbia, Princeton, Cornell, and Colgate Universities.

This project was generously supported by the Open Society Institute of New York. An Individual Project Fellowship from the OSI funded Greenhalgh's work, while a 2003 Soros Fellowship (from the OSI and Columbia University's Mailman School of Public Health) supported Winckler's research and writing. The OSI also provided a publishing grant for the book. Winckler thanks Ellen Chesler at the Institute, Wendy Chavkin at Mailman, and his fellow Fellows for instructive discussions during that project. Greenhalgh's 2003 research trip to Beijing was made possible by a grant from the Science and Technology Studies Program of the National Science Foundation (#217508). Without the generous support of these organizations, this book could not have been written.

Finally, we acknowledge, with gratitude, the support of Muriel Bell, Senior Editor at Stanford University Press, who accepted the manuscript and guided it through all stages of the publication process.

Laguna Beach, CA
Georgetown, NY
April 2005

Governing China's Population

CHAPTER 1

Introduction: Population as Politics

THE LAST FEW CENTURIES have seen a growing preoccupation with human life—individuals and populations as biological entities—among governing authorities and mass publics everywhere in the world. The administration of collective human life, health, and welfare has become a key objective of modern states. Some projects have been life-enhancing, such as the global extension of public health measures and incipient efforts to manage relationships between population, environment, and resources. Others have been life-threatening, such as racist cleansing of ethnic populations and socialist collectivization of peasantries. In the early twenty-first century the world seems to be entering a new phase of vital politics in which rationalized interventions in human life are taking new forms and gaining added significance. The proliferation of new biosciences and biotechnologies, the emergence of novel forms of biological citizenship and biocapital, and bioethical controversies over interventions at the beginning and end of life, and, indeed, what counts as life and death, all exemplify the growing importance of the biological in political life.

The case of population management in the People's Republic of China merits particular attention—and not only because of the gargantuan size of the PRC's population, now over 1.3 billion. China is important also because the PRC's interventions in human life are so broad and deep, and because the shifts in its population politics are so big, so weighty—and so little understood. Since the founding of the PRC in 1949, population has become a central object of power in China. Concern about governing population processes originated in the PRC regime but soon spread throughout Chinese society. Those concerns focused initially on the location of the population (keeping rural people out of cities), but gradually grew to embrace its quantity (slowing growth and limiting size) and its "quality" (enhancing not only health and education but also social morality and political commitment). Meanwhile, the PRC's intervention in reproduction became an object of international consternation and a contentious issue in the PRC's relations with the rest of the world. Over the last half century population has become an ever-expanding domain of Chinese politics.

Preoccupation with Population

All of the PRC's main leaders have regarded the size and "backwardness" of China's population as the fundamental point of departure for development strategy. Under Mao Zedong, a large but "poor and blank" population appeared sometimes an asset and sometimes a liability. Regime intervention remained tentative and intermittent, but the goal of slowing population growth gradually rose on the political agenda. Under Deng Xiaoping, the large size and low quality of China's population loomed unequivocally as a serious obstacle to China's modernization. Post-Mao leaders gave limiting reproduction a central and urgent place in China's new program of national reform and global ascent. Under Jiang Zemin, policy first persevered at limiting population quantity and then, on the premise of maintaining low fertility, shifted toward raising population quality. By the Hu Jintao era of the early 2000s, the PRC is using its newly redefined population-and-reproduction policy domain to address long-neglected social problems of gender imbalance, old-age security, and rural-urban distribution, problems that strict birth limits had greatly aggravated. In partial recompense, in the Hu era "population policy" has come close to meaning "social policy." Limiting the number, raising the quality, and optimizing the location of China's population have become central objects of Chinese statecraft.

During these same decades, population at the aggregate level and reproduction at the individual level have also become major concerns of Chinese society. Ordinary Chinese have long viewed their country as a place of vast territory and abundant people (*difang da, renkou duo*). Under the PRC, these understandings have taken on fresh meanings and significances. As the PRC began first to modernize and then to globalize, enmeshing both regime and society in transnational processes, China's people have become increasingly preoccupied with producing world-class persons: good scientific mothers, exemplary single children, and globally competitive workers. Animating these new concerns has been a dizzying array of developments around "population." The years since Mao's death have brought the proliferation of demographic discourses, the multiplication of population institutions, the commodification of childrearing, and the intensification of interventions designed to "govern" population by an ever-expanding range of actors, from state bureaucracies to professional institutions, capitalist corporations, and the public at large. Over time, couples have come to limit their childbearing ever more stringently and invest in childrearing ever more heavily. Since the 1990s, political tensions between regime and society have eased, as popular fertility culture has begun to converge with state birth propaganda and state programs have begun to respond to emerging popular demands for better and better-delivered reproductive health care.

During these same decades, China has experienced one of the fastest fertility declines in recorded history. During the 1970s, the number of children per woman dropped from just under 6 to just under 3. In the 1980s, fertility hovered somewhat above the "replacement level" of about 2.1 children per woman. By the 2000s, according to the best recent studies, fertility appears to have fallen further to around 1.6. In the last quarter century, individual and societal reproduction has been "modernized" and China has achieved much of the "great power" population structure to which it has long aspired. Internationally, the PRC has been both acclaimed for its responsible slowing of population growth and denounced for its repression of reproductive rights. Despite these apparent certainties, the relationship between state population policy and social-demographic change remains unclear. Given the close connections between a locality's program strength and socioeconomic development, it is impossible to estimate with any precision the relative contributions to fertility decline of program and development. A back-of-the-envelope calculation suggests perhaps an equal influence in the 1970s and 1980s and a decline in the program's influence in the 1990s and 2000s. Within the birth program's contribution, it is even more difficult to distinguish between the impact of the conventional components—educating the public, providing contraceptives—and the coercive components that distinguished the PRC's approach to slowing population growth from those of other developing countries. As discussed in the Conclusion, these uncertainties greatly complicate assessments of the program's contribution to China's spectacular economic and social development of recent decades.

Govermentalization of Population

Western scholarship has reported much about the demographic change accompanying the PRC's rapid development and institutionalization of population policy, but little about the political dynamics animating it or about the place of population in the regime's larger agendas of rebuilding the economy and securing its own power. Equally obscure are the political effects of this buildup of governmental thought and institutions around population on the PRC regime, on the Chinese people, and on China's place in the world. Consideration of these political effects poses the still broader yet unasked question of the nature and transformations of the power brought to bear on population within this rising actor on the world stage. For several reasons—including a division of labor between scholarly disciplines that assigns population to demography and a division of opinion that makes Chinese population policy controversial both in China and abroad—population remains a relatively uncharted domain of state policy and political life in China.

This book argues that the PRC's population project has become central to post-Mao politics and power in ways that have not been appreciated. A productive perspective for connecting population to power centers on the notion of "governmentalization." This perspective was first developed by the French philosopher and social critic Michel Foucault as a way to extend the notion of governance beyond solely state-centered processes (1991, 102–103). The governmentality approach has since been developed by others and applied to a variety of areas, including statistics and the social, insurance and risk, health and medicine, crime and penology (e.g., Dreyfus and Rabinow 1982; Rose 1999, Dean 1999; Ong and Collier 2005). This book applies these constructs to population, as Foucault himself started to do.

We argue that the PRC's population project has been a striking case of governmentalization, in the extended sense delineated by Foucault. His schema involves three sets of dynamics. First, governmentalization of population includes intervention by "government" in the conventional sense. Early modern states attempted to manage social processes quite directly, and communism continued that tradition in the Soviet Union and China. This is the first, overwhelmingly Leninist, half of the story of PRC birth planning, which by the Deng era applied Soviet techniques for the state planning of economic growth to the state planning of population growth. However, governmentalization also includes two other dynamics: the disciplining of conduct by nonstate social institutions and the cultivation by individuals themselves of the capacity to regulate their own behavior. Later modern states found it impossible to manage on their own the vast range of problems and processes that population involved. A more economical strategy for the state was to retreat to the role of orchestrating interventions by a variety of forces, including by the state itself, but only when absolutely necessary. That was the core of nineteenth-century liberalism, and it is the core of the neoliberalism that, by the turn of the millennium, had become the globally dominant paradigm for effective governance. This is the second, increasingly neoliberal, half of the story of PRC birth planning. During the Jiang era the program began facing up to the appalling "side costs" (*daijia*) of enforcing strict birth limits and began reforming PRC birth planning in an increasingly neoliberal direction. (These terms are defined later in this chapter.)

In this book, governmentalization serves not only as the central construct guiding our analysis but also as the master historical process informing our narrative of the Chinese population case. The governmentalization analytic helps illuminate the trajectory of the past, the nature of the present, and even the options for the future. Foucault's method was to first identify important features of the present, and then mine the past to discover how they developed. The result was a "history of the present." This book is also concerned to diagnose the prospects for the future, viewed from the middle of the first decade of the twenty-first century ("the early 2000s"). The book charts the trajectory of the PRC's antinatalist population project since its origins in the mid-1950s. The only slow rise of "soft" birth control during the Mao era precipitated the very rapid rise of "hard" birth planning during the Deng era, which in turn provoked the gradually deepening reforms of the Jiang era. This policy evolution defined the problems and opportunities left to the Hu era. We dig into the historical record to identify the enduring features of population politics, tracing how they arose, how they took shape, and how they have been transformed. Happily, many of these developments point the way to a future that will be notably different from the past. In particular, the reforms in the birth program that PRC leaders launched between the mid-1990s and mid-2000s are very promising but remain little reported.

We view governmentalization through two sets of lenses, one analytical, the other practical. The analytical lenses are the authors' own complementary disciplinary approaches, which we tag as "regime capacity" and "biopower." The practical lenses are the alternative approaches to governance that PRC leaders themselves have adopted, which we tag most broadly as Maoism, Stalinism, and Reformism. We briefly introduce these lenses in this chapter and then elaborate them in the next (the Problematique).

Regime Capacity and Biopower: An Experiment in Interdisciplinarity

This book's analytical approaches to studying governmentalization pair the perspective of a political scientist viewing policymaking within the state, with the perspective of an anthropologist witnessing the consequences emerging within society. Our subject—the governance of population in a country of more than one billion people in the midst of a momentous transition from socialism—is one of those domains of modern life that is so big, so complex, and so protean that no single approach can do it justice. The social facts we seek to illuminate demand new methods and new approaches that stretch across conventional disciplinary, methodological, and theoretical divides. Today, interdisciplinary work in the social sciences usually joins fields whose intellectual premises are quite similar. Political science's borrowings from economics and the convergence of anthropology and history are prime examples. In this study we develop a new type of interdisciplinarity. We offer this not as a finished product but as a methodological and theoretical experiment that we hope others working on similarly complex modern issues, in China and elsewhere, might find stimulating. One disciplinary approach employed is the historical and rational institutionalism of political science, summarized through "regime capacity." The other disciplinary approach is the broadly Foucauldian social constructivism of anthropology and women's studies, summarized through "biopower." These are quite different approaches to modern power and politics and many might regard them as incompatible. They do contrast—not only rationalist versus constructivist but also state-centric versus sociocentric and empirical-explanatory versus discursive-critical. Yet remarkably, these two approaches converge on finding the same development—governmentalization—intriguing and important.

The problematique of *regime capacity* emerges from the political science literature on state capacity (e.g., Jackman 1993, later developments summarized and critiqued by Fukuyama 2004). In this book, "regime" signals the multipillared nature of the PRC state—not only the government but also party and military—and its intrusive extension into society. The regime capacity approach focuses on how the PRC regime came to grips with a new domain of governance, framed the problem in relation to other problems, and created institutions to solve the problem. The problematique of *biopower* emerges from the investigation Foucault sketched out of how, historically in the West, "population" arose as a central domain of modern power, creating a new *biopolitics* around the administration and optimization of the processes of life. The resulting biopower entailed the increased ordering of human life itself in the name of improving the life, health, and welfare of the individual and population (Foucault 1978). This approach directs attention to the PRC's biopolitical achievement—the emergence in a few short decades of a large edifice of discursive, bureaucratic, legal, and other forms of power around the issue of population, and the resultant increased organization of human life. These approaches differ in their evaluation of the emergence of modern population governance. The regime capacity approach, which was developed mainly to remedy "state failure" in Africa and elsewhere, accepts the elaboration of modern techniques of governance as essential to the running of complex societies. The biopower perspective, which was developed mainly as a critique of liberal governance, takes a critical stance toward the consequences of modern power, seeing the effects not as necessarily and categorically pernicious, but as ambiguous, problematic, and in various ways dangerous.

Despite their dissimilarities, these two approaches do converge in some important respects. The point of departure for both is an insistence on not taking for granted the existence of the elements of governance, whether institutions and policies or discourses and practices. Instead, both approaches seek to account for these elements, either by explaining them in rational-strategic terms or by tracing their emergence in cultural-historical terms. Also, the two approaches highlight many of the same analytical elements, such as monitoring/surveillance and sanctions/punishment, and their patterning into distinctive institutions for regulation/discipline. Elements of the two approaches can also be combined in the analysis of specific issues. For example, in this book, the positing of policy "tendencies" (explained in Chapter 2) draws both on social-scientific repertoires of social "mechanisms" and on discursive-critical attention to the language in which policy is conceived. To the extent that the political science approach in this book is an example of historical institutionalism, it is also sociocultural and macrohistorical, like the discursive-critical approaches of anthropology. For its part, the critical approach features some "rational actors," particularly Chinese families who, following the logics of the peasant family economy and the market, make hard-edged calculations concerning the birth and disposal of different children. The two approaches thus align rather well, complementing and enriching one another. When used together, they speak across what are usually wide disciplinary divides and expand the terrain of the political in new and, we think, provocative ways.

Bringing these two analytic approaches together offers important advantages. Because each illuminates different parts of a sprawling and complex political reality, using them together enables us to see more of Chinese population politics, and from more angles, than has been possible before. The result is an account much more inclusive than anything now available. This broadened perspective also allows us to use the case of population and reproductive politics to probe some central questions in the study of contemporary China and of communism and modernity more generally. We outline these issues at the end of this chapter and elaborate them in the book's Conclusion.

Alternatives within Chinese Leninism: Maoism, Stalinism, and Reformism

The practical approaches to governing population are what we call alternative versions of the Leninist project in China. In the course of its rule, the Chinese Communist Party (CCP) has drawn on several different approaches to governance that it has applied to most policy domains, including birth planning (Solinger ed. 1984). As used here, "approaches" refers mainly not to the goals pursued but to the methods employed—to the kinds of "policy instruments" or "institutional capacity" that a regime selects, builds, and uses. In these terms, the CCP's approach has always been Leninist in the broad sense of relying on strong leadership by an organized party which claims that its "scientific" ideology "democratically" represents the most progressive forces in society and shows in what direction the country should go. However, the CCP has experimented with a spectrum of variants within Leninism, ranging from left through center to right. On the left is the CCP's own largely indigenous approach, commonly referred to in China studies as Maoism. This was a lean-and-mean "revolutionary" Leninism for guerilla warfare before 1949, coordinating dispersed forces through ideological agreement and a minimum of bureaucracy. In the center is the approach that, after 1949, the CCP borrowed from the Soviet Union, commonly referred to in Soviet studies as Stalinism. The aspect of Stalinism emphasized in this book is its rather ponderous "developmental" Leninism, coordinating a centrally planned socialist construction through an elaborate technocratic bureaucracy. On the right is what post-Mao leaders themselves have referred to as Reformism—an "adaptive" Leninism that attempts to correct problems in both Maoism and Stalinism by borrowing from "advanced Western experience" so that China might become internationally competitive, both economically and militarily.

In these very broad terms, during the Mao era (roughly the mid-1950s to the mid-1970s), the CCP's basic approach to all policy domains was mainly a varying combination of Stalinism and Maoism, but the CCP applied that approach to birth control only tentatively and intermittently (Chapter 3). During the Deng era (roughly the late 1970s through the early 1990s), the CCP finally got around to applying this approach to birth planning (Chapter 4). Meanwhile the Deng era's approach to most other policy domains became Reformism. However, senior Deng era leaders did not allow much Reform of Stalinist-Maoist birth planning, which after all was still under construction at that time. Thus the Deng era represented the height of *Leninist* biopolitics— a politics of the administration of life by predominantly bureaucratic and mobilizational means. It was only in the Jiang era (roughly 1993–2003) that CCP leaders gradually began a progressively deepening Reform of birth planning (Chapter 5). Until about 2000 that Reform consisted mostly of getting rid of the outmoded part of the Maoist legacy (periodic crash campaigns) and completing the construction of the Stalinist approach (continuous professional work). Meanwhile, in most other policy domains, the Jiang era had gradually discarded some outmoded parts of the Stalinist legacy, in particular transferring the coordination of most economic activity from central planning to market mechanisms. Jiang era leaders were adamant that management of population growth must remain a government function. However, from around 2000 they did begin changing the form of government management from directly planning couples' reproduction to indirectly regulating it through law. The Hu era (2003 –) has continued that basic approach, though with some very significant modifications in terms of both method (less coercion, more rewards) and objective (more social policies to guarantee people's economic security).

This book argues that the Hu era has continued to shift the PRC's basic approach toward neoliberalism, which is now the globally dominant approach to governance (Chapter 6). Neoliberalism recognizes the need for government to regulate social activities. However, it requires that intervention be grounded in full understanding of the complexity and autonomy of subsystems of society, such as the economy or population. Intervention should then be as limited and indirect as possible, in the mode of central banks adjusting interest rates to regulate complex economies. The analogy in PRC birth planning would be reducing regime intervention to mild disincentives and strong incentives for complying with birth limits, which the Hu era has set out to do. A neoliberal regime works strenuously to transfer as many responsibilities as possible to communities, families, and individuals. It does so in part by constructing "neoliberal subjects" capable of governing themselves in ways deemed appropriate by the regime. Instead of underwriting extensive entitlements to government welfare payments, as socialism would do, neoliberalism regulates insurance schemes through which supposedly autonomous social actors can provide for themselves. In the Hu era, PRC social policy—including population policy—combines socialist and neoliberal approaches. Thus the Hu era has brought about a profound if partial shift from Leninist to *neoliberal* biopolitics—a politics of the administration of life by increasingly market-oriented means. The current question is: How far can the CCP carry the neoliberal approach, both in general and in population policy in particular? How far will political and practical limits allow the PRC to develop a "neoliberalism with Chinese characteristics"? Can the CCP develop a neoliberal approach within a spectrum of Leninist possibilities, extending the spectrum still further to the right? Or will the PRC adopt enough neoliberalism to carry China's transition from communism beyond Leninism to something else? It is too early to answer these questions, but it is high time to use dramatic developments in PRC population policy to explore them.

Diverse Sources

This book culminates many years of research and engagement with China's population affairs on the part of both authors, but particularly Greenhalgh.

The study is a product of a series of unique research opportunities spanning twenty years. Between 1984 and 1994 Greenhalgh served as analyst of China's population policy for the New York-based Population Council, a leading international scientific organization in the population field. The personal contacts formed during that decade have given the authors exceptional access to many of the central players in China's population policy establishment. In 1993 both authors were asked to participate in a high-level United Nations mission to China to explore charges of coercion in the birth program. During 1998–2002, both authors were invited to lecture in an Advanced Leadership Program that brought six groups of two dozen top Chinese birth program officials to the United States to learn of new thinking in the international population community. The actors we interviewed, and in some cases ethnographically observed, include individuals situated at virtually every key node in China's birth project below the national political leadership: top policymakers at the national birth planning commission, central- and provincial-level birth planning officials, the state's scientific advisors, community implementors, and the program's individual targets (now "clients"). Both authors had the extraordinary opportunity to carry a draft of this book to Beijing in late 2003 and to query key participants in our story on questions of fact and interpretation. These contacts have also placed in the authors' hands unusually complete documentation on the origins and development of China's birth project within the leading bodies of the regime itself. Drawing on this variety of personal experiences and written materials, only a fraction of which we can cite, we have attempted to convey the perspectives and voices of the Chinese who have been engaged in this giant project of social engineering in different ways—as policymakers and implementors, propagandists and critics, compliers and resisters.

Part 1, on policy formulation and implementation, takes the perspective of actors within the state. Written by Winckler, a political scientist, these chapters are based on his close reading and analysis of the state's own record of what it has done, as reflected in speeches, policy documents, and official reports selected for their importance by the birth program itself. Winckler's analysis of these materials is informed by a decade of research on the program, including field trips to China in 1993 and 2003 that involved visits to field sites in Shanghai, Jiangsu, Anhui, and Shaanxi (in 1993) and Heilongjiang and Qinghai (in 2003). His analysis also draws on extensive interviews with top Chinese birth planning officials who visited the United States between 1998 and 2002, updated by interviews in China in late 2003. These officials, who occupy key positions in national and provincial birth planning organizations, are the very people now formulating and implementing the reforms reported here, the people to whom PRC leaders have entrusted the future of the program.

Part 2, on the social and political consequences of the birth project, views developments in good part from the vantage point of cadres and ordinary people at the level of the rural village and urban enterprise trying to cope with the ambitious project the state has assigned them. Written by Greenhalgh, an anthropologist, the chapters in Part 2 are based on a broad review and synthesis of anthropological and other literatures on contemporary China, press accounts of China's population affairs, and, most important, her own research in and on China over twenty years. That research included two periods of ethnographic fieldwork in three Shaanxi villages (1988 and 1993) and extensive interviews with national-level population policymakers and their scientific advisors (especially in 1986, 1987, 1989, 1993, 1999, and 2003). The fieldwork also involved visits to sites in Guangdong and Hebei (in 1985), as well as Shanghai, Jiangsu, Anhui, and Shaanxi (in 1993). Since the mid-1980s, Greenhalgh has also been actively engaged with some of China's population specialists, especially those concerned about the social costs of the one-child policy.

PRC birth program officials have displayed an admirable commitment to leaving as complete a record of program history as possible, particularly recently, by declassifying as many historical materials as is politically possible. The authors have been impressed by the willingness—even eagerness—of most program officials to assist foreign scholars in compiling a record that outsiders can regard as complete and accurate. The program sources we use are not only the program's own record of *how* it has been run but also the documents *from which* it has been run. They are not, by and large, materials concocted mainly for domestic or international political consumption. There has been no "second set of books" available for coordinating the program's hundreds of thousands of operatives—though, of course, the written record has always been supplemented in practice by superiors' oral instructions and subordinates' interpretations of what leaders wanted.

Despite the considerable candor shown by our hosts and their histories, we maintain a reflexive attitude toward our texts, keeping in mind how they have been constructed, for what ends, and with what effects. As many students of Chinese politics have noted, wordsmithing is a fundamental technique of PRC statecraft (e.g., Schoenhals 1992). It has been crucial in the population domain. The 1,500-page *Encyclopedia of Birth Planning*, the program's main compilation of documents and our single most important source on policymaking, illustrates the range of purposes for which such compendia have been assembled. This 1997 compilation appears to have had several purposes, with contradictory consequences for reliability. Arguably the most general purpose was to document regime authorizations for the existence and autonomy of the program, which have periodically come under threat from government downsizings and mergers of ministries. For this purpose the *Encyclopedia*, like other program compendia, scours leaders' speeches and official documents for any remarks relevant to the program, often tearing those remarks out of their original contexts and inflating their importance, particularly for the Mao era. Undoubtedly another purpose was to demonstrate to national political leaders that the program had paid meticulous attention to their instructions and had done a good job of following them, with good results. That intention is reflected in the exasperating (but telling) arrangement of the materials in the *Encyclopedia* according to the order of official precedence of PRC leaders and institutions. Certainly a third purpose was to provide a complete, detailed, and accurate record of the instructions and regulations governing the program, as an important part of improving its efficiency and efficacy through institutionalization.

We use contemporary materials, such as the *Encyclopedia*, to understand the past with full awareness of the methodological problems involved. In China, as elsewhere, history has been constantly rewritten in response to changing circumstances. Having ourselves lived through the historical transformations from the tough-talking Deng era to the soft-speaking Hu era, we are keenly aware of how Chinese stories about Chinese population policy have changed with the times. Our experience with these materials suggests that who writes the history makes a big difference. Program histories crafted by hardliners and softliners emphasize different past events and reach different conclusions about issues such as the necessity of retaining versus abandoning the one-child policy. Recent softer accounts foreground earlier attempts at reform that hardliners had frustrated and that earlier harder accounts had downplayed. To get outside these stories, we read *across* texts, comparing the different facts marshalled and interpretations offered by different authors. We also read *against* our texts, trying to understand what part of the historical record is being suppressed for what purpose.

This reflexive approach to our materials extends to the journalistic items used in Part 2. Clearly the stories Western journalists have told about China's population policy have been crafted to fit larger Western narratives about China. Similarly, the individual cases they have presented as emblematic were selected to fit those stories (cf. Madsen 1995; Weston and Jensen eds. 2000). Thus, in the mid-1980s, the dominant news story in the West was of a coercive totalitarian regime, the cases of journalistic interest those of individuals suffering from the brutal enforcement of the one-child policy. In the late

1990s and early 2000s, the story has been of a modernizing, increasingly capitalist China, the cases of interest "quality" single children with consumerist tastes and global aspirations. In Part 2, we mine the Western news items for both types of cases—suffering villagers and spoiled city singletons—in full awareness of the changing narrative context that drew journalists' attention to them at different times.

Faced with length limits, we have tried to economize on the length of citations while still meeting the needs of both specialists and general readers. In order to provide a fresh view, Part 1 was written directly from primary sources. In-text citations to chronologies take the form "(ME 570227),"providing the reader with the exact date of occurrence and referring to the entry under that date in one or another of several main chronologies. Whenever possible the reference is to the most up-to-date and readily available chronology (*Main Events*, abbreviated ME, in the references as Yang, Liang, and Zhang 2001). Citations to documents also concentrate on the few most complete collections, taking the in-text form "(EBP, 22–23)." Whenever possible the reference is to the program's most recent, most authoritative, and most widely available 1997 compilation, *Encyclopedia of Birth Planning* (abbreviated as EBP). Space constraints have dictated not providing long Chinese titles and their English translations. Instead, we have specified each document's nature in the text, enabling specialists to consult the source cited. In both parts, authors' interviews are cited in the form "(SG 25Dec03 BJ)," with the last two letters indicating the place where the interview was held (BJ for Beijing). Most interviewees are left anonymous because of the sensitivity of our subject and the potential dangers some informants might face were their identities made known. However, in some cases we do identify informants: where clearly they would be happy to be identified, where they would run no risks as a result, and where the source was particularly authoritative. In those cases the informant's initials are added after the place of interview and the initials are explained in the table of abbreviations at the end of the book. In citations to chronologies and interviews, omission of the day or month in the date reflects the lack of temporal specificity of the event or source.

In Part 1, on birth planning itself, citations to secondary sources do not so much specify sources of information as indicate the main previous contributions, so that general readers can find more on the topic in English. However, the secondary literature does provide the basis for the summaries of political context, albeit reformulated into the policy tendencies framework employed in this book. Part 2 follows standard citation practices.

A Look Ahead

This introductory chapter has stated some main themes, enough to enable readers to proceed directly to the body of the book if they wish. Chapter 2, the Problematique, provides a fuller statement of the concepts used in this book, a statement to which some readers may wish to return only as they feel the need to do so. The body of the book consists of two main parts connected by a bridge chapter. A Conclusion returns to the main themes and briefly outlines the implications of our research for U.S. policy.

Chapter 2, the Problematique, lays out key concepts that are crucial to understanding the analysis that follows. A first section elaborates on our central analytic theme, governmentalization, and the two perspectives (regime capacity and biopower) through which we approach it. A second section elaborates three variants of the broad Chinese-Leninist project of which PRC birth policy is a part, explicating Maoism as Revolutionary Mobilization, Stalinism as Bureaucratic Professionalism, and Reformism as Socialist Marketization. Analysis of the changing mix of Leninist approaches will be central to our discussion of population policy in Part 1. These approaches provide the larger political context within which birth policy evolved, as well as the specific mechanisms or instruments for use in birth policy implementation—most broadly, mobilization, bureaucracy, and markets. A third section stipulates three dimensions of population that structure PRC population policy: location, quantity, and quality. Each of these is important in itself, but together the three dimensions define distinctive population policy regimes.

Part 1 on policy represents a view "from the top" of the regime's governing apparatus. It traces PRC policies toward reproduction and population since the founding of the regime in 1949, embedding the many shifts in China's population policies into the changing political and social imperatives of the PRC regime. The part's introduction notes the actors involved in the policy process, and outlines the guiding and operational components of Chinese birth policy. The terms introduced here inform the analysis throughout the book; so we urge readers to peruse the introduction to Part 1 before turning to the individual chapters. Chapter 3 traces the erratic ascent of advocacy of "soft" birth control during the Mao era from the mid-1950s to the mid-1970s. Chapter 4 takes a fresh look at the best-known period of China's birth planning history, the Deng era of "hard" birth limitation from the late 1970s to the early 1990s. As PRC leaders aggressively pursued their goal of modernizing China by century's end, the PRC became infamous for its heavy-handed enforcement of the one-child policy. That effort went through successive phases of advance, consolidation, and re-enforcement. Chapter 5 documents the successively deepening reforms of hard birth planning launched during the Jiang era from the mid-1990s through the early 2000s. In an era of sweeping social and economic change, the PRC has done its best to gain popular support for birth planning, effecting reforms that have been increasingly far-reaching yet are still little known outside China. This effort produced first state-centric administrative rationalization, then some movement toward client-oriented deregulation and, finally, Comprehensive Reform.

Chapter 6 serves as a bridge between Part 1 and Part 2. It describes Comprehensive Reform, the general framework for many specific changes in the program to be made in the first decade of the twenty-first century and beyond. More analytically, this chapter uses Comprehensive Reform to illustrate an epochal shift that the whole PRC regime is attempting, toward some form of neoliberalism. Finally, as it sketches the several levels within Comprehensive Reform, this "pivot" chapter carries the reader down from the national level of Part 1 to the community level of Part 2.

Part 2 maps the view "from the bottom" of the state apparatus to report social reactions and effects, then switches to a view "from outside" to make more comprehensive assessments. This part focuses on the post-Mao era, when the governmentalization of population proceeded apace. The introduction to this part maps out its analytic terrain and highlights three cultural logics—culture as lived practice, as discourse, and as (bio) ethics—that, together with scientific and market logics, help make sense of the surprisingly broad effects of China's population policy. Chapter 7 analyzes the politics of enforcement at the community level in urban and rural settings. It documents a transformation from Leninist to more neoliberal biopolitics that has involved shifts from quantity to quality, from state regulation to self-regulation, and from concentration of power in the state to its dispersal to other actors. Chapter 8 explains how the birth program inadvertently produced vast social suffering and some little known positive effects. In the process, it restratified Chinese society along reproductive lines, reinforcing old inequalities between urban and rural, male and female, while introducing new inequalities based on categories in the birth program itself. Chapter 9 explores the effects of post-Mao population policy on Chinese politics writ large: strengthening the socialist party-state, remaking state-society relations, and reestablishing China's global position in complex and contradictory ways. Overall, analytically, this part explores how in the reform era the rapid development of population science and scientism—the exaggerated belief in the efficacy of science—worked to redefine the state's population project and reorganize relations between state and society, producing effects never imagined by China's policymakers.

Chapter 10, the Conclusion, uses our application of the governmentalization perspective to Chinese population politics to explore some wider questions about Leninism and modernity. One is whether Leninism in China has been a success or a failure. During the twentieth century the Leninist project undertaken throughout the communist world was meant to revolutionize society in a broadly socialist direction under the strong leadership of a Leninist party guided by Marxist-Leninist ideology. In China, post-Mao reforms have peeled away Maoist and Stalinist layers, revealing the PRC's persisting "late Leninism," which now must come to terms with global neoliberalism. When communism fell in the former Soviet Union and Eastern Europe, influential Western analysts pronounced Leninism a "grand failure" and a great tragedy (Brzezinski 1989; Malia 1994). PRC leaders' decision to engineer a gradual transition from communism suggests that it was largely a failure in China as well. This book's close study of birth planning—a large-scale Leninist project launched in the midst of reforms dismantling Leninism—provides insight into these big questions and large processes.

A second broad question concerns the nature of Chinese modernity. When China's leaders launched marketizing reforms in the late 1970s, they sought to restore China's historic greatness by rapidly transforming a poor backward society into a modern nation and global power based on the principles of science and democracy. Motivated by these same goals, the post-Mao birth planning project invites us to ask what kind of modernity China's leaders have made and whether—or rather, how—the promises of "science" and "democracy" have been fulfilled. Finally, the critical literature on modern power suggests that in Western Europe the modern political era brought the emergence of biopower—the increasing power over and ordering of the production and cultivation of life itself—as a central domain of modern power, a domain that increasingly eluded the grasp of the state. The study of post-1949 Chinese population politics provides an opportunity for us to trace the evolution of this power over life in a very different setting, asking how Chinese biopower developed, what it produced, and how the particular configuration of state, disciplinary, and market power that emerged in China differed from the configurations of power seen in the West.

A Statistical Overview

There are many studies of China's demography, but clearly this book is not one of them. As students of population politics, we are keenly interested in the numbers, but not for what they reveal about population dynamics. Instead, we mine the numbers for insights into the underlying politics of population policy, as well as for evidence of the policies' intended and unintended effects. Accordingly, tables are used sparingly. There is one table that deserves special note, however. Table 1 provides an overview of trends in population size, growth, and fertility over the first 53 years of the PRC. In reading the chapters, especially those on the history of population policy, the reader may wish to consult this table occasionally for grounding in the demographic dynamics of different eras.

TABLE 1

Basic Demographic Data for the PRC, 1949–2001

(Total Year-end Population, Crude Birth Rate, Crude Death Rate, Natural Increase Rate, and Total Fertility Rate)

Year	Total population (in millions)	CBR	CDR	NIR	TFR
1949	541.67	36.00	20.00	16.00	6.14
1950	551.96	37.00	18.00	19.00	5.81
1951	563.00	37.80	17.80	20.00	5.70
1952	574.82	37.00	17.00	20.00	6.47
1953	587.96	37.00	14.00	23.00	6.05
1954	602.66	37.97	13.18	24.79	6.28
1955	614.56	32.60	12.28	20.32	6.26
1956	628.28	31.90	11.40	20.50	5.85
1957	645.63	34.03	10.80	23.23	6.41
1958	659.94	29.22	11.98	17.24	5.68
1959	672.07	24.78	14.59	10.19	4.30
1960	662.07	20.86	25.43	−4.57	4.02
1961	658.59	18.02	14.24	3.78	3.29
1962	672.95	37.01	10.02	26.99	6.02
1963	691.72	43.37	10.04	33.33	7.50
1964	704.99	39.14	11.50	27.64	6.18
1965	725.38	37.88	9.50	28.38	6.08
1966	745.42	35.05	8.83	26.22	6.26
1967	763.68	33.96	8.43	25.53	5.31
1968	785.34	35.59	8.21	27.38	6.45
1969	806.71	34.11	8.03	26.08	5.72
1970	829.92	33.43	7.60	25.83	5.81
1971	852.29	30.65	7.32	23.33	5.44
1972	871.77	29.77	7.61	22.16	4.98
1973	892.11	27.93	7.04	20.89	4.54
1974	908.59	24.82	7.34	17.48	4.17
1975	924.20	23.01	7.32	15.69	3.57
1976	937.17	19.91	7.25	12.66	3.24
1977	949.74	18.93	6.87	12.06	2.84
1978	962.59	18.25	6.25	12.00	2.72
1979	975.42	17.82	6.21	11.61	2.75

TABLE I
(*Continued*)

Year	Total population (in millions)	CBR	CDR	NIR	TFR
1980	987.05	18.21	6.34	11.87	2.24
1981	1000.72	20.91	6.36	14.55	2.63
1982	1016.54	22.28	6.60	15.68	2.87
1983	1030.08	20.19	6.90	13.29	2.42
1984	1043.57	19.90	6.82	13.08	2.35
1985	1058.51	21.04	6.78	14.26	2.20
1986	1075.07	22.43	6.86	15.57	2.42
1987	1093.00	23.33	6.72	16.61	2.59
1988	1110.26	22.37	6.64	15.73	2.31
1989	1127.04	21.58	6.54	15.04	2.25
1990	1143.33	21.06	6.67	14.39	2.17
1991	1158.23	19.68	6.70	12.98	2.01
1992	1171.71	18.24	6.64	11.60	1.83★
1993	1185.17	18.09	6.64	11.45	1.78★
1994	1198.50	17.70	6.49	11.21	1.73★
1995	1211.21	17.12	6.57	10.55	1.68★
1996	1223.89	16.98	6.56	10.42	1.65★
1997	1236.26	16.57	6.51	10.06	1.59★
1998	1247.61	15.64	6.50	9.14	1.59★
1999	1257.86	14.64	6.46	8.18	1.58★
2000	1267.43	14.03	6.45	7.58	1.55★
2001	1276.27	13.38	6.43	6.95	—

SOURCE: *China Statistical Yearbook* 2002.

NOTE: Because of the large increase in the underreporting of births from the late 1980s and, even more so, the early 1990s, estimates of the total fertility rate for 1991–2000 vary widely. The unadjusted TFR from the annual State Statistical Bureau surveys fell from 1.82 in 1991 to 1.46 in 1995 to 1.22 in 2000. Since an annual average of 27 percent of births were underreported in the 1990s, those figures need to be adjusted upward rather substantially. A careful review of all the large-scale data on births and underreporting in the 1990s suggests that the TFR is likely to be on the order of 1.5–1.6 (Zhang Guangyu 2004; also Retherford et al. 2005). Because of these data difficulties, the State Birth Planning Commission does not publish TFRs. In planning documents and public statements it uses the conservative figure of 1.8.

★Based on time-series reconstructed by Zhang Guangyu 2004.

CHAPTER 2

Problematique: Governmentalization of Population

ONE OF THE MOST impressive accomplishments of the People's Republic of China in the last quarter of the twentieth century was to bring population within the orbit of state management. Equally impressive but less noticed, by the twenty-first century Chinese society has begun taking over the rationalized governance of its own reproduction.

In 1950 most PRC leaders had opposed limiting births on ideological grounds, while most of the Chinese people opposed it on "traditional" grounds. Chinese culture was essentially pronatalist and population in all dimensions was largely unregulated except by the family.[1] Nevertheless, starting around 1975 the PRC began actively building an enormous bureaucratic apparatus for the centralized planning of reproduction (at the individual level) and population (at the aggregate level). That apparatus proved remarkably effective, though its effects did not always match its intended goals. Eventually PRC leaders began reforming it. Meanwhile, driven largely by sweeping social, economic, and political change, China's people were increasingly limiting childbearing and perfecting childrearing on their own. By the early 2000s population had been governmentalized—in the broad sense that reproductive conduct and population process had been brought under various forms of rationalized conscious control. Within that overall process, governance was rapidly shifting from state to society. These have been momentous changes, with broad implications for China and the world.

That is the bare outline of our story. Certain parts of it are now illuminated by a sizable literature on China's population. A first group of studies, by demographers, charts the striking changes in China's population over the last few decades.[2] A second set of studies, again largely by demographers, describes the evolution of the PRC's population policies and programs.[3] A third and smaller body of work, primarily by anthropologists and women's studies specialists, examines the social consequences of those policies in particular times and places, tracing local contests over reproduction and their effects, particularly on the bodies and lives of women and girls.[4] The fourth and smallest body of literature connects the PRC's population policies to the larger political dynamics of the post-1949 regime.[5] These works provide many valuable insights, yet the processes of governance and power surrounding population in China remain relatively unexamined. Accordingly, this book focuses not on demography but on politics. By bringing to bear perspectives from both political science and anthropology, it reveals more of Chinese population politics from more angles than has been possible before. The book aims to make two kinds of contribution: descriptive and interpretive.

Descriptively, this book fills many of the gaps in the existing literature. On policy, contemporaneous Western observers of the Mao and Deng eras did a remarkably good job of inferring national policy from subnational reports, but now many national policy documents are available from which to confirm, correct, and elaborate their accounts. During the Jiang and Hu eras, though birth rules have not changed, policy on other matters has evolved further than most foreigners realize. Emphasis has shifted from limiting quantity to improving quality—not only of the population but also of the program itself. This book documents these important shifts. On consequences, existing scholarship emphasizes the sociodemographic effects of the birth program on fertility, population structure, and the life chances of young girls. For many outside the academy, China's birth program is virtually synonymous with human trauma and social suffering, yet those costs have not been much assessed. Drawing on a wide range of materials, this book catalogues the enormous social suffering imposed on the peasantry by the rapid and essentially coerced fertility decline of the 1980s and early 1990s. The book then turns to some little-known groups of beneficiaries of the birth project who have emerged in the 1990s and 2000s. Moving beyond the more widely recognized social effects, the book also charts the broad political consequences of the governmentalization of population for the regime and for China's place in the world.

Interpretively, the book deepens both explanation and evaluation. Taking advantage of our complementary disciplinary locations, we move the analytic focus beyond the state-institutional and domination-resistance approaches that prevail in the small literature on China's population politics, adopting instead the broader interdisciplinary approach of "governmentalization." This approach enables us to bring into view forms of governance beyond the state—other institutions and discourses—and to trace broad shifts in governance from state-socialist toward more neoliberal modes. This broadened framework allows us to address important questions: Why did PRC leaders adopt the policies they did and how did the CCP find the capacity to implement them? What were the effects on individuals and society and how did couples respond to state intrusion? None of these questions has been explored in adequate depth, particularly not in terms that are consistent across the PRC's history as a whole.

No single book can cover everything. Any of the main episodes of policy formulation and implementation could usefully receive more detailed treatment or comparison to other episodes in other policy domains or other countries. The book explores social, cultural, and political effects of China's strict policies, but leaves economic and environmental consequences for specialists in those areas.[6] Feedback to the next round of policymaking too deserves more attention, particularly the "politics of numbers" surrounding the reporting and misreporting of vital events.[7] Finally, the book implicitly poses many issues for outsiders—of performance evaluation, ethical concerns, and possible policy responses—that we could not address explicitly at length (though we briefly address policy issues at the end of Chapter 10, the Conclusion).

Approaches to Population and Power in China

Most existing work on Chinese population policy is grounded in the Western liberal tradition. In general, in that work power is viewed as concentrated in the state and as fundamentally negative or repressive. State-society relations are often represented as antagonistic, while modern science and the professions are seen as liberating forces that exist outside of any power relations. This book moves beyond that liberal perspective to one that problematizes it by illuminating additional forms of power, including ways in which even liberal states exercise control, albeit indirectly. This broader approach was originally outlined by Michel Foucault, the French historian of systems of ideas, who traced the genealogy of modern power in the West under the rubric of governmentality (Foucault 1980, 1991, 1997a). That approach, which is known as an "analytics of government," has since been elaborated by social theorists in various disciplines (Burchell, Gordon, and Miller eds. 1991; Dean 1999; Rose 1999). In the governmentality perspective, modern power is not only negative and repressive but also positive and productive, circulating widely in and through the state, the disciplinary institutions of modern society, and society itself. State and society are interpenetrating and mutually constitutive. Science and the professions exist within networks of power relations, creating new kinds of rationalities and individuals that are useful to modern governance. The governmentality perspective offers fresh understandings of transitions to liberalism and neoliberalism and new ways to understand

China's early twenty-first-century attempt to incorporate some neoliberalism into its Leninist project. This project has replaced Maoism and Stalinism with Marketizing Reform but remains socialist in some ways. An analytics of government is particularly useful in the study of population, which is a central object of power and governance in modern societies.

GOVERNANCE, GOVERNMENTALITY, AND GOVERNMENTALIZATION

In our account of Chinese population policy, the central analytical construct is governmentality and the central historical process is governmentalization. These are concepts developed by Foucault for his own critical histories of the West. He offered these ideas not as parts of an overarching history or theory but as analytical tools, interpretive frameworks, and historical questions that others could refashion as they found necessary. What is interesting about this cluster of concepts is that they point to an enormous preoccupation with population. We begin with the broad concept of governance, which indicates the range of topics addressed by the other two terms.

Historically the word *governance* has had a wide range of meanings. With an ancient Greek root sense of "steering," in French and English the term has referred to everything from sovereign-state power, to formal nonstate supervision over social activities, to individuals' informal sway over each other, to individuals' regulation of themselves. Recent international development literature preserves some of this breadth by using "good governance" to imply moving beyond a top-down statist approach to managing development to an approach that draws on as wide a range of types of actors and forms of power as possible (UNDP 1999; Burns 2003). That is the wide semantic domain that Foucault, in order to establish a broad analytical and historical perspective, deliberately invoked by using the word "government" not in its conventional modern state-centered meaning but in the broad early-modern sense of "the conduct of conduct," which included virtually any form of regulating human behavior. A useful formal definition of this broad sense of governance is "any more or less calculated and rational activity, undertaken by a multiplicity of authorities and agencies, employing a variety of techniques and forms of knowledge, that seeks to shape conduct *by working through our desires, aspirations, interests, and beliefs,* for definite but shifting ends and with a diverse set of relatively unpredictable consequences, effects and outcomes" (Dean 1999, 11, emphasis added). This book uses "governance" to refer to this broad range of activity, while using "government" in its ordinary modern state-centric sense.

Arising in modern societies, *governmentality* is a particular regime of government that takes population—its health, welfare, security, and prosperity—as its primary end. Governmentality is a form of rule that goes beyond old-fashioned sovereign state power to draw on three forms of power that, analytically, constitute a triangle (Foucault 1991, 102–103). These forms of power all incorporate the notion, invented around 1800 by the new science of political economy, that society is composed of "autonomous systems" that the state should regulate only indirectly. The first is governance over and through government in the conventional sense. State bureaucracy can intervene in macrosocial processes such as population dynamics, preferably through indirect regulation, and can also intervene in individual behavior such as reproduction, preferably by helping shape individuals' own sense of their identities and desires. The second form of modern power is governance through "intermediate" disciplinary institutions, usually run by professionals on the basis of particular expertise. Main examples of these disciplinary institutions are schools, hospitals, armies, and prisons. Some of these generally are state institutions, others generally are not. The third form of modern power is self-governance by individuals of themselves. That self-governance is often promoted and guided by states and professional experts.

Governmentalization is the historical process by which that distinctive modern form of rule came about. Narratively, the three forms of power compose a series, in the course of which the whole complex of governmentality has gradually achieved preeminence over older, separate versions of state sovereignty, institutional discipline, and self-cultivation (Foucault 1991, 102–103). The modern form of governance does not eliminate earlier versions of these but instead retains and utilizes their techniques, rationalities, and institutions by reorganizing them within a new concern for population and its optimization. Thus the process of governmentalization includes building formal organizations for regulating behavior through political-economic mechanisms such as monitoring and sanctioning. These are the focus of the institutional literature in social science on which Winckler draws. However, governmentalization also includes the development of various mentalities or rationalities of government—bodies of knowledge and expertise (especially those based on "science")—and the elaboration of sociocultural discourses and practices for such governance. These are the focus of the Foucauldian literature on which Greenhalgh draws.

As earlier in the West, the process of governmentalization in China has been occurring in two stages that can be clearly discerned in the domain of population. The first stage was the construction of state-bureaucratic capacity. In birth planning, that happened during the Deng era. The second stage has been a shift toward professional disciplines and individual self-governance. In birth planning, these shifts gathered momentum from the Deng through the Jiang to the Hu eras. In the population domain, this accelerating downward shift in the locus of power resulted in part from regime success at building professional institutions to instill in individuals a new norm of fewer but higher-quality children. The shift also stemmed in part from society's own creation of new institutions and norms surrounding population and reproduction. These trends in society were stimulated by broader regime policies toward economic and social development, in particular those spurring the emergence of the market. The governmentalization of population in China is particularly impressive because it has occurred so rapidly—essentially, within the few decades since 1980.

The second stage of the process of governmentalization, the downward shift in power, has been especially dramatic because in the first stage power had become so heavily concentrated in the state. This devolution of power to professional disciplines and individuals is also highly significant because it challenges the widespread view that power remains concentrated in a top-heavy state. Compared to the Western nations that have been studied most closely, however, power in China has indeed been relatively state-centric. For most of the time since the founding of the PRC, bureaucratic statism has dominated professional institutions and deeply penetrated individual self-governance. That dominance was true for most of the history of PRC birth planning as well.

POLITICAL SCIENCE AND REGIME CAPACITY

Winckler's approach to governmentalization is largely through "regime capacity," drawing heavily on the institutionalism—both historical and rational—of contemporary political science. Both help explain why the policy narrative in Part 1 unfolded as it did. Historical institutionalism highlights the multiplicity of strategies that the CCP has adopted in the course of its Leninist project and how tensions between those strategies have produced change. Rationalist institutionalism illuminates the logic of each of those strategies considered individually. The two approaches complement each other. For example, much of the story of PRC birth planning can be viewed as the rational use of political-economic mechanisms to instill new sociocultural norms of childbearing and childrearing in Chinese society for the next period of PRC history—a process analogous to the gradual establishment within Chinese politics of a new norm of regularized retirement by aging leaders (well analyzed by Manion 1993).

The historical-institutional approach to regime capacity emphasizes that it is a cumulative composite of different paradigms left over from different time periods. Real regimes include overlapping cohorts of institutions, introduced at different times, pursuing different purposes, and operating on conflicting logics. It is this dissonant diversity that explains both systemic robustness and systemic change, both regime capacity and regime incapacity. Moreover, real institutions are not neutral mechanisms but rather embody purposes and exert control. (See Steinmo et al. 1992; Orren and Skowronek 1995.)

This approach illuminates much about PRC regime capacity, both in general and in birth planning in particular. As Chapter 1 explained, the CCP has successively adopted three broad approaches to constructing regime capacity: Maoism, Stalinism, and Reformism. As this chapter further explains, those approaches can be characterized more analytically as Revolutionary Mobilization, Bureaucratic Professionalism, and Socialist Marketization. The two terms in the names of each approach stand for separate tendencies that existed in changing proportions and tensions within each approach. Those six policy tendencies have provided the repertoire of policy instruments on which the CCP has drawn to construct regime capacity at successive points in time. In historical-institutional terms, what explains PRC regime capacity are the strengths and weaknesses and waxing and waning of those approaches and their interaction (Skinner and Winckler 1969; Suttmeier 1974; Solinger 1984; Solinger ed. 1984; Bachman 1991).

The historical approach to institutional capacity shares much with Foucault's account of governmentalization. Both argue that the best explanation of the present is a sharp analysis of the past. This is particularly so for the PRC, where little in regime history has been definitively repudiated and many institutions and discourses persist across the entire history of the regime, even as their functions and meanings change in new circumstances. It is appropriate, therefore, that both the historical-institutional and Foucauldian approaches emphasize historical specificity. Explanation must be grounded in particular circumstances, even though it draws on general processes. Finally, both approaches are sociocultural, holding that discourses and practices create institutions as much as formal rules and regulations do.

The rationalist-institutional approach to regime capacity is essentially the application to politics of the neoliberalism in economics that provoked Foucault to further elaborate his idea of biopower (Lemke 2001). Like classical liberalism, neoliberalism is skeptical about state capacity. Neoliberalism wishes to identify what tasks bureaucracies do poorly and what tasks they do well and to limit state bureaucracies to undertaking only the latter. At the least states should stop producing harm. States should also limit themselves to selective and indirect regulation of societal "systems," whose autonomy and complexity the state must understand and respect. In the areas in which it continues to operate, the state should remake itself into an efficient machine—lean, mean, and clean. In the course of the Jiang era, such an effort got underway in China, at first mainly in the economy, but eventually also in birth planning as well. (See Hughes 2003; Fukuyama 2004.)

The rationalist-institutional approach to "macro" regime capacity identifies particular "meso" mechanisms from which such capacity can be constructed, such as the mobilization, bureaucracy, and markets that this book uses to characterize the CCP's variants of Leninism. The neoliberal approach to regime capacity achieves its intellectual authority by grounding those meso-mechanisms in a "micro" analysis of particular arrangements of information and incentives (e.g., Eggertsson 1990). To be effective and efficient those arrangements must be tailored to the demands of particular tasks. The most precise form of such analysis explores the role of information and incentives in relationships between "principals" and their "agents." Such models map directly onto post-Mao PRC "responsibility systems," which have emerged as the main tools through which PRC leaders steer both regime and society, particularly in birth planning (Winckler 1999). Since this book does not treat implementation in any detail, it provides little opportunity to develop such models, but in principle they underlie the analysis. (Classic discussions of meso-mechanisms include Dahl and Lindblom 1953; Etzioni 1961; Williamson 1975; Hedstrom and Swedberg eds. 1998. On China, see Winckler ed. 1999; Naughton and Yang eds. 2004; for responsibility systems, Whiting 2001, 2004, Edin 2003).

"Regime capacity" is, of course, a grandiose term with many potential aspects. One might think of institutional capacity as residing mostly in nuts-and-bolts details of administrative organization and implementation processes, topics that we cannot discuss in detail here because of limited space. Nevertheless, one might also think of institutional capacity as originating in the aptness of earlier stages of the policy process: the ability to address problems squarely, to air issues openly, and to formulate policies in detail. Evidently the international development community has come to that conclusion, emphasizing detailed project protocols and evaluation procedures. In any case, the first half of this book makes that argument, tracing the gradual emergence of the main components of birth policy across the last half of the twentieth century.

At the beginning of the twenty-first century—despite a historical-institutional legacy of conflicting policy tendencies and despite many other obstacles to designing rational institutions—the policy process in the PRC has become increasingly robust and effective. Moreover, it has done so through a neoliberal process of governmentalization that has kept the regime's own role as limited as possible while mobilizing as much other institutional and social capacity as the regime can manage to orchestrate and can bring itself to allow. Overall, the progressive institutionalization of the PRC regime has become evident not only in its capacity to conduct smooth successions but also in its capacity to conduct a capable policy process. As a result, whereas in the long sweep of PRC history the main distinctions were between eras defined by the rise and fall of paramount leaders, by the turn of the millennium changes of administration began to have increasingly identifiable effects on the substance of policy and on the increasing capacity of the regime to formulate it.

ANTHROPOLOGY AND BIOPOWER

Greenhalgh's approach to biopower is informed by broadly Foucauldian approaches to forms of power that exist in and beyond the state. These approaches, favored by contemporary critical anthropology and women's studies, are concerned with institutions, but their distinctive emphasis is on *discourses*—historically specific bodies of knowledge that structure how things can be said. Discourses are politically productive, working to constitute population, programs, politics, and power itself. In his seminal study, *The History of Sexuality, vol. 1*, and in later lectures, Foucault proposed that the modern political era (in Western Europe beginning in the eighteenth century) has given rise to a new form of power that is no longer concentrated in governmental institutions of the state but is instead increasingly dispersed throughout society in disciplinary institutions such as medicine, education, and the law (Foucault 1978, 1980, 1997a,b,c, 2003). Grounded in modern science and technology, whose claims to authority rest on their apprehension of and mastery over "nature," this modern power over life focuses on and works through the body. It operates at two interconnected poles, the regulations of the population as a whole and the disciplines of the individual body. Although Foucault's writings on biopower were fragmentary, his concepts have exceptional relevance today, when this power over biological life is expanding into ever more domains. These concepts are particularly useful in understanding the politics of life at the collective level of the population, a domain of politics that has been little explored.[8] We begin by clarifying how we use key Foucauldian terms and suggesting how they might inform anthropological and feminist understandings of the workings of modern power.

Biopower is the calculated power over human life, especially at the level of the population. Biopower is aimed at the administration of the vital characteristics of human populations and exercised in the name of optimizing individual or collective life, health, and welfare. Biopower entails the increased ordering of life at all levels. It is the characteristic form of power in the modern era, when life itself becomes a central object of power. *Biopolitics* is a field of politics concerning the administration and optimization of the vital attributes of human life, particularly at the aggregate level. This modern politics of life involves rationalizations (formulations of population problems), interventions (techniques or strategies designed to optimize population), contestations (between governing agents and between governors and governed), and a broad range of consequences for individuals and societies.

Foucault's writings have inspired the development of numerous bodies of work on the politics of life in the modern era. In the area of population/reproduction many have explored the reproductive disciplines of the individual body in various locales (e.g., Ginsburg and Rapp eds. 1995; Lock and Kaufert eds. 1998). Feminist scholars in history, philosophy, anthropology, and technoscience studies have taken up this part of the Foucauldian project, uncovering the particular importance of these modes of power for women's bodies, lives, and subjectivities. (Classic works include Martin 1987; Sawicki 1991; Tuana 1993; Oudshoorn 1994; Keller 1995; Clarke 1998.) The feminist work has shown modern science to be a uniquely powerful vehicle for inscribing biopower into women's bodies and lives. Drawing on cultural assumptions about male and female, science has depicted women as the natural reproducers of the species and thus the "natural" objects of regulation and discipline. In this way, science both builds on and reinforces gendered divisions within society. Science gains its power from its position as the ultimate arbiter of "truth" in modern societies. When science speaks in the name of nature, it depoliticizes beliefs and practices that are often eminently political, removing them from the arena of contestation.

Only very recently have scholars begun to examine the regulation of the population as a whole from Foucauldian perspectives. Researchers in this emerging area have treated selected topics within that broad domain, including the discourses of demography, family planning, and population control (Anagnost 1997a; Greenhalgh 2001a; Chatterjee and Riley 2001; Paxson 2004; Krause 2005), the development of population science (Greenhalgh 1996), rationalities and/or technologies of population governance (Rabinow 1989; Horn 1994; Sigley 1996), and the unexpected effects of population programs as they interact with local cultures and societies (Ali 2002; Greenhalgh 2003a).

Of particular interest to students of biopower are the population control programs that have proliferated in the Third World since the 1960s. These programs, which the historical Europeanist Foucault did not attend to, present some of history's most striking examples of the regulations of the social body. Focusing on one of those programs, in this book we seek to take the Foucauldian research program on population/reproduction to a new level. By combining a political science study of the state with an anthropological study of society, we are able to see the emergence and workings of population regulation from the perspectives of the governors and the governed. By placing the regulations of population and the disciplines of the reproductive body within the same framework, we aim to produce an overarching account of the historical emergence and transformations of biopower in one historical site. Finally, by combining the insights of feminist work on gender, science, and culture with a Foucauldian analysis of the governmentalization of population, we hope to create a relatively comprehensive account of the consequences of the rise of biopower for women in one national site. That site, the PRC, is the world's most notable case of the rapid politicization of population, and a case in which regulation has encompassed not only the quantity of population but also its quality. As noted above, that regulation has resulted in a broad governmentalization of life. We explore three aspects of this process.

First, we are interested in the historical emergence of an institutionalized politics of life—when and how the production and cultivation of life come to be major foci of organized power and social control in China. We examine the development of political activities and institutions at both poles of modern power: at the macrolevel of the state, the regulation of the population, or social body; and at the microlevel of the enterprise, village, family, and individual, the practices or "disciplines" of the individual body and mind, especially those directed at women as reproducers and mothers and at children as embodiers of population quality. Though space constraints preclude a detailed analysis of their workings, we also discuss the mesolevel institutions (the clinic, the market, and so on) through which these disciplines are produced. By showing how the regulations of the population are achieved—and challenged—through the production of various disciplines of the individual body and mind, we create an overall account of the evolution of modern power over life at macro- and micropolitical levels.

Second, we are concerned with shifts in the power to regulate and discipline life. In studying these transformations, the key concept is the *norm*, the modern standard established by the human sciences for all members of society to follow. The key process is the *normalization* of society to eliminate deviations and anomalies. The political question is: Which social forces get to define and instill the norms governing life? Historically, the emergence of a politics of life has been intimately connected to the rise of capitalism, when newly disciplined bodies and newly educated minds were needed to form a new labor force for the expanding capitalist economy. With the development of capitalism, the power to create and instill the norms guiding the cultivation of life, particularly its health and education, drifted from the state to other social forces, including the medical, educational, and legal disciplines. In China, too, these new powers over life were born in the state, but with China's rapid integration into the capitalist world economy other actors with other kinds of norms and disciplines came flooding into the political arena. To see the new politics that emerged, we focus on the shift from the norm of population quantity to that of population quality, which dominated the 1990s as the state intensified its efforts to fashion a modern labor force that would be competitive in the global marketplace. We examine the contests between various social forces as they struggled to shape the norms on health and education and to persuade individuals to adopt their norms, practices, and products. We chart too the negotiations and struggles between these social forces and individuals embracing and resisting the spread of normalizing power. In studying these contestations we look for shifts of two sorts. The first is the shift from external regulation to self-regulation and self-cultivation. The second is the shift from "state disciplines" to "medical disciplines" to "market disciplines" of child economics, consumer desire, and consumption fantasy (Ong 1999). Population turns out to be a productive site from which to trace the broad shifts in the locus of regulation from state to market.

Finally, we are interested in the social and political effects of the governmentalization of life. Since this new power over life is created in society, it profoundly alters society and its individual members. In examining the social processes and effects of a politics of life, the Foucauldian work stresses the positivity, or *productivity*, of modern power (in contrast to the negativity or repressiveness of old-fashioned sovereign state power). Modern power, it suggests, gives rise to historically new objects of power and new sites of struggle. In China there are three categories of persons who, because of their centrality to the success of the state's population projects, have become major new objects of power and sites of struggle: *the reproductive woman*, charged with reducing the fertility rate; *the quality single child*, responsible for the future of family and nation; and *the good mother*, tasked with nurturing that quality child. By exploring the institutional and cultural processes through which these new categories have been produced and the impacts of this politics on their bodies, lives, and selves, we can see the ways in which the governmentalization of life has both remade the social order and created in individuals new kinds of bodies and subjectivities that ready them for participation in modern life and the global capitalist economy.

We are also concerned with the broad political effects of the governmentalization of population. The work on governmentalization directs attention to the many unintended effects of modern programs of social change. Indeed, it posits that such projects rarely achieve their intended goals, but are politically productive in other ways (e.g., Ferguson 1990). In China, the low quantity–high quality policies launched around 1979–1980 were designed to modernize Chinese individuals, families, and society, to strengthen the regime, and to help transform the PRC into a global power. To a remarkable extent, the post-Mao population project accomplished those goals. But it accomplished much more in the process. A broad review of the project's consequences reveals a host of surprising effects that were not only unpredicted but also unpredictable. The effects could not have been predicted because the regime was interacting with a society and culture that it sought to transform, not understand; because that society and culture were undergoing rapid change; because the mode of governing society was shifting from state to market; and because China was joining a world it understood poorly. Teasing out these hidden dynamics, we explore both anticipated and unanticipated political effects of the population project on the regime, on regime-society relations, on the nature of power, and on China's connections to the world.

FOUCAULT AND CHINA STUDIES

Other students of Chinese modernity have also found Foucault's ideas productive, adapting them to understand crime and punishment, China's "exemplary society," and even the official and popular discourse on sexuality and population (Dutton 1992; Dikotter 1995, 1998; Sigley 1996; Anagnost 1997a,b; Evans 1997; Twohey 1999; Bakken 2000). Although many China anthropologists and humanities scholars now use Foucault's ideas, the China field as a whole has been slow to embrace Foucauldian perspectives. While this is not the place for an extended discussion of the relevance of Foucault to China, by identifying and responding to some of the main objections, we can show how our work relates to that of others in China studies. Simplifying, we can identify three sets of objections, each associated with one of three major paradigms in China studies: culturalism, modernization, and Marxian political economy.

The *culturalist objection* holds that Chinese history and culture are too different from those of the West to allow use of these constructs. In particular, some have argued, population has been a concern not just of the modern state, but also of ancient Chinese states; China lacks the flourishing professions and self-governing subjects of the liberal societies Foucault studied; and, most generally, power is more centralized in the Chinese state than in modern Western states. While these concerns are important, the first two need to be reconsidered in light of the historical record. The imperial and republican states were indeed concerned about human numbers, but it was not until the PRC that the state was able to create the institutions that allowed population to emerge as a major domain of governance. The PRC drew on and reworked earlier logics and techniques, building them into a massive and relatively effective apparatus of governance unlike anything that existed before. As for liberal modes of governance, research conducted in the early 2000s illuminates neoliberal trends in professional governance and self-cultivation that have been developing since around the mid-1990s. With regard to state-centrism, as discussed earlier, power in China is indeed more concentrated in the state than it is in the West. But far from making Foucault's ideas irrelevant, we take this political fact as our entry point into a study of the histori-

cal specificity of power over population in China. In response to the culturalist objection, then, we argue that although China's modern political trajectory takes a distinctively Chinese form, far from being outside modern power
relations, since around 1980 and especially since the early 1990s, China has
become ever more enmeshed in them.

The *modernization objection* maintains that the modernization of reproduction in China—the shift toward raising few, well cultivated children—is part
of the rationalizing changes based on scientific knowledge that are associated with socioeconomic modernization everywhere. Rather than subjecting
people to onerous power relations, science-based rationalities and behaviors
liberate individuals from an oppressive tradition. Our research certainly supports the notion that the modernization of reproduction in recent decades has
freed China's people from an oppressive tradition. At the same time, however,
it suggests that these changes have enmeshed them in a new type of power—
the power of the modern, science-based norm—that is especially insidious
because it is masked by the apparently neutral language of science. Spread by
a wide range of disciplining forces (the professions, the market, and so on) and
society itself, those modern norms are particularly constraining because they
are internalized by people themselves. Our investigations also reveal that
modern science, far from being external to power relations, has been fundamental to the construction of the modern state and modern power while
working to mask that power in the language of truth, rationality, and progress.
By rethinking the assumptions underlying the modernization model, a Foucauldian perspective opens up the important yet rarely asked question of
whether the development of modern science and the spread of modern reproductive norms do indeed liberate the Chinese people or instead amount
to a new form of domination.

The *political economy objection* holds that the Foucauldian perspective, with
its emphasis on discourse and the workings of power at the local level, neglects
the large-scale organization of power in the capitalist world economy and the
gritty materiality of power relations. While not analyzing the workings of the
capitalist economy, this book views China's incorporation into the global
economy and its rapid marketization as major forces behind the state's rationalization of its birth program and behind society's growing desire for
fewer, better raised children. Moreover, with its emphasis on the body as the
site where the large-scale organization of power links up to individual lives, a
Foucauldian analysis can bring out the concrete consequences for women and
infant girls of the reorganization of power in Chinese modernity. This study
documents not only the centrality of discursive formulations, but also the materiality of their effects. The classical Marxian perspective, while useful for
many purposes, is not especially useful for understanding population politics,

because its concept of power is too narrow and too negative and because it lacks a notion of subjectivity, which is essential to understanding individual motivation. The research reported here shows that power over population has been not only negative, but also positive, producing new bodies and selves readied for insertion into the capitalist world economy. By broadening the notion of power and focusing on the productivity as well as the negativity of power relations, a Foucauldian perspective allows us to see whole new domains and dimensions of power that the classical political economy perspective overlooks.

Alternative Projects within Chinese Leninism

The overview in Chapter 1 introduced three main approaches within Chinese Leninism: Maoist, Stalinist, and Reformist. Here we elaborate. More analytical terms for these approaches are Revolutionary Mobilization, Bureaucratic Professionalism, and Socialist Marketization. Each approach contains two policy tendencies in tension with each other, corresponding to the two terms in its name. Each of these six policy tendencies has distinct and direct implications for birth planning.

The two tendencies within Maoism were a destructive Revolutionary current on the extreme left and a more constructive Mobilizational current on the moderate left. The Mobilizational side attempted to construct centrally controlled work methods and cadre corps for propagandizing birth planning (as began in the early Mao era and continued intermittently thereafter). The Revolutionary side attempted to tear down that central regime capacity (as occurred during the Cultural Revolution, to some extent). Nevertheless, the Revolutionary current did contribute something positive to birth limitation by transferring many health resources from city to countryside and by promoting community-based approaches to providing health care and governing reproduction. The Deng era purged the Revolutionary current and the Jiang era largely moved beyond Mobilization as a policy instrument, even in birth planning (though rather slowly).

The two tendencies within Stalinism were Bureaucracy on the center-left and Professionalism on the center-right. On one side was a central planning bureaucracy concerned primarily with meeting plan targets for limiting births (the tendency that dominated during the Deng era). On the other side was a professional medical establishment concerned primarily with delivering reproductive health services (a tendency that revived and gradually began to prevail during the Jiang era).

The two tendencies within Reformism have been a Socialism that remains concerned to maintain at least minimal economic equity and social security (on the moderate right) and a Marketization that allows relatively unregulated economic growth regardless of social consequences (on the extreme right). One side seeks to limit population growth as stringently as possible to facilitate economic development (as continued throughout the Deng and Jiang eras). The other pays greater attention to social objectives, particularly economic security in old age (as the Hu era has begun to do).

Depending on the issues at stake, each of the three general approaches can give rise to more specific policy tendencies that conflict within that approach. The more specific pair of tendencies that mattered most for the *origins* of PRC birth planning arose within the economic sector during the Mao era, between "Industrialists" and "Financialists" (Bachman 1991). The Industrialists accepted more of Stalinism as practiced in the Soviet Union, particularly its emphasis on the high-speed development of heavy industry in cities. That was the approach of the PRC's First Five-Year Plan and an impulse that reappears in other attempts at rapid industrialization, such as Mao's Great Leap Forward in the late 1950s. At first many Industrialists probably opposed limiting births, partly because Soviet Stalinism was pronatal, partly because at first many Chinese Industrialists thought they could use all the manpower they could get. However, after the failure of Mao's Great Leap, evidently most Industrialists began to favor the regime's promotion of birth control. Financialists, after observing the initial workings of the First Five-Year Plan, concluded that it was necessary to adapt the Stalinist approach to China's conditions, by giving more attention to agricultural production and consumer needs, making some use of managed-market price signals, proceeding at a more deliberate pace, and better coordinating different parts of the economy. This policy provided the main early support for birth planning, as a way to coordinate economic development and population growth.

The specific pair of tendencies that matters most for the *future* of PRC birth planning arose in the post-Mao period in the political sector over the extent of democratization. Post-Mao PRC leaders have restricted democratization to what we will call "Elite Pluralization": they have encouraged a more robust policy process within the regime, in order to produce policy that is more scientific in the sense that it reflects the views of a variety of elite experts (Gilley 2004). This tendency is visible in birth policy both in its increasing openness to input from a variety of elites (including foreigners) and in its continuing refusal to alter basic birth rules, regardless of what the populace might think. Post-Mao PRC leaders have eschewed the alternative of Mass Democratization. They have pursued some "village self-government," but that has remained a form of what we call "managed democracy" (explained in Chapter 6).

Fully elaborating and documenting these variants of Chinese Leninism lies beyond the scope of this book, which uses them simply as an economical way to summarize the evolving political setting for PRC birth planning. Identifying such policy tendencies is a standard method in the analysis of both authoritarian and democratic regimes (e.g., Skilling and Griffiths eds. 1971; Sabatier ed. 1999). Many of the specific formulations used here have been standard in studies of communist China for two decades (e.g., Suttmeier 1974; Solinger 1984; Solinger ed. 1984; Bachman 1991). These approaches, currents, and tendencies are, of course, vast simplifications—shorthand for myriad concrete actions and ideas, not suprahistorical abstractions driving actors' behaviors. Moreover during PRC history they have recombined continuously into a kaleidoscope of changing coalitions, with alliances between tendencies from different approaches, though some tendencies were more compatible than others. The Mao era ran mostly on a combination of Mobilization and Bureaucracy, which the Deng era applied to birth planning. Post-Mao eras involved a deepening tension between Bureaucracy and Marketization, which increasingly affected birth planning. Sometimes the approach taken to birth limitation was out of sync with the dominant mix of approaches within the regime as a whole at the time. Nevertheless, although these labels are simplifications, they do identify discourses containing definite ideas held by powerful leaders that had definite material consequences. For example, each general approach has had its preferred technique for steering direction and correcting problems. The "powerful magic weapon" of Revolutionary Mobilization was rectification campaigns. Bureaucratic Professionalism aspired to "socialist planning" and "scientific management." Elaborating that, Socialist Marketization has relied heavily on "management by objectives" through "responsibility systems." In the early twenty-first century, these techniques are evolving into ever-more-sophisticated procedures for evaluating personnel and programs, which are the core of "neoliberal reflexive government," preoccupied with minimizing the size of the state apparatus and perfecting the operation of what remains (Dean 1999). Change in the mix of policy instruments employed has been central to the history of PRC birth planning.

At this point, again, some readers may wish to skip forward to the last section of this chapter (on location, quantity, and quality) and then proceed to the body of the book. The rest of this section provides a fuller statement of the three main approaches within Chinese Leninism (Revolutionary Mobilization, Bureaucratic Professionalism, and Socialist Marketization). On the one hand, we treat the six policy tendencies within them as discursive strategies connected to larger rhetorical themes such as science and democracy. On the other hand, we locate the tendencies within the overall institutional structure of the PRC regime, which we now briefly introduce.

In 1949, for convenience of vertical oversight, PRC leaders organized domestic policy into three main sectors, which correspond remarkably well to the distinction in organizational sociology between order, economic, and ideological goals. These three sectors contained a half-dozen main sets of policy domains, which PRC leaders coordinated through "leading groups" and government staff offices. For convenience in horizontal coordination, PRC leaders made the same parallel divisions within party, government, and legislature. PRC leaders divided among themselves the task of overseeing these groupings and the systems within them, major leaders sometimes having more than one functional "system" in their portfolios. Accordingly, arrangements have been somewhat fluid, allowing reassignment of functions and powers as politics and practice required. Nevertheless, rather remarkably, in the early twenty-first century, the PRC's original basic organization of regime capacities still provides the framework for the policy process. Indeed, as the former birth program's mandate expanded to include population, in 2004 birth minister Zhang Weiqing used exactly this sectoral framework to map the broad potential scope of the expanded program's responsibility and authority. (See Etzioni 1961; Lieberthal 1995, 192–207; Wang 1995; Winckler ed. 1999, conclusion.)

Under this sectoral system of oversight, for any particular program it obviously matters greatly how its function is defined, to what ministry it is assigned, to what system that ministry has been assigned, and to what grouping that system belongs. To a significant extent, those assignments determine how the program's tasks are defined, how its performance will be evaluated, and by whom. Thus, these arrangements have affected birth planning in several ways. They have created the institutional landscape on which birth planning had to establish itself, and they have provided institutional homes for the alternative approaches to regime capacity used to implement birth planning. Many of the individuals who played striking roles in the history of birth policy were major leaders of these institutions, which helps explain their influence on population matters.

REVOLUTIONARY MOBILIZATION

Revolutionary Mobilization was designed for the chaotic situation of guerilla warfare, in which it was impossible to deploy a comprehensive bureaucracy, so coordination was achieved by inspiration through a few general guiding ideals. Because its main steering mechanism is ideals, Revolutionary Mobilization was particularly concerned with ideology and with maintaining pre-1949 revolutionary values. As an approach to creating regime capacity, revolutionary mobilization can be remarkably economical and effective, largely in proportion to public support for the regime or a particular policy.

That helps explain the Mao era's success at promoting birth control in Chinese cities even without building a bureaucracy dedicated to that purpose. However, Revolutionary Mobilization does not permit precise calibration of the amount or kind of effort desired. Under this approach, the function of plan targets is more inspirational than operational or indicative. Implementors tend to compete to overfulfill their assignments, resulting in cycles of advance and consolidation. General slogans implemented by amateurs are not a good way to coordinate delicate operations on women's bodies. This helps to explain the damage this approach did when extended to promoting birth control in rural areas.

Institutionally, Revolutionary Mobilization ideals were lodged mainly in the systems for party affairs and for propaganda and education, which constituted the cultural and social policy sector of the PRC regime. On the party side, that sector corresponded to the CCP's party affairs grouping, which was usually the most powerful. Ideology was fundamental to the legitimacy of the regime and its leaders. It was supervised by party ideological specialists, who during the Mao era tended to be radicals with a close relationship with Mao (such as Mao's personal secretary, Chen Boda, and his security advisor, the intellectual Kang Sheng). On the government side, these functions were supervised by the State Council's Culture and Education Commission (*wenjiao hui*), later the Council's Second Office (*di'er bangongshi*). A survey of PRC regime structure by a PRC scholar says the broadest purpose of that commission was to raise the "political consciousness" and "cultural level" of the population (Wang 1995, 29–30). That purpose eventually appears in birth planning as the goal of raising the quality of China's population. The Revolutionary Mobilization tradition also became strongly entrenched in the security sector, both military and police. At least initially, this tradition within the military—along with its sheer peasant conservatism—may have contributed to the extensive resistance that state intervention into reproductive matters faced during the Mao era. Later, Mobilizational methods of police work—including policing by the local militia—contributed to the Deng era's vigorous enforcement of birth planning.

Discursively, Revolutionary Mobilization was in principle both scientific and democratic. A vanguard revolutionary party uses its "scientific" ideology to correctly diagnose the current "situation" and to lay down the general "line" for addressing it. The vanguard party is also supposed to practice "democratic centralism" within the party and, in China, the "mass line" in relations between party and public. In both cases the party extensively consults lower participants on their needs before centralizing and synthesizing that information into an authoritative statement of the current best interests of the party and public. In practice, the application of this approach is often the prerogative of the currently dominant party leader, whose authority it legitimates. The mass line approach—including its partyist, personalist, and populist aspects—has always been fundamental to the CCP's claim to legitimacy for itself and its policies. In the early twenty-first century, aspirations for the birth program to be scientific and democratic remain main themes of Comprehensive Reform of population work (Chapter 6). Maoism's approach to reproduction and sexuality was that the less said about it in official media, the better (Evans 1997). Instead, collective communities regulated the conduct of their members directly. Consistent with this quiet approach to reproduction, even though Mao himself had coined the term "birth planning," he did not authorize the creation of an elaborate ideology and organization for that purpose. Consequently, PRC leaders who favored slowing population growth were able only to "advocate" only "birth control," and to do it only through relatively restricted health media and face-to-face interaction.

BUREAUCRATIC PROFESSIONALISM

Bureaucratic Professionalism was designed for very orderly environments, in which a large bureaucracy not only makes detailed plans but actually runs everything. In principle, plan targets do try to calibrate exactly the amount and characteristics of what is to be produced. During the heyday of PRC birth planning, this meant "birth according to plan"; bureaucracies decided not only how many children a couple could have but also exactly when they could have them (and even whether the resulting child achieved the regime's minimum standard for genetic quality). Because Bureaucratic Professionalism combines organization and expertise, it can be quite effective. Some of it is indispensable for any purpose and in the twenty-first century for those attempting to reform PRC birth work it is helping to institutionalize "quality care." However, the Bureaucratic Professional approach finds it is difficult to collect the vast amount of information required and to include everything it wants in plan targets. Implementors tend to concentrate on the main goals for which they are most rewarded (such as quantitative goals for population growth or contraceptive operations) and to neglect other considerations (such as qualitative ideals of health and rights). In addition, when extended to running an entire society, Bureaucratic Professionalism creates huge "transaction costs," pervasive corruption, and popular resistance.

Institutionally, Bureaucratic Professionalism found its stronghold in the finance and economics system, which constituted the economic sector of the PRC regime, including planning for both economic development and population growth. That sector corresponded to the CCP's own "government work" grouping. Within the government, economic functions were divided between two commissions, one for industry, headed by Bo Yibo, and one for finance and trade, initially headed by Chen Yun. These two commissions provided the institutional homes of the Industrial and Financial tendencies, of course. Both Bo and Chen became important advocates of birth planning. As a main part of the socialist approach to governance, Bureaucratic Professionalism was also the mainstay of other sectors as well. In the security sector, Military Professionals eventually supported birth limits because the military had plenty of potential recruits and came to prefer quality to quantity. Police Professionals ran the household registration system that contributed to controlling population along both location and quantity dimensions. In the ideological sector, Bureaucratic Professional institutions, such as the science establishment and the education and health systems, often suffered because the sector was run by the regime's ideologues.

Discursively, the Bureaucratic Professional approach is even more scientistic than Revolutionary Mobilization, using physical sciences such as engineering and mathematics to give socialist construction a modern rationale and erstwhile effectiveness. The Bureaucratic Professional approach also claims to be democratic. Scientific planning is the most effective way to meet social needs, so it must represent public interests, a rationale revived by Deng and elaborated by Jiang. That "socialist legality" is superior to "bourgeois democracy" is another argument revived by Deng and maintained by Jiang. On population, because Russia was relatively underpopulated, the Soviet Union had emphasized Marx's rejection of Malthus's pessimistic view that population would tend to outrun resources, making anti-Malthusianism the orthodoxy of international communization. In 1949, the PRC officially endorsed Marx's and Stalin's optimism that socialism could make better use of people than could capitalism. This official anti-Malthusianism continued to inhibit birth limitation for the rest of the Mao era, particularly during radical periods. Discursively, the Bureaucratic current tended to treat people as dehumanized objects of material planning, whereas the Professional current wanted to treat them as human beings with a need for "scientific knowledge" about their own sexuality (Evans 1997).

SOCIALIST MARKETIZATION

Socialist Marketization permits the less costly and less intrusive approach of selective indirect regulation, which among many advantages provides fewer opportunities for corruption. General rules tell people what they are allowed to do, and the regime intervenes only when people don't do it, to enforce compliance, fairness, and equity. To the extent that there is planning, it is not mandatory but indicative, mostly forecasting what services government will need to deliver, but not telling society what to do. The Jiang era accomplished much of the transition from operation to regulation in economic policy and initiated that transition in social and cultural policy. State planning persisted longest in the population domain, but the post-Jiang era has begun switching from operation through "birth according to plan" to regulation through "birth according to law." Regulation is economical and effective, particularly when supplemented by social self-regulation through private consumer aspirations and private professional advice. The main difficulty about governance through regulation is that, to be optimally effective, it must be quite sophisticated, allowing a variety of stakeholders to participate in fashioning rules that optimize such values as economic efficiency, social equity, and public accountability.

Institutionally, Socialist Marketization originated in the financial side of the financial and economic system and has gradually built its own institutional locus in the PRC's emerging financial system. The process has involved a struggle against the previously dominant economic planning establishment. As reported in Chapter 5, the struggle eventually helped open more institutional space for "strategic planning" of population by an updated population-and-birth commission that is replacing mandatory central planning of individuals' behavior with indicative planning to guide future government policy and investment. PRC leaders instructed all sectors to adapt to Socialist Marketization, but they instructed birth planning to do so without turning over to the market the regulation of population, which PRC leaders insisted must remain a macroregulatory function of government. Birth planning had to adapt not only to Marketization itself, but also to the adaptations to Marketization within other policy sectors—or, more specifically, to the adequacy or inadequacy of those adaptations. For example, in the area of enforcement, at least some birth policy planners would like to convert disincentives for noncompliance with birth rules from "fines" or "fees" to "taxes" but cannot do so yet because the system for collecting taxes from individuals remains too weak. In principle the birth system has already turned enforcement of the payment of the existing Social Compensation Fee over to the courts, but evidently many local courts are reluctant to enforce full payment on couples who refuse to pay. Meanwhile, the adaptation of the police system to Socialist Marketization has included the decision that the state must be willing to register all newborns, whether they are authorized under birth rules or not, thereby undercutting another implicit sanction against couples who do not comply with birth rules.

Discursively, like the first two Leninist approaches, Socialist Marketization is scientistic. It aspires to world-class physical science and technology and wishes to apply the social sciences to the management of both state and society. State administration draws on recent Western theories of scientific management, particularly management by objectives. This approach also claims to be democratic, particularly at the elite level. It wishes not only to complete the technocratic-bureaucratic project of constructing a socialist legal system but also to use the consultative and oversight capacities of legislative bodies. However, so far the proponents of Socialist Marketization have limited political reform to Elite Pluralization, eschewing Mass Democratization. Thus it has declined to progress much beyond the limited village-level "managed democracy" initiated in the early post-Mao period. However, by the 1990s, Socialist Marketization was applying "village self-government" to community supervision of birth planning. Socialist Marketization promotes open discussion of reproduction and even allows for the pleasurable aspects of sexuality (Evans 1997).

Constructing Population Policy: Location, Quantity, and Quality

Over the last half century, PRC policies have addressed three successive key dimensions of population—in the order in which they historically emerged: location, quantity, and quality. China is most famous for its efforts since the Deng era to limit the quantity of population by the state's planning how many children each couple could have. However, birth limits were preceded in the Mao era by locational policies confining the rural population to the countryside. Since the Jiang era, birth limits have been followed by increasing emphasis on the population's quality—its health, education, and welfare. These policies, some highly unusual, have borne the marks of Chinese culture and of strategies for managing population developed by earlier Chinese regimes.

LOCATION: URBAN VERSUS RURAL

The PRC has had strong spatial policies that have changed drastically during its history. Most of the time the population's geographic movement has been severely restricted. Originally, PRC "population policy" did not include these locational regulations and practices, yet they strongly affected it. By the early twenty-first century, one of the main tasks of the PRC's population-and-birth program is to do strategic planning for China's population future, including location. Accordingly, location is a basic dimension of the story told in this book.

The PRC's most direct spatial regulation of population has been the restriction of rural residents to the countryside. Early in the Mao era those restrictions were institutionalized through a nationwide system of household registration that created radically different political-economic regimes in China's cities and villages. In terms of socioeconomic modernization, the result was gradation in space. That is, most rural residents were poorer than most urban residents, but some rural localities were poorer than others, depending largely on their distance from urban markets and transportation lines. (For a precise model see Skinner, Henderson, and Yuan 2000.) In terms of political demography and reproductive culture, however, the result approached dichotomy. Institutionally, people were registered as either urban or rural, and their life chances differed dramatically as a result. Post-Mao population policy built on this urban-rural divide, creating different birth rules and enforcement mechanisms for those officially registered as urban and rural residents. In the process population policy widened that divide, creating two worlds of population control and two sets of social, political, and bodily consequences. The urban-rural dichotomy is not only a central category of state bureaucratic practice, it is also the central construct in a cultural politics of population in which the "modern, low quantity, high quality" urban populace has been constituted in opposition to the "backward, high quantity, low quality" peasant population. Both institutional and discursive practices of urban-rural division have had powerful effects on the population politics charted in this book.

The Deng era began relaxing locational restrictions, gradually allowing ever larger flows of temporary migrants to the cities (Solinger 1999). To some extent this mobility made birth planning more difficult because migrants tended to slip beyond the control of both their locality of origin and their locality of residence. To a greater extent, however, rural-urban mobility made birth planning easier. Most migrants went to cities to make money, not to parent unauthorized children. Migrants soon adopted urban attitudes toward childbearing and childrearing and carried those attitudes back to their villages. The Hu era has begun exploring how to reduce rural-urban dualism and how to better incorporate migrants in cities as citizens with full rights.

QUANTITY: NUMBER AND TIMING

From roughly 1970 to 2000, PRC population policies, like those elsewhere in the world at the time, focused almost exclusively on slowing population growth. Yet China's policies toward population quantity were unique in two crucial ways. First, the PRC approached limiting population growth as a matter of the state planning of births. This differs from the Western liberal notion of family planning in that the role of the state is paramount: the regime plans births to bring the reproduction of human beings in line with the production of material goods. The Chinese invented the historically unique concept of state birth planning and institutionalized it with extraordinary relentlessness.

The political and institutional life of this construct constitutes another big part of our story.

Second, the PRC attempted direct state intervention not only in the number of children that couples had but also in the timing of marriage, the initiation of childbearing, and the spacing between children. This multifaceted approach is well captured in the 1970s slogan "later-longer-fewer" (*wan xi shao*, or later marriage, longer spacing, and fewer births). In 1980, policy made explicit another dimension that had long been implicit, adding quality to make a four-part slogan: "late marriage, late birth, few births, quality births" (*wanhun wanyu shaosheng yousheng*). Throughout most of the 1980s and 1990s, policy emphasized mostly "few births," trying to prevent third and higher births while aspiring to limit most couples to one. In the course of the 1990s, China's fertility fell below replacement level. By the early 2000s, the emphasis of state policy and public concern had decisively shifted to quality.

QUALITY: HEALTH, EDUCATION, AND WELFARE

Much has been written about the PRC's policies on the location and quantity of population, but little is known about the regime's third population project—enhancing the quality of China's people to prepare them for participation in a modern globalized economy. In China, population "quality" is a polysemic term, whose meaning has broadened considerably as it has been taken up in popular culture (Anagnost 1997a, 1997b). For the state birth planning system, quality refers in the first instance to the health of the child at birth. Yet even in official discourse, quality extends to the lifelong health of the mother and child and to the education and well-being of the younger generation.

State and popular efforts to promote quality began on a modest scale in the 1980s. Preoccupation with population quality grew during the 1990s and should grow even more during the 2000s in both state and society. For the regime, quantity has been brought under tentative control, permitting a shift of resources to problems of quality and welfare. In the early 2000s, PRC leaders have felt particularly responsible for ameliorating negative side effects of the regime's earlier policies on quantity, such as distorted sex ratios, accelerated aging, and the resulting need for old-age support, particularly for couples with no son. Attention to these issues signals the new administration's concern both with the population's quality (by regularizing the age and sex structure) and with its welfare (by delivering services to enhance the well-being of young girls and the childless elderly). For society, rapid economic development has created resources for addressing quality goals and strong social demand for the relevant services. Far-reaching changes in Chinese society and its aspirations for the young have also fueled an intense popular interest in nurturing a new generation of "superior" children equipped to compete in the modern world.

The quality issue is especially interesting because the forces regulating it—or attempting to regulate it—extend well beyond the state. Some quality goals, particularly those most directly related to childbearing, do fall within the responsibility and competence of the birth system. Others, including maternal and child health care, fall under the jurisdiction and capabilities of the health system. Still other quality goals belong to other branches of government, such as the education system. However, with child quality embracing so much, nonstate actors have played growing roles in defining the norms and practices governing child quality. Capitalist corporations, international and domestic, have become particularly important. Involving not only state intervention but also nonstate social forces and market logics, the politics of population quality has developed quite differently from the politics of quantity.

PART ONE

Policy Formulation and Implementation

Policy Actors and Policy Components

BY THE EARLY TWENTY-FIRST CENTURY, PRC policies toward reproduction and population had completed three major eras. The Mao era (from the mid-1950s to the mid-1970s) started from only tentative approval of individual "birth control" (*jiezhi shengyu*), progressed to relatively "soft" advocacy of couples' practicing birth control, and ended with increasingly "hard" enforcement of state "birth planning" (*jihua shengyu*). The Deng era (from the late 1970s through the early 1990s) started with the formulation and ended with the re-enforcement of a significantly harder version of state birth planning: the increasingly strict enforcement of quite restrictive birth rules. The Jiang era (from the mid-1990s to the early 2000s) eventually initiated and progressively deepened the reform of hard birth planning. In the current Hu era, PRC policies toward population and birth planning may be entering a new epoch during which classic PRC state birth planning will be gradually phased out and population-related social programs gradually phased in.

The three chapters in Part 1 tell the story of policy during the three completed eras, directly from the main policy documents, largely from the point of view of the policymakers and implementors themselves. The policy documents include not only formal declarations of policy but also program work reports and less formal speeches. Implementors conveyed to policymakers what the concrete problems were and policymakers conveyed back to implementors what local examples they wanted followed. Some previous accounts have provided this inside perspective for particular episodes (e.g., Greenhalgh 1986, 1990a; White 1994a, 1994b). Part 1 of this book is the first account to cover the entire history of PRC birth planning from the "inside," indicating not only what policies were adopted but also some of the process through which they were formulated. Thus in addition to providing the fun of eavesdropping on PRC leaders as they tried to figure out how to manage China's huge population, this perspective provides comparable coverage across periods and brings out continuities and variations between them.

Policy Actors: Formulation and Implementation

The ultimate purpose of the policy narrative in Part 1 is not simply to report the evolution of PRC birth policy but rather to illuminate the evolution of the PRC regime's general capacity for policy formulation and implementation. This does involve the definition of formal institutions and processes. Indeed our policy narrative is particularly concerned to note when top PRC leaders did and did not directly address issues of population and reproduction through their highest formal forum for making decisions and did or did not produce what they themselves would have regarded as formal policy. However, much of regime capacity emerged through less formal processes. Procedurally, the narrative sketches the resulting interactions between the main categories of policy actors (defined later in this section). Substantively, the narrative highlights the gradual emergence of the main components of policy itself (defined in the next section). These components are important elements of the regime's capacity for implementation because they tell implementors how to approach the problem and exactly what to do. The narrative does not, however, attempt to follow in any detail the extent and manner in which policy was actually implemented in particular instances. (To do so would require another book.)

ACTORS IN POLICY FORMULATION

Over the past fifty years, the documents embodying PRC birth policy were generated by the interactions between three sets of actors: national political leaders, national program leaders, and subnational program leaders.

The first and by far the most powerful actors are the *national political leaders*. Individual instructions and, particularly, collective decisions by national political leaders tell both national and subnational program leaders what, in general, they are supposed to do. From 1949 to 1976, birth policy was dominated in practice by the PRC's "paramount leader," party chairman Mao Zedong. As we shall see, he invented the idea of state birth planning but remained ambivalent about it and prevented it from getting fully under way until after he died. During that first half of the story, government premier Zhou Enlai was also important, as the chief advocate of actually putting state birth planning into effect as quickly as possible. After Mao and Zhou died, the most important single actor was Deng Xiaoping, who eventually became their de facto successor as leader of both party and government. Deng strongly favored state birth planning, which he institutionalized and implemented very vigorously. Also important are the views of other senior revolutionary leaders and, to a lesser extent, their designated younger successors. However, except for Mao, and perhaps Deng, ultimately what made the views of any of these individuals into official policy was a decision by the Standing Committee of the Politburo of the party's Central Committee to incorporate their views into a document issued by the Central Committee and/or the government's State Council, the most authoritative voices of national political leaders. In addition, the PRC's legislature, the National People's Congress, has been important in principle and eventually also in practice. Finally, relevant intellectuals, such as economists, and relevant professionals, such as doctors, have been an important source of policy ideas. However, those ideas were important mainly only insofar as they were adopted—or conspicuously rejected—by national political leaders and their authoritative media.

The second most important category of actors is *national program leaders*. Within the parameters set by national political leaders, they worked out specific policies for implementation and reported back on the results (in both the superior-subordinate and professional-informational senses of "report"). Work reports written by national program leaders—either for submission to national political leaders or for delivery as speeches at national conferences of subnational leaders—summarize instructions from above and reports from below. At the beginning of our story these work reports are somewhat sketchy; by the end they are elaborate with program jargon. In between they are often remarkably candid, reasonable, pointed, and succinct. They are almost always carefully crafted, usually exemplifying PRC administration at its best.

During the Mao era the relevant national program leaders were top officials of the health ministry, particularly of its maternal and child health department. The health ministry started off in 1949 opposed even to contraception, let alone abortion and sterilization, not to mention compulsory versions of any of those. Party leaders soon converted the ministry to advocating voluntary contraception and to trying to deliver that and other reproductive health services, particularly to cities and densely populated rural areas. Nevertheless, there were many in the health ministry who always opposed its participation in mandatory mass birth limitation, which in any case exceeded the health ministry's organizational and technical capabilities. Accordingly the Deng era established a separate national ministry for birth planning, along with a separate subnational ministerial system for implementing it.

The third set of actors, *subnational program leaders*, is in charge of health administration or birth work at the provincial level. (In the PRC, the roughly thirty provincial-level units include a few major cities directly administered by the national level—originally just Beijing, Tianjin, and Shanghai.)

Subnational program leaders translate national guidelines into provincial programs and report the results to national program leaders (but only in the professional-informational sense of "report"—what the PRC calls a "professional relationship," or *yewu guanxi*). Such work reports become historically visible and nationally important when national political leaders approve them and circulate them to all subnational leaders as models. Eventually, as institutionalization of birth administration worked its way downward toward society, this category of subnational program leader also includes program officials below the provincial level, particularly at the prefectural or district level (300 – 400 *diqu* nationwide). Those units are typically small city-regions, containing a central city and surrounding counties (2400 – 3000 *xian* nationwide). A crucial part of the process of building the administrative capacity for state birth planning has been establishing and training officials at these intermediate levels that connect the national state to society. Part 1 refers to the prefecture and county as "localities" or the "local" level.

ACTORS IN POLICY IMPLEMENTATION

In addition to these three sets of actors, there are another three sets that remain largely off the stage of policy formulation: subnational political leaders, community cadres, and the public. These become increasingly significant to birth policy as implementation progresses from state to society. They also become increasingly significant to this book as it too progresses from the state in Part 1 to society in Part 2. These actors are not main participants in policy formulation but, as problems of implementation come to the fore, policy increasingly focuses on them and they acquire some indirect influence on it. So we need to introduce them here.

Subnational political leaders are the individuals whom the national party and government personnel systems place in charge of the party and government at the provincial level, constituting party committees and government "cabinets." The principals are the provincial party first secretary and the governor, but deputy party secretaries and vice governors are also important, particularly those whose portfolios include supervising health work and birth work. These are the people to whom, at each level of administration, subnational program leaders report (in the superior-subordinate sense of "report"—what the PRC calls a "leadership relationship," or *lingdao guanxi*). During the Mao era, subnational political leaders increasingly included party and state leaders at the district and county levels. During the Deng and Jiang eras, the instruments of national party and government personnel systems were increasingly brought to bear on progressively higher levels, first to enforce birth limitation, then to reform it.

Community cadres are the policy implementors at the street or grassroots level, where state meets society. It is an axiom of Leninist systems that, along with "correct" party leadership, "basic-level" cadres are crucial to success. Because basic-level units are sufficiently small scale to permit face-to-face interaction, Part 1 refers to this as the "community" level. In urban areas these basic levels include both territorial units such as administrative districts and neighborhoods, and functional units, such as factories and bureaucracies. For most of its history, the PRC absorbed most urban community activity into direct state administration, making the state responsible for most urban residents as dependents but also giving the state much leverage over them. Consequently in urban areas the regime could implement both voluntary birth control and mandatory birth planning quite quickly. In rural areas the basic levels are principally the rural township or town and the rural village (several tens of thousands of townships and roughly a million natural—as opposed to administrative—villages). Although the PRC has always exercised strong administration over rural activities, during the Mao era it left most of them in a self-reliant collective sector and during the Deng era it turned many of them over to the private sector. That made the state less responsible for financing rural services but also gave the state less leverage— and declining leverage—for enforcing mandatory birth planning.

Instead of imagining a sharp dividing line between state and society, it is more accurate to visualize a transitional zone in which the state's reach gradually becomes weaker and social influence becomes stronger as one moves from county to township to village to neighborhood to household. The loyalties of community cadres similarly shift according to the level of their positions, as the PRC has recognized quite clearly. Ideologically, birth work has always included educating cadres as well as masses. Organizationally, the main problem for birth planning has been securing the financing for local personnel and services and training the personnel to deliver those services to communities.

Finally, *the public* is the vast majority of the population on whose behalf the CCP has claimed to be acting. The PRC's original revolutionary tradition defined the public as "the masses" (*qunzhong*) while its later-emerging constitutional tradition defined them as "citizens" (*gongmin*). The CCP summed up its revolutionary political-administrative theory as "the mass line," or "from the masses, to the masses." The party is supposed to ascertain public needs and desires, subject that information to the scientific analysis of Marxism-Leninism, then transmit the results back as "party policy" to guide the public. When party research and analysis is done well, party policy is, by definition, "correct," both in constituting the best possible analysis of the "objective situation" and in reflecting the long-term best interests of the masses. Particularly in social policies where the objective is to change public behavior, the key to successful policy implementation is therefore the propaganda and education that is necessary for explaining to basic-level cadres and the public what is in their best interest. Then they can comply "self-consciously" and "voluntarily" (*zijue, ziyuan*). In large part, PRC birth policy is the application of this political-administrative theory to the problem of limiting births. Because of their extensive experience in applying the mass line to other problems, PRC policymakers had a good idea of the general dynamics of what such limitation would require. Nevertheless, applying the mass line to the particular problem of limiting reproduction required much experimentation and involved some bad mistakes, of which arguably the greatest was the one-child policy. (Chapter 7 describes the workings of the mass line in both rural and urban areas during the implementation of the one-child policy in the 1980s.)

Policy Components: Guiding and Operational

Like many kinds of PRC policy, birth policy has six major components: three "guiding" components of ideological line, party leadership, and directional policy, and three "operational" components of plan, rules, and enforcement. Full-dress policy statements by national program leaders in any major policy area usually include most of these components, usually in approximately that order.

GUIDING COMPONENTS: IDEOLOGY, LEADERSHIP, AND DIRECTION

The guiding components consist of, first, a guiding *ideology* defining a general party line during a particular period (*zhidao sixiang*); second, the party and government *leadership* necessary to articulate and animate that line (*dangzheng lingdao*); and third, a general statement of policy *direction* for each specific policy area (*fangzhen zhengce*). Roughly speaking, it takes a national party congress or plenum to effect a change in overall line and a meeting of the Politburo Standing Committee to adopt changes in the directional policy within particular policy areas. Either the party Secretariat or the government State Council then formulates more specific policies, which program leaders must then figure out how to implement. Once national party leaders issue such guiding components, it becomes virtually impossible for others to dispute them, particularly for issues that national party leaders declare to be a matter of party line. One of the main facts about the history of PRC population policies is that, because of conflicts with other ideological premises, they began to receive their ideological rationale only after the end of the Mao era. Until then, lack of ideological legitimacy inhibited the activation of party leadership, the statement of policy direction, and the institutionalization of birth work.

OPERATIONAL COMPONENTS: PLAN,
RULES, AND ENFORCEMENT

The operational components of policy tell both subnational implementors and the general public what to do. The operational components of PRC national birth policy emerged only gradually. The first component to appear was the kernel of a *plan* in the form of numerical targets for national population growth. Until around 1980 those targets were expressed mostly as growth rates, after that also and more dramatically as an end-of-century total that population must not exceed. In the middle 1970s the incipient birth program found it advisable to translate these macrodemographic targets into specific *rules* for microindividual behavior concerning the timing of childbearing and the number of children in order to make policies more concrete for both cadres and public. During the Deng era the gradually strengthening birth program developed increasingly elaborate methods of *enforcement*, mostly through provincial regulations.

Conclusion: Policy Formation

Policy analysis in political science has involved models ranging from the extreme top-down model of "leader-in-command" to extreme bottom-up models that attribute policy to social forces. In the authoritarian PRC, the most relevant models focus on elites, as in classic models for analyzing decisions in American foreign policy (Allison 1971). In these terms, PRC policymaking has involved a mix of leader-in-command, competition between competing bureaucratic programs, and rivalry between the "principals" within the PRC revolutionary elite. As in any large organization, the top leader steers the system by assembling successive "dominant coalitions" from competing power groupings and policy tendencies within the system. At any given time, policy consists of a package of compromises between the main policy tendencies within the dominant coalition, a package often skillfully crafted to appear to be a seamless and consistent ideological whole. Over time, policy has ratcheted to left or right as the more extreme members have gradually been dropped from one side of the dominant coalition and added on the other. These policy tendencies have in turn been aggregations of many specific ministerial and provincial interests that bargained continuously with each other in a fragmented way. (See Lampton ed. 1987; Lieberthal and

Oksenberg 1988; Lieberthal and Lampton eds. 1992; Hamrin and Zhao eds. 1995.)

The demarcations between leadership eras have been substantively important for the policy domain of population and reproduction because the views of the paramount leader have mattered greatly, even though the power of the top leader declined from Mao to Deng to Jiang to Hu. Most of the time, policy toward population and reproduction was in fact largely aligned with the views of the principal leader, whose prerogative it was to define ideology and agenda. For example, during the Mao era population policy reflected Mao's ambivalence about population size; during the Deng era it reflected the determination of Deng and his colleagues to limit growth in that size. Within eras, demarcations between "administrations" have also been quite significant. For example, during the Deng era the change from the Hu Yaobang–Zhao Ziyang administration (1981–1986) to the Zhao Ziyang–Li Peng administration (1987–1989) produced a distinct toughening of enforcement of birth limits. During the Jiang era, the change from Jiang's first full administration with Li Peng as premier (1993–1998) to Jiang's second full administration with Zhu Rongji as premier (1998–2003) produced a pronounced deepening of reform of the birth program. The transition from the Jiang-Zhu administration to the Hu Jintao–Wen Jiabao administration has produced a significant reorientation of the now "population-and-birth" program from limiting births toward orchestrating population-related social programs.

In all of this, society was both absent and omnipresent. On the one hand, mass associations run by the party preempted most niches in which society might attempt actively to participate in policymaking. For high-priority objectives, policymakers could and did choose to override public disaffection for years at a time. On the other hand, policymakers usually responded eventually to mounting political costs. These included the unwillingness or inability of basic-level cadres to implement policy, the indifferent compliance or passive resistance by the mass public and—of greatest concern to PRC leaders—the potential for open public demonstrations and mass political instability.

CHAPTER 3

The Mao Era: From Soft Birth Control to Hard Birth Planning

DURING THE MAO ERA (mid-1950s to mid-1970s), the PRC defined a policy domain connecting reproduction and population and began intervening in those processes in society. Before 1949, population and reproduction had not been major issues for the Chinese Communist Party because the CCP had been preoccupied with surviving Nationalist attacks, repelling Japanese invasion, and conquering the country. After 1949, at first PRC leaders saw both advantages and disadvantages to having a large population and consequently alternated between allowing and limiting its growth. During the 1950s the PRC began national economic planning and endorsed birth control—policies that converged in the notion of "birth planning." Then the Great Leap Forward first interrupted birth work, then made it more urgent by creating famine in rural areas and enlarging the cities with migrants whom the state had to feed. During the 1960s PRC leaders resumed efforts to slow population growth by promoting birth control, which spread quickly in large cities but only began to penetrate rural areas. For whatever reasons, fertility did begin to fall. Then the Cultural Revolution again interrupted birth work, slowing the decline. During the 1970s PRC leaders again resumed efforts to plan population and promote birth control in both urban and rural areas. This time, those efforts were not interrupted and gradually became more systematic and intense. Again, for whatever reasons, fertility continued to fall (Table 1).

The Mao era is long past and during that era the CCP pursued birth planning only intermittently. Nevertheless the legacy of that period remains significant in the early twenty-first century in ways that are not merely historical. Most concretely, because the PRC did not consistently promote quasi-voluntary birth control during the Mao era, births increased from the late 1950s through the late 1960s (interrupted only briefly by the Great Leap famine). That baby boom then threatened to produce an echo boom in the late 1980s and early 1990s, which was the main reason the Deng era considered it urgent to enforce mandatory birth limits on that generation. Despite the reduced fertility of that cohort, their children will still produce a minor peak in new childbearing couples in the 2010s, which is one reason the PRC has left mandatory birth limits in place. Demographic booms and busts that originated during the Mao era will have continuing effects—economic, social, and political.

The relatively low level of activity in birth planning for most of the third quarter of the twentieth century under Mao throws into sharp relief the high level of activity in birth planning throughout the last quarter of that century under his successors and the struggle to reform the results of that activity in the first quarter of the next century. Nevertheless, it was the Mao era that imagined the goal of mandatory state limits on number of children, limits the Deng era codified and that by the Jiang era most Chinese accepted. The Mao era also innovated many of the methods of central population planning and mass birth work that the Deng era used and that the Jiang era began to reform. Thus the Hu era did not start from a blank slate with a free hand, in either goals or methods. On the contrary, their continuity across more than half a century has been remarkable, reflecting the gradual succession of CCP leaders, the incremental evolution of policy discourse, and the growing institutionalization of population policy and birth work.

The father of the concept of "birth planning" for limiting the quantity of China's population was Mao Zedong. However, the godfather who repeatedly rescued that nearly abandoned offspring was Zhou Enlai, the premier of the PRC government under Mao. Both Mao and Zhou understood from the beginning that, ultimately, reducing fertility requires cultural change, to which educating the public might contribute, but only gradually. As Zhou told Edgar Snow in late 1958 (Shi 581000), "we are confident that putting birth planning into practice is correct (*zhengquede*), but to do so immediately in China is difficult (*kunnande*)." Nevertheless, Zhou knew that the sooner the PRC began slowing the rate of population growth, the less haste and coercion would occur later. Accordingly he wanted to proceed as soon as possible with a relatively gradual and voluntary approach to limiting quantity, based on educating the public about reproduction and providing couples with contraceptive services (EBP 295). Whether vigorous promotion of rural birth limits would have been possible during the Mao era is debatable, given the technological unavailability of cheap and effective contraceptives and the social resistance based on the cultural conservatism and practical labor needs of rural families. Mao maintained a complex position on these issues. At the "micro" pole of individual behavior, he wanted to extend modern conduct to the countryside but insisted on only cautious intervention against peasant resistance. At the "macro" pole of population and development, he weighed alternative assessments of China's future manpower needs, ranging from labor-intensive defense and development, which would require as many people as possible, to agricultural and industrial mechanization, which would make a large labor force redundant. Mao's temporizing contributed to Deng's feeling that he had to adopt the "catch-up" scenario that Zhou had feared. Under Jiang the PRC began to move beyond Dengist "hard" birth planning, but under Hu the struggle for Comprehensive Reform continues.

Continuity of goals involves not only quantity but extends also to location. As noted in Chapter 1, it was the Mao era that locked most of the population into the countryside in a collective sector of self-reliant communities that needed labor power. The communist revolution, ostensibly intended to elevate peasants into prime movers, instead relegated them to a supporting role in socialist development. The Hu era is only beginning to come to grips with the inequalities and indignities involved.

Continuity of goals also extends beyond quantity to quality. From the very beginning of the CCP in 1921, its leaders wanted to raise the cultural and political "level" of China's population. From the very beginning of the PRC in 1949, its leaders considered such cultural construction essential to national wealth and power. During the Mao era, national political and health leaders did want to provide women, including rural women, with modern reproductive health care. Doing so would improve not only the immediate health of mother and child but also the later health and education, employment and prosperity of family and community—and ultimately of state and nation. The means were supposed to include choice from a range of contraceptive methods and were supposed to ensure quality care tailored to individual needs. During the Deng era these ideals were largely superseded by preoccupation with limiting the quantity of population, but they never entirely disappeared. The effort of the PRC birth program that began during the Jiang era to shift from limiting births toward delivering services has been in part a reversion to the health system's original objectives, although elaborated and legitimated by new international ideals. The late reassertion of such ideals gives their early articulation a particular relevance and poignancy.

Many of the components of state intervention in social reproduction that originated under Mao persist in the early 2000s. The ambition of the Mao era to set grand numerical *plan* targets for national modernization to be achieved by 2000 remained alive after 2000 in new targets for the twenty-first century, even though the targets became indicative not mandatory. The idea of linking national population goals to individual reproductive behavior, which also originated in the 1950s, remained an objective after 2000, even though the link shifted from plan to law. *Rules* about timing of marriage and number of children that originated in the Mao era entered Deng era planning and Jiang era legislation and, in the Hu era, remain in place. As for *enforcement*, the Mao era quickly adapted the CCP's general methods for fomenting revolution to the specific task of changing reproductive behavior. Ostensibly these mobilizational methods of birth work relied on persuasive propaganda and education, but they easily slipped into coerced abortions and sterilizations. Facing what it considered a national emergency, the Deng era vigorously applied those methods. The Jiang era gradually proscribed them in favor of a more professional approach, but the Hu era continues to struggle against them in backward localities.

In terms of the governmentalization of population, in a complementary relationship with the state that had lasted for a thousand years, during the Mao era rural reproduction remained largely under the governance of extended families—extended in the sense not only of actually operative kinship relations but also of embeddedness in family-based economic production and in a definition of family identity that stretched over generations of time. For their part, CCP leaders' long-term agenda was equally broad, aspiring to control location, limit quantity, and raise quality. As evidently Mao understood, a frontal assault on the traditional Chinese family system by old-fashioned sovereign state power was unlikely to succeed in fundamentally altering reproductive behavior—or could succeed only at immense political cost. Crude physical coercion would not work because the threat of the new revolutionary regime to kill those who resisted it should be applied only to "class enemies," not to "the people." Persuasion or incentives would not work until the institutions intermediate between state and households began to shift from extended families to socialist collectives or to a more diverse array of quasi-capitalist enterprises, professions, and associations.

Regime capacity, both Mobilizational and Bureaucratic, would remain relatively inefficient until individuals—in China, more than in the West, in the context of their families and communities—cultivated conscientiousness in governing their own reproduction, as Mao himself might have said. However, to be maximally effective, the necessary disciplining institutions and professional discourses would have to be allowed to proliferate freely, as Mao would not allow. In particular, the regime could not intervene efficiently or effectively until it recognized the quasi-autonomy of population processes, which obeyed the "laws" of demographic dynamics posited by western or Marxist political economy. Such laws were constraints on his freedom of action that Mao would not abide. It was only toward the end of the Mao era that the PRC regime would begin to adjust its approach to promote a more encompassing biopower that—as the PRC birth program itself eventually came to argue—drew on the capacity for governance not only of the political regime but also of professional institutions and private individuals.

Introduction: Linking Levels

The invention of state planning of births during the Mao era required the gradual linking of three levels of problems, which we will tag "micro," "macro," and "meso." Micro and macro are of course conventional terms in mainstream social science for large-scale versus small-scale phenomena; Foucault used them as well, to identify the two poles of biopower, individual and societal. The term "meso" is less common but refers to a variety of middle-scale mechanisms—in this book both institutional and discursive—for linking micro and macro. We note these levels in roughly the order in which the CCP addressed them as policy issues in the population domain.

At the micro level of individual reproductive behavior, after 1949 the CCP soon encountered a "birth control problem" (the party's term). Simply as a matter of individual health and morality, should the CCP discourage or encourage contraception and the related medical procedures of abortion and sterilization? Before 1949, in its revolutionary base areas, the CCP had straddled the issue by favoring mass population growth while allowing its elite cadres to practice contraception (Shi 1988, 49–52). In the course of the Mao era, needing a consistent overall public policy, the CCP shifted quickly from discouraging contraception to allowing it, and then gradually from promoting it to enforcing it. This microindividual level involved many concrete questions: the ethical acceptability and medical effects of contraception, sterilization, and abortion; the production and distribution of the necessary supplies and facilities; and the provision and regulation of access.

At the macro level of the relationship between population and development, the CCP soon encountered a "population problem" (again the party's term). The founding of the PRC, by ending civil war and permitting the resumption of normal economic activity, had permitted renewed population growth. Should the CCP adopt the optimistic view that the more economic and military manpower the better, or the pessimistic view that China already had too many people? As the PRC state began planning development and allocating manpower, it assumed overall responsibility for employing and provisioning the population, which turned out to be daunting tasks. Under Mao, in principle the CCP continued to vigorously deny the universal validity of Malthusian pessimism, maintaining instead a Marxian optimism that socialism could always make good use of more people. In practice the CCP shifted from optimism to pessimism, though with some flip-flops along the way. This macrosocietal level too involved many concrete questions: employment and migration, food and clothing, housing and education, and, eventually, overall resources and environment.

At the meso level of institutions and discourses, the CCP soon encountered a "socialist birth problem" (our term). As the CCP socialized first urban and then rural areas, it discovered that, by providing modest subsidies to urban areas and by helping secure basic needs in rural areas, socialist institutions tended to encourage more births than socialist institutions could support. Should inadvertent incentives for reproduction be removed and countervailing disincentives be adopted? This would be a complex question anywhere because public policies in different domains typically conflict. It proved to be a very complex question in the PRC, where the government intervened so heavily in so many domains and in such rapidly changing ways. In any case, the PRC needed an institutional bridge and discursive formulations to connect its population plans to individual behavior. The particular institutions that the PRC adopted strongly shaped the results that policies produced. For most of the Mao era, to the extent that it pursued birth planning, the PRC did so by mobilizing the public through existing institutional channels that had been created for more general purposes, mainly the propaganda and technical capacities of the public health system, and eventually through the mobilizational capacity of generalist local cadres as well. The reliance on periodic campaigns through nonspecialized channels contributed to the on-again, off-again pattern of policy and implementation under Mao. This mesoinstitutional level also involved many concrete questions: work and reward, entitlements and responsibilities, and party leadership and work methods.

These three levels of problems first arose as active issues and first became linked through actual policies in the mid-1950s (1953–1957). The notion that the state might need to limit population already had a significant history in both late imperial and Republican China (Sun 1987, 33–50; Dikotter 1995, 102–121). Several CCP leaders probably had a commonsense understanding of many of the problems involved (particularly Deng Xiaoping). Several nonparty intellectuals articulated detailed analyses and solutions (particularly senior nonparty economist Ma Yinchu). Nevertheless it was Mao, as CCP leader, who was most responsible for floating a grand vision of "birth planning." In several speeches during 1957, Mao raised the possibility that a socialist society might plan not only economic production but also social reproduction. He did not concede that China had too many people or that socialism could not provide for them. Instead, he bypassed those arguments by implying that planning births would be the rational and scientific thing to do. In February 1957 Mao addressed the Supreme State Council on the implications for China of recent turmoil within the Soviet bloc and of China's shift from revolution to development, prescribing "the correct handling of contradictions among the people." In that speech he famously deplored the "anarchy" of human reproduction and its likely disastrous consequences (a theme he had mentioned as a youth—Shi 1988, 49). Accordingly he raised the possibility of the PRC's establishing a government department for birth planning, or a government committee on birth control, or a people's organization to advocate birth control—all of which were later created (ME 510227). Mao also noted the need to solve "technical problems," presumably designing and delivering the necessary propaganda and services.

Using language that had been used by some intellectuals, Mao spoke in general of "childbearing with planning" (*you jihua de shengyu*), whose abbreviation (*jihua shengyu*) can be translated as either "planned birth" or "birth planning," with a range of possible meanings. It could refer to "family planning" by couples, as in the West, which evidently was how some Chinese initially interpreted it and a meaning that even Mao's initial thinking embraced. It could also be read as "collective planning" by communities, which may have been the early interpretation of at least some local cadres and perhaps the later preference of the extreme left during the Cultural Revolution. However, clearly what Mao soon envisioned for the long run was "state planning" for the nation as a whole, as many regime cadres may have immediately understood (White 1994a, 268–269). The Mao era did make much progress toward state planning of births, particularly in large cities. Nevertheless, Mao repeatedly indicated that it would take many years for the regime to figure out how to do birth planning throughout the whole country and how to persuade the public to go along with it, which he considered essential for success (ME 571009, 571013). In any case it did take another five years before other PRC leaders officially adopted the idea and began to try to implement it. It would be another ten years after that before PRC state birth planning began uninterrupted development (starting in 1973). It was not until the subsequent Deng era that the regime began building the institutions necessary to regulate births (starting in 1980).

Thus, although the Mao era invented both the concept and practice of state planning of births, during that era PRC leaders issued few formal instructions and endorsed few program reports on the subject. The three main guiding components of PRC birth planning for which the national political leadership was responsible—ideology, organization, and directional policy—remained relatively underdeveloped. Consequently the three main operative components of PRC birth planning—plan, rules, and enforcement—emerged only gradually, mostly from subnational experiments. The regime's primary contribution was technical: the development, manufacture, and provision of the necessary birth control devices and services, including the suction abortion machine, which was later adopted for use internationally. The regime also gradually began making a social contribution: propaganda and education to gradually change reproductive culture. However, for most of this era the party did not place much emphasis on advocating birth control and in fact declined to campaign for it through the party's most authoritative general national media (principally the *People's Daily*). Birth control propaganda was restricted largely to the dissemination of knowledge about contraception through specialized health publications (principally the *Health Daily*) and through subnational channels, preferably face-to-face.

1950s: Preinitiation

In the course of three decades of revolutionary struggle, what had emerged as the CCP's key to survival and victory was Maoism, providing a set of strategies and methods for mobilizing China's largely rural-agricultural population for warfare against the Nationalists and Japanese. In 1949, suddenly faced with the task of developing all of China, for lack of much alternative, the CCP began by relying on Stalinism, a Bureaucratic-Professional approach to rapid development of heavy industry, particularly in cities. The combination of Maoist mobilization and Stalinist bureaucracy provided the basic mix of mechanisms for the Maoist era in general and for birth planning in particular. Stalinism brought with it Marxist and Soviet pronatalism, which became the PRC's initial stance on population issues. However, the CCP soon concluded that Stalinism required some adaptation to China, expressed in midcourse corrections to the first Five Year Plan (1953–1957) and in the preliminary version of the second (intended for 1957–1962). During 1956 and 1957 economic policy seemed to move toward the preference of the Financial tendency for gradualness and balance, including some interest in slowing population growth. Instead Mao later endorsed using Mobilization to pursue Industrialization, the formula for the Great Leap Forward. Mao may also have considered China's large population a hedge against atomic weapons, as he shocked Khrushchev by suggesting. (On politics see MacFarquhar 1974, 1983; Harding 1981, 32–194; Bachman 1991; Teiwes 1993; Zheng 1997, 53–158; Huang 2000, 159–210.)

The CCP's heritage from before 1949 was mostly pronatal and anticontraceptive. Marx had argued that different social systems had different population dynamics: in capitalist systems population might outrun resources, but in socialist systems population would be a valued resource. The Soviet Union had encouraged childbearing because Russia was relatively underpopulated and because its population had been reduced by war. In China, the CCP had conducted revolutionary war from poor rural base areas where it needed the military and economic support of as many people as possible. Most of the party and army came from a rural culture that assumed the desirability of many children. A presumption against limiting births became entrenched in the CCP's major institutions—party, military, and government. (On pre-1949 program background see Sun 1987, 16–51.)

In 1949 the CCP was preoccupied with revolutionizing China and establishing the PRC, so population and reproduction were not yet priority issues. China's new leaders might have had little reason to pronounce on population, if a White Paper by the U.S. State Department had not argued that population was China's primary problem, which no regime would be able to solve. This provoked the New China News Agency to a rebuttal, later attributed to Mao (Shi 490916; Aird 1990, 20). China's big population was "a good thing," bourgeois pessimism was "utterly groundless," and the CCP would "achieve miracles" with people, who are "the most precious thing in the world." In early 1952 *People's Daily* carried its first editorial on population, explaining that limiting it would ruin the country (Shi 520100). (On 1949–1962, see Sun 1987, 52–116.)

The party's longstanding commitment to liberating women did result in one major policy act related to reproduction, the 1950 Marriage Law (Diamant 2000). For the rest of the Mao era, it remained the first of the three main legal bases for state intervention in reproduction, through state regulation of family life. Its main relevance to controlling births and limiting population was that it helped to raise marriage age, a goal that in the late 1950s some PRC leaders endorsed (Shi 570400; EBP 287–288, March 1957 speech by health vice minister Fu Lianzhang). However, the Marriage Law minimum age was rather low (20 years old for males and 18 for females) relative to what many leaders wanted (mid to high 20s for both), in order to promote health or extend education, mobilize manpower or slow population growth. As in much else about birth planning, a gap developed between legal foundation and administrative policy. A second relevance of the Marriage Law to birth planning concerned the premarital medical checkup that the law required. The health system tried to implement this provision, but "the masses were not yet ready for it and we had to give up" (EW 12Nov03 BJ-LXZ). This was another indication of early social resistance to the regime's intervening in reproduction and perhaps a lesson to health leaders on the need for caution in doing so. Fifty years later, the national health ministry was still trying to universalize premarital medical checkups—for eugenic among other reasons—and to force subnational levels not to charge couples for undergoing them (PI 040820). A third area of initiative resulted from the longstanding interest of some party leaders in reducing the maternal and infant mortality produced by traditional methods of childbirth, which the leaders had noticed in revolutionary base areas. In 1950, the PRC promptly began propagating more modern methods of childbearing as a main means of promoting maternal and child health.

During the middle 1950s issues of reproduction and population arose, first in meeting immediate needs of party members and state personnel, then in middle-range planning for urban areas, and finally in long-range planning for rural areas as well. (On program see Aird 1972; Shi 1988, 115–141; White 1994a; Scharping 2003, 43–50.)

REGIME ORIGINS

As is often the case with the origins of social policies throughout the world, the earliest origins of PRC birth planning lay within the regime itself, in the need of the regime's own personnel for access to reproductive services. This "micro" need was expressed first by elite women cadres through the regime's internal channels for communication, formal and informal.

Before 1949, despite Marxism's pronatal stance, the CCP's Revolutionary-Mobilizational legacy had included some antinatalism. In the revolutionary base areas, the concentration of party members in poor regions clearly had strained local resources and elite party members had needed to limit their own childbearing in order to devote themselves to their work (particularly women, of course). Evidently the elite issue was addressed most explicitly in 1942 at CCP headquarters in Yan'an, during the rectification campaign through which Mao established his ideological hegemony over the party. He criticized his rivals for too-literal application of Soviet ideas to China, presumably including Soviet population policies. Between late March and late May 1942, the base area newspaper, *Liberation Daily*, carried a series of articles discussing in effect how to reconcile Soviet pronatal ideology with Chinese Yan'an realities. The articles concluded that under wartime conditions—for the sake of revolution, work, and study—party members should postpone marriage and, once married, should practice contraception (Shi 1988, 49–52). It is worth noting that many of Mao's leading allies and agents in Yan'an later played important roles in the PRC, including roles in population policy (Huang 2000, 119–125). The contributions of Liu Shaoqi, Zhou En-lai, Deng Xiaoping, and Chen Yun will appear in this chapter and the next. In addition, Kang Sheng and Chen Boda remained leftist political advisers of Mao who helped orchestrate campaigns against antinatalists, such as Peking University president Ma Yinchu (Zhu 1999, 132–175). Hu Qiaomu remained one of Deng's leading intellectuals and helped launch the one-child policy (next chapter). (On politics see Selden 1971; Dorris 1976; Huang 2000, 119–125.)

After 1949, the PRC needed a consistent policy on contraception and, somewhat inadvertently, began extending its officially restrictive rural mass policy to everyone, including urban elites (White 1994a). Early reproductive policymaking evidently involved some lack of synchronization between the sociocultural and military-security sectors of the regime, on the one hand, and the economic-developmental sector on the other. Thus the earliest reproductive regulations were issued jointly by the health systems of the government and military for the newly occupied Beijing military district (Shi 500420). Because at first contraception was not a priority issue, the matter devolved to the health ministry, which was run by pronatal communist military doctors and staffed by anticontraceptive holdovers from the Republican period (Lampton 1977). The health ministry drafted regulations that narrowly restricted access to birth control, particularly abortion and sterilization (Shi 520531). The government commission in charge of sociocultural policy (Culture and Education) approved those regulations "for reference" for big hospitals (Shi 521231; EBP 59–60). The health ministry even instructed PRC Customs to block imports of contraceptives from abroad (Shi 530112).

However, it was just at this time, in January 1953, that the PRC declared a change in priorities from revolution to development and called on women to participate in "socialist construction" (Shi 530101). In April 1953 some women party members wrote a report to the All China Women's Federation arguing that such participation required access to contraception. According to the recollection of Li Xiuzhen, the woman who ran the health system's maternal and child health work for much of the Mao era, the report was passed to the federation's leader Deng Yingchao (the wife of government premier Zhou Enlai), who passed it to vice premier Deng Xiaoping (Shi 1988, 20n1). In the PRC's earliest turn toward contraception, in August 1953 Deng wrote on the report his instruction that birth control should be "advocated" (*tichang*). This judgment by the man who was later to sponsor the one-child policy was pivotal: Li Xiuzhen judged that it laid the basis for the CCP's ensuing endorsement of birth control, a policy that Zhou later credited Deng with inventing (ibid.). In the PRC's first official statement of a turn toward contraception, the State Council instructed the health ministry to facilitate public access to contraception (Shi 530811). During August Deng "repeatedly" instructed the health ministry to lift its import ban, which it did not do (Shi 530800).

This incipient policy shift did not immediately solve the "birth control problem" for regime cadres who wished to practice contraception. In May

1954, after the second national meeting of the women's federation discussed maternal and child health, Deng Yingchao wrote Deng Xiaoping stating the case for contraception (Shi 540527). In reply, Deng Xiaoping instructed that contraception was "necessary and appropriate" and that the government should "take effective measures" to provide access to it (Shi 540528; CTBP 6). In July 1954 the health ministry admitted that it had "lacked a correct understanding" of the matter, the State Council approved the health ministry's relaxation of restrictions on contraception, and the state pharmaceutical company began supplying some contraceptives (Shi 540720). In November the health ministry officially recanted its previous restrictiveness, citing both demand from the public and orders from superiors (Shi 541110). The state commerce bureau began participating in the distribution of contraceptives, which transferred control of access from doctors to stores (Shi 541130).

Further progress on this issue required a clear statement of party policy to government ministries. In December 1954 party leader Liu Shaoqi convened the PRC's first official meeting on the "birth control question," summoning relevant ministries to the office of the State Council's organ for coordinating sociocultural policy (renamed the Second Office, or *di'er bangongshi*). Liu declared that the party approved contraception (*zancheng jieyu*). The Second Office then convened a series of four interministerial workshops during January 1955 to work out details. (Shi 541227 regards these consultations as providing the preconditions for birth planning.) The party committee of the health ministry then wrote a report that "approved *appropriate* birth control" (*zancheng shidangde jieyu*). The report declared opposition to birth control to be a serious mistake in political line that required thorough correction (EBP 1–3). Access to contraception should be unrestricted and the government should develop the relevant technology, production, and supply. In contrast, access to abortion and sterilization should remain restricted (abortion because it was deemed harmful to women's health, sterilization because it was so drastic). These more drastic measures would be available, evidently mostly in urban areas, only on application to relevant medical or administrative departments and only for definite medical or social reasons.

In February 1955 the health ministry report went to the party Central Committee, which approved it at the beginning of March, issuing an instruction "on the question of controlling population." Thus an issue of reproduction had already morphed into an issue of population, and the party Center had for the first time declared itself in favor of "control" (Shi 550301). However, these inner-party decisions remained secret at the time; instructions for implementing them emerged only gradually over the next several years. It was not until August 1956 that the health ministry instructed its subnational organs to propagandize contraception and strengthen technical guidance, initiating an actual campaign (Shi 568000; Aird 1972, 236–275). It was not until 1957 that regulations were issued on abortion and sterilization for regime personnel, somewhat loosening restrictions and specifying associated benefits (ME 570515, 571012; Scharping 2003, 44–45).

URBAN ORIGINS

A second origin of PRC birth planning extended to the entire urban proletariat for which the CCP claimed to be the vanguard and which it soon granted urban residence and state employment. On the one hand, like elite regime cadres, mass women workers discovered that more participation in socialist production required less devotion to reproduction. A party campaign against government "bureaucratism" allowed the urban public to use the standard communist mechanism of "letters and visits" to complain about this practical problem (White 1994a). On the other hand, regime leaders soon became increasingly concerned about the "burden" (*fudan*) of employing, provisioning, housing, and educating all these people.

A key problem was employment. In 1949 China had been ravaged by civil war and economic disruption, causing inflation and unemployment, particularly in cities (Shi 500300). The CCP's main strategy was "low wage, high employment," stretching available resources to create as many jobs as possible (Shi 510226). These problems quickly assumed a statistical form, as the PRC initiated registration of households, partly intended to restrict new rural-to-urban migration (Shi 510716). By late 1951 the new State Statistical Bureau had used such administrative data to estimate the total population at 564 million (Shi 510000). By 1952 the health ministry began to try to keep records of births (Shi 510000).

The main spokesperson for this macroperspective was Zhou Enlai, an early and active advocate of slowing population growth through both late marriage and birth control (Shi 590900). As government premier he was responsible for provisioning urban party and government cadres, whose numbers had expanded enormously. Zhou's first expression of the "burden" theme came in connection with the formulation of the regime's First Five-Year Plan at a central party work conference on organization (ME 530929). By February 1955 Zhou was musing that generous treatment of party cadres might encourage them to have too many children. He proposed to limit the number for which the government would raise cadre family allowances. "One of these days when we implement a salary system, they will have to bear those burdens themselves, and they may have a period of difficulty. Nevertheless, for the overall good, they themselves ought to control their fertility a little. . . . [I]n the initial period . . . we will still give people with many children a little help. Within three [children] they can manage themselves;

for those above three, we will subsidize two at most; those with five or more, we will just ignore (*wuge yishangde, jiu buguanle*)." The party must advocate the contraception that some nonparty intellectuals had long recommended (EBP 133). Other enduring Zhou themes were that planning births was a matter more of public responsibilities than of private preferences, more of economic planning than of health work, and more of education than of compulsion.

At the mesoinstitutional level, the specific forms taken by the PRC's new urban socialist organization shaped the specific forms taken by problems of population and resources. In the middle 1950s, as the CCP turned from revolution to development, it relied heavily on Soviet economic models: managed by government, striving for speed, oriented to heavy industry, centered on cities, and designed for a relatively underpopulated country. Following Soviet institutions, the PRC socialized industry and collectivized agriculture in the service of industrial development and military modernization. The PRC's new urban institutions made the state responsible not only for cadres but also for most of the urban population, most of which was employed in what were now state bureaus and enterprises. In particular, 1951 labor insurance regulations (revised and implemented in 1953) extended generous social benefits to those employees (Shi 510226, 530102).

The specific way in which the PRC addressed these problems was further affected by its distinctive combination of a Stalinist penchant for Bureaucratic-Professional central planning and a Maoist preference for Revolutionary Mobilization. Scientific planning was to be the secret to socialist development, overcoming the fluctuations and scarcities, imbalances and inequalities in capitalist economies. The First Five-Year Plan (1953–1957) required more accurate information about the size of the population and, particularly, its rate of increase. Consequently, in 1953 the PRC conducted its first national census (Shi 541101). It showed that the population was about what the statistical bureau had already estimated, confirming the magnitude of China's population problem. However, the census also showed that by the mid-1950s the population was growing twice as fast as it had immediately after 1949, confirming the urgency of the problem. In addition to being informative in itself, the census helped regularize the work of household registration and statistical collection, including periodic sample surveys of population dynamics by the statistical bureau (Shi 531100). Also, during the winter of 1953–1954, Deng told the health ministry that it should "have some measures" (*you xie banfa*) on contraception, which finally prompted the ministry to begin researching the subject (Shi 1988, 120n1). The health ministry prepared a plan for "controlling population" that it forwarded to the State Planning Commission (Shi 540720).

As PRC leaders realized that they had a "population problem," evidently they encouraged intellectuals to help analyze and solve it. China's most prominent advocate of birth control, a doctor from the Republican period named Shao Lizi, argued that the government should not only advocate contraception but also actively provide the necessary "technical guidance" and contraceptive supplies (Shi 540918; Aird 1972, 227–228). In September 1954 the first session of the government legislature, the National People's Congress, provided an important forum. Shao addressed the NPC and his speech was reprinted by the intellectuals' newspaper, *Guangming Ribao* (Shi 541219). Also during 1954, senior economist Ma Yinchu, in his capacity as a member of the NPC, had observed development in his native Zhejiang, where he noted the presence of many young children. In 1955 he raised this problem at the NPC in remarks to the Zhejiang delegation (Shi 550700). Ma said it was acceptable for state policy to support second births, but third births should be taxed, and fourth births should be taxed heavily. According to Ma's own account, the reaction of other delegates was so hostile that he set his ideas aside until a more favorable moment (Ma 1957 in Ma 1997, 67–107). Nevertheless, Ma had already anticipated financial disincentives that the PRC would adopt a quarter century later. Moreover, he envisioned implementing such disincentives in the form of taxes, a more sophisticated method toward which the birth system may move later in the twenty-first century.

Around 1956 a second round of economic planning began to adapt the Soviet model to Chinese realities, particularly to China's dense and still largely rural population. The formulation of the Second Five-Year Plan pitted three alternative versions of the Leninist project against each other (Bachman 1991). In the center, the Industrial tendency favored continuing the high rate of investment and high speed of development in heavy industry of the First Five-Year Plan. On the right, the Financial tendency favored steadier and balanced development, with more attention to consumption and its per capita requirements, which implied the desirability of limiting births. On the left, the Mobilizational tendency favored quickly organizing peasants into progressively larger collective units, to facilitate the collective pooling and state extraction of resources.

In 1956–1957 PRC leaders briefly tried the balanced approach to development, providing the first brief public heyday for leader advocacy and public promotion of birth control. The first public statement of a "population control" policy was by Premier Zhou to the NPC (Shi 560600). About the same time *Health Daily* published what was probably its first editorial on implementing contraception through educational propaganda and technical guidance (EBP 560615 and 397–398). A more famous public statement by Zhou was his slightly later report on the Second Five-Year Plan to the Eighth

Party Congress (Shi 560927; EBP 3). A clause in the section of the plan on public health endorsed "appropriate" birth control, calling it a matter of the health and prosperity of Chinese as a nation (*minzu de jiankang he fanrong*). This article remained the second of the three main legal bases that the PRC claimed for birth planning during the Mao era. The congress elected a central committee, which during the mid-1950s met in a series of important plenary sessions, in the course of which virtually all CCP leaders progressed from "approving" birth control to "advocating" it.

Not least, the main spokesman for the Financial tendency articulated many of the rationales and methods of birth planning. In August 1957, senior party economic planner Chen Yun spoke to the standing committee of the State Council on pressing economic problems, including the increase in migrants to urban areas and the decrease in urban food supply (EBP 570820). Noting the connection to population growth, Chen asked provinces to create committees for birth work, particularly propaganda to overcome peasant reluctance to buy contraceptives. He proposed lowering the price of contraceptives, even to the point of free distribution. "Most striking, he made what was perhaps the first reference to a general limit on childbearing, suggesting a 'call on communist party members not to give birth to a third child'" (White 1994a, 269–270). This foreshadowed not only the more restrictive policies of the 1980s but also the use of a direct appeal to party members as a way of implementing them (the 1980 Open Letter, adopted in another period of high Chen influence). (On Chen see Lardy and Lieberthal eds. 1983; Bachman 1985.)

RURAL ORIGINS

A third origin of PRC birth planning extended to the relationship between city and countryside and to the countryside itself. Urban provisioning required rural procurement, which strained rural supplies. Rural collectivization revealed a rural demand for limiting childbearing, or at least so the regime claimed.

The 1953 census had shown that China's population was 87 percent rural and that population was growing faster than agricultural output (Shi 541101). In the mid-1950s new socialist procurement institutions enabled the state to transfer grain and other supplies from the countryside to the cities. Meanwhile new socialist institutions for agricultural production had not yet proved that they could make up the resulting deficit, causing rural anxiety and potential political unrest. Thus, from the beginning, rural issues—agricultural planning, rural economic development, and relations between the party and its rural political base—provided a main locus for the politics of birth planning. From the beginning, in these national deliberations, rural interests had little representation—not even a mass organization for farmers. During the Mao era it was Mao who, as the party's expert on rural revolutionary strategy, played the key role in rural development strategy, appointing himself the ultimate arbiter of rural interests. Unfortunately Mao's definition of rural interests was sometimes utopian and caused real rural interests huge harm. Nevertheless, when it came to population, to some extent Mao did say what the male heads of farm families might have said if they had been asked, that they were not yet ready to limit their childbearing (Stacey 1983). In any case, most of Mao's remarks about birth planning related it to the rural population, which was the main challenge.

In the mid-1950s Mao switched, in principle, from opposing an effort to limit population growth to endorsing it. However, he maintained a complex position about how much of what sort of effort was immediately desirable or feasible. As a result there remain many ambiguities about what he meant by what he said and about what he endorsed at what time. The later birth system has interpreted these ambiguities to give birth planning as early and firm an endorsement from Mao as possible. One major example of ambiguity is worth noting. Mao's switch from antinatalism to pronatalism *may* have occurred during his 1955–1957 efforts to accelerate the socialization of rural agricultural organization in the context of expectations that, on the Stalinist model, rural mechanization would soon reduce the need for rural labor power (White 1994a, 265–269). The major evidence for this is supposed to be that a positive reference to birth control was included in the Twelve-Year Agricultural Plan (1956–1967), whose drafting and presentation to a meeting of the Supreme State Council in January 1956 Mao supervised. Thirty years later, the first edition of the *Birth Planning Yearbook* began with two large photographs of that meeting, with a caption stating that the plan included an article endorsing birth control (*YB86*, 4). However, that draft of the plan did not contain that article, which was added only in October 1957 when the plan was revised—at whose initiative it is not clear (Bowie and Fairbank eds. 1965; 119–126). This later date for official inclusion of birth control in rural planning is more consistent with the apogee of advocacy of birth control from mid-1956 to mid-1957, during a period of "opposing rash advance" rurally (Teiwes and Sun 1999, 20–52). Actually Mao's first-ever quasi-public statement favoring birth control came in November 1956, when he remarked to a visiting delegation of Yugoslav women: "In the past some people criticized us for advocating birth control, but now the number of people who approve has increased. Spouses should make a family plan, deciding how many children to have. That kind of plan should be coordinated with the national five-year plan (*yinggai . . . peiheqilai*). Society's production has already become planned, but humankind's own reproduction remains in

a state of anarchy, unplanned. Why can't we also implement planned reproduction of mankind itself? I think that is possible (*keyide*)." (See ME 561012;
EW 6Nov03 BJ.)

Mao's February 1957 "contradictions" speech to the Supreme State
Council was his first statement to other regime leaders of the possibility of
birth planning (ME 570301). It encouraged a series of supporting events.
Learning of Mao's ruminations, Ma Yinchu quickly repeated his 1954 ideas
to another meeting of the same body (Shi 570302; Ma 1997, 108–123). Mao
attended the meeting and praised Ma's analysis, noting that Shao Lizi and
health minister Li Dequan also supported birth control. Also after Mao's
statements, *People's Daily* printed its first antinatal editorial, endorsing "appropriate" birth control, now said to be needed not only by workers but also
by farmers (ME 570305). Two days later, the paper carried a speech to the
Chinese People's Political Consultative Conference by health minister Li,
who explained that "contraception is difficult and complex work" (ME
570308; EBP 288–289). *Health Daily* followed with an editorial on the "responsibility" created for the ministry by CPPCC suggestions that the government control population and implement birth planning (ME 570315, 570300;
EBP 398–399). Later in the year, the health ministry finally somewhat loosened restrictions on abortion and sterilization and the State Council finally
issued regulations on contraceptive operations for regime personnel (ME
571012, EBP 60–61). (Bowie and Fairbank eds. 1965, 295–299 has the Li
speech in English.)

The year 1957 also produced the most public media discussion about population and reproduction of any year in the Mao era. Early in the year the
party encouraged intellectuals to express their views on many issues, and
some experts advocated government promotion of birth control (Shi 570000;
EBP 530–558; Aird 1972, 239–242). Ma expanded his March talk into a
short book on *New Population Theory* that he presented to the NPC in June
and that *People's Daily* published in July (Shi 570600, 570705; EBP 551–557;
Ma 1997, 67–107). In October 1957, at the Third Plenum of the Eighth Central Committee, Mao elaborated on the possibility of birth planning, suggesting that three years of experimental propaganda, three years of pop-
ularization, and four years of universal implementation would add up to a
ten-year plan for that policy area. However, until society agreed and cooper-
ated, "it won't do" (Shi 571009; EBP 132). The plenum revised the Twelve-
Year Agricultural Plan, with the biggest change the addition of Article 29,
calling for propagation of birth control in densely populated rural areas (ME
571025; EBP 3; Bowie and Fairbank eds. 1965, 119). Passed by the National
People's Congress in 1960, that article provided the third of the three main
legal bases for birth planning for the rest of the Mao era (ME 600412).

In early 1958 some movement within the government toward active advocacy of birth control continued. In March the health ministry, by then converted to promoting contraception, held a national work conference in Beijing on birth control, addressed by an assistant to the health minister, Li Qizhong (ME 580328; EBP 289–291). The conference compared provincial experiments already underway, particularly in rural areas, evidently attempting to fit maternal and child health work into the emerging Great Leap Forward (EBP 399–400, the *Health Daily* editorial on the conference, titled "Maternal and Child Health; Big Steps, Leaps Forward"). The health ministry submitted a thorough report on the conference to national leaders through the Second Office of the State Council (EBP 125–128). The report remains quite significant in showing what the health ministry was trying to do at the time through its incipient system for delivering maternal and child health services and promoting birth control. That is what, as circumstances have permitted, the health system has continued to try to do ever since.

First, the health ministry report connected the sharp rise in population growth to the success of socialism at stabilizing livelihoods and health. In effect the masses were already having their own demographic great leap forward. Second, for health purposes the health system wanted later marriage, longer spacing between children, and fewer children—exactly the policy rules advocated in the 1960s and adopted in the 1970s. (The report remained adamantly opposed to using abortion to limit population growth.) Having fewer children would improve the quality not only of people's health but also of their education, their livelihoods, and—of greatest immediate importance to the state—their work. Thus, third, the state would benefit from birth control because it would transfer women's energies from reproduction to production, tapping a huge labor pool. In the future, agricultural mechanization would replace any lost manpower. Fourth, because birth control benefits both individuals and state, it could be voluntary. Contrary to previous assumptions, the provincial experiments had shown that many rural women were eager to practice it. Fifth, while the health ministry already envisaged national "birth planning" under strong party leadership, it expected a strong role for community initiative. Finally, voluntary "planned birth" by families themselves was the "crux" (*guanjian*).

Meanwhile, however, the Financial approach to development had not produced immediate results and was soon abandoned—birth control along with it. By July 1957 Mao had decided that intellectuals had gone too far in criticizing the party and he had launched an "antirightist" movement against them (managed by Deng Xiaoping). Targets soon included advocates of birth control, particularly Ma (Aird 1972, 242–244; Walker 1964 in Walker 1998, 333–355). By late 1957 a coalition between the Industrial and Mobilizational tendencies was moving the country toward attempting a Great Leap Forward in economic production (Bachman 1991). The Leap would need all the manpower it could get. The health ministry's April 1958 plans were adapted to support the emerging Leap, but the Leap submerged birth control nevertheless. In the winter of 1957–1958, successful labor mobilization for construction of agricultural infrastructure made it appear that communization could drastically increase agricultural output and that socialism could obviate Malthusian fears about food supply. By January 1958 Mao concluded that, for the present, a large population was still useful (EBP 1406). Besides, Mao opined—evidently addressing any colleagues who favored immediate active advocacy of birth control—doing so was not yet feasible. Rural people were not yet ready to accept late marriage and birth control, and it "would not do to force" them. He also observed that the regime itself was not yet prepared: both party propaganda work and government contraceptive capacity remained insufficient. (Mao might have added the inadequacy of budget and personnel, except that evidently he assumed, along with his proadvocacy colleagues, that birth propaganda and services could be delivered through existing channels, mostly within the health system.) At the August 1958 Beidaihe party conference, Mao said that a population of over one billion would be "no cause for alarm." People would practice birth control on their own initiative as their education level increased (White 1994a, 273).

Nevertheless, Mao said, he still favored birth control. Propaganda work and contraceptive production should continue. This became the basic official policy until Mao died in 1976. However, Mao's other projects created drastic variation in the extent to which the government could pursue that basic policy.

1960s: Initiation

Externally, the middle period of the Mao era was a period of "dual adversaries" for the PRC, during which it was in hostile confrontation with both superpowers. The PRC's split with the Soviet Union was not explicitly about population, but population was implicitly involved: Mao had used his more Mobilizational approach to adapt Stalin's more Bureaucratic approach to China's greater manpower. China's isolation from technologically advanced countries left it having to pull itself up by its own bootstraps, a situation to which a labor-intensive approach to development was a plausible response. Internally, after the failure of the Great Leap Forward, centrist party and government leaders partially sidelined Mao and Maoism, switching back toward more orthodox Stalinism. However, in light of the Great Leap experience, most PRC leaders, including Mao, now moved further away from Soviet pronatalism. In response to being sidelined, Mao co-opted some leftist leaders within the military to help gradually revive both the Revolutionary policy tendency and his own personal power. Eventually, with their assistance, he unleashed the Cultural Revolution at the government and party, paralyzing Bureaucratic Professional development in all but a few sectors that Mao favored, mostly military industry. Birth planning first revived along with Bureaucratic planning and then succumbed to renewed Revolution along with it. Nevertheless the Revolutionary policy tendency—which emphasized the self-reliance and even autonomy of rural communities—may have made some further progress toward building rural health infrastructure, including some reproductive health services, at least in some areas. (On politics see Harding 1981, 195–295; Lardy 1987a, 1987b; Sun 1987, 117–138; Shi 1988, 135–152; Lieberthal 1993; Harding 1993; MacFarquhar 1997; Huang 2000, 211–266.)

EARLY 1960S: URBAN EXPERIMENT AND IMPLEMENTATION

The Great Leap Forward sponsored by the Industrial and Mobilizational tendencies had produced just the imbalances that the Financial tendency had feared. Accordingly, in the early 1960s, Financial planners reemerged to restart and rebalance the economy, bringing their antinatalism with them. By now many Industrial planners too had probably become antinatal, because the Great Leap had discredited Mobilization enthusiasm for unlimited labor power. Nevertheless, Mao began reviving the Mobilizational approach to politics and development, calling for renewed attention to class struggle and rural areas (from 1962). However, evidently Mao did not object to the resumption of birth work, now formally under his rubric of "birth planning."

In population the most immediate problem was locational. During the Leap, urban economic boom had attracted many migrants to the cities, increasing the number of people that the state had to employ and provision. After the Leap, following Chen Yun's advice, the Center instructed cities to return migrants to the countryside, to begin annually "sending down" excess urban youth to rural areas, and to resume promotion of birth control (Shi 610500). Restrictions on movement locked returned migrants, sent-down youth, and the rest of the rural population into place. During the Great Leap, disruption of agricultural production had produced widespread rural famine that had sharply depressed rural fertility. Therefore extending birth control to rural areas was not necessary immediately but would resume after rural fertility rebounded.

Even at the height of the Great Leap, the party had not formally repudiated birth control. In November 1959 Ma Yinchu had still been allowed to publish an article emphasizing the need to raise quality as well as control quantity (Shi 591100). In March 1960 Ma was finally removed from the presidency of Peking University (Shi 600300). After that, for more than a decade, no one dared research population questions. Nevertheless, in April 1960 the National People's Congress had passed the Twelve-Year Agricultural Plan with its Article 29 authorizing advocacy of planned birth in densely populated rural areas. Some experimental propagation of birth control may have continued during the Great Leap or may have been revived immediately thereafter in some localities, particularly Shanghai. However, it was only in March 1962 that Premier Zhou reported to the National People's Congress that, as a matter of national policy, the government "earnestly advocated restricting births" (Shi 620328). In April 1962 the health ministry, citing the authority of the agricultural plan, issued a notice on "further extending" the work of both propaganda and technical guidance for birth control, urging health departments at all levels to continue striving to implement Article 29 (Shi 620405). The health ministry's official organ, *Health Daily*, famously instructed the health system to "actively advocate planned birth," and followed with a series of authoritative articles on sterilization, contraception, and abortion (Shi 620718, 620822, 620919, 620929, 621107).

Still more authoritatively, but still rather restrictively, in December 1962 the party Central Committee and government State Council jointly issued a directive on "earnestly advocating planned birth" in cities and densely populated rural areas (Shi 621218; EBP 4−5). According to the directive, the party advocated "birth control and planned birth," but birth work had relaxed in recent years. Now, advocacy should be earnest, emphasizing benefits to maternal and child health. On the same day *Youth Daily* carried an article advocating late marriage (with first child at 26−27), spacing between children (three to five years), and limited numbers (normally two, no more than three). That formula quickly became known as "later, longer, fewer" (*wan, xi, shao*) and was put into practice by several localities in the mid-1960s, long before the program adopted it as a slogan in 1973. The health ministry finally established a separate bureau for birth control, run by veteran health administrator Li Xiuzhen (ME 621200; EW 12Nov03 BJ-LXZ). Provinces began establishing birth commissions at the beginning of 1963 and continued throughout the year (ME 621218; EW 4Nov03 BJ).

Nevertheless, PRC leaders were not yet pushing comprehensive compulsory "birth planning." Advocacy of planned birth should not be very open, with propaganda limited in scope (as astutely inferred by Aird 1972, 285). According to the directive, first, relevant areas should strengthen their guidance of birth work and periodically conduct discussions and surveys. Local newspapers and the publications of relevant ministries and mass associations could "appropriately" publish "some" articles about planned birth and contraceptive methods. However, central newspapers should *not* carry such propaganda. Second, there should be "appropriate guidance" over both propaganda and technology. Propaganda should aim mostly at married couples and should emphasize health benefits to individuals, respecting folk sensibilities and avoiding "vulgarity." Propaganda should be mostly small-scale and face-to-face. Mistaken methods such as raising slogans, setting targets, and conducting contests were strictly forbidden. Contraceptive clinics should be reopened or established. The health ministry could issue pamphlets about contraception but contraception should not be openly introduced through newspapers. Third, work on manufacturing and supplying contraceptives should be done well. Fourth, given the current lack of contraceptive knowledge on the part of the public and given the current lack of manufacturing capacity on the part of the state, in order to avoid unsafe abortions, the health ministry should take measures and set conditions for making abortion and sterilization available to the public.

In May 1963 the Central Committee approved a health meeting report in which the ministry said that, in line with the emphasis that the September 1962 Tenth Plenum had placed on rural work, in 1963 planned birth work should emphasize rural experiments (EBP 5). In July 1963, a health ministry report to the State Council summarized progress and problems since the December 1962 directive (EBP 128). The rather sharp gist was that, while calling for advocacy of planned birth, national political leaders had failed to write the necessary agencies and resources into state organization and state plans. The very success of preliminary advocacy had already overloaded existing systems and created unexpected negative side effects. The Center should establish a national organ to guide birth work, should establish a separate system for delivering the necessary propaganda and services, and should provide the necessary funding. In September 1963 the Central Committee and State Council convened an important conference on urban work, which included attention to birth planning, indicating the urban focus of birth work at the time (EBP 630912). A report by health vice minister Xu Yunbei elaborated the ministry's July suggestions and stated that in 1963–1964 the ministry was extending "technical guidance clinics" from the eight largest cities to all provincial capitals to all cities over a million in population. Many of the ministry's recommendations were included in the conference report, which the Central Committee and State Council endorsed (ME 630918, 631011; Shi 631022). Birth planning was an important mission for which the national and subnational levels localities must establish commissions to exercise concrete leadership. Both mass movements and technical guidance must be strengthened. Related ministries must do their part and localities must meet urban and rural control targets (EBP 5–6 and 291–292).

Throughout the early 1960s Premier Zhou remained the main individual spokesman for birth planning (EBP 134–135). "Having a lot of people is a good thing but, as the world's most populous country, we already have plenty of them" (Shi 630201). Childbearing was not just a matter of maternal and child health, it was "necessary to see that the state's burden is great" (CTBP 630700). Shanghai was already achieving success at birth work, proving that China's problem was "not that it couldn't, but that it hadn't" (*fei buneng ye, shi buwei ye*—Shi 630709). Perhaps to preempt ideological criticism that limiting population was Malthusian, Zhou argued that the PRC needed to do birth planning in order to *combat* Malthusianism, presumably meaning that success would show that socialism did not have the demographic problem that capitalism did (Shi 651116). Zhou indicated the need for research toward a socialist theory of population, while setting out some of his own practical ideas (EBP 149–151). He provided the rudiments of all three operative components of birth planning—plan, rules, and enforcement.

The need for a *plan* for population in socialist systems was a problem that Marx and Lenin hadn't encountered and therefore hadn't solved. Doing so in China was now "a major mission for agriculture and health, and also the most difficult plan to make" (Shi 630226). Evidently Zhou was impressed by the experience of Japan, whose population growth rate had fallen from 2–3 percent to one percent or below. Zhou called that "a great accomplishment" and said that, if China could control net increase to one percent by the end of the century, that would be "extraordinary" (*liaobuqi*). However, he said that China must create its own experience, which still required "groping" (*mo-suo*—Shi 630721; EBP 152). The health ministry report to the second urban conference had recommended incorporating "earnest advocacy" in national and provincial plans. It also proposed urban population growth targets that the conference adopted, that the State Council endorsed, that Zhou often cited, and that China largely achieved. Urban growth should fall to under 2 percent within a three-year readjustment period (by 1965), to under 1.5 percent by the end of the Third Five-Year Plan (1966–1970), and to under one percent by the end of the Fourth Five-Year Plan (1971–1975). Population later played a role in the Third Five-Year Plan, the first to set a quantitative target for end-of-plan total population: 800 million in 1970. Calculations showed that achieving this would be a huge task, requiring the reduction of natural increase from 2.7 percent to 1.7 percent or less (combined urban and rural) (EBP 8).

On *rules*, in February 1963 Zhou proposed a slogan of "two children per couple is enough," the earliest formulation of such a principle. Although not official government policy, it had a definite influence (EW 6Nov03 BJ). Zhou argued that the solution to China's population problem should include late marriage as well as contraception (Shi 630708). "In his personal view," after people had two children they should be sterilized (CTBP 630200). Encountering a woman worker with only one child, he told her that she was a model for birth planning and that everyone should emulate her (ME 650000). Zhou's "personal views" presaged later official policy.

On *enforcement*, Zhou offered a rather complex formulation. Compliance should be voluntary, with individuals themselves exercising some "conscientious restraint" (*zijue yueshu*). On the other hand, he did call for effective regime policies and measures. "Formerly in this area we just advocated, now we must add restrictions" (Shi 630708). Policies that created perverse incentives for noncompliers to have children should be revised (Shi 630708). Compliers should receive preferential treatment in such matters as wages, housing, and commodity supply (CTBP 13). But the regime should not use coercion (e.g., EBP 152, a 1965 Zhou talk). "Coercive commands won't do, but neither will leaving people to themselves. It won't do not to have propaganda, not to have model demonstrations, and not to have experimental localities" (CTBP 651100). Reportedly, one reason Zhou took the "end of the twentieth century" as the time horizon for "solving the population problem" was to avoid being in a hurry and using coercion (according to birth office director Yang Zhenya). "Wouldn't it be better," Yang reported that Zhou had asked, "to start to practice [planned birth] a little sooner [rather than later]?" (EBP 295). Zhou felt that although birth control could proceed in the cities, to avoid coercion the emphasis in the countryside should be on propaganda through the ongoing socialist education campaign (Shi 650221).

Local innovations began to accumulate. For example, Hebei "groped" its way toward a "definite experience" of "great significance" to later birth work (Shi 631120). The provincial government and party committee issued a notice instructing local parties and governments to "grasp production on the one hand and birth planning on the other." The notice recommended the propaganda device of "comparative calculations" in which peasants computed how much better off they and their communities would be with fewer children. Hebei alone deployed some 350,000 propagandists—150,000 urban, 200,000 rural. Shulu—within the prefecture run by Hebei's capital Shijiazhuang—was an early rural pilot and model county. By 1965 it claimed an extraordinary contraceptive rate of 70 percent, versus national averages of 50 percent urban and 20 percent rural. Nationally, by 1965 about 400 of about 2000 rural counties had begun birth planning, though in only several dozen did it begin to have significant demographic effect (EW 4Nov03 BJ). (Blecher and Shue 1996 treat 1980s Shulu.)

MIDDLE 1960S: TOWARD NATIONAL INSTITUTIONS
AND RURAL EXPERIMENT

In the middle 1960s most national party and government leaders continued to pursue a centrist version of the Bureaucratic-Professional approach to development. The Financial tendency's program for economic recovery having succeeded, the Industrial tendency reemerged to draft a Third Five-Year Plan (1966–1970). However, a struggle soon developed between the Stalinist center and the Maoist left (which was actually hyper-Stalinist). Mao assembled his own economic planning team and substituted his own Third Five-Year Plan, which concentrated investment on inland military industry (Naughton 1988). Rural communities were told to become "self-reliant" through Mobilization. Mao wanted to transfer most health resources from urban to rural areas and then begin rural birth work, but under mass Revolutionary rather than elite Professional auspices.

Birth policy finally began to achieve some separate Professional institutionalization at the national level. In January 1964 the State Council did finally establish its first Birth Planning Commission, formally chaired by the State Council's secretary general Zhou Rongxin. Simultaneously the State Council established its first Birth Planning Office, headed by Yang Zhenya, brought in from Tianjin where he had run public health and been deputy mayor (EW 12Nov03 BJ-LXZ). In principle the office was independent of the health ministry but in practice relied on it for administrative and medical capacities. The health ministry's Li Xiuzhen was in charge of technical guidance, and the ministry soon issued a notice on strengthening it: personnel should adopt a comprehensive approach that did not over-rely on remedial medical procedures, that allowed voluntary choice, and that guaranteed the competence of personnel and the quality of procedures (Shi 640000, 640512). The new commission quickly achieved some interministerial cooperation. A meeting of the health ministry, chemical ministry, and science and technology commission prepared a report on technical research needed for birth planning, which the State Council transmitted (ME 640327; EBP 61–64). The ministries of health and finance worked out arrangements to fund services, which the State Council approved (ME 640404; EBP 61). Costs to clients for basic medical procedures were to be reduced or eliminated, and other procedures were to be subsidized. In June 1964 the State Council finally created an independent budget item for birth planning, to be allocated by the birth office but administered by the health ministry (EBP 997–998; Shi 142–152). In June 1964 the government conducted its second national census—really only a sample survey, but confirming the resumption of growth in China's population after the Great Leap Forward.

During the mid-1960s birth work began to shift from urban to rural areas. It intensified in urban areas, beginning to have some demographic impact and reducing urban population growth rates below those of rural areas. It began to extend from city to countryside, promoted as part of the rural "socialist education campaign" but still supervised from the top down by Professionals. In June 1965 the Central Committee and State Council jointly transmitted a report by the Shanghai party and government on their birth work, "for reference" (EBP 6–8). Shanghai had already reduced its population growth rate to below 1.5 percent, the urban target that the 1963 urban conference had set for 1970. The Center said this was a "great achievement," proving that good political leadership and good propaganda work could reduce childbearing "without using tough regulations" (*bu gao yingxing guiding*) and "without using coercive commands" (*bu gao qiangpo mingling*). Meanwhile, in counterpoint, Mao expressed dissatisfaction that birth work had not yet been extended to rural areas (Shi 650109). On June 26 he issued his famous "626" instruction to the health ministry, telling it to move the focus of health work to the countryside and to reassign most medical personnel there (Shi 681005). Receiving ministry personnel, Mao told them that after expanding health work in rural areas, the ministry "must do birth control" (*yao gao jiezhi shengyu*—Shi 650626). In October a party central work conference endorsed a shift of birth work to the countryside (Shi 651000).

In the mid-1960s the health ministry held four national conferences on birth work. The first two were in Beijing. A February 1963 conference concerned maternal and child health work (ME 630201). A January 1964 conference was the first on technical services, issuing the first regulations on the medical quality of birth control procedures (ME 640106). The second two national conferences were held in the field. A February 1965 rural field conference met in the Shandong county of Wendeng, which from 1963 began advocating "later, longer, fewer," reducing its growth from 4.5 percent to 2.9 percent (ME 650200). A July 1965 urban field conference met in the major city of Tianjin, which had adopted a series of measures to promote birth planning (ME 650700). From 1963 it had been providing contraceptives free of charge, along with other incentives in both urban and suburban areas, the first locality in the country to do so (Shi 650700, 650717). The city had used the socialist education campaign to extend birth work from urban to suburban districts. The conference made several recommendations: universalize propaganda, train birth workers, and build the necessary institutions. Party committees should strengthen leadership and basic level units should grasp both propaganda and technical work (ME 650700). Receiving health minister Qian

Xinzhong, Mao praised Tianjin's free provision of contraceptive services, saying it was worth the cost to the state (ME 650820).

In October 1965 Qian reported to the Central Committee on experience and progress to date (EBP 8–10). Experience had shown that success
at birth limitation required the following elements: active party leadership
across government departments and administrative levels, careful ideological preparation of the masses, both a propaganda corps and a technical
corps, improving the quality of medical procedures for birth control, and
improving the quality and availability of the necessary technologies and
equipment. Progress so far had been mostly urban, and it was now time to
apply urban lessons to rural areas. In January 1966, as a sequel to its long 1962
instruction, the Central Committee endorsed the Qian paper and circulated it with a brief instruction. Intervening experience had shown that accomplishments were possible "if methods were on target (*fangfa duitou*) and
if the masses were willing (*minzhong ziyuan*)." Propaganda and reports in the
media on birth work should continue to follow 1962 instructions—that is,
remain relatively restricted (EBP 8). Nevertheless, PRC leaders had again endorsed birth planning and the program appeared headed toward further
expansion.

LATE 1960S: NATIONAL INTERRUPTION

Toward the end of the middle 1960s, to restore his personal political control and to promote his military-industrial priorities, Mao resorted to the
destructive side of Revolutionary Mobilization, using the Revolutionary
tradition to attack both government and party. In the process Mao largely
destroyed national planning, including for population and births. Politically, the dominant coalition consisted of leftist military and leftist civilians
who were probably sincerely pronatal and in any case took the opportunity to attack their centrist party and government enemies as antinatal. Administratively, central population planning was supposed to be connected
to central economic planning, but no one did any of either, completely dis-
rupting the Bureaucratic-Professional approach to birth planning, which
Revolutionaries denounced as "bureaucratism (*guan*), obstruction (*ka*), and
oppression (*ya*)." (On politics see Harding 1993; Marfarqhuhar 1993; Shi
660000.)

According to histories by birth Professionals, a few leading cadres were
designated "capitalist roaders" and "revisionists" and sent to detention in
"cowpens" (Shi 660000). After the Cultural Revolution few of these cadres
reassembled as a program leadership team (EW 12Nov03 BJ-LXZ). In 1967
the newly established central-to-local birth system was abolished and personnel—on temporary loan in any case—were transferred to other organs.

Technical personnel were sent down to villages, where they were forced to accept education from poor-and-lower-middle peasants (Shi 670100). Most birth workers and activists suffered attacks by leftist movements, and birth work was, from the point of view of the Professionals, "completely destroyed" (Shi 660000). To the extent that the Revolutionaries had their own approach to birth planning, it may have been based on autonomous communities and virtuous classes. However, the general chaos probably weakened any kinds of controls (Shi 153–258).

Thus from 1966 through 1968 official histories of birth work contain virtually no reports of constructive activity. However, there were a few exceptions, at both the elite and mass levels. Two elite exceptions concern the development and trial of oral contraceptives, in which Mao had expressed interest. Then in late 1968, as Mao moved to restore political order, the State Council established a "leading group" (*lingdao xiaozu*) for birth planning. The general affairs section of the health ministry—now under military administration—established an "office" (*bangongshi*) under Li Xiuzhen, though she had no formal title (Shi 680905; EW 12Nov03 BJ-LXZ). In March 1969, at meetings to revive economic planning, Premier Zhou reiterated the need for birth planning and contraception, citing Chairman Mao's previous interest (Shi 690300). However, there is no evidence of follow-up to these administrative developments at that time. One reason may be disruption by violent factionalism (Unger 1998), first in urban areas (1966–1968) and then in rural areas (1968–1970). During the 1960s fertility had been declining from its high during its post-Leap recovery (a TFR of 7.5 in 1963). It rebounded slightly at the height of Cultural Revolution disturbances (from 5.31 in 1967 to 6.45 in 1968). It then resumed its decline, which continued throughout the 1970s. By about 1965 urban rates of increase had fallen below rural rates of increase and were leading the decline (EW 6Nov03 BJ).

At the mass level, both urban and rural areas may have provided some exception to the official account of complete cessation of activity. Some level of birth control operations continued, probably mostly in urban areas; when available data series resume in 1971, they show 13 million operations in that year (Tien 1991, 156). Moreover, the Cultural Revolution did somewhat increase rural health resources by rusticating urban health professionals, who helped train paramedics in newly organized community health services, including some training in contraception and birth control operations (Shi 680000). Fieldwork—in the kind of "densely populated rural area" near a city area where the Agricultural Plan authorized birth work—found that rural women remember this as the time when they first gained access to contraception (SG 1988, fieldwork near Xi'an). In any case, after 1968, average national fertility resumed its decline.

1970s: Re-Initiation

In the late Mao period, externally, the PRC gradually initiated relations with the West and its "international regimes," including a nascent one for management of population growth in developing countries. In 1949, U.S. comments on China's population had provoked official PRC endorsement of pronatalism. In 1974, the PRC's international demographic debut at the Bucharest population conference elicited a PRC updating of "Marxist population theory," in formulations personally reviewed by Zhou Enlai (ME 740416; EW 5Nov03 BJ, ZMC). The PRC now straddled the anti-Malthusianism of international Marxism and the PRC's need to slow China's population growth. On the one hand, the PRC delegation repeated Mao's 1949 line that, as a socialist country, China could not have a "population problem" (ME 740311, 730819). Nevertheless the PRC was becoming increasingly concerned about population growth and was reviving its domestic effort to slow it. Accordingly, on the other hand, the PRC delegation advocated including population in socialist planning. As program leader Peng Peiyun later said while commemorating Deng Xiaoping's contribution to PRC birth policy, there was no model available for managing population, so China had to find its own way (ME 970308). The international regime for population policy was not yet fully developed. The international environment could not yet provide cheap and effective contraceptive technology. Nor was there any foreign assistance available to China for building institutional capacity.

Internally, the Revolutionary tendency remained ascendant throughout the late Mao period. Civilian leftists continued to impose Revolutionary discourse on the official media, including on the promotion of birth control. In practice, Stalinist planning gradually revived, birth planning along with it. However, Bureaucratic planning remained combined with a Mobilization approach, as exemplified by the heroic workers in the Daqing oil field. In the early 1970s ideological campaigns by the Gang of Four against Zhou Enlai inhibited the elaboration of a Bureaucratic Professional rationale for birth planning, but birth work resumed, at least at the subnational level. In the middle 1970s an ideological rationale for planning reproduction together with production began to emerge and both economic planning and birth planning were further formalized. In the late 1970s, after Mao's death, efforts intensified at both accelerating economic growth and slowing population growth. (On politics see Harding 1981, 296–328; Sun 1987, 139–172; Shi 1988, 159–177; Orleans 1972, 1974; Perkins 1991; MacFarquhar 1993; Huang 2000, 267–349.)

EARLY 1970S: RURAL EXPERIMENT

In the early 1970s, the Revolutionary tendency began to fragment as Mao purged his leftist military allies (Lin Biao and company, whom he had come to consider a threat). That created an opening for revival of the Industrial tendency. Zhou masterminded the gradual revival of planning within the economic ministries he controlled, becoming again the main spokesman for birth planning (Shi chronology entries for 1970–1973). Nevertheless, as a counterweight to Industrial technocrats, Mao left civilian Revolutionaries in charge of ideology and media, which impeded Zhou's revival of birth planning.

In 1970 when preparing the Fourth Five-Year Plan (1971–1975), as though reminding Mao of his earlier promises, Zhou remarked that "the population is now large and in the 1970s we must pay attention to birth planning. . . . It's good to have lots of manpower but only if it is coordinated with economic development" (ME 700200). The plan contained a sentence on recommending late marriage and planned birth and on free supply of oral contraceptives (EBP 64). It set 1975 targets for population growth of under one percent in cities and under 1.5 percent in the countryside. Nevertheless birth work remained ideologically questionable, struggling to achieve legitimacy. Zhou told representatives from the health ministry—then still under a military control commission—that planned birth was not a health matter but a planning matter. "If you can't even plan population increase, how can you do national planning?" (Shi 700626). This may have been not just a philosophical observation about the relationship between production and reproduction but a lament that reproduction fell under military jurisdiction, not his. Mao said little on the matter. Reflecting his preoccupation with lowering barriers to rural use, he did tell the health ministry that it was not enough that contraceptives be free, they must be delivered to couples' front doors (Shi 721000), actually a long-standing principle of revolutionary health work in general. National political leaders neither formulated nor broadcast a theoretical rationale for birth planning. The national government's main role was to develop contraceptives and equipment and to supply them to local governments. However, Zhou complained that rural leaders remained unwilling to use these free supplies and that neither propaganda nor technical work was done adequately (Shi 710131).

It was in commenting on a report by the ministries of health, commerce, and chemicals that in July 1971 the State Council issued its only central directive in the early 1970s specifically devoted to birth planning (EBP 64–65). Overall, Document 51 suggests a program not much more ambitious or vigorously implemented than population limitation programs in other developing countries during that period (Warwick 1982). In the absence of national action, the document urged localities to get on with the job, by complaining that birth work was "uneven" (because "we have not learned from Mao's instructions on planned birth"). The directive reauthorized subnational experiments, by commending some local experiences, particularly that of the Hebei county of Leting, a model of strong party leadership of birth work. Ideologically, propaganda "of all kinds" should build public motivation for planned birth and knowledge about contraception. Organizationally, the health system should establish "a small administrative apparatus" for planned birth work, but within the existing administrative structure. However, provinces must pay for their birth work themselves. At the end of the year, the State Council further signaled its renewed interest in birth planning by issuing an article that called it a "profound revolution" (Shi 711230).

To get things rolling again, evidently the Center instructed two advanced provinces—one southern, one northern—to convene meetings of provinces at which Li Xiuzhen could explain national policy to subnational program administrators. In November 1971 the Jiangsu county of Rudong hosted a conference attended by 13 southern provinces (Shi 711116; EBP 482). Rudong exemplified strong party leadership of interdepartmental cooperation, good mass work through promoting models, good technical training of birth workers in combination with maternal and child health work, and good supply of contraceptives to rural users combined with examinations for some women's reproductive health problems (ME 711116; Orleans ed. 1979, 210–223). In January 1972 Hebei's model county of Leting hosted an analogous conference attended by 17 northern provinces (Shi 720000, EBP 482). Li's speech to that conference issued work targets for 1972 and stated her "personal views" on some issues that evidently national policy had not yet formally decided but that the conference had discussed (detailed immediately below). In August 1972 the health ministry submitted a report to the State Council, based on an investigation in preparation for an expected September 1972 national conference on birth work (EBP 129–130). The report noted the subnational models that were emerging and outlined the policies that Li had stated in January as her personal views. Curiously, the Center did not endorse that report and did not circulate it as an instruction, perhaps reflecting the continuingly problematic status of birth planning as a policy project. Moreover, the expected national conference did not occur until December 1973, at least formally. Instead, informally, in November 1972 the Shandong prefecture of Changwei hosted a conference attended by 24 provinces (Shi 721101; EBP 297–298). That conference summarized work since 1970, emphasizing "comprehensive measures," particularly the dependence of birth planning on good training and good maternal and child health work.

The rather laid-back slogan the conference proposed was "marry a little later, space a little more, have a little fewer, raise a little better." (The fourth item on quality was not included in the main slogan for the 1970s but was reemphasized in late 1979—CTBP 791200; ME 791215.)

Li's 1972 speeches and the health ministry report show that by 1972 all the operational components of birth planning—plan, rules, and enforcement—had reemerged in full form, putting the statist aspect of governmentalization back on track. Li's formulations are worth summarizing because they set the parameters for birth work for most of the rest of the 1970s. They are surprisingly moderate and flexible, retaining many of the health care ideals of quality care and client choice that had been advanced in the late 1950s and that reemerged in the late 1990s. Thus as regards *plan*, in her January 1972 Hebei speech Li asked first, "what should really be the target for natural increase? The lower the better?" Li answered that in July 1971 the State Council had made clear the national target for the Fourth Five-Year Plan. Consistent with that, provinces should establish their own targets in accord with their own circumstances. To stabilize national population growth at around one percent would require much difficult and meticulous work (EBP 296–297). Nevertheless, as Li said more explicitly in December 1976, "What we favor (*zhuzhang*) is that population should have planned growth, not that the lower the target the better" (EBP 299).

Li's next several topics in her Hebei speech concerned *rules*. Thus as regards "the marriage age question," "based on public willingness," the state was now recommending 23 and 25 for rural females and males, 25 and 27 or 28 for urban females and males. But these were just the "advocacy slogans"—special individual circumstances could be accommodated. "How many children should each couple have, with how many years of spacing?" Stabilizing natural increase at around one percent would require an average of no more than two per couple. For the health of the mother and child, spacing of four to five years would be optimal. As for method of birth control, there are many available and the client should choose according to her situation: "Don't force uniformity." Our policy is to advocate contraception, Li said. Abortion is only a supplement. However, if the masses demand it, that demand should be satisfied. Medical personnel should do a good job of birth control procedures, ensuring cleanliness, guaranteeing quality, avoiding medical "incidents," and doing follow-up work.

Finally, *enforcement* should be through positive incentives: free contraceptive operations and oral contraceptives, together with rest periods after operations, with pay. This showed the party's concern for people's livelihood. Infertile couples should be given positive treatment to the extent that existing levels of medicine permit.

MIDDLE 1970S: RURAL EXTENSION

In the middle 1970s, as first Zhou and then Mao sickened and died, PRC politics polarized along several dimensions—ideology, economy, and sheer personal power. Ideology and propaganda remained under the Gang of Four (Revolutionary tendency). Mao rehabilitated Deng Xiaoping to assist and off-set Zhou (Industrial tendency). Meanwhile Mao began promoting an alternative both to the Gang on the left and to Deng on the right: rising younger centrist Hua Guofeng (Mobilization tendency). (On politics see Harding 1987, 11–69; MacFarquhar 1993, 278–319; Baum 1994, 27–48.)

Amid these cross-currents, birth policy made some progress at the national level. Ideologically, although the PRC now officially favored birth control, so long as the civilian leftists still controlled propaganda, policy still could not be elaborated theoretically and implementation could not be pursued vigorously. Nevertheless, in 1974 a few local institutes began working on a version of a Marxist theory of population that would legitimate limiting births. Organizationally, in July 1973 after most provinces had already established leading groups to coordinate birth work, the State Council finally reestablished a national leading group for interagency coordination (ME 730716). The director was Mao's center-left protégé Hua Guofeng, then also in charge of agriculture. As in 1965, the administrative office of the leading group remained in the health ministry, under Li Xiuzhen. Importantly for implementation, from March 1973 the State Planning Commission included population targets in economic plans, in 1973 recommending growth rates of about one percent for cities and 1.5 percent for rural areas (Shi 730300; EBP 65).

In December 1973 the first official national birth conference of the 1970s finally convened, attended by vice premier Li Xiannian and birth director Hua Guofeng (ME 731211). National program leaders formally announced a national policy emphasizing late marriage (*wan*), long spacing (*xi*), and fewer children (*shao*). Each component carried specific numbers: minimum marriage ages of 23 for women and 25 for men, spacing between children of at least four years, and number of children not to exceed two (ME 731211). The slogan was kept simple to make it easy for cadres and masses to grasp the relationship between macropopulation and microreproduction, while the specifics were provided so that cadres and masses would have some concrete numbers for guidance (CTBP 20). Remarkably, national political leaders did not endorse and circulate a report on that conference and its policy, not even through an editorial in the *People's Daily* (still controlled by the civilian leftists).

As Zhou's health failed, a vigorous Deng increasingly took over the de facto running of the government. The years 1974–1975 constituted a watershed during which Zhou revived the goal of achieving the Four Modernizations by 2000 and Deng supervised planning to do so (MacFarquhar 1993, 288–296). Thus in late 1974 Deng helped Zhou embody his modernization goals in annual, five-year, and long-term plans, all containing targets for population growth rates. It was on the draft of the 1975 annual plan that Mao scribbled his last authorization of birth planning: "It won't do not to control population" (*renkou fei kongzhi buxing*—ME 741229). At that time the Central Committee issued the first substantive official communication from national political leaders to subnational levels since early 1966 that dealt exclusively with birth planning (Shi 741231). A "notice" circulated reports by Shanghai and Hebei, implying them as urban and rural models (EBP 10–12). In phrases later repeated often, the Central Committee remarked that the crux of accomplishing birth planning was that "party committees at all levels" must "include this work on their agendas," "effectively strengthen leadership," and "grasp" it "frequently and tightly" (CTBP 21). In February the party Central Committee, transmitting the 1975 economic plan, instructed subnational party committees to put birth planning on their agenda and to put someone in charge of it, presumably meaning some party secretary (Shi 750210). In May 1975 the health ministry convened a national conference on health work that discussed health targets, including population, for the Fifth Five-Year Plan (Shi 750522). The State Council endorsed the conference's report, thereby giving some indirect authorization for the "later-longer-fewer" slogan (Shi 750805; EBP 65). Meanwhile, Hua Guofeng became vice premier and minister of public security, leaving the birth planning leading group. Its new head was vice premier Wu Guixian, a well-meaning but uneducated woman model textile worker whom the Cultural Revolution had catapulted to national position (Shi 750100; EW Nov03 BJ).

After Mao died in September 1976, a centrist coalition purged the party leftists and helped centrist Hua emerge as Mao's apparent successor as leader of party, government, and military (Macfarquhar 1993, 305–316). Ideologically, the shift from leftist Maoism to centrist Stalinism was reflected in elaboration of "Marxist-Leninist-Stalinist" theories of development, including of population. At the end of 1976 the health ministry held another national meeting on birth work (Shi 761213). The conference lamented the damage that the Gang of Four had done to health work before their recent deposition. The conference also reissued the population theories of Marx, Engels, Lenin, and Stalin, and the instructions of Mao and Zhou. Still, Li Xiuzhen's wrap-up speech remained straight-spoken (at least as printed in EBP 300–301). She said that in 1976 the birth system had begun attempts to staff the community level of rural service delivery (but clearly those attempts remained experimental and preliminary). Another main development had been the extension of "population theory" classes for cadres. Li reaffirmed the adequacy of the policy of "later, longer, fewer" for achieving Fifth Five-Year Plan targets. Nevertheless, to avoid future birth "peaks" resulting from unusually large cohorts of child-bearing women, she said that it might be necessary to make "appropriate adjustments," principally through propaganda. This was the first of many future references to population "peaks" as adding urgency to birth work.

LATE 1970S: NATIONAL INTENSIFICATION

Mao's adventurism had cost China twenty years of development, and the succession politics accompanying his demise had complicated the beginning of the Fifth Five-Year Plan. China's centrist post-Mao leaders were now in a hurry to make up for lost time. In February 1977 they relaunched the development plans drawn up in 1974–1975, continuing their combination of Industrial goals and Mobilization style. Slowing population increase became increasingly central to Industrial attempts to maximize investment over consumption. Practicing birth control became part of the exemplary behavior displayed by Mobilization models, such as Daqing and Dazhai. (On politics see Macfarquhar 1993, 316–339; Baum 1994, 48–65; White 1994b, 141–144.)

Birth planning began to assume a higher profile, featured in several national meetings during 1977. Curiously, so soon after December there was another national "work report" meeting in February (Shi 770206). In May Li Xiuzhen addressed a national conference on learning from Daqing, and the meeting distributed materials claiming that advanced industrial units practiced birth planning. In September a meeting of provincial directors included a cross-section of other ministries to get birth work on their agenda as well (Shi 770923). Reflecting the post-Mao consciousness of the need for neo-Maoist ideological rationales, the meeting stressed theory. Li's concluding speech was uncharacteristically ideological and complex (EBP 300–301). It deftly combined not only Maoist nostrums and anti-Maoism but also both the social-mobilizational and technical-medical sides of birth work. The result was a series of multifaceted and tightly packed instructions, seemingly endless and often mutually contradictory. Such baroque formulations are characteristic of mature policy domains in the PRC and became characteristic of birth planning from then on. Substantively, on the one hand, Li reiterated the health ministry's preference for technically sound and client-centered maternal and child health work. On the other hand, she foreshadowed the momentous shift from soft birth control to hard birth planning that was already under way.

Given the ideological transition at that time, Li began by directly address-ing the question of whether the "line" in birth planning was correct. She re-peated five times that "we certainly must respect Mao's instructions," once for each of her five main points, often stretching what he had said to cover ob-jectives that he never really endorsed. First, because Mao had favored birth planning, it was now a matter of "line" both for China's socialist revolution and for its socialist construction. Second, because Mao had always said that the party must lead everything, party leadership over birth planning must now be strengthened to achieve a "dialectical relationship" between economic construction and population development, to "truly" incorporate birth work into economic development, and to achieve a mass movement of scientific and technological modernization. Third, because Mao had once spoken fa-vorably of "open" education about planned birth, now all possible channels and means of propaganda should be "forcefully strengthened" (*dali jiachang*) to raise the self-consciousness of both cadres and masses about birth planning. Fourth, because Mao had favored cultivating a medical corps that was both politically solid and technically excellent, by implementing the party's policy on intellectuals, the technical capacity for planned birth should be strength-ened. Fifth, because Mao had once said that planned birth might require a ten-year plan, birth work should now include research-based population plans, which should be incorporated into economic plans.

Li continued with some remarks about overall mission. Birth work must achieve the objectives of the Fifth Five-Year Plan in three years. From 1980 to 2000 the birth program would be threatened by "high peaks" in childbearing, which would make birth work "far more difficult" than at present. There-fore, to meet plan targets, the party must strengthen its leadership over birth work and the birth system must strengthen its role as the research and plan-ning "staff" to the party. Accordingly Li concluded with "some views" on concrete work matters. In hindsight the most significant new nuance was a shift in emphasis from the timing of children to the number of children: from now on a central work task should be "fewer" children, preventing three and more. Planned birth work should be preventive, reducing abortions in order to protect women's health and to advance maternal and child health work, which must not be slighted.

In June 1978 the State Council upgraded its leading group for birth work (Shi 780600, 780626). Though part of a gradual intensification, the reor-ganization crossed a threshold between the cautious approach of the Mao era and the aggressive approach of the Deng era. It further detached birth work from the health system and further reoriented it toward economic plan-ning. Looking back, the first meeting of the strengthened leading group summarized past experience in a cumbersome thirty-six character slogan: "party secretary in command *(shuji guashuai)*, whole party acts *(quandang dongshou)*, propaganda and education *(xuanchuan jiaoyu)*, models show the way *(dianxing yinlu)*, strengthen scientific research *(jiaqiang keyan)*, improve [medical] technique *(tigao jishu)*, implement measures *(cuoshi luoshi)*, mass movements *(qunzong yundong)*, persevere *(zhizhi yiheng)*." This was the legacy of the Mao era that Mao had hesitated to apply with full force, as Deng would now do resolutely. The governmentalization of China's population would now proceed rapidly, but still in a statist direction. Looking forward, top leader Li Xiannian told the meeting that, although the emphasis within "later, longer, fewer" was now on fewer, it was still necessary to do a "good job" and not use coercion. The governmentalization of China's population would continue under a statist approach that in principle recognized the need for voluntary compliance by autonomous individuals, but in practice slipped into the self-defeating commandism it nominally disavowed.

CHAPTER 4

The Deng Era: Rising
Enforcement of Hard Birth Planning

DURING THE DENG ERA (late 1970s to early 1990s), population and reproduction were major issues for the Chinese Communist Party. To senior revolutionaries and their conservative protégés, a renewed struggle to modernize China demanded a particularly "hard" version of birth planning, with draconian limits and strict enforcement. At the end of the 1970s and beginning of the 1980s, national leaders adopted and implemented such a policy. However, severe enforcement produced strong disaffection among both cadres and public. In the mid-1980s policy went through both deliberate adjustment and inadvertent relaxation, then increasing debate and eventual stabilization. By the late 1980s, through trial and error, national political and program leaders had arrived at a version of hard birth planning that they believed was not only necessary but also worked. In the early 1990s they reenforced that version. Thus, during the Deng era, PRC birth policy went through a classic CCP policy cycle of advance (*qianjin*), followed by consolidation (*gonggu*), followed by renewed advance. Many of these hard policies and institutions remain in place after 2000. One cannot understand what they are or why it is so difficult to get rid of them without understanding where they came from and how they became so firmly entrenched.

As with the Mao era, the processes initiated under Deng during the "long" 1980s remain significant in the early twenty-first century in ways that are not merely historical. One very broad legacy for population policy concerned *location*: the distinction between urban and rural first sharpened and then began to blur. By decommunizing rural areas, accelerating urban development, and introducing market mechanisms, the era of "reform and opening" gradually unleashed a flood of migrants from the countryside to the cities. This "floating" of population made it more difficult for birth planners to monitor and sanction reproduction. However, it also contributed to an urbanization of rural attitudes that lowered rural fertility aspirations more profoundly and permanently than state birth planning propaganda ever could have done alone (Chapter 8). In the twenty-first century, continuing urbanization will remain a fundamental fact for population planning—creating huge locational needs for infrastructure and social programs but, on balance, facilitating reduction in quantity and increase in quality.

A second broad legacy for population policy was the beginning of a shift from quantity to *quality*, the preoccupation that became dominant in the early twenty-first century. Deng era leaders considered raising the quality of China's population central to modernizing China. One component of this was eugenics, which in China did include some elements of "racial hygiene," but which consisted mostly of what the West would call "human capital." Accordingly, at the beginning of the Deng era, the birth program changed its rubric from "advocating planned birth" to "controlling population quantity and raising population quality" and added a fourth item on quality to the three-part 1970s slogan of "later-longer-fewer" (Shi 791215). From the beginning the Deng era envisaged a series (*yixilie*) of concrete policies for achieving quality objectives. At a minimum, having fewer children would enable couples to do a better job of rearing them, as couples increasingly have done. Government services for maternal and child health could be improved, as the PRC finally got around to doing toward the end of the Jiang era. More ambitiously, the government could adopt negative measures to discourage people with hereditary diseases from having children—measures that remain on the books and continue to receive some attention. Still more ambitiously, the government could adopt positive measures for promoting health, education, and welfare—measures that the PRC continues to adopt to the extent that local governments can afford them. Meanwhile, however, the regime's own policies of reform and opening promoted economic marketization, which produced social modernization, which contributed to couples' concern for the quality of their children (Part 2).

In practice the Deng era's main preoccupation remained reduction in *quantity*, leaving a strong legacy for the operational components of population policy, particularly in birth *rules*. Stringent limits emerged from calculations of what would be required to meet the goal of preliminary modernization of China by the end of the twentieth century and from projections of the consequences of population growth for the twenty-first century (Shi 841006, quoting Deng). Quantitative objectives now included rapid slowing of population growth rates, limits on ultimate population size, and increases in per capita income. All of these seemed to require limiting Chinese couples to only one child, at least for one generation. During the Deng era the main issue in birth policy concerned how many exceptions for second children to allow to the one-child ideal. The eventual upshot was to permit about half of rural couples—those whose first child was a daughter—to try again for a son. That birth rule remains in effect in the early twenty-first century, subject to informal debate, but evidently not yet to formal reconsideration. The main mechanism that the Deng era envisaged for transition beyond that rule remains in force as well. Most of the 1980–2000 generation should be "only children," at least in cities. Allowing urban couples composed of "only children" to have two children of their own would allow a gradual transition to an urban two-child policy, without any change in rules (PI 040806, ZWQ). In the 2000s this transition would apply only to the roughly 30 percent of Chinese who are urban residents; by the 2020s that proportion might rise to 60 percent (PI 041019, YXJ).

The Deng era legacy in *enforcement* was to supplement persuasion with coercion and with economic incentives and disincentives. Persuasion and remuneration provided legacies to build on; coercion, a legacy to overcome. During the Mao era the main means of inducing compliance in rural areas had been propaganda and education (normative), combined with making birth control services as inexpensive and accessible as possible (remunerative). In early 1979 Deng told the Politburo that there should be legislation to control population growth, presumably in order to make birth limits legally enforceable (ME 790323). Two months later Deng declared that "it is ok to use economic and administrative methods, just so that [fertility] declines, that would be the greatest victory" (*yong xingzhengde, jingjide banfa dou keyi, zhi yao neng xianxialai, jiushi zui da shengli*—Shi 790505). Thus the Deng era added the "economic constraint" of a steep fine for extra children (remunerative coercion), in principle backed by legal enforcement (institutionalized coercion), but in practice backed by ad hoc administrative measures (uninstitutionalized coercion). In rural areas the main method of implementation was periodic campaigns in which political generalists mobilized citizens for mandatory technical services delivered by visiting medical teams, further enforced through ad hoc administrative measures. However, the early Deng era also initiated a transition to a new method: continuous routine technical work by community paraprofessionals, backed by enforcement through standardized legal rules and proceedings. The Deng era initiated that transition but did not complete it and in the early 1990s itself again resorted to crash campaigns. Institutionalization resumed during the Jiang era and continues in the twenty-first century.

The Deng era legacy in *planning* was some improvement in the capacity to make mandatory population plans, a legacy that has since been largely abandoned. Though at the time touted as the application of science to population, the projections that around 1980 called for drastically limiting population size and that stampeded national leaders into adopting a one-child birth limit turned out to have little basis in science or fact (Greenhalgh 2005b). In the early 1980s the birth program began to develop some capacity for conducting surveys and making projections, a capacity that grew only slowly over the ensuing two decades. Meanwhile the program did begin compiling national and regional population plans, whose population targets were then disaggregated to the local and community levels, where community cadres decided exactly which couples qualified to use the quota allocated to each township and village. By the middle 1980s some national economic reformers (e.g., then premier Zhao Ziyang) began advocating a shift from mandatory planning (enforceable on both cadres and citizens) to guidance planning (indicating to cadres how they might need to allocate resources), a shift that evidently would apply to birth planning as well (Naughton 1995, 176–187). In the late 1980s and early 1990s, conservative planners managed to maintain mandatory population planning, at least formally. Nevertheless, as it became clear that the original 2000 target of "under 1.2 billion" could not be met, reformers succeeded in loosening it, first to "about 1.2 billion," then to "under 1.3 billion." The Eighth Five-Year Plan (1991–1995) was the first under which birth work achieved—even overachieved—its demographic targets, establishing the major precondition for eventual reform (SG 23Nov99 BJ).

In terms of the governmentalization of population, then, the most conspicuous legacy of the Deng era was the construction of the regime capacity for more effective party-state intervention—and the destructive consequences of that achievement. China's biopolitics began to move from revolutionary Leninism toward developmental Leninism. Policy formulation remained personalistic but gradually moved toward more professional review. Policy implementation remained highly mobilizational but began to move toward some institutionalization. The increases in both capacity and damage were facilitated by a narrow focus on limiting quantity and by doing it through direct quantitative limits.

However, the Deng era also did something equally fundamental: it finally began to allow the emergence of at least one component of modern neoliberal biopower and biopolitics—quasi-autonomous professional discourses concerning quasi-autonomous societal processes of population and economy, reproduction and sexuality. Unfortunately one cannot say that the revolutionary elders who dominated this time made much progress toward the second component—modern forms of state governance over society. Nor did they show much sensitivity to either the normative prerogatives or the practical potential of the third component of biopower—autonomous self-governance by individuals, families, and communities. Instead senior Leninist PRC leaders adopted and implemented a mechanistic central birth planning that left little room for neoliberal agency on the part of its "targets" (Chapter 7). The result of rolling the PRC regime apparatus over China's social landscape was to largely destroy the traditional Chinese family system. The regime achieved the capacity to impose birth limits, but at the high cost of creating political problems that the late Jiang era realized and addressed and of exacerbating social problems that the early Hu era began to try to remedy.

Introduction: Population and Politics

During the Deng era, externally, the PRC joined the new international population regime as an increasingly active and proud member. At the 1984 Mexico City decennial population conference, the PRC delegation strongly favored limiting population growth through state intervention. The U.S. criticized that, favoring an approach through marketization. The PRC rejected the criticism, insisting that population was a domestic matter. Nevertheless, at about this time the PRC began experiments at adapting its statist approach to the early stage of its own marketizing economic reforms. The international population regime began contributing ideas and resources for building the institutional capacity to manage population affairs. Foreign funds have been only a tiny proportion of PRC expenditures on birth planning, but they have been crucial for promoting change. In the 1980s the United Nations Fund for Population Activities (UNFPA) helped the PRC conduct a modern census and train demographers, who began to give the PRC its first real capacity for analyzing population dynamics and policy. In the 1980s and early 1990s, UNFPA helped improve Chinese contraceptives to make them safer and more reliable, thereby better protecting women's health and preventing unnecessary abortions. (On program see ME 840806, 840815; Shen et al. 1990.)

Internally, during the Deng era, the course of population policy reflected the interplay of the rival Leninist projects that had emerged during the Mao era but lagged behind their transformation of the PRC system as a whole. After Mao's death most PRC leaders rejected most of the Maoist project of Revolutionary Mobilization. As a strategy to accelerate development, the most immediate reaction of post-Mao PRC leaders was to resume the Stalinist approach of Bureaucratic Professionalism. Later, as renewed Stalinist development encountered difficulties, the reaction of many PRC leaders was a Reformist approach that resorted to market mechanisms. These economic reforms largely succeeded, by the Jiang era evolving into Socialist Marke-tization. Deng era political reforms quickly self-destructed, forcing Deng to sacrifice his reformist junior lieutenants Hu Yaobang and Zhao Ziyang. (On politics see Solinger 1984; Harding 1987; Solinger 1993; Baum 1993; Shirk 1993; Baum 1994, 25–243; Fewsmith 1994; Naughton 1995; Sun 1995; Huang 2000, 350–410.)

Birth planning continued its mixture of Maoism and Stalinism: mobiliza-tion through propaganda for mandatory "technical services," in order to meet centrally planned population goals. Even the most reformist Deng era leaders believed that marketization made regulation of population all the more necessary, even while making it more difficult. After intensification of birth planning encountered problems, reform was limited to a modest re-laxation of birth rules and an only temporary moderation of implementa-tion. However, if Zhao had survived politically, he probably would have relaxed birth rules much further, and he almost certainly would not have re-sumed harsh enforcement in the early 1990s, as his victorious hardline rivals proceeded to do.

In the late 1970s Deng's main weapon for unseating Mao's nominal suc-cessor Hua Guofeng was ideological. Deng used an old slogan of Mao's—"seeking truth from facts"—to displace Hua's exaggerated Maoism. Devel-opmentally, Deng's empiricism showed a country woefully behind where it could have been and dangerously behind advanced countries. Accelerat-ing China's material and cultural modernization became the main theme of Deng's tenure as leader. Demographically, Deng's empiricism showed that the large size of China's population was a central fact on which future development strategy must be based. Politically, Deng's empiricism sug-gested that, for the post-Mao CCP to regain enough legitimacy to remain in power, it must raise living standards to a "modestly comfortable level" (*xiaokang shuiping*). Therefore Deng set a goal of quadrupling annual per capita income by 2000 (originally to US$1000, later reduced to US$800). Because the output of some essential resources and products could grow only slowly, limiting the growth of population could contribute to raising consumption per capita. Deng weighed in heavily with these ideas at major central party work conferences in early 1979 that set the ideological and practical direction of the ensuing era (Shi 790323, 790326, 790330, 790505). These are the ideas that, as the justification for maintaining a strict birth pol-icy, the Jiang era canonized as "Deng Xiaoping Population Thought." As birth program leaders put these ideas into practice, they spoke openly of "conveying Deng's instructions" (ME 810110). Nevertheless, Deng never publicly committed himself to any particular birth policy, leaving that to his lieutenants to work out.

Accordingly the adoption of hard birth planning requires a more political explanation than one man's cryptic insights. Even before Deng had completed his political comeback, birth planning had begun to rise in priority, presumably with the support of the immediate post-Mao troika of top party, army, and government leaders (Hua Guofeng, Ye Jianying, and Li Xianninan). Birth policy gradually became tougher during the last half of the 1970s, evidently with the endorsement of the leaders of all of the major policy tendencies of the time. Overall, the likely explanation for the adoption and persistence of hard birth planning during the Deng era is that most senior members of Deng's coalition agreed it was necessary. They considered Mao's failure to limit population growth a grave mistake in development strategy that they now had the opportunity and obligation to correct. Doing so could constitute another grand contribution by their generation to shaping China's destiny. Doing so even gave some of them jobs after Deng succeeded in forcing them to retire from mainline regime positions. To the extent that arguments persisted within Stalinism between Industrialists and Financialists, evidently the imperative to limit population growth was not one of them. Propagandizing compliance gave Mobilizationists something to do during an era in which Maoism was being phased out of any role in economic development.

After Mao's death, as the ranking of leaders by their revolutionary status reasserted itself, the main support for intensified birth planning came from senior leaders of the Financial tendency, particularly senior political "survivors" Li Xiannian and Chen Yun. Since the 1950s Li Xiannian had been a main representative of the Financial tendency and, by the late 1970s, of the Industrial tendency as well. Li was the main post-Mao centrist government leader and the early Deng era's chief public articulator of specific targets for population policy. It was Li who in mid-1978 told the government's newly strengthened birth planning leading group that controlling population growth had become a major "strategic task" and that emphasis within the national birth policy of "later, longer, fewer" must shift to "fewer" (ME 780628). It was Li who in early 1979 told a party central work conference that the target for population size at the end of the century should be "under 1.2 billion" (Shi 790405, 800115). It was Li who in late 1979 suggested to a meeting of the planning commission that the goal should be one child and that policy could not permit "the slightest slackening," remarks whose quick endorsement by the Central Committee provided its earliest official adoption of those policies (ME 791220, 800104, 800315). In early 1980 Li complained that the annual national population plan had not been achieved in 1979 and that there could not be the slightest relaxation (*sihao songjie*). He repeated Deng's early 1979 call for reducing the rate of population growth to a half percent by 1985 and added the goal of achieving zero population growth in 2000. Plans must be made quickly to achieve this objective (Shi 790323, 800210). Nevertheless, technically these remained calls for "advocating" one child; it was not until June 1980 that policymakers decided to make the one-child limit mandatory and to enforce that demand on the whole country—except national minorities—as quickly as possible (EW 12Nov03 BJ).

The most senior leader of the Financial tendency, Chen Yun, emerged once again as a major proponent of birth planning as an adjunct to development policy. Like Deng, Chen said the central problem was the contradiction between China's poverty and the imperative of achieving the Four Modernizations, a contradiction that could be overcome only by restraining population growth (Shi 790321). In 1979 Chen reappeared alongside Deng to "readjust" the "Great Leap Outward" (plant imports financed by oil exports), a policy of the Hua-Ye-Li troika. Chen achieved a significant reallocation of resources from heavy industry toward agriculture and light industry (Naughton 1995, 67–76). One reason Chen favored a tougher birth policy may have been to ensure that the new investment going to rural areas was not simply consumed by population growth. As Chen later remarked, somewhat sourly, "some other East Asian nations have been quite successful economically, but they don't have the problem of 800 million peasants" (Shi 801216). Accordingly early Deng agricultural policy included birth planning (ME 790928, 820101). As soon as Chen reemerged he set out, in his usual terse style, the agenda of birth policy for the entire Deng era: to legitimate widespread discussion, to legislate "one-couple, one-child," and to provide preferential social programs for those who complied (Shi 790308). Those remarks were published later, after a big struggle over important details had produced policies that could be officially adopted (ME 810525; Greenhalgh 2005b). In the course of the 1980s Chen and his protégés became the main advocates of continuing stern enforcement of a one-child policy, as Chen's increasingly conservative adherence to central planning became the main economic alternative to Deng's increasingly aggressive pursuit of marketization.

Among junior leaders, the key figure for birth planning was Hu Yaobang. A long-time associate of Deng Xiaoping, during the Mao era Hu had headed the party's youth organization. After Mao's death, Hu assumed important posts—in the party organization department, the central party school, and the informal party secretariat—from which he helped rehabilitate Deng. In 1979 the Secretariat of the Central Committee was formally restored to its pre-Cultural Revolution role as the party's main body for researching policy and for the first half of the 1980s as the main forum for deciding policy as well.

As general secretary of the Secretariat, Hu became the head of the party, with particular responsibility for sociocultural policy. Both his Secretariat position and his sociocultural portfolio gave Hu particularly direct responsibility for birth policy. The party was also the key to securing implementation of birth policy by subnational leaders. As early as June 1979 the Secretariat discussed birth work and Hu suggested writing an "open letter" to party and youth league members in order to use them to set an example (*chi mofan daitou de zuoyong*—Shi 790626). Given the commitment of senior leaders to a strict birth policy, Hu had little alternative but to support it. Nevertheless, how avid an advocate Hu was of trying to reach the one-child goal remains unclear. Evidently at first he had some doubts and later he may have favored more exceptions rather than fewer (EW 6Nov03 BJ).

The role of Zhao Ziyang in birth planning remains obscure, partly because it was not his direct responsibility, partly because his successors have largely erased him from the record. In the middle 1970s Zhao was provincial party leader in Guangdong when it was pioneering research and training in population theory. In the late 1970s Zhao was provincial party leader in Sichuan when it was pioneering harsh enforcement of birth limits in a relatively undeveloped region. Therefore it is likely that Zhao favored relatively strict birth planning, even though those accomplishments are never mentioned among his credentials, and even though he may have learned some cautionary lessons in achieving them. After Deng promoted Zhao to replace Hua Guofeng as premier, Zhao loyally upheld strict birth limits (e.g., Shi 811130). Nevertheless, in the mid-1980s Zhao was the main potential backer of attempts to reform the one-child policy, reforms that in the end did not go as far as he probably hoped. (On Zhao see Shambaugh 1984.)

A third major actor within the younger generation was the relative hardliner Li Peng. A Zhou Enlai protégé and junior technocrat, he succeeded Zhao as premier (1987–1998), then headed the National People's Congress (1998–2003). Li does not cut a sympathetic figure, with his backing by conservative seniors, background in hydroelectric engineering, commitment to central planning, and association with the Tiananmen repression. In the population domain he consistently supported hard birth planning and, once that policy was in place, insisted that fundamentals should not be changed. (His Three Givens were existing birth rules, existing plan targets, and existing systems for forcing subnational officials to enforce them). On the other hand, at least before Tiananmen, Li could be remarkably unstuffy and straightforward, as in several speeches he made to subnational birth program officials that explained national political leaders' thinking about birth policy. Moreover, policies over which he presided as premier were relatively centrist for the time, combining basic stability and harsh enforcement with some compromises and even some innovations, such as the integration of birth planning with antipoverty work.

1979–1983: Advance

In the early 1980s Chinese politics completed a shift from left to center, then stalled and polarized as leftists counterattacked. In the center, the December 1978 Third Plenum had inaugurated the Deng era and initiated economic reform to liberalize economic organization. During 1979 and 1980 Financialist Chen Yun reemerged to shift attention from reforming organization to readjusting the proportions of investment, away from heavy industry and toward agriculture and light industry. By the Fifth Plenum in February 1980, by purging leftists and promoting centrists, Deng had achieved a majority on the Politburo and its Standing Committee. It was this centrist majority of reformers and readjusters that officially launched hard birth planning. In 1981 through 1983 leftists counterattacked centrists by raising ideological issues. To placate the left and to protect his economic gains, Deng reaffirmed his ideological commitment to Leninism. However, by the end of 1983, the left's ideological campaign jeopardized economic reform, so Deng terminated it. The leftist campaigns did not conspicuously challenge birth planning, but they may have distracted key leaders just as hard birth planning was being operationalized and given its first main nationwide implementation. (On politics see Perkins and Yusuf 1984; Harding 1987, 40–69; Shirk 1993; Solinger 1993, 27–62; Baum 1994, 121–163; Zheng 1997, 161–254.)

Meanwhile birth planning proceeded ambitiously—first to general formulation, then to further specification, and finally to full-scale national implementation. (On program see Orleans ed. 1979, 203–209; Banister 1984; Sun 1987, 173–263; Shi 1988, 172–285; White 1990, 57–60; White 1994b, 141–149; Sharping 2003, 50–58; Greenhalgh 2003b, 2005b.)

FORMULATION

Post-Mao leaders finally gave PRC birth policy its guiding components of active party leadership, legitimate ideological rationale, and directive party policies. First, PRC leaders finally provided *party leadership*, by becoming directly involved and making necessary decisions, by approving and circulating national program reports, and even by deputing some of its members to act as program leaders. The renewed involvement had begun in early 1977 to early 1978 when the State Council approved reports of the national work conferences on birth planning that had been held in late 1976 and late 1977 (ME 770205, 780224; EBP 65–67). This involvement deepened in June

1978 when the State Council upgraded its birth planning leading group, appointed vice premier Chen Muhua to run it, and sent senior regime leader Li Xiannian to participate in its first meeting. In October 1978 the party Central Committee quickly approved the report of the meeting, which recommended a birth rule of "one is best, two at most" (Shi 781029; EBP 12–14). This was the party Center's first direct action exclusively on birth planning since December 1974 (when all it had done was to transmit subnational work reports). It is from this October 1978 authorization by the Central Committee that program histories date the beginning of many efforts at program building. In February 1981, citing the long-term nature of the strategic task of controlling population growth, Premier Zhao asked the standing committee of the National People's Congress for permission to upgrade the temporary leading group to a permanent birth commission, a request soon granted (Shi 810224; ME 810306). In July the State Council established the State Birth Planning Commission with a mandate to build a stand-alone system for delivering birth control services and with some mandate to coordinate related work in other ministries (ME 810713). Chen Muhua continued as the first birth minister until May 1982. Then, on becoming a state councillor, she gave government oversight of birth work to vice premier Wan Li and relinquished the running of the birth ministry to former health minister Qian Xinzhong (ME 820504). Later, in the run-up to attempting nation-wide enforcement of the one-child policy in 1983, the Secretariat assigned party oversight of birth work to its new female deputy secretary, Hao Jianxiu (ME 821011). Hao had started in the early 1950s as a textile worker in Shandong with a flair for technological innovation. She had gradually risen through the provincial and national government and party to a significant role in national planning that extended into the early 1990s.

Second, PRC leaders finally provided *ideological legitimation* for birth policy. In line with Dengist empiricism, legitimation shifted to science as espoused by professional intellectuals, who had not been heard from on population issues since the late 1950s. The Central Committee approved Peking University's reversal of its late 1950s verdict that Ma Yinchu was a "rightist." As commentators remarked, "[We] mistakenly criticized a Ma Yinchu, [and as a result we] produced more than 300 million extra people (*cuo pile yige Ma Yinchu, duo shengle sanyi duo ren*). This is a painful lesson" (Shi 790925). To dramatize the urgency of developing a Marxist social science of population, the regime inaugurated periodic conferences on population theory and established a population studies association (Shi 781101, 791207; Greenhalgh 1990b). Thus reinstated, social scientists elaborated a Marxist theory of population that helped legitimate this new policy domain but also questioned extreme policies (Greenhalgh 2003b). Meanwhile the media propagandized these new scientific rationales for policy. *People's Daily*, having in the previous thirty years only intermittently run authoritative pieces devoted exclusively to promoting birth control, ran at least ten of them between 1978 and 1983 (six editorials and four commentaries, according to EBP 11). The titles of the first few editorials reflect the rapid evolution of leadership thinking, from influencing individual behavior to controlling aggregate outcomes. The earlier ones called for more attention to "birth planning" (ME 780709, 790127); later ones introduced the theme of "controlling population" (ME 800211, 820823). Emphasis was shifting from micro discipline to macro limits.

Third, PRC leaders finally provided active and authoritative *directional policy*. The substance of the policy was ostensibly based on highly scientific planning that demonstrated the urgency of action and dictated a tightening of both rules and enforcement. The form of policy was not only party pronouncement but also government legislation by the National People's Congress. The 1978 state constitution stated that the PRC "advocates and promotes" birth planning, an article that had a "big effect" (Shi 780305). The 1982 constitution went further, making it a duty of citizens to practice birth planning, an obligation that campaigns quickly used to justify enforcement of birth limits (ME 821204). Meanwhile PRC leaders very much wanted the NPC to put details of a one-child policy into an enabling law. The Secretariat called legalization the "central problem" for making birth planning "sustainable," calling on all levels of government to produce "effective and realistic" regulations and laws within two years (ME 821011). The Deng leadership did succeed in revising the Marriage Law. Provisions relevant to birth planning somewhat raised the legal minimum age for marriage, added eugenic restrictions on marriage, and made it a duty of both spouses to practice birth control (ME 800910). The State Council then issued a notice on using the revised Marriage Law to regularize and intensify subnational marriage work through the formula "since there is a law it must be followed, enforcement of the law must be severe" (*youfa biyi, zhifa biyan*—ME 801210). Lacking a national birth law, the PRC was not able to do the same for birth work until the early 2000s. Repeated efforts to draft such a law—or even national birth regulations that the State Council could issue—failed repeatedly. Ostensibly the problem was the difficulty of framing a law that could apply to diverse localities. Actually the problem was the reluctance of lawmakers to legislate one-child families and legal punishments. As a result the Deng era had to get by on provincial administrative regulations, later passed by provincial people's congresses as provincial laws.

The Deng era also formalized the operative components of birth policy (plan, rules, and enforcement). The formulation of a population *plan* for the rest of the century contributed crucially to the overall tightening of guiding policy. Mathematicians from the PRC's space program volunteered to help draft the Sixth Five-Year Plan and longer-range perspective development plans (SG 24Dec03 BJ). They projected China's likely future population using the advanced mathematics of control theory, derived from missile science and western population cybernetics (Greenhalgh 2005b). The results suggested that China's population could reach 1.5 billion by 2020, which was viewed as a disaster that could be avoided only by quickly adopting a one-child limit for all. The 2000 population target that would allow reaching Deng's goal of quadrupling per capita income was about 1.2 billion, which also required a one-child rule (Shi 841006). Chinese social scientists protested that such a drastic policy would impose severe costs on society—both microindividual frustration of fertility aspirations and macrodemographic distortions of age structure. Nevertheless, between late 1979 and mid-1980 cyberneticist Song Jian gradually persuaded national political and program leaders to shift from a policy that advocated one child but allowed two, to a policy that allowed only one, with very few exceptions (Greenhalgh 2005b). At a meeting with the regime's mass organizations on a new propaganda campaign for new styles of marriage and childbearing, Chen Muhua said that the only way to control population at "about 1.2 billion" (*12 yi zuoyou*) was "gradually" (*you jubude*) to achieve 95 percent one-child couples in cities and 90 percent in the countryside, a prescription that *People's Daily* repeated the next day (Shi 800202, 800203). In the context of the times, "gradually" probably meant by 1985.

Trying to impose a one-child *rule* that rapidly was extraordinarily ambitious. Specific policies evolved over time. First, the new rule was applied in stages: initially to regime personnel (the September 1980 Open Letter), then to urbanites (as some legal basis was established in the 1982 Constitution and local regulations), and finally to rural residents (in the 1983 campaign). This sequence recapitulated the development of birth planning during the Mao era. Second, application was to be discriminating. By 1980 when they adopted the one-child policy, PRC leaders realized that at least some couples would require exemptions permitting a second child. By 1984 they realized as well that different kinds of localities required different rules. Third, PRC leaders phased in implementation through progressively more intense winter campaigns conveying the new policy, its rationale, and regime determination to implement it. Only in 1983—after some preparation and after bad news from the 1982 census—did they attempt all-out nationwide enforcement.

Fourth, no sooner had PRC leaders adopted the one-child rule than the policy environment began to change, particularly through liberalization of rural organization. PRC leaders' main response was a limited increase in exceptions. Fifth, when the one-child policy finally was strongly enforced during 1983, the regime had not yet built the capacity for controlled implementation. The result was disastrous, not only for women's health and dignity, but also for political relations between the party, its community cadres, and the masses. The regime responded with more exceptions, finally codified only in 1988.

In their early deliberations, policymakers extensively explored issues of *enforcement*. As Chen Yun had implied in 1978, because rural families rely on children for labor power and old-age support, limiting them to one child would be implementable only if the government compensated them for their loss of labor power and guaranteed their old-age security, which Chen proposed to do (Shi 790308, 800615, the latter a letter to Chen Muhua formalizing the former). The birth program had already begun to institutionalize positive preferential treatment for only children and their parents (paid for by subnational governments, particularly by communities themselves). Eventually couples who already had one child and promised not to have another were issued a "one-child certificate" that entitled both child and parents to a series of benefits, at least to the extent that their local governments could afford to provide them. But the main additional enforcement tool became strong economic disincentives: not only steep fines for unauthorized children but also the refusal of state services to them. As Chen's astute formulations also implied, inducing compliance with such a demanding policy would require all forms of power the regime had available. Accordingly, at the beginning of 1980 the central committee called for "legislative, administrative, and economic" measures to "encourage" one child (Shi 800104). In the policy parlance of the time, literally and quickly restricting virtually all couples to one child was called "one-child-ization" (*yitaihua*). Much of the spring 1980 discussion was about whether that was feasible and about how to achieve it (Greenhalgh 2005b). Reportedly Hu Yaobang and some other younger leaders kept asking "Will it work? Will it work?" (*Xing buxing? Xing buxing?*). Some program insiders—and many social scientists—told political leaders from the beginning that literal one-child-ization was not feasible. That is why, from the beginning, the policy included the possibility of exceptions, whose extent then became the main issue. (Based on EW 6Nov03 BJ and 12Nov03 BJ; SG 15Dec03 BJ and 19Dec03 TY.)

To put these operative components of policy into effect, in May 1981 the State Council elevated its birth planning leading group to a State Birth Planning Commission. Not only did the SBPC have ministry-level status, but it even had some claim to coordinate any work relevant to birth planning in all ministries. Chen Muhua stayed on for a year as the first birth minister, probably to supervise the transition from leading group to commission. Her successor Qian Xinzhong had been health minister in the mid-1960s, and again vice minister and minister of health starting from the mid-1970s. He had become concurrently vice minister of the birth commission when it was established in 1981. Meanwhile the SBPC quickly held its first meeting and set about staffing its several departments. The process of organizing the new SBPC continued for the next year or two, including July 1981 State Council approval of the SBPC's views on division of labor (EBP 69) and a March 1983 directive from the administrative office of the State Council on the SBPC's missions and responsibilities (EBP 70).

SPECIFICATION

In early September 1980 Hua Guofeng, leaving the premiership, announced to the National People's Congress that "after much research" the government had adopted a one-child rule and a target of keeping population under 1.2 billion in 2000 (Shi 800907). Then, at the end of September, the party Central Committee issued a dramatic Open Letter to members of the party and its youth organization, in effect telling them to take "the State Council's" one-child slogan seriously (EPB 1617; White ed. 1992, 11–16). The Letter explained the need to keep population under 1.2 billion in 2000, citing the cyberneticists' alarming projections. The Letter also raised and refuted concerns that had been raised and dismissed within the policy process, such as possible shortfalls in manpower, accelerated aging of the population, and distortions in sex ratio. For birth control, the letter emphasized contraception, with choice of method. Significantly for policy evolution during the mid-1980s, the letter noted the possibility of exceptions to the one-child rule that would allow some rural couples with the "real difficulties" specified in local regulations to have a second child (at first only about five percent of couples who already had one child, with third children strictly prohibited). The letter endorsed preferential treatment for only children and their families, noting a series of specific policies that the party and government had already resolved to adopt and execute. Significantly for policy evolution in the early twenty-first century, the letter noted: "In the future, when production is more developed, and people's livelihoods have improved, there ought to be continuous increase and improvement in social welfare and social insurance." Finally, the letter asked party and youth corps members to lead the way by setting an example, by modernizing their own ideas, and by persuading others.

National program leaders quickly convened a national conference of provincial directors to discuss how to implement the Open Letter's demands. The conference agenda was extraordinarily complex, including exceptions and benefits for the one-child rule, old-age insurance and social welfare, late marriage and late childbearing, long-term population planning, and enforcement of the resulting targets. Not surprisingly, subnational program leaders were overwhelmed by the enormity of the task and the complexity of the details. Veteran program leader Li Xiuzhen told them that until the Center defined more policies they would just have to figure out measures on their own! The meeting prescribed a propaganda campaign for early 1981, during the winter slack season in farm work, the usual main time for birth work. (See ME 801007; EBP 303–305, Li closing speech.)

Meanwhile the policy environment began to change, as private memos and public announcements reflected (Shi 810411, Hu Qiaomu phone call to Chen Muhua; ME 810818, *People's Daily* article). The 1980 revision of the Marriage Law, although somewhat raising the legal minimum marriage age, left it below the age that birth policy called for and still further below the age that some localities actually enforced. This discrepancy, together with the new emphasis of the Deng administration on legality, temporarily allowed the beginning of the new "peak" of young people to marry and reproduce earlier. Also, just when liberalization of rural organization was reducing regime leverage over farmers, rural marketization was increasing the value to rural households of male labor power, making enforcement of birth limits more difficult. Some provinces rushed to add exceptions for two children to their rules, so that second children would be allowed under the Open Letter's formulation (EBP 472–473, the Chen report cited immediately below). The result was therefore not a tightening of rural implementation as policy demanded but instead some slackening. In 1981 birth control medical procedures slumped to only 23 million and a post-1971 low of less than 10 percent sterilizations, compared to about 30 million and 20 percent in the previous two years.

In September 1981 Chen Muhua reported these problems to the party Secretariat (ME 810910; EBP 472–473). The meeting concluded that birth policy faced a "new situation" that required "further research" on the party's "directional policy" to ensure that it "accorded with reality." The meeting formulated two proposals on *rules*, one advocating one child but allowing a second, the other advocating one child and allowing a second only to couples with "real difficulties" (*shiji kunnan*), meaning mostly rural couples whose first child was a daughter. Relevant experts and subnational leaders should discuss this and report to the provinces in October. They would then react at a central work meeting in November. Whether and when that follow-up meeting occurred is unclear, but the upshot was the tougher second policy, with a narrow definition of "real difficulties" that applied to only about 5 percent of couples who already had one child. Reportedly the majority of provinces voted for the tougher "micro" birth rule, probably to make it easier for them to meet their "macro" population targets (EW 3Nov03 BJ; SG interpretation). This crucial decision was then incorporated in a pivotal central document in February 1982.

Meanwhile, on *enforcement*, at the September 1981 meeting Chen said that although good propaganda preparation was still primary, it would be necessary to have economic incentives and disincentives that were "effective and implementable." For example, she said, one could pass new legislation imposing an extra child "tax" on excess children. This was then done during the 1980s by the provinces as a "fine" on excess children, nationally standardized in 1992, and further formalized as a "social compensation fee" in the 2001 national law on population and birth planning and in accompanying regulations. Actually, like Ma Yinchu's suggestions in 1955, Chen's formulation remains ahead even of the 2001 law because the social compensation fee it imposed may eventually in fact evolve into a tax, in the context of introducing systematic taxation of personal income when that becomes feasible.

After the late 1981 round of consultations over the one-child rule, in February 1982 the Central Committee and State Council jointly issued a directive to subnational leaders on "doing a better job of birth work" (ME 820209; EBP 18–20). This pivotal Document Eleven was the first from the Center exclusively devoted to the one-child policy and the first to specify current operational details. The directive contained a hint of impending urgency: Some progress had been made since the 1980 Open Letter, but the "new situation" had made progress difficult. Moreover "some people" were "damaging" birth work, and the directive said they should be "dealt with severely." In April the Secretariat met to discuss birth work and complained that "not a few" localities were controlling population poorly: localities must grasp this matter tightly and under no circumstances relax (ME 8304215). As a result, enforcement became more severe in 1982 and still more severe in 1983. (White ed. 1992, 17–26 provides Document Eleven in English.)

IMPLEMENTATION

In August 1982 the birth commission convened a work conference on how to implement the Center's instructions (ME 8208910). It noted the need both to enforce birth limits and to solve problems in work methods. It decided on a campaign at the beginning of 1983, between Western and Chinese New Year. In September, laying the public ground for severe enforcement, Hu Yaobang told the Twelfth Party Congress that birth planning was now a "basic national policy" affecting people's economic security, "perhaps even society's stability." . . . "Under no circumstances could birth work relax, particularly in villages" (ME 820901). In October, the party Secretariat approved the August birth conference report (ME 821011). The administrative offices of the Central Committee and State Council transmitted it as an instruction, requesting a progress report from each province during the first quarter of 1983 (ME 821020; EBP 21–23).

Meanwhile the policy process received sobering news from its demographic environment. In July 1982 the PRC conducted its first modern census, and in late October the State Statistical Bureau issued some main results (ME 821027). As with the 1954 census, the size of the population, though staggering, was not a surprise. The shock was that, after years of decline, in 1981 the birth rate and growth rate had rebounded (to 2.09 percent and 1.46 percent, respectively). The next day the birth commission said that the census results showed that the rate of population increase was too fast, that there had been a rebound in fertility, and that the task of slowing population growth must be grasped (Shi 821028). Many national leaders mentioned the census results in late 1982 when launching the 1983 campaign. Also, in September 1982 the birth system conducted a 1-per-1000 fertility survey (EBP 820901). Analysis revealed still greater disaster: previous data on fertility and population growth had been off by a wide mark. These results were crucial to PRC leaders' resoluteness in enforcing harsh measures during the 1983 campaign (SG 18Dec03 BJ; Greenhalgh 2005a).

In November 1982 the birth commission and the propaganda department of the Central Committee convened a work meeting on the impending campaign (ME 821101). Leading Financialist Bo Yibo addressed the meeting, calling for, among other things, achievement of the Three Basics. These were an emerging standard for professionalizing birth work that advocated primary reliance on education over coercion, routine work over crash campaigns, and contraception over abortion. After the meeting, birth minister Qian Xinzhong issued more specific instructions to the provinces (Shi 821122). In his capacity as the party secretary of the birth commission, he wrote directly to the party leading groups for birth planning in the fifteen provinces with more than 30 million people, which accounted for 80 percent of China's population: "The Center has decided on a propaganda month. We recommend that you combine propaganda month activities with tightly grasping the implementation of birth control measures for fertile females, particularly rural ones who already have two children, with the exception of minorities, the ill, and couples who have already been using IUDs effectively for five years. In general [the campaign] should mobilize one or the other of the couple to implement sterilization. This winter to next year [the campaign] should basically fulfill all sterilization targets. At the same time [the campaign] must abort out-of-plan pregnancies firmly but early. [This] should be done well, guaranteeing safety." A propaganda meeting in Beijing kicked off the campaign. Wan Li included opposing gender prejudice and raising women's status among the objectives (ME 821222). Hao Jianxiu urged that "everyone come participate" in creating a new phase (*xin jumian*) of socialist development in China. *People's Daily* commented that birth work must be done to the point where "every household and individual understands" (ME 821223).

Hu Yaobang explained the rationale for these active measures to the visiting president of Turkey (Shi 821228). "We made a mistake in population. It was only three or four years ago that we began to grasp the work of controlling population. This work relies first on political mobilization, second on law, and third on technical procedures. In these [last] few years we have had accomplishments, but there are still great difficulties." Later a *Health Daily* editorial called this formula the Three Firsts (Shi 831004). Policymakers also gave some attention to professionalization of birth work, advertising the Three Basics. Nevertheless, it would take another decade before the professionalism of the Basics could begin seriously reforming the politicization of the Firsts.

In February, obeying the Secretariat's earlier instruction to report back on progress, the birth program convened a meeting in Tianjin to "exchange experiences" about the campaign (Shi 830223). The meeting recommended that propaganda and sterilizations should continue beyond the winter season. Qian then reported to central leaders that the campaign had been effective and should continue (Shi 830224). Hao Jianxiu gave Qian's letter to Wan Li, who personally issued instructions (Shi 830226, 830229). "We can't have the slightest relaxation or wavering. . . . The accomplishments of the propaganda month must be wholly affirmed" (*chongfen kending*). Effective methods must be maintained. "Grasp tightly, grasp well" (*zhuajin, zhuahao*). Thus even Wan, who inveighed against coercion immediately before and after the 1983 campaign, endorsed the campaign while it was occurring (ME 821124, 840227). However, evidently national leaders did receive some alarming feedback on problems, at least some of which they did try to correct. For example, *People's Daily* devoted a commentary to infanticide, child-abandonment, and infant sex-ratio imbalance, calling them "a big problem that deserves serious attention" (ME 830407). In May, with the assistance of the United Nations Fund for Population Activities and the International Planned Parenthood Federation, the birth program convened a large field conference in the home town of birth minister Qian Xinzhong

(ME 840507). Rongcheng in Shandong had pioneered the Three Basics. Qian urged that they become the standard for improving birth work while reducing population growth to 1.3 percent (EBP 313–315).

Nevertheless, the 1983 propaganda and sterilization campaign became a human tragedy, traumatizing millions of women and ending the lives of uncounted numbers of infant girls (Chapter 7). An indicator of the intensity of the effort is that in 1983 birth control operations reached an all-time high of 58 million, 36 percent of them sterilizations, both about twice the normal number (Table 3). The campaign was also a political disaster, harming relations between party, cadres, and masses, and even threatening sociopolitical stability. The debacle was a defining moment for PRC birth planning, defining what political and program leaders wanted never to repeat and deepening the division between hardliners and softliners within the birth policy process.

1984–1988: Consolidation

In the mid-1980s Chinese politics shifted from center-left to center-right and then back to dead center. Deng finally succeeded in forcing the semiretirement of most of the moderate left, the remnants of the Mobilization tendency within Maoism. They thought that "reform and opening" had already gone too far and wished to roll it back in some aspects. Their semideparture allowed Deng to initiate further reform. However, those initiatives opened a rift within his centrist reform coalition. The center-left was the remnants of the Industrial and Financial tendencies. They had supported economic "reform and opening" but now thought that reform—particularly political reform—should proceed only slowly if at all, and only to the extent that it did not threaten stability. Elder Chen Yun took this position, along with less senior planners such as Yao Yilin and Song Ping, and their main junior protégé Li Peng. The center-right was the Reformists, who wished to extend economic reform from rural agriculture to urban industry and to revive Deng's proposals for reform of elite political institutions. Deng's junior lieutenants Hu Yaobang and Zhao Ziyang were the main representatives of the Reformist position. During most of this period Deng leaned to the right of center and authorized his lieutenants to proceed. However, urban economic reform produced an inflation of prices, and elite political reform produced an inflation of mass participation. By the late 1980s, these instabilities allowed the center-right gradually to regain the initiative, while Deng attempted to maintain an at least centrist course. (On politics see Baum 1994, 164–224.)

As a Maoist-Stalinist project advancing amid de-Maoization and de-Stalinization, birth planning converged only gradually with these systemic swings. In the early 1980s the initiation of hard birth planning had coincided with the launching of economic and political reform, but its harsh enforcement had coincided with a slowing of that systemic reform. In the middle 1980s birth policy entered a phase of consolidation: first deliberate adjustment, then inadvertent relaxation, and finally stabilization. The adjustment and relaxation coincided with renewed systemic reform that, if it had continued, might have pushed birth planning itself into such drastic reforms as abandoning the one-child policy. Instead another slowing of systemic reform restabilized birth policy around a much more modest adjustment of birth rules. In the course of all this, controversy became bitter over how to fix the problems that too-harsh enforcement had created in 1983. Controversy also became protracted, persisting with greater or lesser openness into the early 2000s. As adjustment slipped into relaxation, hardliners demanded firm adherence to the target of keeping population under 1.2 billion in 2000, demanded a retightening of birth rules back to the original one-child policy of few exceptions and resolute re-enforcement of that rule. Softliners regarded the 1.2 billion plan target as simply impossible and succeeded in loosening it to "about 1.2 billion." They hoped that such loosening would allow a shift to a largely two-child rule and a more gradual approach to gaining public acceptance of that limit. In 1988 national political leaders endorsed a centrist compromise: a one-and-half-child policy and gradual but resolute re-enforcement. (On program see Greenhalgh 1986, 1990a, 1993, 1994a; Shi 1988, 286–348; Aird 1990, 35–87; White 1990, 60–68; White 1991; White 1994b, 14–154; White 2000a, 2000b; Wang 1991a, 1991b; Scharping 2003, 58–63.)

1984: ADJUSTMENT

After remaining inscrutable during 1983, the policy process reappeared in January 1984 as one of "perfecting" (*wanshan*) birth policy. Birth minister Qian Xinzhong having been fired, the party Secretariat received an oral report from the new minister Wang Wei (ME 840119, EBP 24). He was a former administrator of the youth association, therefore probably associated with Hu Yaobang. If so, presumably it was Hu who had assigned Wang as vice minister of the birth commission when it was established in 1981. The Secretariat also received a written report from the birth commission that diagnosed what had gone wrong in 1983, suggested what to do about it, and evidently requested instructions. The commission's report was rather abject, accepting the blame for 1983 excesses and promising to strengthen administrative supervision and basic-level implementation. The report also recommended additional second-child exceptions to the one-child rule that would raise the proportion of couples who could proceed from one child to two from about

5 percent to 10 percent. The Secretariat prescribed a careful process of policy review, under which the birth commission convened a national directors' conference to refine recommendations, revised its original report to the Secretariat, and resubmitted it (ME 840227). The Secretariat then met again to review the revision and a week later issued the historic Document Seven. It set the broad parameters for birth policy ever since (ME 840405, 840413; EBP 24–27).

The Secretariat's January reaction to the 1983 debacle had been scathing. In 1983 the performance of many basic-level cadres had been appalling, but the fault was not theirs. Part of the blame lay with birth system administrators, for failing to provide cadres with adequate training and timely supervision. The other part lay with an interpretation of the one-child policy that was too inflexible to implement. Particularly in rural areas, somewhat more couples under somewhat more circumstances must be allowed to have second children. The Secretariat invoked the most fundamental test possible within Leninist ideology: "The party's policies cannot depart from reality" (EBP 474).

As for new policies, the Secretariat's main point was that birth policy must be "established on a foundation that is both firm and implementable" (EBP 840227). Birth work would have to "capitalize on its accomplishments, deal with its shortcomings, and solve its problems." Birth policy must be built on a foundation "that was acceptable and reasonable, that was supported by the masses, and that enabled cadres to do their work." Based on the current actual situation, concrete policies must be improved. First, rural rules must open a "small hole" to allow more second children, after application and with permission. Second, the opening of a "large hole" must be resolutely prevented—no second children that were not in accord with the rules, and no third children or beyond. Third, corruption was severely prohibited and any cadres guilty of it in connection with birth planning should be punished. (See EBP 473 and 24–27.)

Within these parameters, the birth policy process began absorbing information through elite reports, mass letters, and program experiments. On the elite side, in February Liang Zhongtang of the provincial party school in Shanxi had written a report to the Central Committee on how to "build birth planning work on the foundation of the laws of population development" (ME 840200). Liang's recommendation was to allow couples two children, but spaced eight to ten years apart. Policy could continue to advocate one child, but Liang recommended a proportion of single children of only about 30 percent. In July two birth commission staffers wrote a research report to the Central Committee and State Council on "some issues of population control and population policy." They recommended that the 2000 plan target of "within 1.2 billion" should be relaxed to "about 1.2 billion" and, like Liang, that the birth rule should be relaxed to two children with long spacing in between (ME 840730). The staffers were a researcher at the birth system's China Population Information and Research Center (Ma Yingtong) and a cadre at the birth commission (Zhang Xiaotong, son of health minister Cui Yuili, who had opposed the one-child policy). The report argued that a one-child-for-all policy was unenforceable and that the looser target would reduce pressure on implementers and the public (SG 17Dec03 BJ). In August government leader Zhao and party leader Hu approved the Ma-Zhang report. Although there "continued to be different views at the Center," Zhao instructed the birth commission to switch to a two-child policy. The commission called a meeting with Yu Jingyuan, a colleague of the control theorist Song Jian, whose calculations had underlain the original one-child policy. Yu redid the new report's calculations, showing that the Ma-Zhang plan would produce a 2000 population not of 1.23 billion as it claimed, but rather of 1.26 billion (1.29 billion including the military). At a second meeting most experts agreed that relaxing policy would be a demographic disaster, so Zhao's two-child instruction was not transmitted to lower levels (SG 21Dec03 BJ).

On the mass side, the birth system held its first meeting on "letters and visits" (*xinfang*), the channels through which the public was allowed to register complaints, which provided useful feedback, particularly on maladministration (ME 840616). Complaint work was supervised by the birth commission's administrative office, which under Liang Jimin was a significant source of new thinking during this period. The administrative office also supervised local experiments at adapting hard birth planning to regional and local realities. The planning division of the birth commission was gearing up to do more detailed regional plans. It had adopted the principle of "differential guidance" (*fenlei zhidao*) for different types of localities, in order to coordinate economic and social development with resource utilization and environmental protection (ME 841005). The administrative office convened a meeting on local experiments at reforming birth planning, creating an "experimental county coordination group" divided into north and south sections. Evidently treading on thin ice, this effort distinguished between "reform" and "experiment," the former to "improve" policy, the latter to "demonstrate the correctness of Document Seven," evidently referring to its endorsement of allowing more exceptions to the one-child rule. The ensuing experiments tried various combinations of number and spacing of children, including allowing all couples to have two.

Thus birth planning, a late-started Maoist-Stalinist project, became for the first time the object of Reformist experiments. However, the scope for experiment was much narrower in birth work than in economics. Even

Zhao had said that birth planning was not something that could be "enlivened" through liberalization, unlike policy areas such as family farming and enterprise management. Instead, he said, birth policy resembled policy areas such as forestry and the urbanization of farmland, where it was necessary to establish restrictions (Shi 821008). All that was possible in birth planning was to conduct controlled experiments in a limited number of localities in order to explore exactly how large an exception to the one-child rule was possible without causing fertility to rebound. Also, birth policy was not something that could be publicly debated.

1984–1987: RELAXATION

In the classic PRC advance-consolidation policy cycle, national leaders do not intend that consolidation should deteriorate into relaxation, but that often happens. The rather long period of relaxation in birth policy during the mid-1980s is an example. Certainly at first it was in part a deliberate backing-off from the overenforcement of 1983, but national political and program leaders still insisted that enforcement of birth limits "not waver." Later the main cause was the demand of rural community cadres and publics for relaxation. (Chapter 7 describes how, during this relaxation, negotiation of local birth policies between cadres and peasants somewhat modified central rules to accommodate local needs.) However, the later relaxation may also have been in part an unintended by-product of the themes to which birth policy turned during this period. None of these themes appears conducive to national mobilization to enforce the quantitative limits in the one-child policy. Thus in winter 1984–1985 there was no national birth work meeting. In 1985 and 1986 the main national birth meetings concerned initiating birth planning among minority nationalities, training basic-level cadres, and integrating birth planning with cultural construction, respectively (ME 850606, 860308, 861016). Both meetings turned the program's attention from quantity to quality.

Other meetings in 1985 and 1986 introduced the new idea that the standard for evaluating birth work should be "social benefit" (*shehui xiaoyi*—Shi 851118; ME 860900). This concept may have been introduced to the PRC by the World Bank, which at this time made its own more sophisticated projections for China's development (World Bank 1985; Hamrin 1990). As interpreted by program leaders, it implied less attention to long-run population size and mid-run economic payoff and more attention to long-run population structure and short-run political stability. Emphasis on social benefit disappeared in the late 1980s but returned again in the early 2000s. Then it was fundamental to reorienting the program toward "actually delivering positive benefits to people," the new criterion that national leader Jiang

Zemin eventually laid down. The reorientation drew on another theme that originated in the mid-1980s, the connection of birth planning to the regime's emerging emphasis on antipoverty work (ME 860711). Insofar as birth planning produced economic benefit, that should be not so much through aggregate average per capita income as through targeting specific poor households to help them become prosperous (*zhifu*). Such targeting developed gradually during the 1990s and took center stage in the 2000s. In still another harbinger of developments that became central in the 2000s, the birth commission conducted a training session for policy research organs on methods for research and evaluation of birth policy, aided by a representative from the Southeast Asia office of the Population Council (ME 860127).

In late 1985, meetings on south and north local experiments "exchanged experience" in how to "gradually perfect" birth policy in order to "explore a work road for socialist birth planning with Chinese characteristics" (ME 851000). The experiments had included a range of ways to improve birth work and birth services, many of which eventually made their way into national practice. Nevertheless, the centerpiece concerned birth rules: different ways of "opening a small hole." Three kinds of experiments had emerged, one emphasizing different rules for different kinds of localities, one allowing a second child to rural couples whose first child was a daughter (*dunuhu*), and one allowing more second children but with added spacing. In early 1986 the birth commission submitted two reports to the Secretariat, one on "reasonably controlling population growth" and the other on accomplishments during the 1981–1985 Sixth Five-Year Plan and prospects for the 1986–1990 Seventh Five-Year Plan. Discussing these reports, a Secretariat meeting endorsed the need to continue to "perfect" policy, insisted that policy be implemented realistically according to circumstance, stressed the need to coordinate population with resources and environment, reiterated the centrality of improving propaganda, elevated the priority of reducing births of defective infants, and called for better demarcation and cooperation between the birth and health systems (ME 860220). The Central Committee later issued these views as 1986 Document Thirteen (ME 860509). The National People's Congress approved the Seventh Five-Year Plan (ME 860412). Looking back, the commission began to shift attention from over- to underenforcement, its report complaining of cadres who opened "crooked holes" (*wai kou*) in birth limits to favor themselves, family, and friends. Looking forward, these documents insisted on the need for strict control of the impending "third peak" (EBP 27–28; White ed. 1992, 41–50, in English).

Soon after, the administrative office of the birth commission convened a national research meeting on birth policy (ME 860727). Evidently some softline localities had interpreted 1986 Document Thirteen as revising 1984 Document Seven toward greater liberality of opening for second children. The meeting insisted that this was not so, that the Center's directional policy had remained clear. Nevertheless, the meeting left the door open to "improving" operational policy. The meeting discussed "the relationship between policy and instructions," analyzing various local policies, evidently in order to maintain both the integrity of national policy and the validity of local variants. A few months after that, the administrative office's Experimental County Coordination Group convened a second pair of north and south meetings, involving 46 counties in 27 provinces (ME 860900). These meetings discussed how to increase social benefit by improving birth policy's "form" (*xingshi*). Again, this may have been an effort to appear not to tamper with basic policy direction while at the same time considering significant modifications in actually operative policy. On the other side of the argument, at about this time the space scientists used data from the 1982 survey to calculate the alternative demographic effects of some of the policy options that the local experiments were considering. In 2000 "two children with spacing" would overrun the 1.2 billion limit to 1.25 billion, while the "only daughter household" exception would produce only 1.19 billion (Shi 860720).

Deng Xiaoping himself seems to have remained abreast of such calculations (ME 861101). He provided the visiting premier of Italy with a remarkably detailed briefing on how China would achieve the "middle rank" of development (another World Bank concept that entered PRC parlance at this time). Deng told the president of Mexico that U.S. criticism of PRC birth policy was a plot to keep China underdeveloped (ME 861206). "It's very simple: if the growth rate of the Chinese population remains 1.5 percent or 2 percent, it will eat up all the fruits of economic development."

In December 1986 the State Council itself held a pivotal annual national program work conference (ME 861201). One importance of this meeting was that by convening the meeting itself, the State Council could summon not only subnational program leaders, as the birth commission was limited to doing, but also subnational political leaders responsible for supervising birth planning in their provinces. National political leaders could thereby deliver their rather nuanced instructions—some adjustment of policy but no relaxation of enforcement—directly to the subnational political leaders in charge, thereby further involving them in national policy. A second importance of this meeting was that, on population policy, it officially loosened the 2000 plan target to "about" 1.2 billion. At the conference, Premier Zhao Ziyang said that this target was more realistic but that it absolutely did not mean any relaxation of enforcement.

A third importance of this meeting was to keep the door open to further improvements in birth policy. "The purpose of perfecting policy," the meeting argued, "is to control population better." On the one hand, the conference insisted that "we must continue to firmly grasp birth planning work and we absolutely cannot waver" (the title of Premier Zhao Ziyang's speech to the conference as excerpted in White ed. 1992, 59–60; not reprinted in EBP). On the other hand, what needed to be enforced was not the original hard policy but an improved version of it that was more sustainable and that therefore would best control population growth in the long run. Unnamed "central leaders" (presumably again Zhao) instructed that, in order for birth planning to become acceptable to rural villages, they needed a long period of stable policy with more generous exceptions for second children. In addition to the special circumstances already specified in regulations, households with only a daughter could request permission to have a second child, which they should receive permission to do, although only after the necessary spacing (EBP 475). This policy raised the proportion of couples having second children from about 10 percent to about 25 percent, but in practice it may have resulted in still more generous exceptions.

1988: STABILIZATION

In 1986–1987 a previously downward trend in fertility had reversed (from a low of 2.20 in 1985 to a high of 2.59 in 1987—Table 1). Hardliners became increasingly alarmed at what they considered a "loss of control" (*shikong*) over reproduction and began campaigning for retightening of both enforcement and rules. Because even softliners did not favor lax enforcement of existing regulations, some retightening of enforcement began. In 1987, winter campaigns resumed, raising the number of contraceptive procedures substantially, from a post-1983 low of 26 million in 1985 to 35 million in 1987 (Table 3). Meanwhile policymakers became interested in strengthening political leadership over birth planning, not only to achieve more enforcement by the regime but also to deliver more rewards to the public for compliance. This required coordination between ministerial systems that the birth system could not achieve by itself. In January 1987 party elders had persuaded Deng to fire Hu Yaobang as party leader. As Zhao Ziyang succeeded Hu as party general secretary, decision making shifted from the party Secretariat to the Standing Committee of the Politburo. The shift may have deprived Zhao of the authority over birth policy that Hu had possessed. As Li Peng succeeded Zhao as premier, evidently supervision of birth policy shifted from party general secretary to the government premier. This may have given Li leverage over birth policy that Zhao had never had.

After Li Peng became acting premier, he attended the next national meeting of provincial birth directors, where he said that policy could not be changed and that exceptions for villagers "with difficulties" should be strictly controlled (ME 880116). He called birth work a difficult task of "social systems engineering," reflecting a new concept of policy that established itself at that time (Qian 1987). Foreshadowing a major development of the early 1990s, Li said that performance in birth planning should be a major aspect of evaluating the performance of the leaders of subnational levels of government. Implementing a collective decision, Li convened some birth policy meetings within the premier's office itself (ME 891212, 900831).

For birth policy the pivotal meeting was the first major one, in March 1988, when the Politburo Standing Committee (PBSC) tried to end disputes between hard and soft liners by adopting a compromise (ME 880331). The meeting's rather long minutes began by reviewing the history of birth policy in the 1980s to underline that the Center's intention had always been—and its decision categorically now remained—that birth policy must be established on a "firm and implementable" basis. The Center had always allowed for some flexibility in the one-child policy, the PBSC said, because when such flexibility was denied, cadres found policy simply too hard to implement and just gave up. The Center had stated this in the 1980 Open Letter and had reemphasized it in April 1984 when it opened a "small hole" (about 10 percent). The Center had reemphasized flexibility again in December 1986 when it had opened a somewhat larger hole (about 20 percent). In the light of local experiments, the PBSC now "stabilized" policy at a new middle position. On the one hand, leadership should be strengthened in order to limit population to "about 1.2 billion" at the end of the century. On the other hand, birth rules should be loosened, but only to allow rural daughter-only couples a second child so that they could try for a son (a quite large increase to about 50 percent). Rules definitely should not be further loosened to allow all rural couples to have a second child (100 percent).

In early 1988 the birth program received a new leader, Peng Peiyun (ME 880121). She had exceptional political credentials, as the daughter of conservative senior revolutionary Peng Zhen, who during the early post-Mao period was in charge of rebuilding the PRC's legal system. She had exceptional political experience, stretching back to the 1950s and 1960s, when she had been the party secretary at both Qinghua and Peking universities. When she was appointed as birth minister, she was a member of the party's powerful Central Discipline Inspection Commission. During her tenure as birth minister she became a government state councillor (almost equivalent to a vice premier). She had substantial administrative experience and was regarded as a good manager (EW 3Nov03 BJ). Most recently she had been vice minister of education, which would help her strengthen the program's educational work. One of her earliest appearances as birth minister was at a meeting of the research offices under the birth commission's administrative office, to which she "transmitted the spirit" of the PBSC's recent instructions and called for "strengthening policy research" in order to "make decision-making more scientific" (ME 880407). The meeting endorsed the PBSC's choice of the daughter-only policy, saying that in the 22 counties in 13 provinces in which it had been tried it had both permitted a "tight policy with good results" and improved cadre-mass relations. Though a few local experiments with birth policy continued, emphasis in experiments shifted to implementation, for example through the program's new local "service stations" (ME 911024).

Peng made her main debut at a national conference of provincial directors (ME 880509). Her closing speech to that conference reflected thoughtfully on what the conference—and she personally—had learned from studying the minutes of the March PBSC meeting, along with recent important reports by party general secretary Zhao Ziyang and by premier Li Peng (to the October 1987 Thirteenth Party Congress and March 1988 National People's Congress, among other speeches). Her conclusions are worth summarizing because they guided program policy for the rest of her tenure (until 1998), even though much of her agenda she could not actively pursue until the mid-1990s (EBP 344–346, translated in White ed. 1992, 80–96).

The PBSC had needed to meet, Peng said, because of continuing disagreement over birth policy, particularly among some leading cadres. Nevertheless central policy is clear: to promote a one-child goal but to allow some exceptions that will make the policy acceptable to the public, particularly exceptions for single-daughter households. "If our policy is one that is not acceptable to the majority of the peasants, then it would be difficult for us to implement it, and even if we did implement it, it would be hard for us to maintain it for long. The peasants, including the grassroots cadres in the countryside, would thwart us in all sorts of ways" (White ed. 1992, 87).

In a riff on the perennial claim that adjustments to birth policy "neither tightened nor loosened" birth rules, Peng said that for the few localities that had too rigidly enforced a one-child rule the re-enforcement of central policy was a relaxation. For the majority of localities that had allowed more second children than existing policy permitted, re-enforcement was a tightening. The birth program had experimented with allowing couples to have second children, but national political leaders had ruled that these experiments could not be extended because they might result in too much population increase. Bringing now disparate subnational policies into conformity with national policy will require "a process of transition." In this process, the key is strong party leadership. Experience should be exchanged from local experiments in allowing single-daughter households to have second children, but the spacing requirement must be rigorously maintained.

Peng summarized four things common to successful birth work. First was strong party and government leadership, guided by a rigorous system of management by objectives. The birth program itself must do a good job of lobbying for support from all sectors of government and society. Second was an adequate and stable corps of cadres. The birth program would strengthen cadre training—particularly on-the-job training of cadres already in service—and would welcome subnational suggestions on how to do that. Third was to lead with ideological education. Cadres in all localities must master the Three Basics of birth work (propaganda, contraception, and routinization); education in population and reproduction must be extended to the public, including secondary school students. Fourth was good technical work. To supplement health ministry capacity, the birth program was establishing a birth planning "service station" in each locality, work that must be done well.

Not mentioned in her May 1988 speech was another thing that Peng did during her tenure, giving China's new demographers a policy role by convening annual meetings of population experts and having experts attend national work meetings. Some of these experts, particularly the natural scientists, were hardliners who advocated retightening. Others, particularly the social scientists, were softliners, some even quietly advocating a return to a two-child policy, as some foreign scholars were recommending (Bongaarts and Greenhalgh 1985). One way the social scientists had a softening effect was by clarifying the demographic processes at work. For example, the demographer Zeng Yi's "decomposition" of a recent slight rise in births enabled the March 1988 meeting of the PBSC to reach the rather balanced conclusion that the cause was not somewhat relaxed birth rules or even just lax enforcement but also rising numbers of young people—thereby averting a return to a very strict one-child rule (EBP 476; SG 28Nov01 NC). Even national political leaders began speaking in terms of "total fertility rates" and other statistics more precise than overall population growth rates. However, perhaps inadvertently, this new precision did highlight "peaks" and other problems that hardliners could use to justify stern measures.

1989–1993: Re-Enforcement

In the early 1990s Chinese politics first leaned center-left toward revived central planning and then lurched right toward renewed marketization. As center-left central planners and political authoritarians had feared, in the late 1980s even just rumors of economic and political reform had caused mass instability and brought the PRC regime to the brink of collapse. The fall of communism around the world confirmed center-left determination to freeze both economic and political reform and to use Stalinist central planning and Leninist political controls to correct imbalances and instabilities. In China's still senior-dominated political system, the center-left succeeded in reversing proposed elite political reform, repressing the Tiananmen demonstrators' demands for political liberalization and placing the party back in direct control of government operations. That political victory removed the center-right from the policy process and placed the center-left in control, facilitating attempts to recentralize the economy and to re-enforce birth planning. However, in China's increasingly mixed economic system, center-left attempts at economic consolidation and readjustment threw the economy into recession. Deng switched dramatically from center-left to center-right, restarting economic marketization, but not political pluralization. (On politics see Baum 1994, 225–382; Lam 1995; Fewsmith 2001, 21–156.)

After its phase of consolidation in the mid-1980s, birth policy moved gradually into a new phase of advance—of Maoist-Stalinist re-enforcement, not of Dengist reform. PRC leaders had restabilized birth rules, but there remained some *uncertainty* about how forcefully to re-enforce them and about how to accomplish that re-enforcement. Uncertainty remained also about what population targets were feasible and about what public form policy should take. A further compromise emerged in which birth rules remained unchanged, enforcement was tightened, but plan targets were loosened. PRC leaders finally achieved *formalization* of this compromise in a major decennial 1991 decision on policy for the 1990s. National leaders applied management-by-objective "responsibility systems" to subnational leaders to induce them to fund birth work and to compel local cadres to enforce birth rules. The PRC also completed construction of a mass association to mobilize and monitor public compliance. However, professionalization of services proceeded more slowly. Consequently *re-enforcement* took the form of a new round of crash campaigns. The results exceeded expectations, as fertility appeared to fall abruptly to below the replacement level of slightly more than two children per couple. (On program see Aird 1990, 59–87; White 1992; Greenhalgh 1994a; Scharping 2003, 63–80.)

As for the policy process, because national leaders were ordering subnational leaders to raise the priority of birth planning on their agendas, national leaders could hardly omit it from their own. They decided to assign a Politburo member to supervise ongoing coordination and to have the State Council convene a meeting of the premier's office twice a year to research how things were going and to resolve any problems (EBP 172—LP). At the turn of the decade a schedule gradually emerged of the PBSC itself hearing a report on birth policy near the beginning of each year. The meeting was followed by an annual summit of national political leaders with subnational political leaders (in conjunction with the annual spring sessions of the "two meetings," the National People's Congress and Chinese People's Political Consultative Conference). That was in turn followed immediately by a national birth work conference of subnational program leaders. This arrangement emerged during the transition to full Jiang leadership (1989–1992) and continued through the Jiang era into the Hu era.

1989–1991: UNCERTAINTY

Despite the apparent definitiveness of the March 1988 PBSC decision, arguments between hardliners and softliners continued over population targets and birth rules. Birth minister Peng remained uncertain how to pursue hard birth planning while avoiding coercion. Performance during the Seventh Five-Year Plan had to be assessed and the Eighth Five-Year Plan prepared. Questions remained about how to induce subnational leaders to re-enforce existing policies. Differences persisted over how far and how fast to intensify that re-enforcement. For the kind of integrated approach national leaders had in mind, subnational political leaders were crucial. Inducing their compliance required some formal and authoritative statement of national policy. It also required some institutional mechanism for making that compliance central to their career prospects. Evidently it took some time to work through alternatives for how to formalize national policy and how to motivate subnational political leaders.

These uncertainties were reflected in Peng Peiyun's several inquiries to the Central Committee, as she took over direction of the program, about what policy should be, including a formal "request for instructions" (*qing shi*). The PBSC's response to Peng's query was that policy should remain stable, that performance at implementing policy should be a major indicator for evaluating subnational leaders, and that existing policy should be made into a national law (ME 890223). Until such a law became possible, the State Council could issue national regulations. In the event, neither national regulations nor national law proved feasible. In mid-1990 a meeting in the premier's office decided that for the time being birth planning should progress toward "lawful management" (*yifa guanli*) by helping the remaining provinces pass birth laws as 24 provinces had already done (ME 900831). With neither a national law nor national regulations, at the beginning of the 1990s PRC leaders substituted a party and state "decision" laying out policy for the decade.

Toward the end of the 1980s, drafting the Eighth Five-Year Plan (1991–1995) required that a series of policy questions be addressed. In population, the third postwar peak in childbearing was nearing its own peak. Evidently Li Peng considered some hardline options, but the policy that finally emerged was, though not softline, at least some compromise. Because China was already approaching 1.2 billion, birth minister Peng Peiyun succeeded in further loosening the 2000 target from "about 1.2 billion" to "under 1.3 billion." When Peng took over the birth commission, she had discovered that there had been no solid empirical basis for the 1.2 billion target proclaimed in 1980. Using new data, the PRC's demographers prepared new projections. These were based on the assumption that, on average, couples would continue to have nearly two children, so the plan would implicitly contain a new two-child rule (Gu 1996, 48–59 and 122; EW 28Oct03 BJ). Those projections became a commission report to the Politburo that, over much objection from hardliners, approved the relaxation of the 2000 target to "under 1.3 billion" (SG 23Nov99 BJ). Reportedly Peng said that "her concern had been cast from her mind to the ground," and Li Peng exclaimed that, if population could indeed be kept under 1.3 billion, "the grace will be immeasurable" (*gongde wuliang*—EW 28Oct03 BJ).

Hardliners failed to prevent this change in *plan*, though the PBSC did later remark, as though to forestall any further loosening, that "targets cannot be changed lightly" (ME 920312). Hardliners also did not succeed in tightening the *rules*: permission for rural "only daughter households" to have second children remained in effect. Nevertheless, hardliners did succeed in further intensifying *enforcement*. When China's population reached 1.1 billion, *People's Daily* editorialized that implementers "certainly must grasp" policy "very, very tightly" (ME 890414). The number of contraceptive procedures had slackened in 1988 and 1989, but only somewhat (to 32 million and 29 million, from its brief resurgence to 35 million in 1987—Table 3). However, during 1988 a birth commission survey showed PRC leaders that the country was not meeting their demographic targets. In late 1988 the program issued the first of a series of four formal annual instructions for winter "propaganda months" (also issued in late 1989, late 1990, and late 1991). As a result, most provinces launched major new "crash campaigns" to abort all out-of-plan pregnancies and to sterilize one member of all couples who had reached their childbearing limit. Procedures rose to more than 38 million in 1991—the highest since 1983 and the second highest in program history—an unusually high proportion of them sterilizations (Table 3). The late 1980s crackdown coincided with a brief conservative effort to recentralize control over the economy (Naughton 1995, 274–279).

For several years the new party leader Jiang Zemin had little to say about birth policy, and what he did say concerned mostly not quantity but quality—particularly avoiding the social and personal costs of defective births (ME 890910, 891115). In contrast, Premier Li Peng continued to play an active role both in steering birth policy and in promoting mechanisms for forcing subnational leaders to enforce it. Addressing governors in spring

1989 Li said that population remained in a race with grain, the outcome of which would affect the survival of the Chinese race. To achieve subnational compliance, policy must be supplemented with more detailed management by objectives (ME 890406). At a meeting on birth policy in the premier's office, Li Peng explained that such targets would be neither "mandatory" (à la socialist command planning) nor "guidance" (à la capitalist indicative planning) but "evaluative" (in the spirit of modern business management—ME 891212). Thus Li Peng, though generally regarded as a conservative and certainly determined to enforce strict birth limits, nevertheless was helping provide the framework for a later shift toward neoliberal techniques of optimizing government performance. The Politburo member in charge of birth planning, Li Tieying, appeared to play a role subordinate to that of Li Peng, representing the leadership mostly at technical conferences. However, in spring 1989, at another forum in conjunction with the NPC, he made one of the earliest references to "comprehensive governance" (*zonghe zhili*), referring to the need not just for the birth system but for all local departments—and eventually also for all social forces—to participate in the imposition of birth limits (ME 890406). This idea may have originated during the early 1980s (in the Shandong prefecture of Weifang). It was incorporated in the 1991 Decision and resurfaced in the early 2000s as a main component of the Comprehensive Reform of birth planning (Shi 830802; Chapters 5 and 6). This idea too is consonant with neoliberalism in the sense of extending the practice of governance beyond the state to include associations and individuals.

1991: FORMALIZATION

National political leaders formalized these compromises in a decision issued jointly by the Central Committee and State Council. In March 1991 the PBSC—personally chaired by party general secretary Jiang Zemin—met to hear birth minister Peng report the current population "situation" (ME 910319). Given the arrival of the peak of the "third peak," the PBSC ruled that "grasping" birth planning absolutely could not be delayed. Subnational party first secretaries should inquire into the matter often. Governors, as deputy party secretaries, should "grasp" this work effectively. "It would not be excessive" to increase expenditures on birth planning from one to two yuan per capita (reportedly a Peng proposal). The resulting May 1991 Document Number Nine on "strengthening birth planning work and strictly controlling population growth" stated the general direction of policy for the next decade and specified institutions for achieving compliance by subnational political leaders. Thus the main targets of "strengthening" were subnational political leaders, who would be subject not only to management by objectives but also to a "one vote veto." Failure to perform well in birth planning could completely negate good performance in other areas, giving performance in birth work decisive weight in evaluation for bonuses and promotions. At the mass level, the main target of re-enforcement was couples who already had unauthorized children, particularly in China's nine most populous agricultural provinces, and particularly couples with three or more children.

To further promote the compliance of subnational leaders, the PBSC decided that every spring the Center would convene a summit meeting on birth planning that all provincial political leaders must attend. In other words, top leaders were taking direct responsibility for birth policy and setting an example in personally supervising it. Every year they would communicate face-to-face with subnational political leaders, who would be held responsible for implementation. The PBSC under Jiang Zemin was taking birth policy to a still higher plateau, not just re-enforcing policy but also reinforcing the institutions that would guarantee that policy would be enforced. The basic reason for doing so was that virtually all other formal and informal incentives strongly propelled subnational leaders into preoccupation with promoting the economic development of their localities. For subnational leaders to "simultaneously grasp both production and reproduction" required very heavy emphasis by national political leaders on reproduction.

The annual summits began in April 1991 and continued in the early 2000s, though expanded in the mid-1990s to include the other related "basic national policies" on resources and environment. Participants report that the summit is an awesome occasion because these are the only national policies that bring all of the country's most powerful politicians together every year to focus on one set of programs—a policy domain institutionalized with unique theatricality. Moreover, the message of national to subnational leaders could not be more pointed: this is the only regular occasion on which the entire PBSC meets subnational leaders. Then the PBSC reviews their performance, not in the economic development domain in which subnational leaders would prefer to excel, but in the population-resources-environment domain on whose regulation national leaders insist (EW 6Mar02 NJ).

The summit provided a forum for party general secretary Jiang Zemin to play a personal role in leading birth planning. He had become active in inspecting the performance of lagging provinces such as Henan and Hunan (ME 910205, ME 910311). However, he had not yet made a major speech on the subject in a national venue. In his debut at the 1991 summit, Jiang sounded the main themes of the moment. Strict control of population was essential for achieving the 2000 goal of the Four Modernizations. Subnational leaders were now personally responsible for enforcing that control.

However, that control should be achieved through the propaganda and education prescribed by the party's mass line. Jiang repeated the same themes at the 1992 summit: the need to "stay the course," to steer the regime apparatus through "management by objectives," and to guide the masses through "thought work." A further indication of the intensity of policy pressure at the time was that six months later the State Council itself convened a national telephone conference on birth work (ME 920914). It was chaired not by a health specialist but by one of the nation's top economic planners, vice premier Yao Yilin. (In the early 1990s central economic planners featured prominently in the birth program's yearbook as well.) All of this further intensified the campaigns already under way.

RESULTS

The early 1990s re-enforcement evidently produced its *intended* result of preventing any rise in fertility and of accelerating decline instead. However, the re-enforcement also produced unintended results that helped pave the way for later program reform. Evidently the combination of formal responsibility systems and the informal summit had a bigger effect on subnational leaders than anticipated. They began competing to outdo each other at limiting births, with all provinces trying to remain above average. The resulting heavy pressure on community cadres and the public produced an immediate sharp drop in reported fertility that also probably exceeded what policymakers had expected. The pressure also produced undesirable medical, social, and political side effects. Outcomes were being driven not by policy but by the dynamics of implementation. The concern about coercion that birth minister Peng had thought she had escaped now returned (This and the following paragraph based on SG and EW 2–7Jul93 BJ and 20Jul93 BJ—including JZH and ZEL. Also SG 16 and 23Nov99 BJ; EW 28Oct03 BJ; Greenhalgh et al. 1994; Winckler 1999).

A 1992 program survey showed a drop of fertility to 1.4, much lower than anyone had imagined possible, provoking both domestic and international concern about overly strict enforcement. A mission UNFPA sent to assess the validity of the survey cast doubt on its extreme finding but did confirm the severity of the crackdown. (Both authors of this book participated in that mission.) National *political* leaders, unable to be sure of the true extent of the decline, preferred to err on the side of caution. Even if a sharp drop had been achieved, it probably ran ahead of socioeconomic change, so that if pressure were relaxed, fertility would rebound. Clearly there were many localities in which fertility remained above the level that policy permitted. Furthermore the original plan for dealing with the 1980–1995 peaks had required temporarily driving fertility not just to replacement level but below it. So national policy became not only to "consolidate low fertility" but also to "continue its stable descent" (ME 940320). Nevertheless at least some national *program* leaders concluded that re-enforcement might have been overdone. As it turns out, fertility did remain below replacement for the rest of the 1990s, declining continuously (Table 1). Part of the explanation was that socioeconomic development reaccelerated during the early 1990s, perhaps to some extent "catching up" with an early 1990s sharp decline in fertility. Part of the explanation was continued administrative pressure. By 2000 fertility may have fallen as low as 1.5–1.6 (Guo et al. 2003). That was far ahead of what socioeconomic change alone probably would have produced but virtually identical with the "policy rate" (the level of fertility that would result if everyone exactly complied with birth rules). At the turn of the millennium, with China having largely completed its transition to low fertility, PRC leaders could begin reforming the hard birth planning that had helped produce that result. (See Retherford et al. 2004; EW 4Nov03 BJ.)

The *unintended* nondemographic results of re-enforcement also helped pave the way for later reform. First, with great pressure on cadres at every level to achieve targets, in many places the campaigns involved exactly the kinds of abuses and shoddy surgical procedures that program leaders officially decried (SG 23Nov99 BJ; Chapter 7). Second, in the early 1990s the program suffered a rising tide of upward misreporting, as lower-level administrators felt forced to report on paper the results they could not achieve on the ground. This misreporting demonstrated continued resistance to harsh enforcement not only within the public but also among lower-level administrators. Third, the program also suffered a rising tide of misdirection and misappropriation of funds. At best, local governments used birth planning revenues to fund general expenses; at worst, local cadres used birth revenues to fund their collective but personal consumption. There were some indications of these problems in the early 1990s but PRC leaders largely brushed them aside, ordering that they be corrected—but not by relaxing harsh birth rules (ME 920312, 940217).

A final legacy of the early 1990s for later reform was the first of the three main policy slogans that were to guide birth policy during the rest of the 1990s: the Three Givens (*sange bubian*, literally the three "unchangeables"). This slogan—coined by premier Li Peng, approved by the Politburo, and announced by Li Peng at the second annual summit in March 1992—was intended to make hard birth planning permanent. The first Given was existing birth policy, meaning particularly the *rule* about one child for all except rural couples with one daughter. The second Given was existing *plan* targets, meaning particularly no more loosening of the 2000 target of under 1.3 billion. The third Given was the lynchpin of the new institutions for *enforcement*, the practice of subnational party and government leaders taking personal responsibility for reaching program goals. Hardliners succeeded in keeping the slogan in place through the 1990s, but by the early 2000s it was seldom invoked. The Bureaucratic corner of the governmental triangle had fulfilled its historic mission. During the Jiang era, through arduous struggle against conservative resistance, Reformers began to transfer some initiative to Professionals and individuals.

CHAPTER 5

The Jiang Era: Deepening
Reform of Hard Birth Planning

DURING THE JIANG ERA (roughly 1993–2003), population and reproduction remained significant issues for PRC policymakers. In the early 1990s the Deng era had ended with a phase of renewed advance toward hard birth planning. In the middle 1990s the Jiang era began with a phase of controlled consolidation: state-centric reforms to correct program maladministration, to professionalize birth work, and to improve positive incentives for citizen compliance. However, unlike the middle Deng period, that quasi-consolidation did not involve inadvertent relaxation of enforcement. In the late 1990s, if there was renewed "advance," it was not toward reintensification of hard birth planning but towards increasing reform of it. Against great conservative resistance, reformers within the program succeeded in launching and expanding experiments with more client-centered approaches, particularly "quality care" involving "informed choice." By around 2000, finally convinced that stable low fertility had been largely achieved, national political leaders finally shifted their priority to maintaining that stability by "strengthening" the birth program: strengthening not the control of local programs over the public but the management of local programs themselves. The early 2000s formalized this new direction of linear evolution beyond cycles of advance and consolidation. National political leaders not only endorsed Comprehensive Reform, they personally insisted on it and participated in its formulation and implementation. At the same time they finally expanded the program's mandate from "birth planning" to include "population." New future missions included providing more reproductive health services, designing social programs related to birth planning, and correcting distortions in population structure such as the rising sex ratio at birth (many more males than females).

Thus the Jiang era too left legacies for the future. One is the demographic environment. Quantitatively, China's population will be smaller and slower-growing than it otherwise might have been. During the 1990s the program continued to reduce fertility where it remained above policy limits and by the turn of the millennium China largely completed its transition to stable low fertility. China achieved the reduction of natural increase to about 1 percent in 2000 for which Zhou Enlai had hoped, and it achieved the revised Deng era goal of remaining "under 1.3 billion." Resolute enforcement may have helped consolidate the fall in fertility aspirations that socioeconomic change was producing, further establishing a social norm of very few children. Qualitatively, China's population will be healthier and better educated but will contain significant distortions. The continuing resolute enforcement of birth limits during the 1990s produced worsening sex ratios and accelerated aging. Locationally, China's population will be much more mobile and urbanized, not only in the physical sense of residence in towns but also in the psychological sense of adopting urban-global aspirations and practices.

Another legacy of the Jiang era is in program organization. The gradually deepening reforms that the birth program undertook in order to adapt itself to Socialist Marketization evolved into a permanent "change to change." In the early twenty-first century, the program will continue to perfect itself within a framework of Comprehensive Reform. Overall, the entire concept of the birth program began to shift from direct control to indirect regulation: from "birth according to plan" to "birth according to law." Thus the most fundamental change was in the *plan*, which shifted from mandatory toward indicative. Instead of imposing a schedule on which communities and their couples were allowed to have births, planning increasingly became policy analysis for the government to use in allocating its own resources: projections of likely demographic outcomes, analyses of related social problems, and proposals for solving them. Because national political leaders stubbornly maintained their 1988 "one-and-a-half-child" limit, reformers were unable to change birth *rules*. As planning weakened, making those rules legally obligatory became the main means for enforcing birth limits. However, that also meant that, increasingly, whatever citizens were legally entitled to do they could do, while going through fewer bureaucratic procedures to do it. In *enforcement*, hard-bitten old birth-planning cadres yielded to softer young birth-work professionals. Moreover, birth workers themselves no longer administered sanctions. Community governments levied fines on noncompliers and, if a couple did not pay, the community government was supposed to refer the couple to the courts.

The round of policymaking and legislation in the early 2000s was the best that national leaders could do to guide and constrain subnational leaders.

The aim was to give subnational program leaders a basis for lobbying subnational political leaders to continue to support both the traditional birth program and its new reforms and responsibilities. Thus another legacy of the Jiang era is further confirmation that the birth program will remain largely decentralized. The national level still helps by setting standards and suggesting methods, but it is localities that must adapt those to their circumstances and provide the necessary resources.

Comprehensive Reform is a model not only for the birth program itself but also for the governance of all population-related matters by all local forces. It involves both coordination by local political leaders from above and supervision by community citizens from below. This model reflects the studied conclusion of national political leaders that the birth program faces problems that it cannot solve on its own. A question for the future is whether the eclectic components of quality care, Comprehensive Reform, and other initiatives will produce the hoped-for renovation, or simply become vague rubrics under which localities do what they please, including continuing outmoded methods of hard birth planning.

In terms of the governmentalization of population, the Jiang era significantly moved China toward the modern syndrome of triangular governance and bipolar biopower. The PRC began a phased redefinition of this policy domain from "birth planning" to "population-and-birth-planning" to "population." At the macro pole of biopower, the program could then do strategic planning for the future of China's population as a whole, not only in quantity but also in quality and location. The program could then also begin to try to ameliorate the distortions in sex ratio and age structure that it had aggravated. At the micro pole of biopower, the program should gradually shift from limiting births to delivering services. The regime was becoming increasingly "governmentalized" in the sense of preoccupation with the sophisticated management of complex demographic systems and with fostering the development of China's population in both macro-structural and micro-individual terms. For their part, couples were now increasingly convinced of the economic benefits and cultural superiority of limiting their childbearing and improving their childrearing. As for the third side of governmentality, intermediate commercial enterprises and even independent professions flourished, advertising products and offering advice. The regime also began making some limited use of intermediate community self-government and non-governmental organizations—very limited, unfortunately. "Managed science" and "managed democracy," though significantly improving policy formulation and implementation, had not yet reached the full potential of unfettered public debate over public policy and of a genuinely autonomous civil society. By the end of the Jiang era, China's biopolitics had begun to move beyond a merely top-down developmental Leninism, toward a Leninist neo-liberalism in which the party-state shifted toward fostering the vitality of its population and cultivating the lives of its people. Nevertheless, China remained well short of fully pluralistic neoliberalism, in which individuals were ostensibly autonomous and actually responsible for themselves.

Introduction: Origins of Reform

During the Jiang era, externally, China deepened its globalization but still maintained a somewhat independent line in population policy. UNFPA began urging the PRC to soften its approach to birth limitation, but at least officially the PRC responded only slowly. At the 1994 Cairo conference, the official PRC position insisted that "controlling population" was necessary for "sustainable development," a stance opposite from the drastic reorientation that occurred at the Cairo conference from top-down "population control" toward bottom-up women's empowerment (ME 940902, *People's Daily* Commentary). PRC birth policy "would not change for a long time," birth minister Peng Peiyun assured a Xinhua reporter (ME 940902). Yet PRC program leaders had already begun considering how to resume reform of their program and were quite eager to learn from the Cairo process. Subsequently, with international assistance, experiments with quality care showed the program how to increase its institutional capacity, not to control the public, but to control its own operatives. By the Hu era, supranational Cairo ideals for how birth work should be conducted had been officially incorporated into national population policy and the national level had begun struggling to induce implementation of them at subnational levels. Within the severe constraints imposed by existing birth rules, the PRC was even struggling to move toward "free and responsible" decisions by couples themselves on "timing, number and spacing" (ME 940902, 940904, 940905; Winckler 2005).

Internally, by 1993 the PRC birth program had demographic reason to shift from re-enforcement to reform. The "peak of the peak" in childbearing was beginning to pass, five consecutive years of winter campaigns had significantly leveled that peak, and a 1992 survey had suggested that fertility had already fallen drastically. Some program leaders realized that re-enforcement might have gone too far, not only pushing fertility down further than necessary, but also using a degree of coercion that damaged relations between party, cadres, and masses—not to mention damaging women's reproductive health. Program leaders continued to affirm past accomplishments and to maintain that the program's old forceful methods may have been appropriate to their time. Nevertheless, they began to note the high "side cost" (*daijia*) of those old methods and they argued with increasing force that a "new situation" now required new methods. Still more fundamentally, in the early 1990s the country's historical leader in birth limitation—Shanghai—began to experience negative rates of natural increase (more deaths than births, although total population continued to grow, presumably from in-migration). Some program leaders celebrated but others convened a workshop in Beijing to begin to face up to the long-term consequences of negative growth. Even before "Cairo" some began discussing a China "beyond birth planning" (ME 941123; EW 28Oct03 BJ).

During this era the priority of population and reproduction on the national political agenda remained high, PRC leaders maintained close supervision of birth policy, and the program's guiding ideology evolved. Direct interaction between political leaders from the national and subnational levels became institutionalized through the annual summit meetings. As problems of population and program were gradually solved, their priority may have somewhat declined. In the annual summit, population eventually was merged with related basic regime policies, first on the environment (1997) and then also resources (1999). Then the main speech by the party general secretary, now under the rubrics of "coordinated" and "sustainable" development, dealt with all three together, somewhat diluting the emphasis on population. Nevertheless, from year to year, that speech still served to convey gradually emerging new emphases. Thus at the 1993 summit, Jiang introduced the distinctly new themes of using a "reform spirit" to "raise the level" of birth work because it "intimately affected the vital interests of the masses." This clearly shifted the emphasis from "grasping tightly" to "grasping well" (ME 930331). Jiang also introduced the idea of Deng Xiaoping's Population Thought, later explained by birth minister Peng Peiyun—at the Central Party School, for example—in ways that provided some ideological cover for reform (ME 940504). In the middle 1990s the State Council itself convened the two major conferences that began to deepen birth reform (on the Three Basics and Three Links, discussed below). In the late 1990s the new secretary general of the State Council, Wang Zhongyu, began personally supervising reform of birth work and in the early 2000s he personally helped the program formulate and launch a long-term program of Comprehensive Reform.

PRC understanding of the relationship between planning, development, and population also evolved. Early 1990s conservative efforts to reimpose economic planning had largely backfired, sometimes promoting the very loss of economic control they were intended to combat (Naughton 1995, 279–283). Somewhat the same thing happened in population, where progressive loosening of targets somewhat discredited the idea that even a socialist regime could dictate demographic outcomes. The rapidity of China's economic growth made it clear that economic development contributed much more to raising per capita income than did limiting population growth. With the rapid development of the eastern coastal region, PRC leaders turned increasingly toward accelerating the development of the center and west and toward alleviating poverty in China's poorest counties. The early 1990s re-enforcement of stringent birth limits had assumed that a large population impeded development and that political pressure could force down fertility. With the demographic emergency of the "third peak" passing, national leaders began to foreground the reverse analysis, according to which in the long run it was development that slowed population growth. Simply suppressing fertility was too costly politically and too unstable demographically. This changed diagnosis was particularly pertinent to China's poorest areas and households, among which in the middle 1990s the program was still trying to eliminate multiple children. State-assisted poverty alleviation could complement state-enforced birth limits, particularly if assistance from the one was tied to compliance with the other.

Already in the early 1990s there had been some signs of renewed awareness of need for reform. As the Politburo had said in the mid-1980s, the problem was to keep the program implementable. During the 1992 telephone conference that the State Council convened to review emergency re-enforcement, the Politburo member assigned to oversee birth planning, Li Tieying, complained about lack of enforcement in some localities, but also noted the program's need to respond to "new circumstances" of national reform with a birth planning "mechanism" that could be sustained for a long time (ME 920914). At the same meeting birth minister Peng Peiyun warned implementors not to slacken their efforts during the rest of the year, but also introduced a new note, that of providing women with "quality service" (*youzhi fuwu*). This became the program translation of the ideal of "quality of care" that had been formulated at the Population Council in New York City (Bruce 1990). Peng had recently been to New York where UNFPA director Nafis Sadik had suggested to her that the PRC should begin some experiments at less coercive work methods (SG & EW 29Jun93 GV-NS; EW Oct03 BJ). Reportedly Peng asked national political leaders for authorization to do so, but evidently they declined. Nevertheless, eventually they did agree and experiments under the quality care rubric later became a principal road toward reform of birth work.

Meanwhile a pivotal work meeting of the program's policy and law department had sounded other themes that would be important in the future (ME 911111). The meeting discussed problems in achieving "lawful management" and identified Seven Don'ts in current implementation—coercive practices that the program should eliminate (Chapter 6). Convening in Jilin province, the meeting visited a county whose birth program involved other departments in "comprehensive governance" (*zonghe zhili*) at the same time improving relations between party, cadres, and masses. At the next meeting of the same department, Peng Peiyun called for administration that was not just lawful but "civilized" (ME 930714). Another sign of heightened awareness of a need for rethinking was that—reportedly at the suggestion of senior conservative program mentor Song Ping—during 1993 the program conducted three seminars on population issues (ME 930209, 930424, 930928). The second and third seminars concerned sex ratios and women's status. In the course of the 1990s all of these themes gradually worked themselves into program practice, and in the early 2000s they were formalized in the 2001 national law on population and birth planning and in Comprehensive Reform.

Middle 1990s: State-Centric Administrative Rationalization

In the middle 1990s PRC economics became increasingly focused on reform but PRC politics became even more preoccupied with stability. During 1992, in one of his last major acts of national leadership, Deng dramatized his support for progressive economic policies and persuaded his successors to embrace renewed marketization. In addition, Deng persuaded the 1992 Fourteenth Party Congress to endorse the concept of a "socialist market economy" as the main rubric for the ensuing period. PRC leaders began addressing the question of how to adapt regime institutions to this new environment, wrapping the exercise in Deng Xiaoping Thought to legitimate it. PRC economic reform moved from the Stalinist center to the revisionist right of the Leninist political spectrum. Deng also orchestrated a generational turnover toward younger and generally more progressive national political leaders. Powerful conservatives associated with hard birth planning either died (Chen Yun) or retired from the Politburo Standing Committee (planners Yao Yilin and Song Ping, the latter then taking over leadership of the Birth Planning Association). Active younger reformers joined the PBSC. These included "third generation" reformist future premier Zhu Rongji and "fourth generation" future party general secretary Hu Jintao. Meanwhile PRC political reform remained in the center of the Leninist spectrum, limited to leader promulgation of ideology and top-down rectification of organization and society. (On politics see *China Journal* 1995; Fewsmith 1997; Lam 1999, 1–322; Gilley 1998; Fewsmith 2001, 159–189; Lardy 1998.)

Despite the renewed priority to economic work, national leaders told subnational officials not to reduce the priority of birth work, but rather to grasp production and reproduction together. Although the PRC was now using Socialist Marketization to speed economic growth, Chinese population theorists argued that the market was not yet strong enough in China to slow population growth (ME 940120; Zhang, Huang, and Yang 1997). Jiang Zemin told the 1994 summit emphatically that limiting population remained a government function, through macroregulation (*hongguan tiaoli*—ME 940322). Thus he insisted that the government would continue to intervene, but he also implied the beginning of a fundamental shift in method. In neo-institutional terms, the shift was from direct operation to indirect regulation (Winckler ed. 1999, conclusion). In Foucauldian terms the shift was from policing individual bodies toward governing social processes (Dean 1999). For the birth program, the necessity of adapting to marketization was probably the most fundamental force initiating reform. Nevertheless, initially that re-form remained quite statist, constituting a distinct counterpoint to the greater liberalization in other policy domains (Winckler 1999). At a meeting of the policy and law department, birth minister Peng relayed Jiang's "grasp tightly, grasp well" as meaning "using the spirit of reform to raise work level," strengthening village work, and establishing a good international image (ME 930714). (On program see Banister 1998; Ming 1999; Xie 2000; Scharping 2003, 74–80.)

Thus began three pairs of state-centric reforms intended to strengthen the birth program through administrative rationalization. The first pair, govern-ment supervision and party discipline, was directed at the birth program itself, intended to correct negative by-products of the early 1990s re-enforcement, particularly maladministration by community political leaders and program implementors. Corruption and coercion had outraged the public and dis-couraged voluntary public compliance. The second pair of reforms, institu-tionalization and routinization, was also directed at the birth program itself, promoting its positive organizational development, particularly downward into rural townships and villages. Institutionalization involved broad pro-cesses such as legalization, which was necessary to authorize specific processes such as appropriating the money to hire and train specialized personnel. Routinization involved broad processes such as professionalization, which was necessary to provide continuous quality services, in order to avoid both collective enforcement campaigns and individual contraceptive failure. The third pair, "incentivization" and "integration," was directed at the public. Incentivization responded to the program's increasingly marketized environ-ment by raising the economic incentives and disincentives for compliance. In-tegration connected the birth program to other regime departments and pro-grams, particularly alleviation of poverty in the least-developed rural areas.

SUPERVISION AND DISCIPLINE

The first form of rationalization addressed maladministration within the program, principally corruption and coercion. The problem was political, to insulate the program and the regime from public backlash over rising government corruption and party indiscipline. During this period, following the collapse of communism in most other countries around the world, PRC leaders believed they were caught in a life-and-death race between the strengthening of institutions in order to shore up the PRC regime and the erosion of institutions through corruption (Lu 2000). The regime intensified its efforts at government supervision and party discipline, establishing branches of those institutions in all ministries, including the birth commission (ME 930518, 940111, 970425, 981022). In addition to monitoring for violations, such political work had a positive side. For example, within the birth program, the vice minister in charge took the opportunity to elaborate a code of professional ethics for birth workers (EW 7Nov03 BJ-WJC).

The simplest form of corruption was individual—not just lax work but violating rules by favoring intimates or accepting bribes. Technical service workers could forge certification that birth control procedures had been performed. Party and state employees, who enjoyed the privilege of state employment, should assume its responsibilities. The program was most concerned about compliance by party and government leaders themselves, having long since learned that nothing undermined public compliance more than the public's seeing local party and government cadres using their power to flaunt birth limits. That was one reason why the Open Letter had been addressed to party members and had asked them to "take the lead" (*daitou*, which also implies "setting an example" by exemplary compliance with program requirements). Violations by officials were singled out in these disciplinary campaigns of the 1990s and singled out for legal punishment in the program's new 2001 law.

Corruption could also be collective and institutional. Within the birth system itself, arguably the most severe problem was misreporting program performance and public compliance. Within government at large, the problem was that national leaders had created "perverse" incentives for local and community governments to welcome revenue from out-of-plan birth fees, even to the point of encouraging unauthorized births in order to fine them. Moreover, as part of a general pattern of local governments overtaxing rural inhabitants through myriad taxes and fees, local governments might "wildly" levy and collect birth fees, under the guise of enforcing birth planning. So, during the middle 1990s, the program cracked down on extra or exorbitant fees or charges, and on local regulations embodying them (ME 930113, 950721; Bernstein and Lu 2003).

Perhaps the most complex form of maladministration was coercion, in PRC parlance the use of overly harsh methods to enforce compliance. Despite possibly sincere protestations of dedication to voluntary compliance, in the early 1990s PRC leaders had in effect institutionalized strong incentives for community implementors to apply coercion, even though birth workers might not wish to do so. Coercion had become the norm: targets must be achieved, no matter how. Coercion could involve excessive mobilization, such as locking people in township offices until they complied. Cadres sometimes confiscated the property of noncompliers to substitute for unpaid fines. Sometimes they physically damaged the remaining property of violators who had fled—to warn other potential noncompliers, to show their supervisors that they had "done something," or simply out of sheer exasperation. Already in 1991 the program identified seven coercive practices that particularly offended the public; in the course of the 1990s the program severely proscribed them (ME 911111; Chapter 6). Most localities probably largely desisted from using these proscribed enforcement methods, but the overall coerciveness of the program persisted.

The program also reviewed local and provincial slogans and regulations to remove anything objectionable, particularly anything that might encourage clumsy coercion. In the early 1990s the administrative office issued notices on slogans, eventually recommending fifty good ones (ME 910601, 931118). In the late 1990s the policy and law department began stressing that enforcement must be "lawful" and that the program must "serve the people" (ME 971022, 981025). The commission issued views on subnational legislation, including the view that it should promote a good image of China abroad. Local laws should properly treat the relationship between rights and duties, presumably meaning somewhat greater emphasis on rights (ME 981126). When possible—provided they did not permit a rebound in fertility—subnational levels should advance "legislation, reform, and abolition" (of unnecessary red tape). Except for Tibet, by the end of 2003 all provinces had revised their laws to conform with the 2001 national law (PI 040910, ZWQ).

INSTITUTIONALIZATION AND ROUTINIZATION

The second form of rationalization addressed the program's work methods, attempting to phase out methods that harmed society and to phase in those that benefited it. During the middle 1990s a main program objective was to make "crash" enforcement campaigns unnecessary by building adequate routine administrative capacity and by requiring adequate routine implementation work. Crash campaigns were still conspicuous in the early 1990s, particularly in the most populous agricultural provinces that the program targeted at that time. One reason campaigns persisted was that, by neglecting routine work and enforcing birth planning only when ordered by superiors to do so during a campaign, village-level cadres could make it clear to their community that it was the superiors, not they, who were to blame for the policy (Zhang Weiguo 1999). In 1995 program leaders declared crash campaigns impermissible and established targets for phasing them out by the end of the century: in 16 provinces by the end of 1998, 21 provinces by the end of 1999, and all 31 provinces by the end of 2000. At the turn of the millennium national leaders declared that effort "basically" successful. This fundamental "shift in mechanism" not only phased out the Maoist-Mobilizational approach to birth work, but also permitted phasing in reform of the Stalinist-Bureaucratic approach as well.

Institutionalization-and-routinization was a longstanding program goal. It was implicit in the preliminary building of institutional capacity during the 1970s. It was well expressed in the 1980s by one of the program's main slogans, the Three Basics of propaganda and education, contraception, and routine work. All three were intended to avoid the necessity for coercive emergency campaigns to abort pregnancies that good routine propaganda and contraceptive work should have prevented. The long life span of this slogan suggests the difficulty that program leaders have had turning it into reality. In September 1993 the State Council itself convened a national Three Basics meeting to reemphasize the slogan (ME 930916). In the late 1990s, completing achievement of the Three Basics throughout the nation by the end of the century became an urgent objective of the Jiang-Zhu administration (ME 980410, 980616). The State Council itself even convened a national telephone conference to promote the effort, recommending Shandong as a model of relentlessly improving already good work (ME 981007). The birth commission promulgated eight standards that localities must meet in order to have accomplished the Three Basics. In the early 2000s, achievement of those standards became a prerequisite for embarking on Comprehensive Reform. Indeed the 2003 meeting commemorating the twentieth anniversary of the Three Basics described Comprehensive Reform as a continuation and deepening of the earlier movement (PI 030919, ZWQ).

FROM 1995: INCENTIVIZATION AND INTEGRATION

The third form of rationalization attempted to increase other positive benefits that the birth program had been supposed to deliver to society. Given the rise of material incentives that Socialist Marketization produced in the program's task environment, the program needed to provide greater rewards for compliance with birth limits (incentivization). While the program could do some of this by itself, effective incentivization required linking compliance to benefits provided by other government programs (integration). Consequently, in the mid-1990s program leaders elaborated incentivization and integration into the "two transformations" (*liangge zhuanbian*). Introduced by birth minister Peng Peiyun and expounded by her soon-to-be successor vice minister Zhang Weiqing, these were fundamental to program work during the 1996–2000 Five-Year Plan (ME 970308; *YB98*, 35–42, ZWQ). In the early 2000s they were elaborated as part of Comprehensive Reform. (Sometimes the "two transformations" is used to refer simply to a change in thinking and work method.)

In October 1992 the Fourteenth Party Congress formally announced the shift to Socialist Marketization, requiring all ministries to adapt their work to it. The birth program gained an opportunity for new thinking when the official in charge of performance evaluation, Zhang Erli, spent a year studying that problem at the Central Party School, then run by future party leader Hu Jintao (SG 23Nov99 BJ). By December 1992 the birth commission had transmitted a report from southern Jiangsu (*Sunan*) on one county's experience in adapting birth planning to the "new situation" through the slogan of "fewer children, faster prosperity" (*shaosheng kuaifu*), a slogan that a decade later was applied to limiting population and accelerating development in China's backward western region (ME 921208). The "Sunan model" helped the program develop incentivization. In 1994 and 1995 the commission convened two field conferences on the topic on the margins of the Sunan area, the second conference reviewing experiments in twelve provinces (ME 931010 on Wenzhou in central Zhejiang; 940617 on Yancheng in central Jiangsu). At the second conference Peng noted that Yancheng combined birth planning and economic development, established an "interest-guidance mechanism" that internalized motivation for birth planning, and provided "comprehensive quality care" (the first public mention of this concept). These methods "raised the level" of birth work, established a good image of birth planning, and promoted community construction, both material and spiritual. This conference, to which the commission invited foreign experts, was perhaps the first real sign of movement toward progressive reform, several months before the Cairo conference.

In the late 1990s birth vice minister Zhang Weiqing gave "incentivization" a rather complex formulation, which contains the kernel of early 2000s Comprehensive Reform (*YB98*, 35–42). The program must "shift from an implementation mechanism that relied mostly on social constraint to one that combined social constraint and interest guidance." In other words, the program did not renounce educational propaganda and administrative coercion, but wished to supplement them with economic incentives. In addition to one-child payments and rewards from collateral programs, these incentives should include more and better services from the birth program itself. Thus incentivization required that the program reform its implementation mechanism into one that "combines interest guidance, social constraint, propaganda and education, comprehensive services, and scientific management."

By "integration" the program meant that, instead of trying to reduce fertility simply by limiting births, demographic transition must be combined with broader economic, social, and cultural development—and even with political development, through village self-government. As Jiang Zemin explained at the 1995 summit, progress required coordinated development, aimed at villages, particularly women (ME 950318). The birth program must be linked to other, "collateral" government programs. Previously the birth program had collaborated with other government departments, such as health (for maternal and child health services), science and technology (for contraceptive research), pharmaceuticals (for contraceptive production), civil affairs (for marriage work), and public security (for household registration information). Now the birth program must collaborate also with departments such as agriculture, banking, and commerce—and they in turn must collaborate with the birth program. The hope was that linking social reproduction to economic production would make stand-alone negative birth limitation less unpalatable to the general population by connecting it to the delivery of what citizens would regard as more positive services—particularly reproductive health but also poverty alleviation. Pursuit of integration was facilitated by the elevation of birth minister Peng Peiyun to state councillor—similar in level to a vice premier—which enabled her to convene meetings that included ministries other than the birth program (ME 939329).

In the middle 1990s, as part of regime efforts to bolster the development of rural areas, the birth system made integration concrete through another of its main slogans, the Three Links (*san jiehe*, literally the "three integrations"). The first link was developing the agricultural village economy, the second was helping farmers achieve a modestly comfortable standard of living, and the third was to construct "civilized and happy" families. This was a direction of birth reform quite acceptable to PRC planners, but one that drew on both domestic experience with marketization and international experience with development. Domestically, the benefits of such linkages had first become evident through the rapid growth of a socialist market economy in areas such as Jiangsu and Jilin provinces (ME 920507, 921208, 940630). Internationally, the Cairo and Beijing conferences had further impressed on program leaders the intimate relationship between population and development (described below). Birth minister Peng dubbed the Three Links the "road of hope" for rural birth planning and rural development (ME 951214, in *People's Daily*). The birth commission instructed local administrators to design policies that would help families with fewer children get rich faster. Administrators should "give preferential treatment in terms of project selection, capital, technology, materiel, social welfare, and remunerations to rural households that practice birth planning, offering them more material incentives." Community birth planning workers should "place a particular stress on the need to help the masses of peasants resolve difficulties with their production, daily life, and childbirth" (SBPC 1996, 11–32, PPY).

By the 1995 summit both Jiang Zemin and Li Peng endorsed the Three Links, naming it a "major reform and new development" in Chinese birth planning (ME 950318). In the course of 1995 several important meetings occurred. Peng convened a meeting of many ministries, ten of which later issued a joint circular on how villages could practice the Links (ME 950420, 950921; YB96, 91). The birth commission convened a discussion of theory, including the relationship of the Three Links to the Three Basics (ME 951005). Finally the State Council convened a conference on the Three Links, held in Chengtu, the capital of still highly agricultural Sichuan province (ME 951022). Aside from Jiang and Li themselves, practically all other high officials in the country relevant to implementing the Three Links attended, some 260 persons. These included leaders from about thirty national ministries and the thirty subnational political leaders in charge of birth work. (SBPC ed. 1996 is the conference's proceedings.)

The Three Links conference was a major turning point for the birth program. Peng Peiyun delivered a long speech that reflected the program's recent new thinking about reform. Framing the problem as the need to avoid the heavy side costs of previous program methods, Peng explained the Three Links not just as a technique of administration, but also as a version of the Two Transformations needed in program method, and even as a version of the positive impact of development on population. The conference summary said that implementing the Three Links was important to the birth program for many reasons: they respond to the new situation of market socialism, they encourage interdepartmental cooperation on the positive side of birth planning, they integrate the interests of the state and family, they raise the level of birth program performance by requiring scientific management and quality service, they are good for cultural construction, and they promote other things such as mass compliance with birth planning, the liberation of women, and the restructuring of agriculture.

At the 1996 and 1997 summits, Jiang Zemin further developed the theme of integration, declaring that "population affects everything" and noting relationships to sustainable development and spiritual civilization (ME 960310, 970308; Yu 1999). Li Peng averred that twenty years of experience had given China a "complete and effective" set of policies and measures, particularly the "three threes": the Three Givens, the Three Basics, and the Three Links. These policies cannot be changed, though they might be perfected, particularly to adapt them to marketization. At his last summit in 1998, Li declared that birth planning "can't relax or change." Li then moved from the premiership of the government to the chairmanship of the National People's Congress and China received a more dynamic and progressive premier.

Late 1990s: Toward Client-Centered Deregulation

In the late 1990s PRC economic reform moved slightly further to the right, as the 1997 Fifteenth Party Congress endorsed private ownership of property, previously unthinkable in the PRC's socialist regime. The new premier, Zhu Rongji, redoubled efforts to reform Stalinist institutions and shrink government. However, PRC political reform remained in the Stalinist center, with more ideologizing by party head Jiang Zemin and continued efforts to combat corruption. (On politics see Lam 1999, 323–394; Baum 2000; Fewsmith 2001, 190–220; *China Journal* 2001; Lardy 2002.)

In birth planning, at the 1998 summit, Jiang Zemin marked a watershed (ME 980315). In the eight years since the summit had started, the third birth peak had passed and fertility had dropped below the replacement level. The birth commission had drafted new "fighting targets" for the twenty-first century, which the PBSC had approved (ME 980220). The main current emphasis was to "grasp well" populous provinces, poor areas, and migrants. At the 1999 summit, Jiang elaborated a still broader strategic vision of the relationship between population, resources, and environment (ME 990313). "Systems engineering" required macrodemographic regulation appropriate to Socialist Marketization, a better system for managing birth work, and a social security mechanism beneficial to limiting births. More concretely, localities needed "personnel to manage things, money to do things, and regulations to direct things." These ideas become the core of the 2000 decision on policy for the first decade of the new century and the core of the "scientific concept of development" that Hu Jintao announced in 2003–2004 as the PRC's new guiding ideology. Jiang had also completed the definition of a new population-resources-environment policy domain that could prove of lasting value for realizing those guiding ideals.

On the government side, the new premier, Zhu Rongji, said little about birth planning but did convey a rather tart assessment in instructions he wrote on a provincial investigation report (on Shanxi—ME 980926). He noted "not a few problems," particularly party members and cadres falsifying reports and "taking the lead" in having extra births. He hoped that subnational leaders would achieve the "three standards" (*san dao wei*): leaders taking responsibility, adopting effective measures, and providing necessary funds. "Otherwise 'doing a good job' of birth work is just empty talk." At a telephone conference on implementing the Three Basics by the end of the century, State Council secretary general Wang Zongyu said that localities should take the opportunity to raise other work to yet a new level, following Shandong's example in coldly analyzing the inadequacies within an already good performance (ME 981007). Wang and the Shandong example became driving forces behind Comprehensive Reform at the beginning of the new century.

In the late 1990s the birth program launched a second set of reforms that became increasingly client-centered, as reflected in the rising program slogan of "taking people as primary" (*yiren weizhu*). A first process was internationalization. The birth program had long had relations with foreign organizations, but by the late 1990s these became more numerous and influential. The international population regime had recently changed paradigms, from top-down government control of population growth to bottom-up empowerment of women to manage their own fertility. The PRC birth program quickly absorbed and adapted many of these new ideas, which revived and reinforced its own early maternal and child health objectives. Accordingly, a second process concerned quality. The birth program began surveys and experiments toward improving its services and expanding them beyond birth control to some other elementary aspects of reproductive health. What the birth system could do was limited by the jurisdiction of the health system and by limits on local resources, but any improvement in the program's sometimes problematic services was welcome. A third process was liberalization. This did not mean loosening birth rules, but it did mean simplifying how they were applied: couples could produce any child to which they were legally entitled without obtaining a birth quota through a local plan.

FROM 1995: INTERNATIONALIZATION

The PRC regards itself as an important country in the world and considers its program to limit births a major contribution to international efforts to control global population growth (Chapter 9). International discourse provided Chinese domestic discourse with much of the rationale for initiating and maintaining birth limits: in the 1970s and 1980s, "population crisis;" by the 1990s, "sustainable development." Post-Mao "opening" of the PRC allowed foreign organizations to help ameliorate problems within the PRC birth program. National *political* leaders have emphatically rejected hostile public foreign criticism, which they have regarded as politically motivated (e.g., ME 861206, 880524, DXP). Nevertheless, national *program* leaders have been surprisingly responsive to international influences, particularly professional advice offered in private. In the 1980s the program sought mainly technical assistance to strengthen birth planning, such as demographic analysis and contraceptive technology. By the 1990s, however, program leaders became increasingly interested in international experience on social matters such as implementation methods and ethical standards. International discourse began providing domestic discourse with the rationale for reforming the program and for communicating between the national and subnational levels about reforms (ALP 2000).

Foreign ideas arrived through many channels—governmental and nongovernmental, multilateral and bilateral. The PRC takes its membership in the United Nations particularly seriously. At PRC request, from the early 1980s through the early 2000s the United Nations Population Fund (UNFPA) conducted five cycles of programs in China. These programs gradually shifted from slowing population growth to promoting reproductive health, in line with changes in international preoccupations and changes in China's demographic status. In the 1980s UNFPA helped train demographers and improve contraceptives. In the 1990s it lobbied with increasing firmness for the PRC to try more voluntary and health-oriented approaches, delaying the beginning of a fourth cycle of projects until the PRC agreed to do so. In the early 2000s UNFPA has tried to demonstrate to the PRC that it can maintain low fertility by replacing mandatory birth limits with voluntary reproductive health services (Winckler 2005). The PRC also has longstanding relations with the World Health Organization, which in the 1990s collaborated with birth planning research institutes in China on introducing client-oriented international concepts into PRC birth planning.

Foreign nongovernmental organizations and private foundations have also been crucial sources for ideas and arguments, technical resources and political support that were essential to launching reform against conservative resistance (EW 29Oct03 BJ-ZBG). Since the early 1980s, through its own Birth Planning Association, the PRC has had active relations with the International Planned Parenthood Federation. IPPF has often praised the PRC's accomplishments in birth limitation but also has provided a conduit for alternative ideas, such as the "client bill of rights" (Gu 2003a). Bilaterally, the longest-running assistance has come from the Japanese Organization for International Cooperation in Family Planning, which ran local demonstrations of how to combine work on birth control, reproductive health, and community development, among other things (JOICFP 1994). Some of the localities that received early assistance from JOICFP, such as Taicang in Jiangsu and Tai'an in Shandong, have since become model localities in birth planning. (Both authors visited Taicang in 1993, when it was pioneering the establishment of computerized information systems for compiling client data

and tracking client compliance.) Among philanthropies, in 1991 the Rocke-
feller Foundation entered China with an interest in promoting reproductive
health, beginning by introducing new contraceptive technologies, including
"informed choice" in deciding which to use (ME 950427). From around
the same time, the Ford Foundation too emphasized reproductive health, advocating improvement of program services and involvement by domestic
women's NGOs. Ford involved the Population Council to help promote the
"quality of care" standard that the Population Council had articulated (Bruce
1990; Kaufman, Zhang, and Xie, forthcoming).

Reform also received important impetus from major international meetings, such as those held in Vienna, Cairo, and Beijing. The 1993 Vienna conference on human rights helped set the stage. The 1994 Cairo meeting of the
decennial International Conference on Population and Development was
pivotal. The ICPD "program of action" shifted the focus of the international
population community from deploying state power to "control" population
to empowering women to manage their own fertility. Preparation for Cairo
and participation in it helped to shift PRC thinking toward international discourses (ME 930302, 930510). The State Council wrote white papers on
population and women and the birth commission wrote a report on population and development (ME 931226, 9402000, 940401). Chinese demographers translated foreign materials relevant to Cairo for circulation to key
leaders within China (Gu ed. 1996). Also crucial was the 1995 Beijing Fourth
International Women's Conference and the associated NGO forum held in
nearby Huairou. The women's meetings introduced Chinese intellectuals to
new understandings of gender as an active power relationship, rather than
simply as social-structural inequality. They also forced program leaders to
confront international feminists' critiques of the program's impact on women
and infant girls.

Academic exchanges and professional training provided additional channels. For example, another international event held in Beijing at this time
was the October 1997 meeting of the quadrennial General Congress of the
International Union for the Scientific Study of Population, the influential
international association of professional demographers. The IUSSP meeting
multiplied links between Chinese and foreign population specialists, further
acquainting Chinese scholars with international scholarship, some of it embodying Cairo ideals. Meanwhile, on its own initiative the birth program
itself began sending national and subnational program leaders abroad for
advanced professional training. For example, between 1998 and 2002 the
program dispatched six delegations of about two dozen each for an Advanced Leadership Program in the United States that included briefings
by experts and activists on population from around the world. The birth

commission disseminated ALP materials within China, and by the end of the series many new Chinese participants arrived already fluent in relevant international discourses. (Both authors participated in the ALP program.)

In part because these new ideas dovetailed with ideas that were developing domestically, many Chinese intellectuals and some program leaders embraced these new international objectives and began considering how to shift Chinese birth policy in those directions. Nevertheless, reform progressed slowly against hardline resistance, suffering many setbacks (SG 25Nov99 BJ). Already in late 1995, at the beginning of the Ninth Five-Year Plan (1996–2000), the birth commission had officially called for reorienting the program from exclusive concern with demographic targets toward joint attention to population goals and client-centered approaches, and from a narrow focus on contraception toward a broader concern with women's reproductive health (Gu 1998, 2000). The program added questions on reproductive health to its 1997 quinquennial survey and by the early 2000s was attempting to deliver more such services (Winckler 2002a, 2005).

Indeed, by the Hu era, foreigners achieved extraordinary degrees of participation in some aspects of program reform. Significantly, a main example was the design of the program's own internal evaluation systems so that they met international technical and ethical standards (EW 3Nov03 BJ). Thus the birth program began increasing its capacity for evaluation not to force subnational leaders to enforce birth rules but to fine tune the service the program provides to the public, in the direction of international standards of quality care and informed choice. Most remarkably, this included an emphasis by the program itself on human rights, partly to mobilize the public against program abuses, partly to provide birth workers with concrete standards for conduct (Winckler 2005). Such standards are themselves a way to build regime capacity and exemplify one characteristic of the neoliberal world that the PRC is entering: a world of "reflexive government" that is more preoccupied with perfecting the functioning of its own institutions than it is with imposing particular rules on the public (Dean 1999, 176–197).

FROM 1998: TOWARD QUALITY CARE

In the mid- to late 1990s the PRC birth program responded to these new connections and ideas fairly rapidly. One key process was a series of meetings in which the birth and health systems tried to work out a division of labor on reproductive health work. In 1998 the administrative office of the State Council convened a large interministerial meeting on "improving technical services to raise population quality" (ME 980105). State councillor and birth minister Peng Peiyun announced major new principles that would henceforth guide policy. The birth and health systems must cooperate to deliver quality services and "the starting and ending point" of work should be serving the public, taking mass satisfaction as the standard. The meeting discussed the preparation and implementation of relevant laws and regulations. Eventually these new principles were embodied in the State Council's 2001 regulations on technical services (YB02, 33 – 36).

Another key process was a series of local experiments at achieving not just technically adequate "quality service" but socially sensitive "quality care." This new international ideal had first surfaced within China at the major Yancheng conference on adapting the program to marketization, attended by foreign advisers, as noted earlier in this chapter (ME 940617). From 1995 through 1998 reformist program leaders sponsored a first round of local experiments at quality care in six highly developed counties, where changes in program methods were least likely to result in a rise in fertility (ME 950330, 950604, 960328, 961226; EW 28Oct03, 13Nov03 BJ). The Ford Foundation, with technical assistance from the Population Council, then supported evaluation of those experiments to secure their expansion to five more localities (Kaufman, Zhang, and Xie, forthcoming). From 1998 UNFPA supported a related initiative in thirty-two less-developed counties. The experiments included not only more and better material services but also more careful counselling on the risks and benefits of alternative methods of contraception and a freer choice of contraceptive methods. A key threshold was the abolition of mandatory birth quotas at the community level, in order to reduce coercion. Some national political and program leaders feared that giving clients greater choice—even just indicating that the program was considering changing its methods—would lead to a rebound of fertility in the pilot localities. Accordingly the strategy of the experiments was to "fade in" new approaches before "fading out" all the old ones, so that some less objectionable levers for enforcing mandatory compliance remained. (Gu 1998; Gu, Simmons, and Szatkowski 2002; and Kaufman, Zhang, and Xie, forthcoming detail this process.)

Fortunately, as it turned out, improving the quality of care did provide additional incentives for compliance, by both implementors and public. The experiments did not lead to a rise in fertility but instead to fewer contraception failures, fewer abortions, and more normal sex ratios at birth. Local program administrators found the reformed approach much more acceptable to the public and therefore much easier to implement. Consequently, with program authorization, these experiments quickly spread beyond the limited number of formal pilot localities to some 800 counties in the seven provinces involved, nearly a third of China's counties, mostly the more advanced ones. This combination of careful design from above and enthusiastic participation from below remained an important dynamic in Comprehensive Reform in the 2000s.

There has been much room for improvement in the services that the PRC birth program has provided, so PRC claims to be improving their quality are both credible and welcome (Kaufman et al. 1992b; Li 1999). These experimental practices set a new direction for the future development of the program that is unlikely to be reversed. Nevertheless these experiments do have limits. One problem is the difficulty, even for national program leaders, of knowing exactly what the experiments have included. Localities have been allowed to decide for themselves what new methods to try. That approach is appropriate given China's diversity, and it is unavoidable given local self-funding. However, some localities may have simply relabeled as "quality care" some service improvement that they had already planned. A second concern is how far the experiments can be extended beyond the advanced third of localities, particularly in the eastern third of the country, where most of them have been located. Probably it will become progressively more difficult to extend quality care to the middle third of ordinary counties, let alone to the bottom third of backward counties, particularly in central and western China. The difficulty is increased because each locality pays for its own experiments, and therefore the localities that most need improvement can least afford it. The third and most basic reservation is that so far none of these experiments has fundamentally altered either the mandatory nature of birth policy or the top-down nature of its implementation. Unlike the concept of quality care advocated at Cairo, the Chinese experiments do not allow couples—without incurring a heavy fine—to choose not to contracept and to choose to carry an illegal pregnancy to term (Chu 2000 and 2001). As the PRC has adopted international ideas, it has significantly reinterpreted them, particularly as they diffused down to local implementors. In the PRC, "client-centrism" quickly came to mean not that the client should truly be in control but that the service provider, while remaining ultimately in control, should focus on what the service provider takes to be the client's needs. (The sour joke among foreign reformers was that "informed choice" meant that the service provider would choose and then inform the client of the choice.) In the early 2000s reform leaders have been working hard to overcome these problems, but they have a half million birth workers to educate.

Evidently the late 1990s experiments with quality care became embodied in early 2000s Comprehensive Reform and in the 2001 Technical Service Regulations as "quality service" (*youzhi fuwu*). This may in fact be a rather effective way of implementing as much "quality of care" as is possible under PRC political and program circumstances. Progressive national program leaders may have had more latitude for writing quality care requirements into the Technical Services Regulations—written by the birth commission and issued by the State Council headed by reformer Zhu Rongji—than they had for writing such standards into the program's new 2001 national law, which had to go through the National People's Congress headed by conservative Li Peng. The Technical Services Regulations contain many important prescriptions addressed to the technical-medical hierarchy, such as trying to insure that such services are competent and safe (*YB02*, 33 –36). However, they also go beyond purely clinical issues by containing "social" prescriptions addressed also to the propaganda and education hierarchy, for example, a rather rigorous formulation of requirements for informed choice. The Technical Services Regulations also contain prescriptions addressed to the administrative system, such as the requirement that all technical personnel be re-certified to make sure that they are truly qualified to deliver quality service, including informed choice. In addition, both the Technical Service Regulations and the 2001 law require that certain basic reproductive health services must be provided by localities free of charge. Finally, overall, one might regard the incorporation of quality service into Comprehensive Reform and the Technical Services Regulations as another response to the haphazard way in which the late 1990s experiments in quality care played out, attempting somewhat more standardization and incorporating quality service into a larger framework that makes it possible. Further addressing this problem, in November 2003 the program drafted national standards by which to judge whether a locality had or had not achieved quality care. (As of September 2004, those standards still had not been finalized and released, probably at least in part because of the usual dilemma over how specific to make them.)

FROM 1998: LIBERALIZATION OF PLANNING

Ideally, under mandatory planning, compliance by individuals is dictated by direct orders enforced by administrative institutions. In the case of birth planning, the state allocated quotas for children to each community, which told each couple when they were eligible for a quota. In principle, such a process can appear efficient. In practice, however, micromanaging individual behavior is extremely expensive, troublesome to arrange, and frequently distorts behavior, because individuals respond to plan targets and incentives in unanticipated ways. Such micromanagement also creates opportunities for corruption, as individuals purchase exemptions from enforcers. There are several ways in which one can depart from such mandatory planning. The first, working from the top down, concerns the changing nature of the plan itself and the extent to which institutions try to enforce it. The second, working from the bottom up, concerns the number and type of rules with which the state confronts individual citizens. Both sets of processes can be thought of as "liberalization" because they do increase the latitude allowed individual behavior. However, the state is not really surrendering control but only shifting from direct operation, which is clumsy and expensive, to indirect regulation, which is more sophisticated and economical (Winckler ed. 1999, conclusion). The result is not less control but better control (Chapter 9).

At the macrolevel, as regards planning itself, the first step of a reform process is likely to be from mandatory planning that commands behavior to guidance planning that merely coordinates behavior. (Ideally, individuals decide their behavior on the expectation that everyone else will behave in a comparable way that will lead toward the collective target.) A further step is from guidance planning to indicative planning—calculations that are merely informational, just projections of what is likely to occur that are used mostly by the agency making the forecasts. In the late 1980s, planners such as Premier Li Peng argued strenuously that plan targets should be taken seriously as "fighting objectives" in order to motivate implementors to force the population to remain within plan targets. In the early 1990s PRC leaders endorsed this principle, as part of the Three Givens. As recently as the late 1990s a central meeting reaffirmed that national-level "population planning" would continue in some form (EW 11Nov98 NJ).

Nevertheless, during the middle and late 1990s, PRC birth planning started to take at least the first step in reform of planning and, by the early 2000s, also the second. Increasingly, "population planning" appears to mean little more than the creation of macrodemographic projections, with little attempt to impose mandatory limits on the number of births within particular communities. The intention of national program leaders is that population targets should no longer be passed down below the county level. Nevertheless, those same leaders acknowledge that it is impossible for them to know how many localities have carried out those wishes (SG 23Nov99 BJ). Some local leaders retain the targets, knowing their usefulness in the past and perhaps fearing punishment for failure to meet population goals in the future.

In contrast to the early 1990s, when the center attempted to micromanage subnational programs through the use of elaborate indicators of program performance, reportedly in the late 1990s the center largely turned over to the provinces the formulation of program indicators (EW 15Apr99 NJ, 24Jun99 NJ). This downward transfer of authority could have unintended effects. Because few provinces have the technical capacity to formulate and administer such program indicators, local programs may go largely unmonitored. This is all the more likely because many of the functions that the program now wishes to emphasize, such as reproductive health and quality of care, are more difficult to measure than relatively clear-cut demographic outcomes.

At the microlevel of rules governing individual behavior, again the transition away from planning can involve two steps. Each step represents a large saving of resources that would otherwise have gone to enforcement or corruption. An interesting feature of this microtransition is that, instead of having to challenge conservative shibboleths such as macroplanning, progressive program administrators can bill the microchanges as merely technical, even though they can constitute significant liberalizations.

The first step is from direct control through instructions to indirect control through regulations. On particular matters for which the state thinks it can afford to restructure control, the state eliminates specific instructions for each individual action and replaces them with general regulations that participants must follow. The same rules can remain, but now individuals can follow them on their own, instead of the state's having to program individual behavior. At the turn of the millennium the birth system began to take the first step on some matters. For example, some localities no longer required newly married couples who wanted to have their first child to apply for permission under an annual quota. They could simply go ahead and have their permitted one child whenever they wished (EW 24Jun99 NJ, 6Mar02 NJ). By 2004 all provinces except Tibet had dropped that requirement, most had shortened the spacing before a second child, and several had abolished spacing altogether (Shanghai, Jilin, and Hainan—PI 041009, 041018). Dropping the first child permit reduced the cost of administration, the hassle to citizens, and the opportunities for corruption. Indeed, the first recommendation of a program report on how to reduce corruption in the birth system was to eliminate this unnecessary requirement.

The second step—not yet fully taken by PRC birth policy—is from regulation to deregulation, allowing individuals to define their own goals and rules, usually in response either to market signals or to internalized norms. A substantial proportion of the population may already have made this second step on its own, benefiting enforcement of the regulations that remain in place. At least in advanced areas, the birth program may be approaching genuine deregulation, in the sense that much of the public would no longer have more children than the birth program allows, even if left to their own desires. This results from a combination of market signals (such as the high cost of raising even one child, particularly in urban areas) and from internalized norms (such as the conviction, by now widespread, that modernity dictates few children). (See Part 2, especially Chapter 7.)

Early 2000s: Toward Comprehensive Reform

In the early 2000s PRC economic reform deepened, moving from moderately rightist domestic marketization toward radically rightist globalization.

Symbolic of this, in 2002 the PRC finally joined the World Trade Organization, focusing national attention on the domestic reforms that globalization required, including the adoption of international standards and "best practice." The PRC also moved toward a controlled version of political reform, limited to elite policymaking. A more pluralistic policy process encouraged extensive consultation between branches and agencies of government but did not permit open contestation or public dissent. These political parameters were reflected in the population domain in the policy processes that framed the 2000 decision and passed the 2001 law. Mass participation remained highly managed. Nevertheless, before retiring, party head Jiang Zemin did sketch a long-term political strategy for the relationship of the CCP to society. The party could remain in power by realigning itself with an expanded and different social coalition: the advanced elements in the economy (entrepreneurs), the advanced elements in culture (technocrats), and the "vast majority" of the people (not just workers). Jiang's Three Represents used classical Chinese communist concepts to rationalize progressive reforms, such as admitting businessmen to the Chinese Communist Party, raising standards for party and government, and aligning policies with popular preferences—at least the preferences of the winners from China's spectacular economic development (Fewsmith 2001, 229–230). Birth minister Zhang Weiqing quickly applied Jiang's formulation to birth planning, arguing that the program facilitates economic development, modernizes reproductive culture, and promotes the interests of the vast majority of PRC citizens. Indeed the program had begun emphasizing client satisfaction as "a main criterion for judging our work" (FBIS-CHI-2001–0711, ZWQ).

In birth planning the main overall development at the turn of the millennium was a fundamental reorientation, from strenuous and oppressive efforts to reduce fertility to vigilant but more moderate efforts to maintain an already low fertility. The factual cornerstone for this reorientation was the assessment by Chinese demographers that in the course of the 1990s China's fertility had fallen below the replacement level (Yu et al. 2000b). The birth commission's own best estimate was that starting in 1992 the average lifetime number of children per woman had been about 1.8 (SBPC 19 August 2001, based on SSB figures). A 2001 survey found the Total Fertility Rate to be 1.81 children (1.22 urban and 1.98 rural—SBPC 4 March 2002). Informally, program specialists were suggesting that the TFR had fallen to an astonishing 1.5 to 1.6 (at or below the policy rate). According to program leaders, fertility remained "unstable" because in backward areas the policy remained somewhat ahead of economic development and reproductive culture. Meanwhile China has kept within government targets for population growth rate and total population size. In the late 1990s annual population growth fell below 1 percent as planned. As of the November 2000 decennial census, China's population was 1.266 billion, well under the 2000 target of 1.3 billion (Lavely 2001; Table 1 in Chapter 1).

Assured that the birth program had reduced quantity, the Central Committee and State Council reoriented the program's mission toward raising quality. Doing so required "strengthening" numerous aspects of the program, not so much to strengthen its hold on the public as to improve its grip on itself. The March 2000 decision provided a comprehensive rationale for Chinese birth planning and a pointed analysis of what the program had to do to adapt to the advanced stage of marketization and globalization into which China had now entered. The first major central decision on birth policy since 1991, this one was intended to set the direction of birth work at least until 2010. It directed PRC birth planning well beyond a narrow focus on quantitative birth limitation toward a more comprehensive reproductive policy that began to make birth limitation into just one "service" within a wider range of reproductive health services. The scope of the program was broadened still further, from reproduction to "population," authorizing the program to address a range of population-related social problems, particularly any problems that the program itself had helped to create. The program had aggravated the distortion of sex ratio at birth, so the program should adopt a broad range of measures to correct that. The program had accelerated population aging, so the program should help provide old age support for seniors, particularly those in rural areas whom birth limits had prevented from having a son. (See Decision in *YB01*, 33–36; FBIS-CHI-2000–0507; White Paper in *YB01*, 36–41, English version on SBPC website—see under White Paper 2000 in References.)

The 2000 decision appeared to be a political compromise that synthesized stability and change while remaining silent on some issues. On the side of stability, the decision reaffirmed the program's historic mission of party-led state intervention to save China from overpopulation. Birth limits must be particularly strict in developing the relatively backward western region. Only in the very long run will economic, social, and cultural modernization make political regulation unnecessary. On the side of change, the decision added new content to the program's longstanding mandate to improve population quality, which still included premarital health checks and genetic counselling, but now also better maternal and child health care and, eventually, some social programs (White Paper 2000, section 16). By noting the need to "perfect" the leader responsibility system, the decision authorized the adjustment of performance evaluation criteria toward such progressive goals as lawful administration and client satisfaction. The decision noted the need to improve sex balance and to provide pension programs for an aging population, thereby implicitly acknowledging that the program itself had seriously aggravated or accelerated some demographic distortions. On the side of silence, the decision did not address some additional program-induced distortions, such as the program's inadvertent creation of a "black population" of unauthorized "out-of-plan" children not entitled to government benefits (Greenhalgh 2003a; Chapter 9). It did not explicitly acknowledge, let alone endorse, any of the foreign philosophies and feminist critiques that advocate a genuinely client-centered approach that truly empowers women (Greenhalgh 2001a). Finally, not surprisingly, the decision did not reexamine any of the program's basic assumptions, such as the extent to which mandatory birth planning has accelerated China's fertility decline and whether it has been worth the cost in state resources and social suffering.

In 2000 and 2001, Jiang Zemin's summit speech mostly echoed the 2000 decision, though stressing the need to limit the number and reproduction of the floating population (*YB01*, 6−7; *YB02*, 7−8). At the 2002 summit, however, China's entry into the World Trade Organization prompted Jiang to some broader reflections (*YB03*, 7−8). In paraphrase, he said: We have been convening all these summit meetings all these years because the issue of sustainable development is really important, an issue that all countries in the world are having to confront. Now that we have entered WTO, we have to think more about the relationship between domestic and global processes, such as how to cope with the increased internal migration that external globalization induces. Birth planning must accelerate its reform and renovation, particularly by realizing the potential of recently passed laws and regulations. Birth work should be centered on village groups (*cunzu*) in rural areas and on community districts (*shequ*) in urban areas (in other words at the lowest point of incorporation of households into society). Incentive rewards and social guarantees should be improved so that households that practice birth planning "socially have standing, economically have real benefits, and in their livelihood have guarantees" (*zai shehuishang you diwei, jingjishang you shihui, shenghuoshang you baozhang*). Thus Jiang anticipated the broadening of birth planning into a form of social policy—targeted on program participants with "real difficulties" but therefore including many Chinese.

The 2000 decision set in motion three kinds of process: legalization, to provide authorization to the birth program to undertake its new tasks; reorganization, to put the birth program into a position to do so; and the launching of a continuous process of Comprehensive Reform to provide the institutional capacity through which the program could begin to deliver more social benefits.

LEGALIZATION: THE 2001 LAW

A major transition process in the post-Mao period affecting birth planning has been an overall regime shift from reliance on party fiat toward "rule by law" (Peerenboom 2002). From the outset of hard birth planning around 1980, and again when it was re-enforced around 1990, PRC leaders had wanted a national law to legitimate enforcement, as noted in the previous chapter. However, this had proved impossible. One issue was how detailed a national law should be, in view of diverse subnational circumstances and regulations, and in terms of how specific demands on citizens should be (e.g., regarding method of contraception and number of children). Another issue may have been the definition of the policy domain to be covered by the law — just "birth planning" or also "population"? A further issue may have been too great a gap between the constitutional ideals that "rule by law" represented and the way birth planning was actually being implemented. Nevertheless, by the end of the 1990s, several developments made a national birth law increasingly imperative. In principle, for two decades the PRC had been working on giving the regime a legal foundation, and birth planning remained the only major national policy domain not underpinned by enabling legislation. In practice, there was the need to specify responsibilities and procedures as the program moved toward more nationally uniform implementation that relied not on "the plan" but on "the law" and that involved not only program powers but also citizens' rights. Finally, national leaders wished to redefine this policy domain to include "population" and to provide the legal authority for the former "birth" program to undertake new missions such as launching population-relevant social programs. This shift in both methods and mission was finally enough to overcome legislative resistance to putting strict birth limits into law, but even then some resistance remained (EW 30Octo3 BJ).

The drafting process was quite thorough, as the birth commission reviewed previous domestic drafts and relevant international agreements and as it consulted other national ministries and subnational program leaders. Evidently some previous dilemmas were bypassed by leaving the national law relatively general and by authorizing subnational legislatures to fill in details. Some ongoing disagreements may have been bypassed by treating some issues in other national regulations (which did not have to go through the National People's Congress but instead could be issued by the State Council or birth commission itself). Among jurisdictional disputes, clearly the decision was in favor of formally extending the commission's authority to population, but the division of labor with the health ministry remained unclear. Passing this law presumably was facilitated by the fact that at the time no fewer than four vice chairpersons of the National People's Congress had strong previous connections to the birth program. These included former birth minister Peng Peiyun; former vice minister Jiang Zhenghua; the new head of the Birth Planning Association, Politburo member Jiang Chunyun; and He Luli, formerly a Beijing deputy mayor who had overseen birth planning and later became head of the Population Welfare Foundation.

The 2001 law legalized institutions for the state planning of population and births and at the same time placed legal restraints on them. Each chapter balanced state power and citizen protection. Most of the rewards specified were to citizens for compliance, and most of the penalties specified were against officials for maladministration. As in the 2001 decision, the balance between stability and change was elusive, and the participants themselves may not have known for sure which provisions or omissions might prove operatively most important in the future. Clearly the program was no longer just administratively enforced birth limitation, but equally clearly it was not yet entirely client-centered reproductive health care. The 2001 law put in place language authorizing much of both. How much of which prevailed would depend on the power of rival policymakers and the vagaries of local implementation. Thus, like the 2000 decision, the landmark 2001 law too contained much stability, much change, and both progressive and problematic silences.

As in the 2001 decision, the ostensible basic premise of the law was stability, both demographic and legal. As birth minister Zhang Weiqing went out of his way to emphasize, the new law neither tightened nor loosened birth policy in the sense of altering the specific demands placed on citizens to practice contraception and limit their childbearing (FBIS-CHI-2001–1230). Instead the law reiterated that citizens have a constitutional duty to do so and provided legal bases for enforcement. Nevertheless, the 2001 law reaffirmed an existing policy that already included some slight qualifications to previous regime demands on number of children, methods of contraception, and penalties for noncompliance. Thus, like previous national policy statements, strictly speaking the national law only "advocated" having only one child and allowed subnational legislatures to specify exceptions to that ideal. For ordinary citizens, ostensibly the main penalty for having extra children was a steep fine but penalties did not include administrative sanctions (such as salary cuts or loss of job, which could apply to regime personnel) or criminal punishment (which could apply to those who actively resist or obstruct birth planning).

Some of the progressive changes that the law introduced were intended to reduce abuses, increase incentives, and foster women's development. Officials "should conduct administration strictly in accordance with the law, should enforce the law in a civilized manner, and must not infringe upon citizens' legal rights and interests" (Article 4). The law contained punishments for maladministration (Articles 36 to 39) and provision for citizens to appeal decisions or sue administrators (Article 44, as authorized by other laws). Chapter 4 of the law authorized rewards and other preferential treatment for compliance (Articles 23 through 28) but left arrangements and funding to local government and employers (Articles 27 and 29). As for women, birth planning should be linked to their education and employment and to improving their health and raising their status (Article 3). Implementation should include measures to strengthen maternal and child health care (Article 11). There must be no discrimination against female children and their mothers (Article 22), and sex selection of children through ultrasound and abortion was strictly prohibited.

Some of the silences in the 2001 law were quite progressive because the law omitted many things that many Chinese and foreigners have considered objectionable. The national law adopted a much milder tone than existing provincial regulations and omitted many specific prohibitions and penalties on citizens that many provincial regulations had included. Unlike some previous subnational legislation, the national law said only that contraception must be "safe, effective, and appropriate," not specifying exactly what method must be used at what stage of childbearing. (The classic requirement after December 1982 was insertion of an IUD after the first child and sterilization of at least one member of a couple after the second.) Additional examples of silences were not explicitly requiring termination of unauthorized pregnancies and not explicitly requiring sterilization of people who are not supposed to have children (such as couples who already have their authorized children or couples with hereditary diseases). These omissions were highly significant because, at least in principle, they obliged provincial legislatures to remove inconsistent provisions from provincial laws. In practice, though, central reformers did not expect all provinces to achieve complete consistency with national law immediately (EW 6Mar02 NJ).

REORGANIZATION

During his tenure as vice premier and premier, Zhu Rongji said little about birth planning aside from some obligatory remarks at the annual summit, where he mostly just endorsed Jiang Zemin's speech, as protocol dictated. Nevertheless, one can infer Zhu's agenda for birth planning from his agenda for economic planning, and from the person whom he put in charge of both (Wang Zhongyu). Zhu's overall agenda was to continue to reorient China from mandatory planning under Bureaucratic Professionalism to indicative planning under Socialist Marketization, although maintaining a strong public enterprise sector (Yang Dali 1999). In 1992, as part of his initiative to resume reform, Deng Xiaoping had elevated Zhu from Shanghai mayor to national vice premier. Zhu's overall task was to make China's public sector viable, partly by shrinking unnecessary portions, partly by making the necessary portions more efficient. One of Zhu's moves was to begin superseding the classic planning commission with a new economic superministry that would link the domestic economy to foreign trade (like the famous Japanese MITI or Ministry of International Trade and Investment). (Zheng 2004, 102–106 gives a similar account.)

The man Zhu placed in charge of the Economic and Trade Commission was Wang Zhongyu, who had worked on similar problems in Jilin province. When Zhu became premier in 1998, he made Wang secretary general of the State Council, giving him a broad role in helping Zhu restructure the PRC regime, including the extension of reform from the economic to social sectors. Wang therefore played an extraordinarily direct role in the reform of birth planning. Wang became instrumental in crafting the 2000 decision, drafting the 2001 law, and launching experiments at Comprehensive Reform to implement them. (On Wang see Xiao 1999, 197–205 and several bios on the Web, searchable through Google.)

As a further step in the reform of national institutions for economic and social policy, when the Jiang-Zhu administration was going out of office in March 2003, Wang personally submitted to the National People's Congress plans for a further reorganization of government economic management (passed in June 2003). Probably not by accident, this was just when former premier Li Peng—long a defender of the planning commission's hegemony over intersectoral planning—was relinquishing his post as head of the NPC. In the economic sector, the State Planning Commission of the Mao and Deng eras, which had become the State Development and Planning Commission of the Jiang era, now became the State Commission on Development and Reform. Equally dramatic, this reorganization abolished the Economic and Trade Commission over which Wang himself had once presided, transferring foreign trade functions to a new Ministry of Commerce.

In the social sector, Wang's March 2003 proposal included finally adding population to the title of the birth commission. The newly renamed State Population and Birth Planning Commission became the only national agency that retained "planning" in its name—not because it remained committed to central planning but because, after a half-century of use, the term "planned birth" had become standard. Eventually the commission may drop "birth planning" from its name altogether, leaving birth limitation as only one among several main functions of a national "population" program. This reorganization was not so much a transfer of power from the planning commission to the birth commission as a reorientation of the function of all agencies involved, from mandatory to indicative planning. The planning commission never did have a large capacity for social planning and retained the capacity that it did have (EW 31Oct BJ-Chen).

To address its new population functions, the commission established a new department for population planning. However, the Chinese term used for "planning" was not the old mandatory *jihua*, telling the public what to do, but a new indicative *guihua*, telling the government what it needed to do. The new planning was to serve not economic development but human needs, under the slogan of "taking people as the basis" (*yiren weiben*). The former birth commission was to help formulate social policies, particularly those related to population, especially for the vulnerable, and most of all for those who had sacrificed for birth policy. Thus a first task was accelerating the establishment of the social programs that PRC citizens had been promised since 1980 in exchange for limiting their childbearing.

TOWARD COMPREHENSIVE REFORM

The Central Committee and State Council issued the 2000 decision at the beginning of March (Document Eight). Already, later in March, the party propaganda department and the State Council convened national telephone conferences to get implementation rolling (*YB01*, 20–21, 75–77, 82). In May the birth commission authorized Shandong—whose more developed localities have often been in the vanguard of birth planning—to conduct experiments at Comprehensive Reform in three cities (Qingdao, Bingzhou, and Tai'an). In September 2000 State Council secretary general Wang Zhongyu went to Shandong to inspect (ibid., 22–25). He fully affirmed (*chongfen kending*) the experiments and suggested an additional experiment on insurance in a fourth city. During his inspection Wang coined a five-phrase slogan that was to guide much of the ensuing process of local experiments at Comprehensive Reform: "Lawful administration, village self-government, quality service, policy promotion, and comprehensive governance." Wang explained that national political leaders wanted a "breakthrough" in birth work, toward minimizing state interference with private behavior and maximizing social self-regulation, and toward delivering positive benefits to the public in order to produce public satisfaction with the program. (The next chapter describes Comprehensive Reform.)

By the beginning of the twenty-first century, reform of the birth program was comprehensive in another sense: It included several initiatives by several different departments. Evidently in the mid-1990s a main impulse toward reform had arisen within the planning and statistics department, from which Zhang Erli then ran the early internationally connected quality care pilot projects. Reportedly the question arose whether planning and statistics was really the most appropriate department to supervise such experiments, and during the late 1990s they were transferred to the science and technology department (under later vice minister Zhao Baige). In the early 2000s, the quality care initiative moved out of the commission to its China Population Information and Research Center (under vice director Xie Zhenming, with the now retired Zhang Erli as consultant). In the middle 2000s evidently the initiative moved back into the commission, to be run by several vice ministers and department heads (PI 040827). Meanwhile UNFPA was running related experiments (32 under its 1998–2001 fourth program cycle and 30 in its 2002–2005 fifth cycle). The administration department, continuing its long history of policy research and experiments, was masterminding Comprehensive Reform (in the early 2000s ongoing in 19 nationally official localities). The propaganda and education department was running local experiments for its campaign promoting new styles of marriage and childbearing—in the early 2000s some 429 localities. (Number of localities are courtesy of Xie Zhenming, who supervised and evaluated many of these projects.)

To some extent these many different reforms exercise different creativities and mobilize different resources. To some extent they strain comprehension and resources at all levels. Both positive and negative effects are particularly strong when several of them end up in the same locality, as occurs not infrequently (Holcombe 2003; EW 8Nov03 BJ). There is no necessary conflict between any of these reform initiatives, which do add up to quite comprehensive reform. Nevertheless, in the early 2000s the relationship between them remained not entirely clear, so they may not have been as mutually reinforcing as Comprehensive Reform intends. They may even send partially contradictory signals to localities and make competing demands on limited local resources. As an astute foreign evaluator has observed:

> [The birth commission's inherited] "stovepipe" department structure was well-suited to managing population control. For example, the IEC [Information, Education and Communication] Department supported mass education on population control. The Science and Technology Department took responsibility for contraceptives. The Planning and Statistics Department managed the information system that held officials accountable for meeting population targets. . . .
>
> [In the early 2000s] the Planning & Financial Department is currently proposing reforms in the management and evaluation system to support the QOC [Quality of Care] approach. The IEC Department is launching a major pilot effort in 11 provinces to address the issue of son preference and the unbalanced sex ratio

at birth. The Science and Technology Department works with WHO on quality of care demonstration activities that focus on maternal mortality, RTIs [Reproductive Tract Infections], and healthy babies. The multiple initiatives in the SFPC and by provinces, prefectures and counties reflect a broad interest in and ownership of the QOC concept. These initiatives are not yet well-connected or integrated. What is lacking is a mechanism to assure common standards and accountability for quality in implementation. (Holcombe 2003, 7)

Overall, what is most striking about Comprehensive Reform itself are the reasons that birth minister Zhang Weiqing and vice minister Wang Guoqiang offered for it, that a "new situation" urgently demanded new methods of birth work. To avoid a crisis in its relations with society, the program now needed to abandon its exclusively statist approach to governance and to move quickly toward a more balanced formula that acknowledged the emergence of more autonomous institutions and individuals and that relied more on them to govern their own reproductive behavior. In a watershed speech to the birth program's year-end national work conference in December 2000, Zhang said that China was entering a new epoch and that birth planning was failing to keep up (*YB01*, 60−68, particularly 61−62). Wang expanded Zhang's points to the February 2001 workshop that extended Comprehensive Reform from four to sixteen localities (*YB02*, 117−118). In the past thirty years birth planning had accomplished a lot, Wang said. "But we must recognize that those results were achieved by low investment, relying on forcefully restrictive administrative methods (*qiangyouli de xingcheng zhiyue cuoshi*), in exchange for the huge economic and social effect of 'averting' the births of 300 million more people. At the same time, not a few localities (*bushao difang*) also produced the heavy side cost (*chenzhong daijia*) of damaging relations between party, people, and cadres and of damaging the vital interests of women (*sunhai funu qieshen liyi*)."

Zhang himself further elaborated at the September 2001 conference that reviewed the first year of experiments at Comprehensive Reform (*YB02*, 74−81, particularly end of 79):

> Under special historical circumstances, we had no choice but to do that (*bu de yi wei zhi*), the people could understand, could forgive (*neng lijie, neng yuanliang*). But by now, if we again use past methods to do our work, the people won't accept it (*buhui daying de*). . . . People have changed, in the direction of democracy and law, markets and competition. Under the circumstances, in one meeting we can't achieve a consensus on what to do, it will take a long time. It will be like Deng's agricultural reform in 1979: at first there were many doubters but he went ahead anyway and by the third year everyone had come aboard. . . . If we reform early, the situation for the birth system can be even better, the support of the public for birth planning will be even higher, and the attention and support of party and government leaders toward birth planning will be even greater. . . .

Some comrades might complain that they are already overworked and wonder why we are adding this new burden, and without any increase in salary. It's true, the work of experiment cities is in advance of the rest of the province, even of the whole country, so if you don't reform you can still get by. However, although you can wait, this matter can't wait. The birth system has assumed a heavy burden and faces severe challenges. If we don't reform it will be hard to continue, if we don't reform there will be no way out (*bugaige nan yi wei ji, bugaige meiyou chulu*).

The Hu Era: From
Comprehensive Reform to Social Policy

EXTERNALLY, AT THE beginning of the twenty-first century, both the PRC regime and Chinese society were becoming increasingly globalized, as symbolized by China's 2002 entry into WTO and its hosting the 2008 Olympics. Both regime and society aspired to international "best practice." Abroad, they found a tension between neosocialist international ideals of human development and global practices of neoliberal marketization, a tension analogous to the one at home between Socialism and Marketization. On the one hand, Leninist PRC leaders adopted the international human development paradigm and, declaring it "scientific," began using it to update a revived Maoist Socialism. On the other hand, the same leaders began using global neoliberalism to update a revised Dengist Marketization. These internationalizing updates promised to make Chinese development still more successful. However, they did not fully resolve the tension between how to achieve human development and how to allocate scarce resources. (See Lardy 2002; Lampton ed. 2001; Zheng 2004.)

Internally, after more than two decades of spectacularly successful all-out Marketization under Deng and Jiang, the new Hu-Wen administration (March 2003–) began using the PRC's core Leninism to formalize a shift toward problems of economic inequality and insecurity that Marketization had neglected or even caused. The Jiang era had begun to address those problems, mostly by promoting economic development in lagging regions. The Hu era continued that strategy but began supplementing it with more targeted economic interventions and social programs. Some of these were Socialist, involving direct government guarantees of social security and payments of social support. Some elaborated Marketization, using neoliberal insurance mechanisms to transfer responsibility to communities, couples, and individuals themselves. Politically, some tension remained between a Jiang coalition that represented mostly the winners from China's spectacular development and a Hu coalition that wished to include as many of the losers as possible. Distributing social benefits would help the new Hu-Wen administration consolidate support. In any case, the Sixteenth Party Congress defined the PRC's new agenda as making further progress toward achieving a "modestly comfortable standard of living" for the society, particularly in rural areas. The task of the population-and-birth policy domain became to provide "a favorable population environment" for that endeavor. (On politics see Nathan and Gilley 2002; JOD 2003; Gilley 2004, 3–94; PI 030109, 030319, *People's Daily* editorials; PI 030115, 030123, Zhang speeches.)

The Hu era strikingly exemplifies many themes of this book: science and democracy, regime capacity, the two poles of biopower (macro and micro), and the triangular governmentalization of population (public administration, professional institutions, and private responsibility). Hu Jintao elaborated a new ideology for guiding his era, a "scientific concept of development." This new set of discursive practices was not merely hot air. Relative to earlier eras, rhetoric was increasingly accompanied by regime capacity to formulate detailed policies and to implement them in detail. Elite political development turned inward on the regime itself, as the governmentality account of political neoliberalism as "reflexive government" might predict (Dean 1999). The party became preoccupied with cleaning up its own act and with improving its capacity to steer the government (PI 040701). Regime building included strengthening both technocratic expertise and political rectitude, including in the birth program (e.g., PI 040524, ZWQ on evaluation; PI 041015, a two-day political study session by the commission party group). A newly explicit concern with the robustness of the policy process too was reflected in the population and birth system, for example, in improvements to its system of policy information, including training personnel (PI 030424, 040810, 040823). Within the regime as a whole, there was to be democratization, but from the Center outward. Most crucially, the party should become internally more disciplined and more democratic, as a training ground and model for the rest of society. The government too should emulate the party, auditing administrative processes for their probity and democracy, standards now applied to the birth program as well (PI 030819, 040227, 040318). (On politics see Chao and Dickinson eds. 2001; Lee and Lo eds. 2001; Hope, Yang and Li eds. 2003; Miller 2003, 2004; Naughton and Yang eds. 2004; China Strategy 30 January 2004; Naughton 2004b.)

From Reproduction to Population: The Triumph of Biopower

In the former birth policy domain, the Hu era initiated a new epoch—in some respects, but not in others. The Jiang-Zhu administration had issued new long-term directional policies (the 2000 decision), had established a new legal framework (the 2001 law with accompanying regulations), and had initiated a strengthening of implementation capacity (Comprehensive Reform). The Jiang-Hu transition completed the addition of planning population to planning births (PI 030325). The new "population" moniker authorized the program to participate in the regime shift from economic toward social objectives. All of this was great progress with great promise—reformulation of ideas, leading to reorganization of institutions, followed by redirection of action.

The prospect for progress was less positive in the original reproductive domain, where many old premises remained the same and many old institutions and individuals remained in place. The transition from the Jiang to Hu eras was accompanied by rising unofficial discussion among scholars of the possibility of switching to a two-child rule. Early in 2003 a small group of academics submitted such a proposal to the Central Committee and State Council for consideration (PI 041018). Shanghai, which had been experiencing negative rates of natural increase for more than a decade, actually switched to a two-child rule (without spacing) when it issued revised population and birth regulations at the beginning of 2004 (PI 040121). Birth minister Zhang Weiqing allowed that this was a perfectly reasonable local adjustment (PI 040806). However, he also said that Shanghai was a special case that did not affect the overall stability of either policy or fertility. To talk about the possibility of a two-child policy he said "was not helpful to our work," he said (ibid.). Nevertheless, a recently promoted vice minister publicly opined that policy must change with circumstance (PI 041018, ZBG). The new head of the commission's policy and law department said he personally preferred that couples be allowed two children (ibid., YXJ). Senior demographer Wu Cangping retorted that this was just their personal opinion (ibid.). Ensuing events proved him correct. A few days later the same policy and law official explained to a legal journal that the period until 2020 would be a crucial one, during which population growth, labor force, and rural-to-urban migration would peak (PI 041019, YXJ). Allowing everyone two children would mean that China's population would reach 1.6 billion by 2045, a decade earlier than previously projected. Therefore, until at least 2020, "existing birth policy basically will not change" (*jiben buhui biandong*). Instead, "the main thing will be supplementing and perfecting" (*zhuyao shi buchong wanshan*). Evidently, any further adaptations, such as Shanghai's, would have to be local, gradual, and limited. As in the mid-1980s, it remained to be seen how far an un-changing "directional policy" would allow "operative policy" to be adjusted.

FROM POPULATION PROBLEM TO
PROBLEMATIC POPULATION

The transition from the Jiang to Hu eras at first created much uncertainty for the birth program. At the end of 2002, reportedly many birth officials appeared unsure whether the birth system would remain independent or be merged with the health system (EW 3Nov03 BJ). The beginning of 2003 brought very good news: not only would the new Hu-Wen administration continue an independent birth system and the annual summit but also it would proceed with the expansion of the program's responsibilities to "population" that the 2001 law had authorized (PI 030327). Indeed the new population-and-birth program appeared set to become a significant player in the new epoch of socioeconomic development that it had helped pioneer since the mid-1990s. By absorbing international ideals of quality care and client choice, the birth program had helped turn the PRC toward the human-centered development that the Hu era has embraced. Moreover, the population-resource-environment policy domain provided a main institutional locus for the Hu era's new emphasis, not just on social policy but also on the "coordinated" development of economy and environment.

The new balance between policy tendencies in the Hu era found its first concrete expression for population policy in the transitional March 2003 summit. (The Sixteenth Party Congress in 2002 had replaced Jiang Zemin with Hu Jintao as party general secretary, but the March 2003 National People's Congress had not yet replaced Zhu Rongji with Wen Jiabao as government premier.) Hu's speech at the 2003 summit marked the beginning of a significantly new policy era: he repeated the instruction of the 2001 decision to "maintain stable low-level fertility" but added that "at the same time" the program "must address work to balance sex ratios and must actively address problems of population aging, migration, and employment" (PI 030310). That is the classic formula—affirming A but adding B—by which PRC leaders announce a switch in emphasis from A to B. Symbolizing the underlying demographic transition that made that shift possible, India began overtaking China as the most populous country in the world, something the PRC now regarded as a dubious distinction (PI 040116).

"POPULATION SECURITY" IN
A DANGEROUS ENVIRONMENT

In 2003 the PRC suffered a shock from its natural environment that further consolidated the position and enhanced the centrality of its new population-

and-birth system. A series of epidemics erupted: the regional dangers of bird flu, the international emergency of SARS, and the heightened prospect of possible future domestic disaster from HIV/AIDS. The Politburo itself took command, and the Central Committee and State Council revised personnel evaluation systems to include performance in combating SARS (PI 030418, 030423). The crisis demonstrated the incapacity of the health system and the new capacities of the population-and-birth system, which quickly seized the opportunity that SARS presented to demonstrate the usefulness of the program's capacities. With 520,000 personnel and 1.4 million village representatives (*zhuangan*), the program could reach into society in a way that the health system could not—for example, monitoring the movement of migrants that was crucial to the spread of disease (PI 030523, 030527-ZWQ). Moreover, the program had built multiple, interconnected information systems that could get that information back to national policymakers accurately and rapidly (PI 030527). After years of turf wars, when the SARS crisis was over the health ministry even wrote the population-and-birth commission an official letter of thanks (PI 030620). Meanwhile a similar scenario unfolded on HIV/AIDS, with the health system stumbling and the population-and-birth system mobilizing to help educate the public (PI 031119, 031202, 031231, 040510).

A new rubric of "population security" emerged, dramatizing the importance and urgency of the program's apparently mundane tasks. Addressing the October conference commemorating the twentieth anniversary of the Three Basics, birth minister Zhang Weiqing first defined the concept as follows:

> So-called population security (*renkou anquan*) means that a country's overall power and national security [should] not suffer harm because of population problems, [that the country] be able to avoid or resolve either partial or comprehensive crises in the population domain. [The concept's] main content is that in a particular country during a particular period such factors as the quantity, quality, structure, distribution, and movement of a country's population mutually coordinate with the level of economic and social development and with the demands of [further] development. [Those factors should be] appropriate to the carrying capacity of resources and environment, [and they should be] able to realize sustainable development and all-round human development. Population security is a country's most basic and most important security question. (PI 030919)

Reflecting the program's new responsibility for population, the new rubric extended the program's mandate from quantity and quality to structure, distribution, and movement (PI 040712). The new rubric also legitimated program involvement in what had previously been considered exclusively "health" matters, such as public health education, screening, and referral. At the program's year-end work conference, Zhang articulated a new bipolar formula for guiding program work (PI 031226). At the macro pole the population-and-birth system must "attend to population security" (*guanzhu renkou anquan*). At the micro pole it must "promote all-round human development" (*tuizhan ren de quanmian fazhan*). One could hardly imagine a more literal illustration of Foucault's distinction between the aggregate and individual levels at which modern power fosters life. At the aggregate level, the concept of population security also perfectly exemplifies Foucault's definition of the state's role as the establishment of regulatory "security mechanisms" to "optimize a state of life" in the face of environmental perturbations (Gordon 1991, 19–20; Foucault 2003, 246).

A further Foucauldian subtheme that came to the fore in China in the 2000s was the dilemma posed for life-fostering biopower by the birth of infants with "defects" (*quexian*). The logic of biopower is that, in the interests of improving the population as a whole, the state has a responsibility to "defend society" against abnormalities, presumably including such births (Foucault 2003, 261–262). The quality dimension of PRC population policy has embraced that logic since at least 1980 and continues to do so after 2000. Chinese couples themselves have become increasingly preoccupied with a quest for the "perfect child" (Chapter 8). By the early twenty-first century, China had largely completed its "health transition" from communicable diseases to chronic ailments. Aggravated by growing pollution, infant defects had emerged as a significant source of remaining infant mortality and adult disability (PI 040325, ZWQ). Program statements repeatedly noted that about 6–8 percent of births in China are "defective," between 80,000 and 120,000 per year (PI 031215, 041009). The PRC began addressing this problem through "comprehensive governance," involving not only the health and birth systems but also civil affairs and police. The "crux was to head off the problem as far in advance as possible" (PI 040604). One countermeasure was to strengthen marriage registration and accompanying premarital examinations, including "informatization" of that process (PI 030819, 030926, 040518, 040722, 040820). Another countermeasure was to screen pregnancies for defective fetuses (PI 040604, 040906). From 2001 to 2004, about 70 percent of pregnant women accepted such screening and information (PI 041009, ZWQ). The health system continues experiments at deploying equipment for more comprehensive genetic screening, an expensive process that so far has had little payoff because only a small proportion of such problems is treatable (EW 4Nov03 BJ, 6Nov03 BJ, 10Nov03 QH).

A "SCIENTIFIC CONCEPT OF DEVELOPMENT"
AS A NEW GUIDING IDEOLOGY

By March 2004 the new Hu Jintao–Wen Jiabao administration had been in office for a year and had begun to establish its own new direction— indeed, a whole new guiding ideology for the nation's development strategy, including population. During 2003 Hu Jintao began advancing a new "scientific concept of development" (*kexue fazhan guan*) intended to increase the priority of social development relative to sheer economic growth (Fewsmith 2004). The October 2003 Third Plenum included the gist of Hu's idea in its updating of the PRC's economic reform program. In November the Politburo formally approved the slogan itself. Hu announced the new doctrine to the March 2004 National People's Congress and applied it to population at the 10 March 2004 summit (PI 040405). There he explained that "experience had shown," both in China and abroad, that it mattered greatly what concept guided development, which should be "human-centered, comprehensive, coordinated, and sustainable" (*yiren weiben, quanmian, xietiao, kechixiu de*). That concept met the overriding task of "the party leading the government and prospering the country" (*dang zhizheng xingguo*). For the population domain, his concept implied three main tasks that addressed all three of the dimensions of population posited in this book and both poles of modern power sketched by Foucault. Hu's premise was maintaining low fertility (quantity). His first task was strategic research and planning for regional development (location). His second task was the establishment of a new system of rewards and supports for couples whose security in old age had been compromised by their compliance with birth planning (microquality). His third task was special measures, for three to five years, to arrest the rise in sex ratios (macroquality). The population and birth program quickly shifted its attention to these new instructions and within six months claimed some progress toward those goals (PI 040317, 040817).

A Series of Social Policy Initiatives

Hu's instructions well illustrate the "governmentalization of population": the centrality of population to various forms of governance and vice versa. His instructions set the direction of policy in the population-and-birth domain for the mid-2000s, at least. The resulting array of experiments provides a unique window on more general processes.

These experiments deserve outsiders' attention for reasons that go far beyond birth planning or even social policy. They are a leading part of the PRC's ongoing institutional makeover. They bear the stamp of their Leninist origins, but they may provide the way out of some of the dilemmas of the Leninist project in China, particularly as manifested in birth planning. They provide a window, not only on the direct involvement of top national political leaders in birth planning, but also on their early twenty-first century project for China in general. The top-most PRC political leaders have invested considerable personal effort in deciding what to do about the PRC's birth program. After all, birth planning has remained one of the most controversial and politically sensitive policies in China. It also remains the PRC's main social program and a potential asset in associated programs such as public health, poverty reduction, and social security.

Not the least fascinating and consequential aspect is the absorption by these experiments, not only of international ideals of reproductive health and rights, but also of international techniques of project management and program evaluation, which contain the essence of the globalized "advanced liberal" slim state. This does not mean, of course, that the PRC regime has suddenly and fully become such a state, any more than the PRC has been able suddenly and fully to realize international ideals of reproductive rights. On the contrary, these experiments provide a window on the obstacles, contradictions, and dilemmas involved in this further stage in China's transition from autarkic twentieth-century communism toward an internationalized twenty-first-century future. For example, one of the main early 2000s exemplars of Comprehensive Reform was the northeast China city-region of Mudanjiang. One of the things at which it was exemplary was the drafting of many separate and extremely specific protocols for each of the experiments it undertook, often accompanied by feasibility studies and other up-to-date international procedures for policy project management (Mudanjiang 2002, 26–183).

Let us take Hu's three instructions to the population-and-birth program— and the resulting experiments—one at a time.

STRATEGIC PLANNING TO RESOLVE CONTRADICTIONS

Hu's first instruction was to do strategic planning.

First it is necessary to strengthen strategic research on population and to make medium and longterm development plans (*guihua*). It is necessary, on the foundation of stabilizing low-level fertility, to earnestly research resolution of conspicuous contradictions and problems of population development and to research the relationship between population and economic development, social progress, resource use, and environmental protection, offering scientific projections and corrective proposals. Establish a system of targets appropriate to the demands of a scientific concept of development and establish a comprehensive system for supporting national decision-making on population and development. Each district (*diqu*) must also make local population and development plans. (PI 040405)

The commission did not have the capacity to do all such planning itself but began mobilizing specialists who could do it (PI 030115, 040325). A major dimension of such planning was location, in the form of regional planning on a gigantic scale. Rural-to-urban migrants have tended to flow eastward from central and western China into one of three development cores along the coast: Beijing and Tianjin on the North China Plain, Shanghai in the Yangtze delta, and Guangzhou and Hong Kong in the Pearl River delta to the south. Evidently the idea was to facilitate the transfer of manpower out of agriculture and in the process to meet as many of the social needs of the migrants as possible. Heading this effort were key earlier players in birth policy and program. Jiang Zhenghua was originally a regional planner at Xi'an Jiaotong University, then vice minister in the birth commission, then head of a noncommunist party and a vice chairman of one of the PRC's two main representative bodies (the CPPCC). Song Jian was the control theorist whose calculations prompted the one-child policy (PI 030109).

"REWARDS AND SUPPORTS" AND "FEWER CHILDREN, FASTER PROSPERITY"

Hu's second instruction was, in effect, to further shift the program from reliance on negative penalties, such as the Social Compensation Fee, toward positive rewards, what the program has called "interest guidance" (PI 040720, 040726). The shift was particularly difficult and necessary in very poor localities, where peasants really needed the income from extra children and certainly could not pay fines for having them illegally. The regional focus of this effort was western China, whose development the PRC had begun trying to accelerate (Yu et al. 2000a; *China Quarterly* 2004; Naughton 2004a). The birth system selected a few counties in the northwest to begin experiments at "fewer births, faster prosperity" (*shaosheng, kuaifu*, a slogan that originated in east China in the 1990s). Rural couples of childbearing age who decided not to have a second child even though legally eligible to do so would receive payments (PI 040716). In 2004 those experiments were extended in the northwest and to the southwest (PI 041009, ZWQ).

However, the main thrust of Hu's instruction on incentives was more specific, to meet the program's promise that couples who had complied with birth limits when they were young would receive help when they were old if they needed it.

> Second it is necessary to create new thinking and mechanisms for birth planning and to complete construction of a system of rewards and supports for some rural couples who have practiced birth planning. Because presently the level of rural productivity is relatively low and social insurance capacity is weak, some masses wish to have male children and the aspiration to have more children is relatively

strong. Doing a good job of this mass work—aside from relying on propaganda, education, and guidance—also requires renovation of the thinking and mechanisms of birth planning, organically integrating the expansion of deep and meticulous ideological work with solving the masses' practical difficulties, providing rewards and supports for rural families that have practiced birth planning. It is necessary actively and adaptively (*tansuo*) to establish a rural social insurance system that is appropriate to the level of economic development and advantageous to birth planning, with emphasis on implementing rewards to rural families with one or two daughters and on implementing supports to families who have difficulties produced by the disability (*canji*) or death of their only child and by birth planning operations and [accompanying] illnesses (*fazheng*). Continue to organize work on the "fewer births, faster prosperity" project in the western region, increase the scale of support, and continuously expand the breadth of experiments. (PI 040405)

In response to these instructions, the population-and-birth program undertook several efforts to innovate social policies related to population. The project that targeted seniors in difficulty was a new system of "rewards and supports" (*jiangli fuhu*). As older rural couples reached age sixty and retired, those whose compliance with the one-to-two-child limit had prevented them from having a son would receive a "reward" of modest support payments for the rest of their life (the amount differing by locality). In addition, couples whose only child had died or become disabled, or who themselves had been injured by birth control operations or associated illness, would receive "support." Because PRC leaders regarded meeting these needs as a national obligation, the national government paid more than three-quarters of the cost of these experiments, at least in the poorer central and western regions. PRC leaders encouraged eastern provinces to undertake experiments at such a program as well (which many did) but those provinces had to pay the entire cost themselves (PI 040525, finance ministry regulations; PI 041009, ZWQ). Since the reward payments will eventually involve a significant proportion of rural couples the program will amount to the informal beginning, for at least some rural residents, of a long-needed retirement security program. One hope was that such assurances of security in their old age would make younger couples more willing to have daughters. Meanwhile the country continued research on broader self-funding old-age insurance systems (PI 031023, 031119).

CORRECTING DISTORTIONS IN SEX RATIO AT BIRTH

Hu's third instruction was to arrest the rise in the ratio of males to females among newborns.

Third it is necessary to highly emphasize the problem of the rising sex ratio at birth and to develop the necessary activities for special control (*zhuanxiang zhili huodong*). Statistics from the fifth national census [in 2000] show that our country's sex ratio at birth has risen continuously. Population sex ratios have their endogenous laws, and long-term imbalance can produce social problems. It is necessary to enlarge the scale of propaganda, deeply develop the "Action to Foster Girls" (*guan'ai nu'er xingdong*), advocate new social customs of gender equality and of fewer and better births. Complete the policy system [in order to] resolve the worries that families with girls have about problems at home (*hougu zhi you*). Strengthen responsibility systems, combine indicators for population quantity and indicators for sex ratio in evaluation, and strongly strive through three to five years of effort to arrest the momentum of the rise of sex ratios at birth. (PI 040405)

In response to these instructions, the population-and-birth program undertook a multipronged initiative. In collaboration with other ministries—particularly the party propaganda system, the government education system, and the women's association—the birth program was already running a long-term propaganda and education campaign to modernize China's reproductive culture (on new styles of marriage and childrearing). Now the program deepened that campaign through experiments at still more intensive promotion of gender equality in order to "foster" girls." The program targeted the eleven provinces with sex ratios at birth of more than 120 males to 100 females, within each province choosing one pilot county (PI 030411, 030925, 040306, 040325, 040726). After a year of experiments the program convened a large meeting in the quite poor county of Anxi in Fujian (PI 040813, 040817, 040930). Meanwhile the program orchestrated "comprehensive governance" of the sex ratio problem, bringing to bear the complementary powers of various ministries (PI 040906). Some success was declared in suppressing the private clinics that illegally determined fetal sex. Legal experts began discussing additional measures that could legitimately be backed by state enforcement (PI 040305, 040818). The women's association surveyed 242 officials at the ministry and department level who ostensibly should be helping combat the problem but whom the survey showed were gender biased themselves (PI 040903). The sex ratio problem was a daunting challenge because, as minister Zhang explained, although strict birth limits have aggravated the problem, they have not been its sole cause (PI 040813). (Chapter 9 treats the sex ratio issue.)

Comprehensive Reform

Following Hu's instructions would require considerable institutional capacity.

COMPREHENSIVE REFORM: SCIENTIFIC MANAGEMENT AND MANAGED DEMOCRACY

An indicator of the significance of Comprehensive Reform was the direct personal involvement in its launching of Wang Zhongyu (introduced toward the end of Chapter 5). During Jiang Zemin's two main "administrations"—1993–1998 with premier Li Peng and 1998–2003 with premier Zhu Rongji—Wang was one of the PRC's highest political-administrative leaders. He became one of Zhu Rongji's closest associates in restructuring the PRC's public-sector economic institutions, a process that Comprehensive Reform of the birth system extended to public-sector social institutions. During the Jiang-Zhu administration, as a member and secretary general of the State Council, Wang became one of the PRC's principal leaders in modernizing public administration and personnel selection. A main theme was the need for more "scientific management" (their term), particularly more open and competitive personnel recruitment and promotion. In the late 1990s Wang also participated in a task force evaluating how far and how fast the PRC could proceed in democratization. The decision was, for the time being, to continue to limit elections to the community level. Political participation within their own communities could give citizens more say in matters immediately affecting their lives but, if properly managed, need not threaten the authoritarian structures and policies descending from above. Instead, "managed democracy" (our term) could relieve social pressures for broader political participation and make policies more implementable by assigning their enforcement to the community itself.

In the early 2000s Wang assumed supervision of the turn-of-the-millenium review of birth planning and its future (also described toward the end of Chapter 5). The main thrust was to reduce public dissatisfaction at the clumsy enforcement of birth limits and the poor quality of mandatory medical procedures. Conversely, the birth program should increase public satisfaction by legislating and propagandizing not just citizen duties but also citizen rights and by actually delivering positive health and related social benefits. Scientific management would renovate the program itself, enabling it to provide quality technical services, to convey modern reproductive culture, and to exercise lawful administration. Administratively, the crux was better personnel management and evaluation. The birth program must introduce open and competitive personnel selection and revise the criteria for personnel evaluation to emphasize the new objective of public satisfaction. Another important administrative ingredient was informatization, which would facilitate communication between levels, improve management at each level, and reform the old planning statistical system to assess citizens' needs and deliver services. Meanwhile managed democracy would assign the community the job of restraining both maladministration by local officials and the reproductive behavior of community couples, permitting a switch from childbearing according to plan to childbearing according to law. Within the legal limits on number of children, citizens could decide the timing of their childbearing without a plan issuing them permits, thereby saving both themselves and the government much red tape.

COMPREHENSIVE REFORM: GENERAL DIRECTION

Like much of the original idea for the birth program itself, many of these ideas for reforming it derive from the West, particularly the twin emphases on scientific management and on some form of democracy. For the past two decades, the PRC has ransacked the Western literature on many subjects, looking for concepts and methods with which to modernize itself. In birth planning this has of course meant consulting 1990s international standards for national programs of population limitation and reproductive health, including such slogans as "quality care" and "informed choice" and related analyses of the necessary cultural change. However, the literature most relevant to renovating PRC birth planning as an administrative system is that on organizational leadership and public administration. So the complexities in the PRC formulation of Comprehensive Reform, while admittedly half those of understanding Chinese Leninism, are at least half those simply of understanding recent Western ideas about how to run large-scale organizations.

The ideal of scientific management—now somewhat out-of-date in the West—resonates with the Marxist-Leninist aspiration to a social-scientific approach to running society. One of the main tools that PRC leaders have used to try to steer not just the birth program but the entire PRC regime is the Western method of "management by objectives," the trademark of one of the West's leading management theorists, Peter Drucker. The basic idea is that, to keep large-scale organizations on course, managers should carefully formulate the specific objectives that they are trying to achieve and then, in addition to simply communicating those objectives to the organization as ideas, systematically make them the basis for evaluating and rewarding performance. International project management employs the analogous idea of "logical framework analysis," which attempts to identify exactly what mechanisms the project assumes will produce what outcomes, directs the necessary resources to the key mechanisms, and makes them the focus for evaluating both program and personnel. PRC leaders have also picked up on a more recent and complementary theme in Western administrative theory, namely "human-centered" approaches to both service deliverers and clients.

The guiding ideology for Comprehensive Reform has been the Deng Xiaoping Thought concocted in the mid-1990s, Jiang Zemin's Three Represents (July 2001), and Hu Jintao's human-centered "scientific concept of development," all embodied in the "spirit" of successive party congresses and plenums. The main line was set by the 2000 decision and summarized in Wang Zhongyu's five-phrase formula (discussed below). The "main emphasis" was now rural villages (particularly in the central and western regions), and the migrant population (still technically rural but outside their villages). In March 2001 the birth commission issued "guiding views" for Comprehensive Reform that listed four policy directions and principles (*YB02*, 196–198). One substantive direction addressed the statist elements of the birth program, noting the need to preserve personnel and funding in the face of multiple reforms in local government organization and finance. Another substantive direction addressed the client-centered elements, stating that the "beginning and end" of Comprehensive Reform is to energetically solve the problem of "protecting the basic interests of the public of reproductive age and promoting the comprehensive development of individuals." The other two directions were procedural, urging localities to ground their experiments in reality by adapting pilot areas to the level of development and strength of program in particular localities and by phasing implementation into manageable stages. All this, said birth minister Zhang, is not just a matter of leadership style or work method, it is also a question of ideological standpoint and, therefore, "also a major political question" (*YB02*, 74–81).

Being genuinely comprehensive, this reform of PRC birth planning addresses a half-dozen main program "mechanisms," each containing several major subprocesses with their subsubprocesses and so on. The resulting complexity is rather daunting to the outside observer, and must be even more so to local political leaders, particularly because they have much more to do than just to reform birth planning. Nevertheless, this complexity shows that national political and program leaders are determined to reconstruct the program thoroughly and have thought through rather extensively what that requires (Yu, Lu, and Liu 2001). Comprehensive Reform identifies discrete mechanisms but intends that reforms should reinforce each other—across functions, across levels, and even across time. The instructions to localities are actually quite sensible, telling them not to imitate the final model of any other locality but rather to imitate successful examples of the process of analyzing and reforming each of these mechanisms under different local circumstances. As the national leaders say, Comprehensive Reform is a very large and very difficult project of "systems engineering."

COMPREHENSIVE REFORM: THE MUNICIPALITY OF
MUDANJIANG AS A NATIONAL MODEL

This chapter illustrates Comprehensive Reform through one of its main local models, the city-region of Mudanjiang in northeastern China. The point of choosing Mudianjiang as a national model was to show that even a fairly average locality can do Comprehensive Reform, provided it creatively adapts the overall goals to local conditions. Mudanjiang and its surrounding

province of Heilongjiang have done remarkably well. But as Wang Guoqiang, the national vice minister in overall charge of Comprehensive Reform
volunteered frankly "Mudanjiang was a painful process" (EW 7Nov03 BJ-
WGQ). And as the remarkable Mudanjiang birth director Zhao Jiuxiang
explained with equal candor, the city program wrote all the international
standards into its reform protocols and has done its utmost to meet them, but
everything is not possible immediately (EW 1Nov03 MDJ-ZJX).

Most local reports on pilot experiments begin by parroting national formulations, and Mudanjiang too made its lead principle Jiang Zemin's Three
Represents. However, Mudanjiang's formulation was noteworthy for situat-
ing its Comprehensive Reform in both domestic and international population
development. When the local birth director explains the process, he himself
presents it as an interaction of supranational, national, and subnational
influences (EW 1Nov03 MDJ-ZJX). In the mid-1990s a leading Chinese
demographer—the very first one the UNFPA sent abroad for training in the
early 1980s—had translated major international documents on reproductive
health and rights, including Judith Bruce's seminal paper on quality of care
(Gu ed. 1996; Bruce 1990). At that time the national birth commission did not
choose Mudanjiang as one of the pilots for quality-care experiments. Nevertheless the municipal birth commissioner resolved to make Mudanjiang into
a model anyway, using Gu's translations and other international materials.
Who would have thought that on the remote Sino-Russian border in the for-
ested mountains of Heilongjiang a local leader was mastering and critiquing
foreign literatures to adapt them to his local circumstance? With substantial
help from the provincial level, he succeeded in providing the best demonstration that such adaptation is what Comprehensive Reform is all about.

National program leaders chose Mudanjiang as a model for many reasons.
Its birth work had previously been outstanding within both province and
nation, achieving very high levels of propaganda work and service delivery,
public compliance and public satisfaction. Its reform work illustrated com-
prehensiveness, both vertically in a high level of attention from provincial
program leaders and horizontally in a high level of commitment from local
political leaders and a high level of cooperation from other local departments.
Mudanjiang had successfully implemented some of the bolder innovations
envisaged by Comprehensive Reform, particularly in reducing unnecessary
bureaucratic interference in people's lives. Its reform work was remarkably
even across all aspects of Comprehensive Reform, showing that it was possible
to successfully tackle all elements together. Its reform work was also remarkably even across communities—urban, suburban, and rural. It had achieved
extremely high levels of the public satisfaction that, ultimately, is what national leaders want Comprehensive Reform to produce.

Mudanjiang has done all of this in a relatively marginal corner of the country that, unlike the original models of Comprehensive Reform from coastal eastern Shandong, was not exceptionally advanced or prosperous. A glowing report posted in June 2002 by two inspectors from the national-commission seemed genuinely amazed by Mudanjiang's accomplishments, particularly the evenness of the work and the satisfaction of the public (SBPC 6 June 2002). However, Mudanjiang does have a distinctive advantage that has helped it do so well at enforcing birth limits, risking reforms, and pleasing the public. The fact that its northern counties are border ones that permit all couples two children greatly eases tension between local leaders, cadres, and public. It also gives reforms some margin for error, in case they should weaken the controls inducing people to have only one child. The special treatment accorded those border areas makes Mudanjiang a laboratory for how reforms might work in the rest of the country if the whole country were allowed a second child—this without any change in birth rules in Mudanjiang itself, which program leaders fear might de-stabilize policy enforcement not only in Mudanjiang but also throughout China.

Political Leadership across Ministerial Systems

One sense in which Comprehensive Reform is comprehensive is that it in-volves the relationship of the birth program to local political leaders and to other local programs. In the first instance, Comprehensive Reform is ad-dressed to those local political leaders, not to local birth program leaders. As Wang Zhongyu early explained, most of the difficulties faced by birth plan-ning at the turn of the millennium could not be solved by the birth system alone. In the PRC's dual administrative system, subnational birth commis-sions at each level basically report not to higher-level birth commissions but to party and government leaders at each level. Accordingly, to solve problems outside the program's own jurisdiction, subnational birth commissions must lobby local political leaders and other departments for the necessary cooper-ation. This is a difficult task, given the preoccupation of most local political leaders with promoting economic development and the preoccupation of most other departments with their own responsibilities. The task is made more difficult by drastic government reorganizations, shrinking government resources, and rapid socioeconomic development. Consequently Compre-hensive Reform is possible in a locality only if local political leaders adopt it as a major part of their own career performance. Achieving such cooperation from powerful people outside the program makes this the most difficult of the three levels of Comprehensive Reform.

NATIONAL LEADERSHIP

The national level has made three main contributions to helping subnational commissions perform their difficult lobbying task. All three of these contributions must be arduously replicated by subnational levels. However, subnational program leaders couldn't do that without national authorization, and subnational political leaders wouldn't do that without national political leaders themselves setting an example of personal effort.

First, corresponding to Wang Zhongyu's process of *policy promulgation*, the national level has issued a series of laws and regulations, as reported in Chapter 5. The 2001 national law gave the now population and birth commissions at all levels broader functions. More specific national regulations made it clearer what other departments are supposed to do and obliged them to do it. The three most important were the regulations on technical services, on the Social Compensation Fee, and on migrants. Second, corresponding to Wang Zhongyu's *comprehensive governance*, the national level has set an example by defining interdepartmental projects, such as the 1990s "three links" and the 2000s "rewards and supports." Third, the national level has given these demands heavy weight in its system for evaluating and promoting subnational political and program leaders, simplifying the criteria and shifting them from lowering population growth to raising public satisfaction. The national systems for evaluating party and government personnel will reward subnational political leaders for making birth planning and its Comprehensive Reform a high priority and for guaranteeing the necessary interdepartmental coordination and resources. Subnational leaders who fail to do so will receive bad marks in their performance evaluations and be denied awards, bonuses, and promotions. For the birth program too, personnel work is at the heart of Comprehensive Reform, and personnel managers have played a special role in it. To improve its performance, the birth program must recruit younger and better-educated people and provide them with career lines and evaluation systems to motivate them. Competitive personnel recruitment and evaluation is one of the main mechanisms for achieving program renovation (EW 30Oct03 BJ).

By the early twenty-first century, PRC birth planning appears to have moved beyond cycles of advance and consolidation toward a steady state of continuous incremental experiments. These involve much initiative from below and some involvement from abroad. Pilot experiments aim not so much to produce a working model that other localities must copy as to illustrate the process of adapting national policy to local conditions, as in Mudanjiang. Nevertheless the component of top-down social engineering and leader supervision remains strong. A brief review of the process of experiments at

Comprehensive Reform will illustrate an important feature of successful reform experiments—the closer vertical interaction and strong mutual support between the national, provincial, and local levels.

National political and program leaders played a strong guiding role. In September 2000 Wang Zhongyu personally inspected Shandong's three initial experiments. Commission vice minister Wang Guoqiang ran the February 2001 conference extending experiments to the sixteen localities. He listed some things to be tried and required a quite rapid timetable for progress reports by localities, promising that the birth commission would respond quickly to unfolding developments (*YB02*, 117–120). In March 2001 the birth commission issued his instructions as a formal directive (ibid., 196–198). In September 2001 the program convened a larger conference in Beijing that summarized results from the first year of experiments and extended them to additional localities (ibid., 141–142). At that conference birth minister Zhang Weiqing further elaborated the rationale for Comprehensive Reform, sketching some dimensions along which the experimenters should expect trade-offs (ibid., 74–81). In September 2002, just as the new national law was coming into effect, the program convened a national conference at Mudanjiang to review the first two years of experiments (*YB03*, 149–151). Again Wang Zhongyu attended and approved (ibid., 42–45). By then experiments were beginning in 182 localities (100 urban, 82 rural). Shandong had begun extending experiments to the entire province. Subsequently the national level continued to focus on a limited number of experiments, but by 2004 provinces were running experiments in 182 localities, including all localities in nine provinces (Heilongjiang, Liaoning, Shandong, Jiangsu, Zhejiang, Hubei, Hunan, Sichuan, and Guizhou—PI 041009, ZWQ).

Evidently national leaders did not hesitate to indicate what they liked and what they didn't in local pilot projects. Nevertheless a main effort was to facilitate exchange of experience between localities. In the course of 2002–2003 the program posted local plans and reports on its Population Information Network website for other localities to consult. Delegations from at least some experimental localities visited some of the others. For example, a delegation from Mudanjiang traveled to eight experimental locations in east China and to five in northwest China, learning particularly from Yichang in Hubei, from Shaoxing in Zhejiang, and from Bingzhou and Weifang in Shandong (Mudanjiang 2002, 231–256, 257–275). National leaders convened the two-year review in Mudanjiang so that delegates from around the country could see its work. In his speech at that conference, birth minister Zhang Weiqing remarked with evident satisfaction that, having toured the city-region, conference delegates had experienced the public's satisfaction for themselves (*YB03*, 91–97).

PROVINCIAL LEADERSHIP

The provincial contribution to Comprehensive Reform also was great. First, provincial political leaders laid the basis for comprehensive governance, by a series of measures. They included Comprehensive Reform as one of eight big projects in the provincial Tenth Five-Year Plan. They issued regulations on such matters as village self-government, labor markets, and community development. They established a provincial leading group for Comprehensive Reform, specified departmental responsibilities, wrote "guiding views," and designated provincial experimental units in twelve Heilongjiang localities. They even included interdepartmental cooperation on birth planning in the evaluation criteria for all relevant departments (e.g., police, civil affairs, industry and commerce, agriculture, culture, health, and labor). Second, the province launched a province-wide initiative in "management according to law," meaning not simply that implementation should not violate the law but that the whole system of regulating reproduction should shift from "birth according to plan" to "birth according to law." The whole province abolished permits for first children and authorized some experiments in abolishing permits for second children. It guaranteed funding for birth planning despite local finance reform. Third, the provincial birth commission launched elaborate initiatives in propaganda and education and in technical services (which included everything on the national agenda for reforming those subsystems, as discussed in the next section of this chapter). It also launched reforms of local systems of birth work and community recruitment of birth workers. (See SBPC September 2002, 41–50.)

Specifically as regards Mudanjiang, the provincial birth director visited the city some eleven times during its first two years of experiments. In late February 2001 the provincial birth commission convened a meeting in Mudanjiang of the provincial leading group for Comprehensive Reform to discuss the municipality's plans and to suggest revisions. Then in March it convened a meeting of subprovincial birth planning directors. Mudanjiang presented its revised plan and received suggestions (*jianyixing yijian*). Heilongjiang birth planning director Chun-yu Yongjie gave guidance (*zhidaoxing yijian*). (Based on SBPC 6 June 2002; EW Octo3 MDJ.)

MUNICIPAL LEADERSHIP

The contribution of the municipal government also was considerable. The main national report on Mudanjiang declared it a model not just for local birth programs but also for entire city governments, illustrating the effectiveness of comprehensive governance by local political leaders, relevant departments, and social forces. The main local political leader changed in the middle of this process, but the deputy mayor directly in charge of the process remained the same (Gao Fenghua). Besides, the arrival of a new political leader didn't matter, the Mudanjiang birth director said, "they all understand" (EW 1Nov03 MDJ-ZJX). Already by late 2000 the Mudanjiang birth commission had formulated six projects that it wanted to pursue. It presented them to the February 2001 national meeting in Shandong, which endorsed them and requested Mudanjiang to elaborate. After clearing the proposals with provincial program leaders, Mudanjiang program leaders presented their projects to city political leaders. The city government convened a meeting of relevant departments to discuss funding and staffing requirements, which the city then undertook to meet. Many times thereafter city political leaders suggested revisions to the program's experiments or negotiated with relevant agencies on the program's behalf. The city government declared 2002 the year for reforming birth planning and designated 2003 a year of deepening that reform. For their part, Mudanjiang program leaders actively sought the support of city political leaders, taking the initiative in communicating with them, negotiating with them, and hearing their views and suggestions. (See SBPC September 2002, 51–59, Mudanjiang party and government report to the Mudanjiang conference; SBPC 6 June 2002; EW 1Nov03 MDJ.)

Renovation of Subsystems within the Birth Program

A second sense in which Comprehensive Reform is comprehensive is that it involves extensive renovation of the birth program itself. Again, this requires national precedents, but again most of the work must be done at subnational levels. The main overall process is Wang Zhongyu's organizational renovation to deliver *quality service*. For this purpose, all three of the program's three main vertical systems require renovation. Also the program needs to achieve lawful administration, both in the negative sense of not using illegal methods to enforce birth limits and in the positive sense of using law as a sophisticated method of regulating behavior. None of this is easy, either technically in terms of the necessary skills and equipment or socially in terms of the necessary indoctrination and compliance. Nevertheless, because all the processes fall within the program's own jurisdiction, this is the easiest of the three levels of Comprehensive Reform.

PROGRAM SUBSYSTEMS: PROPAGANDA, SERVICES, ADMINISTRATION

One program subsystem needing further reform was the program's original mainstay, propaganda and education. "Quality service" includes "informed choice" and even "modern reproductive culture." Historically, propaganda and education on population and reproduction only slowly overcame the two main obstacles it faced: the problematic status of population theory within CCP ideology and the traditional reticence about sexuality within both regime and society. During different periods the PRC has adopted different approaches to sexuality, which have been reflected in the PRC's approach to birth control (Evans 1997). One was to allow experts to educate individuals about their own bodies for their own good and to propagandize national policy to motivate public compliance for national purposes. That approach prevailed from 1949 until 1958, to a lesser extent in the early 1960s, and to a greater and greater extent again after 1976. The other approach was simply to suppress any public discussion of such matters on the grounds that they distracted energies from socialist construction. That approach prevailed for most of the time between 1958 and 1977. Evidently Mao would not countenance intellectuals intervening between his Thought and the public mind. China paid a high price for that because in modern societies discourses of self-cultivation propagated by experts are much more effective than state propaganda. Since then the PRC has turned toward the more modern approach (Winckler 1998).

At the turn of the millennium, the main new propaganda project was a long-term campaign to introduce "new styles" (*xinfeng*) of marriage and childbearing into as many households as possible. The movement was launched at a large conference in Yan'an, the old CCP base area in northwestern China (ME 981017). The purpose of the campaign was nothing less than to modernize China's reproductive culture, acknowledged to be a task that was difficult and long term. Content included late marriage and late childbearing, fewer but better births, and gender equality—of male and female children, of capacity to carry on family lines, and of participation and responsibility in birth control. One purpose was to correct imbalanced sex ratios (EW 31Octo3 BJ). Most communities now had "population schools," whose curriculum supported reform efforts: political knowledge of the duties and rights in new legislation (necessary to exercise those rights) and practical familiarity with alternative methods of contraception (necessary to exercise informed choice). Introducing reproductive education for adolescents remained a struggle, but educators had produced teaching materials that began to be used, at least in big cities. The birth program also took the lead in assessing the country's knowledge of HIV/AIDS (very low) and began using its formidable propaganda apparatus to correct this (PI 031119, 031231).

A second program subsystem requiring further reform was another of the program's three main pillars, "technical services." Renovation was necessary to guarantee the quality of birth control clinical procedures and to provide other kinds of reproductive health care. The institutional context was the PRC's long-term project of building and maintaining a three-level rural service delivery system: one that combines fairly sophisticated capabilities at the county level (sterilization and treating complications from operations), some capabilities at the township level (abortion, sometimes sterilization), and elementary capabilities at the village level (IUD insertion and removal). The Mao era had relied on an overtaxed health system to provide birth control services, supplemented by paramedical "barefoot doctors." Overall, the legacy was technical capacity that was widespread but low quality. During upsurges in birth limitation this surfaced as waves of accompanying infections and medical accidents, typically followed by a national directive demanding that medical quality be "guaranteed" (e.g., EBP 630131, 640512; ME 740209, 780225; EBP 831215, 840528). The Deng era built a stand-alone birth system that supplemented the health system with some of its own local "service stations" and community clinics (Kaufman et al. 1992a). During the Jiang era emphasis shifted first toward upgrading the quality of already existing facilities and then toward trying to get the now separate reproductive health capacities in the health and birth systems to cooperate (ME 970318, 970620, 971121, 980407).

Finally, in the early 2000s, the State Council's new regulations on technical services instructed the two systems to collaborate on a local "technical services network" (*YB01*, 33−36, Decision; *YB02*, 33−36, regulations). Those regulations also called for recertifying all birth planning technical service workers to make sure that they meet necessary standards of medical competence. Given the checkered origins of older birth workers, that alone could significantly improve reproductive health care. The project of strengthening China's medical delivery system gained urgency as the country entered a crisis in the provision and affordability of health care and as the country suffered a series of progressively more threatening epidemics (bird flu, SARS, HIV/AIDS). Meanwhile, undercutting these ambitions, the birth program had to persuade localities to continue to provide essential birth control services free of charge, as Mao had instructed and as the 2001 Technical Services Regulations required. (For historical background, see CTHW2, 178−229, 230−259; CTBP 162−163; Chen ed. 1984, 203−240.)

To manage renovation of other areas, the third program subsystem requiring further reform was program administration. Program management had evolved from a few dozen health system administrators specializing in maternal and child health (under Mao) to several thousand birth system administrators (under Deng) to many tens of thousands (under Jiang). Effective management became increasingly crucial, particularly through competitive personnel procedures, rigorous management training, and modern information systems. (See CTHW2, 178–229, on MCH work; CTBP 293–308, on birth staff.)

From a modest start in the mid-1980s, the main technical renovation of administration became "informatization": computerization of record keeping and communication, both within the birth system and between it and society. The birth system is computerizing data on both program and clients and is making that data available "in house" to all levels of program administration. To provide information to both other local programs and the public, the birth system is also posting a great deal of information on the Internet: basic program policies, reproductive health advice, current program news and—for the process of Comprehensive Reform itself—local work plans and work reports. Both within the program and between program and society, informatization increases both service and control. On the one hand, informatization enables the program to deliver increasingly complex services to an increasingly complex and mobile society. On the other hand, it enables superiors to inspect subordinates' records and enables the program to monitor individuals' lives (*YB00*, 110–111; *YB01*, 140–141). Inspecting computerization in Shandong in September 2000, Wang Zhongyu expressed hope that informatization would facilitate renovation of management through "scientific decision-making" and "scientific management." However, he also cautioned against overenthusiasm in merging renovation and informatization, remarking that in doing so it was necessary to "start from reality" (*YB02*, 119, quoted by Wang Guoqiang in his February 2001 speech initiating Comprehensive Reform). There are some problems that informatization can't solve and some of the data remain inaccurate, he cautioned (EW 7Nov03 BJ-WGQ).

As noted above, the program's information systems proved their worth during the SARS crisis. Consequently, the program established a permanent nationwide system for monitoring migration that would be available in future emergencies and would in the meantime permit better coordination between places of origin and places of residence in monitoring compliance and delivering services (PI 030617, 041009). The program also set up a special information system to manage the new "rewards and supports" program, which again will eventually provide nationwide information on households (PI 040823, 040827, 041009).

Personnel work is central to power in Leninist systems, because it is through the nomenklatura that they define political positions, recruit incumbents, evaluate performance, and thereby manage careers. By the early 2000s evidently personnel work became central to Comprehensive Reform of birth planning as well. To find the right replacement leaders for its new tasks, from 1998 the birth commission began implementing a new method for appointing leading personnel through competition, the first central ministry to do so. The method involves a sophisticated combination of procedures: evaluating the candidate's previous performance, testing the candidate's mastery of various subjects, and allowing future subordinates to interview the candidate face-to-face. As a result, vice ministerships and department directorships have gradually gone to smart young people eager and able to advance reform. Personnel reform is very significant also for renovating the quality of work at the subnational and community levels. (See EW 6Mar02, 30Oct03 BJ-Cui; *YB02*, 189.)

Reform of personnel work involves not only recruitment but also evaluation. During the Mao era, the performance of personnel was evaluated only as they left one post for another, and then through relatively vague and political criteria. Since then, an elaborate system of management by objectives has become increasingly central to the ability of national political leaders to steer the policy direction of the PRC regime. This system originated in the late 1970s, partly through study of "advanced foreign models" of scientific management, partly through experience with responsibility systems for contracting agricultural output to individual households. First applied at the bottom of the system to farming households, such performance contracts gradually worked their way up the administrative hierarchy to include even provincial party and government leaders. As applied to administrators, the system is cumbersomely called the "management-by-objectives responsibility system" and can involve not only evaluating officials' performance but also requiring them to sign contracts specifying what they promise to achieve. It was by giving population objectives very heavy weight within this system— the power to "veto" any other accomplishments—that in the early 1990s national leaders succeeded in achieving the re-enforcement of birth limits reported in Chapter 4.

What is extraordinary about the application of management by objectives to PRC birth planning is that the same system that was used in the early 1990s to enforce hard birth planning has been used in the early 2000s to induce drastic reform of that hard approach. This is a major test of the ability of PRC leaders to steer their gargantuan regime toward further reform. Reweighting evaluation criteria was a leading feature of the Mudanjiang model, which shifted emphasis from population plan targets toward public satisfaction (though retaining popular compliance with law). In addition, as part of its move away from micromanagement of individual behavior, Mudanjiang loosened its requirements for local leaders. For local political leaders, Mudanjiang left only the general requirement that they should "specially research and solve from three to five difficult problems" and the specific requirement that they should "guarantee a per capita average expenditure of 5.8 yuan." For local program leaders, Mudanjiang substituted indicators for reform of such objectives as lawful administration, village self-government, quality service, and comprehensive governance. Finally, a main purpose of strong party leadership is to achieve interdepartmental coordination, which Mudanjiang has emphasized since the mid-1990s. In the early 2000s Mudanjiang even built incentives for interdepartmental coordination on birth planning into the personnel evaluation systems of other departments, offering the heads of other departments a substantial monetary reward for cooperation (e.g., 800 yuan, about 80 American dollars).

The PRC's growing reliance on personnel and program evaluation systems for steering China is more than a response to problems of Leninism. It is part of an epochal shift in all modern societies from more to less government and from more direct to less direct regulation (Dean 1999). The existing literature on evaluation in China largely fails to note this shift and its importance, although Maria Edin (2003) does refer to the "new public management" literature that is the flagship for this neoliberal revolution. Program leaders themselves note this shift when they correctly emphasize the difference between plan targets and evaluation criteria. Some even distinguish between "examination" (*kaohe*) as reproving and evaluation (*pinggu*) as fostering (PI 030123; EW 31Oct03 BJ-Chen). Thus, as much as possible, "advanced liberalism" replaces regulation of society with regulation of government itself, and it shifts from direct to indirect government support of social security (from government payments for which the state is responsible to insurance schemes for which individuals themselves are responsible). Although still a "late Leninist" regime, in the early twenty-first century the PRC has begun borrowing some of these "advanced liberal" techniques, particularly in its reform of birth planning, and particularly in the agenda of social security to which that program has progressed under its new "population" rubric.

REFORM FROM ABOVE: TOWARD "LAWFUL ADMINISTRATION"

At the interface between program and public, Wang Zongyu's slogan was *lawful administration*. Its first meaning was negative: no clumsy physical coercion.

Under Mao, birth planning lacked much legal basis and "lawfulness" was not a main basis for either citizen compliance or administrative restraint. Under Deng, constitutional provisions and local regulations made it a legal duty for citizens to practice contraception and obey birth rules. Under Jiang, the emphasis gradually became that administration itself must be lawful, respecting citizens' rights. Already in 1991 an important meeting on birth program legal work identified several behaviors that were unacceptable in cadre handling of noncomplying citizens, the Seven Don'ts (*qige bujun*). However, it took until 10 July 1995 for the national commission to rein in subnational behavior through a formal "notice" (*tongzhi*). Implementors were not permitted to: first, arrest or harm violators or their family members; second, destroy property; third, impound property without due process; fourth, add fees and levy fines at will; fifth, detain noncompliers' associates or retaliate against complainers; sixth, refuse permission for a legal birth in order to meet population plans; and seventh, organize pregnancy checks of unmarried women. National political and program leaders instructed the birth association to help monitor compliance with these new restraints (*YB01*, 42–43). By reducing the gap between nominal standards and actual cadre behavior, this notice and its implementation helped pave the way for drafting and passage of the 2001 law. Nevertheless, in the early 2000s even Heilongjiang claimed only that it had "basically" eliminated these proscribed methods (SBPC September 2002, 46).

The birth program's handling of the Seven Don'ts illustrates not only its determination to curb cadre abuse but also the delicacy of doing so. Despite having identified the problem in 1991, evidently the commission felt it couldn't correct it during the early 1990s re-enforcement. When the new rules were finally announced to provincial officials, reportedly many were in anguish over how they could possibly implement the birth policy under so many restrictions (EW 6Mar02 NJ). Nevertheless the Seven Don'ts were added to the performance evaluation criteria for officials in most localities, though serious problems persisted in some (*YB00*, 65). Both the existence and content of the new rules remained confidential, to protect the morale of grassroots personnel. During the late 1990s both the PRC and the program progressed toward "lawful administration," and the public began accepting birth planning more readily. Citing those reasons, in April 1999 the commission finally issued another notice partially declassifying the first one. Community birth workers should post the Seven Don'ts at township and village offices and should take the initiative in receiving relevant oversight from the public. However, they still should not publish the Seven Don'ts in their local newspaper and the commission notice still did not reveal the new rules themselves (*YB00*, 82).

In the early 2000s a main purpose of new national legislation and regulations on birth planning has been to institutionalize such legal standards and sanctions for cadre behavior. Toward superiors, the administration of birth planning should not involve such practices as systematically misreporting local conditions to make program performance and public compliance look better than it actually is. Toward the public, enforcement of birth planning should proceed in a "civilized" manner that does not infringe on the "lawful rights and interests" of citizens through various forms of maladministration, such as coercion and corruption. Corruption could be individual, with program administrators extracting bribes for such services as issuing a birth permit. Corruption could also be collective, with whole community governments extorting and misappropriating birth planning fines, sometimes even allowing illegal births for that purpose. Corruption could also involve both administrators and citizens, such as doctors certifying that medical procedures have been performed when they haven't or using birth system equipment to ascertain the sex of a fetus for the purpose of gender selection. (See Winckler 2002a.)

In the early 2000s vigilance continued against program abuses such as coercive implementation and pecuniary corruption by local cadres. Evidence of abuses derived mostly from Chinese media reports of successful prosecutions of errant local officials, which were intended both to warn officials against misconduct and to inform citizens of their rights (AFP in FBIS-CHI-2000-1116; AFP in FBIS-CHI-2001-0519). Some coercion continued because of cadre overeagerness not to be punished for failing at birth planning (AFP in FBIS-CHI-2001-0102). To combat this, in 2000 the program held a conference on lawful administration and issued circulars on establishing a permanent system for inspecting enforcement and on including lawful implementation in performance evaluation (*YBo1*, 85–86, 106–108). Other coercion continued through local extortion of fines or fees using birth planning as an excuse (AFP in FBIS-CHI-2000-1124). To combat this, the program began experiments with having noncompliers pay fines directly to county finance offices and it issued implementation rules for a crackdown on corruption (*YBo1*, 87–89, 114–115). In 2002 the program promulgated new "methods for collection and management of the social compensation fee" that allowed communities to make their own arrangements for how citizens pay fines but required that all funds be deposited in the county branch of the national state bank (*YBo3*, 46–47). To combat misreporting, the program issued methods for managing program statistics and surveys and sent out a circular on their implementation (*YBo1*, 116–118, 123–124).

FROM "BIRTH ACCORDING TO PLAN" TO
"BIRTH ACCORDING TO LAW"

The positive side of "lawful administration" is a shift from direct operation through central planning to indirect regulation through law. A main example is the abolition of permits for childbearing reported above. This simplification of procedure was initiated by large cities such as Beijing and Shanghai but then spread to many localities. One reason the national birth commission chose Mudanjiang as a model was that, in line with the general direction of national reform policies, Mudanjiang had conducted some bold experiments in this area. In its report to the September 2002 national conference, Mudanjiang called this change the "core" of its Comprehensive Reforms. Mudanjiang gradually abolished birth quotas and birth plans and substituted a practice of "individual apply, villagers review, village birth planning leading group approve" (Mudanjiang 2002, 276–284). Thus it is still necessary to obtain approval, even to have a first child, but the approval now comes from the community through the village government council, and evidently the assumption is that all legal applications should be approved. The result is then written on a public blackboard, in the order of approval and the likely date of delivery, retaining at least the form of "planning" (EW Nov03 MDJ, rural village).

After careful preparation, from 1 June 2002 Mudanjiang even began an experiment at abolishing permits—and even spacing requirements—for second children. Such an experiment is feasible in Mudanjiang's northern counties because all couples there are entitled to have two children, because the area is sparsely populated and on China's border. Within that two-child framework, birth work and popular compliance had achieved very high levels. Mudanjiang accompanied its report of these experiments with examples of citizens who voluntarily chose not to have a second child even though they were legally entitled to do so. This experiment was the only thing about which the national commission report expressed some alarm, noting that it contradicted the Heilongjiang provincial birth planning regulations and that the result would be "unpredictable." National program leaders allowed Mudanjiang to complete the experiment, and Mudanjiang's May 2003 work report confirmed that it did (however, not as a major reform of regulation but tucked at the end of a section on quality services). This is similar to how national program leaders treated 1980s experiments in allowing localities to permit "two children with spacing": then too they permitted localities to complete their nationally authorized experiments but set aside the results when national political leaders expressed reservations (Chapter 3; EBP 344–346, PPY speech). (See SBPC 6 June 2002; PI 050322.)

Village Self-Government and Mass Participation

A third sense in which Comprehensive Reform is comprehensive is that, at the basic level, it aspires to a complete overhaul of relationships between the birth program and the general public. Indeed, as noted above, reducing public dissatisfaction and increasing public satisfaction is the main ultimate purpose of the reform. As just discussed, a main way to do this has been—at the interface between the birth program and the general public—to provide lawful administration and to shift from plan to law. Within the community itself, the main strategy is managing birth work through *village self-government*, another part of Wang Zhongyu's summary slogan. The idea is to try to persuade elected village governments to enforce birth limits using their electorally confirmed authority, allowing village meetings to review village birth work, and urging couples to take responsibility for their own reproductive behavior. Assisting in this effort is the birth program's mass organization, the China Birth Planning Association. Because this level of Comprehensive Reform involves interaction with the general public, it is more difficult than that internal to the program just discussed. However, it is not as difficult as reforming external relations with political leaders and other programs discussed above, assuming birth rules that are not too distant from popular aspirations.

COMMUNITY AS A POLICY INSTRUMENT

All versions of Chinese Leninism have endorsed a "mass line" method of leadership that is intended to maintain—and that has required maintaining—good relations between leaders, cadres, and masses. These relationships are played out at the community level. The community is crucial for implementing a policy like birth planning that directly affects citizens' "vital interests" (*qieshen liyi*). The community level involves at least three basic relationships: overall relationship between regime and community (administration), the regime's use of community to help manage its agents within the community (cadres), and the regime's use of community to help manage individuals within the public (citizens). (See CTBP 250–272; Yang 2003; Huang 2004.)

As a matter of administration, "community" can be thought of as a "policy instrument" that regimes—including democracies—deliberately define and construct (Dean 1999, 170–171). Population programs will be more effective and efficient to the extent that they can enlist community support (e.g., Warwick 1986, on Indonesia). Also, it matters on what principles community is constructed and for what purpose. Different versions of Chinese Leninism have implied different definitions of community and produced different kinds of communities. For example, as an empirical fact, the higher the degree of collectivism in Chinese communities, the more strongly they implement birth planning (Huang and Yang 2004). PRC leaders have continued to devote much effort to "constructing" political community and to instilling some "political quality" into community cadres. For example, in 2004 the population and birth commission, the civil affairs ministry, and the birth association issued joint views on "strengthening and perfecting village democratic management and democratic supervision" (PI 041019). The commission itself established a leading group for training rural party cadres and party members through the commission personnel department (PI 040525).

The community provides the setting within which supervisors in the county and township must control operatives in the village and within which that lowest level of birth workers must attempt to control citizens' reproductive behavior. Technically, some communities will have more of the necessary administrative infrastructure and personnel funding than others. Socially, direct contact with the public exposes village operatives to numerous difficulties and temptations. However, for supervisors the presence of the public also provides an opportunity to enlist it in helping to supervise basic-level birth workers from below. What is crucial for regime purposes is that communities are the lowest possible level of regime intervention, the level at which individuals (or in the Chinese case households) are embedded in society. Communities involve face-to-face interaction and, as the "life-world" of the individuals composing them, are able to influence individuals through peer pressure. The PRC birth program has emphasized building capacity at the local and community levels since the mid-1980s. However, at the beginning of the twenty-first century, the program has declared a still more precise and ambitious focus, the immediate neighborhood within which citizens reside *within* the community. In urban areas this neighborhood is the large residential bloc ("community district" or *shequ*). In rural areas it is sub-village groupings of households (approximately the locus of the imperial *bao-jia* system and of Maoist commune production teams). On the one hand, an integrated service "door" at the residential neighborhood can provide a variety of services from different ministerial systems in a way that is more economical for the government (because delivery is through one outlet that combines many programs, instead of each program separately extending its services all the way to urban lanes and rural households). On the other hand, combining delivery at the community level is convenient for citizens. Mudanjiang has issued cards to citizens, allowing them to pick up contraceptives at any community center anywhere in the city, instead of only in their own lanes as before (EW 1Novo3 MDJ, urban district).

REFORM FROM BELOW: TOWARDS
"DEMOCRATIC SUPERVISION"

Top-down PRC efforts to control cadre behavior sound formidable. They do temporarily suppress some misbehaviors and catch some offenders. Nevertheless, as a permanent cure, they are expensive to maintain, not very effective, and disrupt routine work (Manion 1998). Among other problems, oversight from above through "police patrols" can address only one place at a time (Lupia and McCubbins 1994). Consequently, in the course of the 1990s, PRC leaders began resorting also to oversight from below through "fire alarms" that members of the public, whenever they experience poor implementation, can sound at little cost to the state (ibid.). Though these forms of public supervision are managed to suit regime purposes, they have brought significant pressure to bear on birth workers to avoid clumsy implementation.

One reason such bottom-up mechanisms are important in the PRC is the weakness of supervision "from beside" by parallel institutions, such as the mass media and mass associations. The media have carried some stories about maladministration in birth planning, but usually these have been by-products of top-down administrative investigations, not the product of independent investigative reporting by journalists. Mass organizations provided some feedback on implementation, but during the periods of advance, when such feedback was most needed, the main role assigned to mass organizations was enforcement. Nevertheless one reason the regime revived the women's association in 1983 was to monitor abuses against women and female infants during the strong enforcement of birth limits at that time (SG 20Nov99 BJ-LXJ). With the onset of reform in the mid-1990s, national leaders encouraged the birth association to monitor cadre behavior.

In the PRC one classic form of oversight from below has long been citizen complaints to public bureaucracies through "letters and visits" (*xinfang*). Periodically the regime has considered this a useful mechanism for obtaining feedback and has tried to correct the problems it revealed. Of course, in a Leninist regime it is the regime not the public that decides how much to encourage public complaints and how much weight to give them. Also, individual programs have some latitude for discouraging or ignoring complaints. Nevertheless, when political leaders want programs to take complaints seriously, evidently they can force them to do so. Historically, a high proportion of such complaints have concerned birth planning, and a high proportion of those have concerned botched medical procedures. During the enforcement campaigns in the early 1980s and early 1990s, such complaints were largely suppressed. During the relaxation of the middle 1980s and during the emphasis on public satisfaction since the middle 1990s, such feedback from citizens has been emphasized and the results carefully analyzed and reported internally. By the early 2000s, decline in complaints provided a measure of public satisfaction and of success at reform.

Another new form of bottom-up oversight has been direct supervision of village birth work from within the village itself. Here the primary channel is "village self-government," but village members of the birth association and other mass organizations could serve as well. A main function of village self-government is to make maladministration by cadres more difficult by subjecting implementation to public scrutiny. Mudanjiang has made a particular point of conducting elaborate public evaluations of cadres in those villages that have implemented village self-government and that therefore are able to conduct village self-management of birth planning. For example, in 2001–2003 Mudanjiang ran an evaluation process in which local administrators scored community cadres on seven main aspects of performance, using a numerical scoring system that assigned each aspect a certain number of points out of a thousand, with some of the aspects divided into subaspects (a total of nine), and all aspects divided into items (a total of 48)! The main aspects were propaganda ability (200 points), service ability (170), creativity (150), managerial correctness (100), work accomplishments (170), mass satisfaction rate (100), and items on which the contestant could win "extra points" (110). As usual in the PRC, winners received commendations. Less usual, those whose performance was judged to be particularly poor received punishment, and many of those were put on probation. Evidently the program genuinely does not want public satisfaction sacrificed to poor village birth work. (See Mudanjiang 2002, 89–93; Brehm and Gates 1997; O'Brien and Li 1999; Alpermann 2001; Saich and Yang 2003.)

MASS ORGANIZATION: THE BIRTH PLANNING ASSOCIATION

At the community level, during the heyday of hard birth planning, implementation relied heavily on mass organizations.

Under Mao, the party established mass organizations to secure control and to promote policies among specific population groups, such as workers, women, and youth (but not farmers). During intermittent birth planning campaigns these organizations were enjoined to help mobilize the public, but no permanent organization for birth planning was established. For birth planning, the most important mass organization was the All-China Women's Federation (*fulian*). Its village representative, the village "women's head," has had the onerous duty of enforcing birth policy in her village, which has meant imposing birth restrictions on her neighbors and relatives. Meanwhile the women's association has expressed no more than officially required enthusiasm for birth planning. These contradictions may explain the addition, under Jiang, of a special assistant in the village for birth planning, usually male (Alpermann 2001).

Under Deng, the party established the China Birth Planning Association (*jixie*), originally for elite functions. However, from the mid-1980s, to help promote birth planning at the community level, national leaders began expanding the BPA into a mass organization. Organizationally, it took the BPA the last half of the 1980s to reach the first half of China's three-quarters of a million administrative villages and the first half of the 1990s to reach the last half. By the end of the 1990s the BPA had 1.1 million local membership branches with 83 million volunteers: a branch in each of China's roughly one million natural villages, with an average of nearly ten volunteers in each village. Initially, BPA village branches were composed largely of reliable retirees (the "five olds" of party, government, associations, models, and elders). In the late 1990s, these older people were supplemented by young women of child-bearing age, likely to have better rapport with other such women and able to act as exemplars. BPA members are assigned a few households, usually ones with which they normally have intimate contact. (See CTBP 335–348; EW 4July93 BJ.)

During this stage of its development, from the point of view of the birth program, the purpose of the birth association was to perform key program functions of propagandizing and monitoring. BPA members mobilized the masses to comply with birth policy and to enforce the policy on each other. BPA members mobilized women for periodic gynecological inspections and for any required contraceptive operations, particularly during crash campaigns (EW 4July93 BJ). BPA members also acted as implementors (for example, getting women to report for their checkups) and as monitors (for example, observing whether a woman is contracepting or pregnant (Greenhalgh, Zhu, and Li 1994). One way in which the BPA was constrained to perform these functions at the community level was that, although its national-level headquarters was relatively independent and its subnational hierarchy had some separate funding and staff, at the community level the BPA normally had no personnel of its own and was run on a part-time basis by township birth administrators (EW 28Octo3 BJ).

Nevertheless the BPA soon developed another set of functions. With its huge membership, it has been able to help solve the particular "practical problems" of particular people that made them reluctant to comply with birth limits, thus tailoring enforcement to individual circumstance. China lacks a mass association for farmers, and the BPA began to play some of those roles—in rural areas doing "whatever was necessary" to help people. This was how the BPA helped pioneer the integration of birth work with collateral programs such as poverty alleviation. The BPA did not so much dole out welfare payments as help individuals or groups start small-scale agriculture-based money-making ventures. In addition, the BPA has helped link birth work to individual advancement (literacy and income) and to community development (nursery schools, old-age homes). In the early 2000s the BPA began assuming a potentially large role in combating HIV/AIDS, both educating young people and caring for victims. (EW 28Octo3 BJ). The BPA also mobilized as part of the population-and-birth system's capacity during the anti-SARS campaign (PI 030530).

In the mid-1990s, with the assistance of the International Planned Parenthood Federation and with regime encouragement, the BPA entered a new stage of development, providing an upward channel for public demands (BPA 1999). At first the demands were mostly complaints: early on, mostly against coercion; later, mostly against unfairness (e.g., regime officials' having children out-of-plan). Thus the BPA was starting to help monitor the lawfulness of administration "from below," at least partially switching its surveillance from citizens to cadres. In the late 1990s, public demands turned to constructive suggestions for how to deliver promised incentives and for other improvements, such as sanitation and roads. At the turn of the millennium, when PRC leaders began emphasizing mass satisfaction and democratic participation in birth work, the BPA helped with public supervision and community democratization. As a result of these reforms, to some extent in some places, the BPA has helped launch NGOs and strengthen civil society in China (ibid.).

Nevertheless the BPA has had chronic problems. The most general is, of course, that so far the PRC has allowed little space for organized groups in civil society. Under the slogan "small state, big society," the PRC is shrinking the state but so far not allowing society to expand, leaving a vacuum in between. Within the BPA's own leadership, reportedly factional conflict has significantly crippled the BPA's effectiveness (EW 4Nov03 BJ). At the mass level, despite years of effort to upgrade its community networks, BPA surveys have found only 30 percent of its branches to be highly effective and fully 30 percent to be largely ineffectual, leaving 40 percent only middling (BPA 1999, 43). This is probably approximately the pattern for village birth work as a whole. Subsequent BPA reports have claimed improvement, with the proportion of highly effective branches going up to 40 percent and the number of largely ineffectual ones falling to only 20 percent. Whether there has been much net gain remains doubtful. In 2001, BPA chairman Jiang Chunyun was still calling on BPA branches to "perform competently" in "real terms" (FBIS-CHI-2000–0527, Xinhua).

In 2000, celebrating its twentieth anniversary at its fifth quinquennial national congress, the BPA issued "opinions" on its future work, endorsed and circulated by the general offices of the party Central Committee and government State Council (*YB01*, 42–43). The opinions reiterated the BPA's classic mission of community-level propaganda and mobilization, but also called upon the BPA to continue to help solve citizens' practical difficulties and to participate in the construction of community-level democracy (*YB01*, 42–43). In the future, on the technical side, the BPA hopes to help deliver reproductive health services to the most disadvantaged portions of the population: poorer, younger, rural, or migrant. One BPA focus will be unmarried young people, whom the birth program has largely ignored and whose reproductive health needs are growing as people mature early and marry late (BPA 1999; EW 6Mar02 NJ). On the social side, the BPA's admirable "strategic vision" for the future is "to fill the gap in China between a shrinking public sector and a profit-seeking private sector" and "to position itself as China's major social development NGO" (BPA 1999; Peng 2000). Whether that promise can be realized remains to be seen.

Conclusion

The complexity, direction, and progress of Comprehensive Reform are well summarized by Heilongjiang's inventory of some twenty reforms that it was pursuing at the time of the Mudanjiang conference in September 2002, arranged in ascending order of difficulty and descending order of progress (see Table 2).

There is little reason to doubt that Comprehensive Reform will significantly improve the services that the population and birth program delivers and somewhat reduce some forms of government intervention in people's lives. It should significantly improve public attitudes toward the program. Nevertheless there is some reason to doubt that very many localities will be able to make very many of these reforms and that the parts will interact entirely as national leaders intend. Also, Westerners are likely to wonder whether—because ultimately the conduct and content of the reform is not democratic and because ultimately individuals still must arrive at the legally prescribed reproductive behaviors—such reform can produce genuine public satisfaction.

In any case, the main practical problem is funding (Winckler 2002a, end). Without redistributive subsidies from the national level, the extent to which the population-and-birth program will be able to help orchestrate social programs will differ greatly across localities, depending heavily on levels of development, prosperity, and revenues. In particular, localities with strong collective economies and therefore strong local tax bases, can further raise the level of social services they provide, which in some localities is already remarkable. However, without national redistribution of resources from rich areas to poor ones, poor localities will continue to have poor social programs. The future is therefore in the fine print of the financing. What will be crucial is the balance within Socialist Marketization between a neoliberal Marketizing approach that leaves communities self-reliant (as in classic

TABLE 2
Heilongjiang Population and Birth Policy Reforms
(By Degree of Difficulty and Extent of Progress)

RELATIVELY EASY AND FAR ADVANCED
Implementation of informed choice of contraceptive method
Development of elementary reproductive health service
Implementation of birth planning village self-government
Inclusion of birth planning in community development
Implementation of the "four mechanisms" for village birth workers
"Dual channel" management of birth planning finances
Perfection of propaganda and education for population and birth planning
Deepening the Three Links in birth planning
Perfecting management by objectives

MIDDLING DIFFICULTY AND IN PROCESS
Performance competitions between village birth workers
Creating quality care birth planning counties
Reform of management of technical services for birth planning
Establishing a stable system mechanism for investment in birth planning expenses
Reform of the personnel system in basic level birth planning agencies
Development of informatization of birth planning

RELATIVELY DIFFICULT AND JUST STARTED
Completing the incentive guidance system for birth planning and perfecting the mechanism for managing birth planning for migrants
In cities, promoting the establishment of basic old age insurance, basic health insurance, and social welfare
In villages, experimenting with social insurance for households with one or two daughters
Perfecting methods for management of childbearing

SOURCE: SBPC Sept 2002, 49.

Maoism) and a Socialist approach that redistributes resources to maintain some minimal equity. The apparent commitment of the Hu era to fulfilling the promises made to all Chinese by a previous generation of political leaders holds out some hope for happier future chapters in the history of PRC birth planning.

PART TWO

Social and Political Consequences

Social Politics and Cultural Logics

THE MASSIVE PROJECT of state birth planning charted in the previous part sought to effect radical change in the most fundamental unit of Chinese society, the family. How did Chinese society react to this attempt to re-engineer the quantity and quality of its members? What political dynamics emerged as the state sought to impose its radical new plans of reproductive modernization on society? What were the broad social and political consequences of the politics of population as it played out on multiple levels? Part 2 answers these questions by placing the birth project in its broad social, cultural, and political context. In this brief introduction we map out the analytic terrain, highlighting the constructs we will use and indicating how they fit together and fill out the broader analytic frameworks employed in this book.

Rationalizations, Interventions, Contestations, and Consequences

In examining the social dynamics and effects of the regime's biopolitical project, the governmentality perspective is especially illuminating, for it enables us to see forms of power that conventional state-centric approaches miss. As emphasized in Chapter 2, the governmentality perspective broadens the range of governing authorities to include the state, the professions, market forces, and individuals, placing them in a field of biopolitics that involves diverse rationalizations, interventions, contestations, and consequences. Part 1 focused on the changing rationalizations and interventions of the regime. Part 2 fills in the other parts of the biopolitical field, focusing especially on the contestations and consequences unfolding within society.

Chapter 7 examines the local or community politics of policy enforcement. It begins by mapping out the scientific rationales behind the regime's population project and the techniques of normalization by which policy-makers sought to create a globally competitive society standardized to the modern norms of low quantity and high quality. It then documents the negotiations and struggles that unfolded as the modern scientific norms of the state interacted with the traditional family and gender norms of rural Chinese society. The chapter uncovers a highly differentiated politics around population, which played out differently in the quantity and quality domains, in urban and rural locales, and in different historical eras. Complementing the previous part of the book, which traced the shift from Leninist to neoliberal modes of governance at the level of the regime, this chapter tracks that crucial transition at the level of society and its individual members. Finally, the chapter describes the new modes of subjectification by which birth planners sought to create new categories of persons, or subjects, essential to the success of the biopolitical project.

Chapters 8 and 9 turn to the broad effects of these interventions and contestations around population, focusing on effects of bureaucratic state power since around 1980 when the governmentalization of population has proceeded apace. The governmentality perspective suggests that the effects of biopolitical projects of population optimization will be mostly unpredicted, and in China, these two chapters show, they were. Chapter 8 traces the social and cultural effects, showing how the new modes of subjectification and other interventions not only remade Chinese society, but also reshaped the lives, bodies, and selves of virtually all children and all women of reproductive age. Chapter 8 underscores the powerful and insidious effects of biopower's rise on women. Chapter 9 charts the political consequences of the governmentalization of population for the party-state, state-society relations, and China's position in the global arena. Both chapters highlight the enormous productivity of this new power over life and the ambiguity of its effects, which in China stretched from the indubitably pernicious to the dubiously positive. By broadening the field of vital politics, the governmentality analytic allows us to see how virtually the whole society has come to be engaged in—and in the process remade by—this giant project of administering and fostering life. If the book's first part showed what is at stake for the regime in our choice of analytic perspective, the chapters in this part convey what is at stake for China's 1.3 billion people.

The Cultural Politics of Population

So far our analysis of population politics has emphasized the political-economic logics of the institutions of the regime. To understand the social consequences of the PRC's post-Mao population policies, however, we also need to attend to the logics of Chinese society and culture. Illuminating the cultural dimension of Chinese population politics is also important because each biopolitical configuration is historically, culturally, and politically contingent. In Part 1 we brought out the political specificity of China's project on population. Here we suggest aspects of Chinese culture that gave the PRC's project on life its distinctly Chinese character. In this section we identify three senses in which culture, broadly defined, is used in the following chapters: as official and unofficial discourse, as lived practice, and as ethics. Far from static, these cultural reasonings were actively reworked in response to the development of the market, the in-rush of global capital, and changes in China's international relations.

OFFICIAL AND UNOFFICIAL DISCOURSES ON POPULATION

The analysis of official ideology and discourse has long occupied an important place in the study of Chinese politics (e.g., Schurmann 1971; Schoenhals 1992; Dutton 1992; Apter and Saich 1994; Kluver 1996; Ji 2004). Discourse is fundamental to our analysis of population politics. We understand discourses not as linguistic systems, but as relatively bounded, historically specific bodies of knowledge that are productive—that is, that *do things* and have *material effects* (a point well brought out in Ferguson 1990). In other words, discourse does not simply reflect the world of politics, it also actively constitutes it. The first part of the book paid close attention to the discursive framings used by the state in formulating and implementing its population policies. In the chapters on consequences that follow, we explore the political role—and power—of three forms of discourse. Although they originate in different domains, these three modes of discourse are not distinct but rather cross-reference and sustain each other.

The first is *institutionalized population discourse*, that is, the framings, narratives, and representations produced by, and central to, the regime's population program. These framings reflect a changing mix of party-state, scientific, and "Chinese cultural" logics. Key elements of official population discourse include the putatively scientific framing of the population problem as a crisis of national modernization, the science-based norms of low quantity and high quality, and the official categories of the program, in particular, the central category planned/unplanned birth, which reflected the logics of the socialist state. These and other elements of official discourse had large and direct effects on population politics, for they were embedded in institutionalized policies and bureaucratic practices that were enforced on all citizens of reproductive age and backed by the coercive power of the regime.

A second form of official discourse is the set of *broad political and cultural discourses* that the birth program picked up and harnessed to facilitate enforcement. Many of these were rooted in China's unusual nineteenth- and twentieth-century history of struggles to modernize in response to changing international developments. Important examples include the larger, historically developed discourses on sexuality, which treated gender difference as a product of biology, reducing women to their reproductive bodies. Also consequential are the larger discourses on "the feudal peasant" and "the virtuous wife and good mother," which the program built on in creating its targets of reproductive surveillance and control. A final example is the party's longstanding narrative of "women's liberation under socialism." The birth program drew on this appealing narrative in rationalizing its work and propagandizing its benefits to women.

The third kind of discourse we will analyze is the *popular discourse* circulating in Chinese society, especially that concerning family, children, and gender. Popular discourses that featured importantly in population politics include peasant sayings about the value of children ("many children, much wealth" or, more recently, "many children, big burden") and parents' views about daughters ("goods on which one loses" or, these days, "those we cannot disappoint"). These understandings are especially interesting, because popular culture often reworks discourses propagated by the state, moving population thought and politics in new and surprising directions.

CULTURE AS LIVED PRACTICE

The post-Mao project on population combined Leninism and modern science into a powerful force for population change. Remarkably, both Deng-era strategies of societal transformation—Leninist political transformation and a "Stalinist" scientistic social systems engineering—ignored the role of actually existing Chinese culture in the social dynamics of population. The Leninist project on population framed traditional reproductive culture and social structure in Marxist terms as "feudal remnants" to be eradicated, replaced by modern socialist views and arrangements. While the Marxist-Leninist approach acknowledged the importance of culture if only to transform it, the cybernetic models that underlay the one-child policy were culture-free or culture-blind, excluding social and cultural factors by definition. Treating population as a biological entity existing in nature, those engineering-based systems models treated people like inanimate objects, to be manipulated like grain or steel. Indeed, it was precisely by ignoring Chinese culture and social structure that the creators of the post-Mao policy managed to conceive of the culturally unimaginable and socially unrealizable goal of one child for all.

Yet the targets of these interlocked projects of societal modernization operated by cultural logics that could be ignored only at great peril. Two aspects of popular culture, and especially peasant culture, would prove crucial, a gender logic that accorded males more value than females and an economic logic of intergenerational exchange within the family. As we will see, when the party tried to enforce its culture-modernizing or culture-free policy on Chinese society, these logics asserted themselves with great vigor, impressing themselves on the politics, policy, and effects of the PRC's population project and producing a cultural dynamic that would, if not undermine the one-child project, at least significantly alter its course. We examine these processes in Chapter 7 and their effects in Chapter 8.

NEW TERRAINS OF SINO-BIOETHICS

Westerners have long deemed China's post-Mao population policies ethically troubling. Surprising though it may sound to outsiders, ethical concerns were also central to the makers of China's one-child policy. They saw in population control an opportunity to present China as a global good citizen, a nation that would contribute to the world's welfare by controlling the growth of the world's largest population, and do so not through coercion, but through the socialist means of propaganda and education. The ethical question turned out to be more complicated than expected, however. Far from enhancing the ethical reputation of the PRC regime, the one-child project raised questions around the world about the use of coerced abortion and sterilization. Moreover, it imposed terrible moral quandaries on China's rural people: Is infant abandonment morally tolerable? When does late-term abortion become infanticide? Should women bear full responsibility for health-impairing contraceptive surgery? Although fear of state sanctions generally kept people from articulating these concerns at the level of public discourse, they certainly weighed such matters in private, filtering them through local understandings of right and wrong. This new bioethical field, which is part of the new configuration of power around population, has shaped the politics of population at community, national, and international levels. We examine it in Chapters 8 and 9.

Methods and Materials

The scholarly literature on the social politics and sociopolitical effects of the PRC's population project is growing, but it remains highly fragmented—by discipline (anthropology, political science, women's studies, or social demography), by location (urban or rural), by time period (most studies deal with the mid-1980s, early 1990s, or late 1990s), and by dimension of population politics (quantity control or quality enhancement, the latter much less studied). Thus, we have one set of studies of the politics of birth planning in China's villages and another group of studies of those dynamics in the cities, but the crucial similarities and differences between urban and rural birth planning remain unexplored. Similarly, the issues of quantity and quality have been treated in entirely different literatures, obscuring the intimate connections between the two projects. Despite widespread and warranted concern about the harmful effects of the birth policy, our knowledge of the damaging (and positive) effects is remarkably limited. Existing research has focused on the immediate demographic and social effects, leaving the broader social and political consequences uncharted. In the following chapters, we read in and across these diverse literatures, bringing them together with other materials in an effort to produce an overall assessment of the broad significance of the state's population project for Chinese politics writ small and large.

Because these effects have grown with the growing ambition of the state's projects on population, we focus here on the reform years, roughly the quarter-century from 1980 to the early 2000s, when birth planning was virtually synonymous with the one-child policy. Much of our discussion will deal with the Deng era of "hard" birth planning, the late 1970s to early 1990s, whose contentious politics and troubling effects provide an important part of the rationale for the Comprehensive Reform described in the preceding chapter. With the availability of a handful of ethnographies, many news items, and extensive interviews dealing with the early 2000s, we are also able to include in our analysis some of the striking social and political changes that are occurring in today's era of birth reform.

These chapters tell the story of the sprawling consequences of the one-child policy—some intended, many more unintended—from multiple vantage points outside the state population establishment. To get the broadest possible view of the difference birth planning has made, we draw on a wide array of materials, from our own field research and interviews conducted over many years to ethnographies of birth planning in particular localities, large-scale social, demographic, and health surveys, and accounts from the media. Although they deal with single villages or work units at particular times, the in-depth case studies of anthropologists illuminate the underlying political-economic and sociocultural dynamics involved, enabling us to identify larger trends in population politics that are likely to be more general. Given the limitations of our materials, we cannot document the diversity in local population politics, though the evidence suggests it was substantial (Kaufman et al. 1989; Short and Zhai 1998; Short, Ma, and Yu 2000). Instead, we attempt to identify a dominant pattern from which communities have deviated depending on local conditions. The insights of Chinese scholars and officials, especially those gathered through informal conversations, shed light on broader dynamics and sensitive developments that cannot easily be conveyed in print. The press reports provide compelling, "raw" accounts, often of the traumas and tragedies of individuals targeted for reproductive modernization during major campaigns for which there were no scholarly witnesses.

CHAPTER 7

The Shifting Local Politics of Population

WHEN THE PRC'S POST-Mao leadership created its project to radically "modernize" the quantity and quality of China's 1 billion people, it undertook an enterprise of enormous scope and difficulty. The challenges of putting this project into effect have been monumental. Previous chapters probed these challenges from the vantage point of the regime, looking at problems of policy design as they have appeared to political and program leaders seeking to administer an unpopular program and achieve its targets against great odds. This chapter leaves the state apparatus and drops down into society to view the politics of enforcement from the vantage point of cadres and citizens in local communities trying to cope with the harsh reproductive demands emanating from above.

By now, even China's leaders openly acknowledge that the local politics of population, especially in the villages, has been grim and grievous. The Western media have told heartrending stories of fierce resistance and violent struggle, with grisly consequences for infant girls (e.g., Weisskopf 1985a, 1985b; WuDunn 1991a). The scholarly literature has portrayed rural population politics, and Chinese population politics more generally, as an unending struggle between a coercive state and a resistant society that continues to this day (e.g., Zhou 1996; White 2000b; Scharping 2003; also Aird 1990). Although this standard account of endless contestation captures important dimensions of the politics of population in some places and times (especially the rural areas during the long 1980s), it is a partial picture that neglects three important features of that politics. First, by focusing solely on the state's repressive project of drastically limiting population numbers, it has overlooked the second, more seductive project of enhancing the quality of the Chinese people. The politics of quality has been very different from the politics of quantity that has dominated our views of Chinese population affairs. In part because of this omission, the standard account has also missed the important transformations that have taken place, especially since the early 1990s, as marketization has accelerated and quality has overtaken quantity as the major domain of population politics. Finally, seeing power only as a negative force, the conventional account overlooks the positivity or productivity of power, which has given rise to new or transformed sites of struggle and arenas of contestation.

This chapter traces broad trends in the community (or face-to-face) politics of quantity and quality, in both rural and urban settings, over the first twenty-five years of the reform period. Although some parts of this story have been told before, the parts have never been connected into a larger account of the transformations that have occurred over the reform years. The bigger story we tell involves the rapid governmentalization of population; a shift in mode of governance from state bureaucratic power to professional discipline to individual self-regulation and self-cultivation; and, finally, the emergence of diverse and mostly unpredicted effects.

Our story starts in the central state, with PRC leaders' own views of their agenda and of what was at stake in the creation and imposition of tough new norms on China's people. Central to those views was modern science, a core logic in regimes of modern power. As we saw in Chapter 2, science—or scientistic claims—were key rationales in all the Leninist state-building projects undertaken by the PRC regime since the middle of the twentieth century. In the population arena, "modern science and technology" emerged as a forceful element of policymaking around 1979–1980, when the regime was initiating the construction of a powerful Soviet-style technocratic-bureaucratic state. Because this new and unusual "population science" so heavily shaped how the state's population project would interface with society, the roles of population science and of the larger "scientization" of politics and society in the reform era will be central themes in this and the following two chapters.

As noted earlier, the regime's post-Mao population project was part of a larger endeavor to rapidly modernize the country through selective absorption of Western science and technology. After the depredations of the Cultural Revolution, class struggle was dead, Marxian ideology moribund, the party's reputation nearly ruined. The modernizing Deng regime that came to power in 1978 sought to rebuild the regime's legitimacy by transforming the regime into a scientific modernizer that would draw on Western science and technology to lead the nation to the long-promised wealth, power, and global position. Population policy was a key site for the construction and later expansion of this new scientific authority rooted in nature, biology, and the body. Population was an opportune site for the development of the scientific state because the core constructs involved in its management lent themselves well to definition in biological terms. Reworking a broad set of putatively "scientific" discourses on sexuality fashioned in the early twentieth century, the post-Mao state defined these constructs—population (the quantity issue), race (the quality question), and gender (the instrument of reproductive management)—in starkly biological terms (Evans 1997; Dikotter 1995, 1998). Population was represented as a biological process of reproduction of individual organisms aggregated into a larger population. Race, often conflated in the Chinese discourse with nation (*minzu*), was construed as a biological entity to be eugenically enhanced to promote fitness and competitiveness of the national "organism" in a social Darwinist world of interracial and international competition (Sigley 1996). Finally, gender difference was defined as biological difference in reproductive structure and function, with women being by nature the primary reproducers. The use of these biologized constructs allowed the state to represent these forces of great potential—and, in the post-Mao era, of great threat—as impersonal processes "in nature" that had to be "objectively" investigated and managed by the state "in the interests of the nation as a whole." Through the use of modern population science and reproductive technology, the regime would take charge of these domains, creating a population of optimal size and characteristics that would both facilitate and symbolize China's status as a rising global power. In the late 1970s, modern science thus displaced the older, socialist planning rationale (of "grasping production and reproduction together") that had guided birth planning in the late Maoist years but now lacked force.[1] The socialist planning rationale was not abandoned, for it helped secure the continued legitimacy of the regime, but it took a back seat to the logic of state science.

Though largely ignored in the Western literature, the development of modern population science was crucial to the formulation of China's reform-era population policy and the emergence of a second site of governmental power, the disciplinary institutions of the professions, which in the PRC were closely connected to the state. Drawing on two closely related natural sciences borrowed from the West, population cybernetics and the population ecology of the Club of Rome, in the crucial transition of 1979–1980 China's problem of population was defined as a dual crisis: too many Chinese of too backward a type (for more, see Greenhalgh 2003b).[2] The solution was for the state to construct and energetically promote new norms guiding the production and cultivation of modern persons. The ultimate aim was to transform China's backward masses into a scientifically normalized, modern society (for more, Bakken 2000). In promoting this larger agenda, the post-Mao regime sought first to limit the growth rate and size of the population (*shaosheng*) and then to enhance its physical and mental quality (*yousheng*). Mobilizing a variety of human and life sciences—demography, developmental psychology, sexology, reproductive biology, and many more—to contribute to this new project on life, the state established putatively "scientific" norms of quantity and quality and then promoted them, initially by the time-honored campaign methods of the Maoist state, and then increasingly through the regulatory methods of the Dengist reform state (all detailed in Part 1) and the disciplinary techniques of the medical, educational, and other professions. The community politics of population focused on the negotiations and struggles that ensued as the state and the human disciplines tried to persuade, mobilize, or otherwise induce local society to adopt their norms.

The natural science that produced the new one-child norm defined social and cultural factors as irrelevant. Yet of course it was China's social structure and culture that gave local society the *community reproductive norms* that it would at times staunchly defend against the *scientific norms* of the state. The state labeled those social and cultural forces "feudal" and targeted them for eradication through "modernization." Yet they forced themselves in through the back door, impressing themselves first on informal community policies and then on formal national policy through the workings of the mass line. Social and cultural forces, in particular family socioeconomics and gender values, would come to play critical roles in the Chinese politics of population, leaving their imprint on the nature, intensity, and outcome of those negotiations and struggles. They will play a big part in the story told in this and the following chapter.

During the long 1980s (roughly 1979–1993, henceforth simply "the 1980s"), the dominant norm promoted by the state was one of quantity: one child for all. Because the state's quantity norm was set far below societal desires, the official norm was fundamentally negative, or repressive. For many years, and still today in many areas, efforts to instill that norm were fundamentally coercive, involving state use or threat of force (physical, legal, or otherwise) to impose the official norm on society. While this newly organized power over life was highly coercive, it was at the same time highly *productive* (in the sense explained in Chapter 2, the Problematique), giving rise to historically new (or revived and transformed) sites of struggle and arenas of contestation. In an era in which nature and science were the new grounds of authority, it was the biological reproducer, the reproductive-age woman, who became the object of state control. In this way, the bodies of women—in particular, married women of reproductive age (15–49)—became newly public sites of intense struggle over an array of reproductive issues that had long been matters of family politics but were now swept up into the maelstrom of state politics as well: contraception, the timing of reproductive events, and the number and sex of children. In China's son-loving culture, the struggles over the *number* of children soon became contests over the *gen-*

der of those offspring. In those contentions, infant bodies and even fetuses became a second newly salient site of fierce and sometimes deadly struggle.[3]

Because of the differing roles of children in city and village families, and because of widely varying enforcement environments, during the 1980s the politics of population numbers came to take different forms in urban and rural areas. In the urban areas, the state's continued control over the populace through the institutions of the workplace and neighborhood, coupled with lower childbearing preferences, limited popular resistance to the policy. There, in a classic example of the state's enforcement ideals—"propaganda and education as basic," "state guidance, mass voluntarism"—the politics of quantity took the form of the cadre production of "voluntarism," or politically conscious acceptance of state policy. With the exception of the politics of migrant fertility, which remains a serious challenge to the birth establishment to this day, the urban politics of population quantity was relatively smooth and stable over time.[4] By the early 1990s, if not sooner, the notion of the one-child family had become a staple of urban reproductive culture.

In the rural areas, by contrast, the peasant family's greater need for children, combined with the weakening of community enforcement structures, led to intense opposition to the one-child rule from peasants and local cadres alike. The result was a highly confrontational and unstable politics of population numbers. In stark contrast to the cities, in the villages policy enforcers had to resort to coercive campaigns, the state's least-favored means of enforcement, to suppress dissent and gain compliance. The literature on rural population politics suggests unending conflict, but a closer look reveals a historically variable "mass line" dynamic. In this dynamic the bottom-up preferences of local society, in particular for a son, came to shape central policy, and then that modified, now gendered, policy was reimposed from the top down on local society. Through such a mass-line process, during the 1980s the masculinist values of the peasantry became firmly embedded in national policy.

The 1990s ushered in a new era in the rural politics of numbers. During that decade profound transformations in the economy and the increasingly market-oriented farmer family lowered fertility desires, leading to a gradual convergence of state and villager fertility norms. These changes in rural society worked in tandem with the "client-centered" reforms in the birth program (described in Chapter 5) to produce a significant easing of tensions over birth planning in the more developed rural areas. From all appearances, by the turn of the millennium rural society was on its way to successful reproductive modernization following a one-to-two-child norm. Yet beneath the surface calm, another political storm was brewing over the gender of the one or two children that would get to be born. The politics of gender had not so much eased as been pushed back into the period before birth. By the late 1990s and early 2000s, the politics of quantity had produced a new site of reproductive struggle—the fetus—and a new politics of fetal gender and life.

While the birth commission continued to devote substantial attention to restricting quantity, in the 1990s and early 2000s the second issue, the enhancement of population "quality," has become increasingly central to the politics of population. The state's norms on population quality, far from suppressing desire, stimulated desire by tapping into widespread parental aspirations for the upward mobility (and future filiality) of their one (or two) children. If the one-child norm was repressive, the norm of the healthy, educated single child was highly seductive. In part because of the popular appeal of the quality norm, the politics of quality has followed a distinctive trajectory. Three specific trends can be discerned. First, with the shift to quality, the regulation of population has shifted from the state imposition of its norms on couples to parents willingly, even enthusiastically, embracing the ideals of health and education, and engaging in self-correction of their offspring to these popular norms. Indeed, the quality project has been a major site for the creation of the sorts of self-regulating, "autonomous," neoliberal subjects assumed by both the marketizing capitalist economy and the slimmed down neoliberalizing state described in Chapter 6. The "autonomy" of the self-regulating reproductive subject should not be thought of simply as the exercise of free will. That autonomy should be understood instead as a product of practices of government (deployed by the state bureaucracy, the professional disciplines, and the market) that have shaped individuals into the kinds of subjects who will exercise their freedom to upgrade their bodies and minds responsibly. Second, in the politics of quality, power has come to center on two new or reconfigured objects of societal investment and control: the "quality child" and the "good mother" responsible for cultivating that perfect youngster. Finally, the politics of quality has relocated power over population from the state birth planning bureaucracy to a much wider range of authorities, each striving to define the standards for child health and education and to get parents to adopt their standards and related practices and products.

With the shift to quality, therefore, the power to shape Chinese life has drifted away from the state into the hands of other social forces, most notably, as we will see, those associated with China's new consumer economy and culture. With this, a new set of logics—the logics of the capitalist market—has come to play a role in shaping the "quality" of the Chinese people. Clearly, in the arena of quality, the devolution in the locus of governance (from state bureaucracy to the professions, many state-affiliated, to individuals) has proceeded much faster and much further than in the arena of quantity. The politics of quality, like that of quantity, took root much earlier in the cities, though by the 1990s concern with quality had become an increasingly prominent feature of rural life as well. The basic political dynamics of population quality appear to be quite similar in urban and rural areas.

Between the early 1980s and early 2000s, then, the community politics of population has been undergoing four major if still far from complete shifts: from quantity to quality; from state regulation to professional disciplinary regulation to societal self-regulation; from concentration of power in the state bureaucracy to its dispersal to other, including global and corporate, actors; and from bureaucratic logics to professional/scientific logics to market logics. In producing new or reorganized objects and arenas of struggle, the politics of population has also become more feminized, more corporeal, and, for a time, more differentiated along urban-rural lines. In chronicling these transformations and productivities, this chapter documents at the community level the broad transition from Leninist to neoliberal biopolitics charted in this book. It begins with the struggles over population numbers in the villages, then turns to the conflicts over quantity and quality in the cities.

Creating One-to-Two-Child Families in the Villages: The Long 1980s

When the state launched the one-child policy in 1979–1980, its overriding objective was to create one-child families in the countryside, where roughly 80 percent of the Chinese people lived. If that goal could be achieved, policymakers believed, the problem of population numbers would be largely solved. Yet the norm of one child for all, the product of a biological systems science that excluded culture and social structure, was profoundly out of touch with the realities of rural China. That norm made no room for the central role of children in the peasant household socioeconomy or the gendered nature of personhood in Chinese culture. The social, cultural, and economic untenability of that new norm, coupled with an enforcement environment weakened by the rural economic reforms of the late 1970s and early 1980s, gave rise to a rapidly changing politics of population. Chapter 4 told the story of the oscillations of the long 1980s from the top down. Now we tell that story from the bottom up. As discussed in Part 1, the state sought to achieve its dominant norm of one child per family through the promotion of subsidiary norms, in particular, late marriage, late childbearing, and long child spacing. Yet the timing norms were distinctly secondary to the numerical norms. Throughout the 1980s and even the 1990s, enforcement efforts focused on achieving the one-child norm through the spread of long-term, "effective" contraception—sterilization or the IUD. Our focus then is on the negotiations and struggles over the one-child norm and the contraceptive means by which program leaders hoped it would be reached.

PEASANT REPRODUCTIVE DESIRES: THE SOCIAL
AND CULTURAL ROOTS OF SON HUNGER

Since the early 1980s, the childbearing preferences of China's peasants have become the focus of intense state and scholarly concern. From large-scale surveys to microstudies, all observers of the rural scene in the 1980s found the same thing among the Han majority: a fervent desire for two children and a lingering preference for three. As important as the number was the gender: at least one of those children had to be a son (Davin 1985; Wolf 1985; Whyte and Gu 1987; Greenhalgh and Li 1995; Zhang 2002; Scharping 2003).

Under the banner of Marxist theory, the state viewed peasant fertility preferences that differed from "modern" state norms as remnants of traditional "feudal" culture that could and should be eradicated through ideological persuasion or, if that did not work, veiled force. That approach failed to grasp the fundamental dynamics underlying peasant fertility preferences, with tragic consequences. A closer look at village life reveals that behind those expressed desires for two or three children and one son lay two fundamental features of village life: the central role of children in peasant household social and economic life, a role rooted in an intergenerational exchange of vital resources, and the gendered character of personhood in Chinese, especially rural Chinese, society. These features of rural life were indeed traditional, but they were not remnants of an older way of life that had simply persisted "over 2,000 years of Chinese feudalism," as the official discourse put it. Instead, they were reinvented traditions, traditions that had been actively reinvigorated by the political economy of Chinese socialism (Hobsbawm and Ranger eds. 1982; on the contemporary construction of "traditional" peasant family culture in the Maoist era, see Parish and Whyte 1978; Johnson 1983; Stacey 1983; in the reform years, see Selden 1993; Greenhalgh and Li 1995).

Throughout China's long agrarian history, the peasant family has been the central unit of social life, essential to the socioeconomic security and mobility of its members. The socialist revolution of the late twentieth century changed that only somewhat. Despite the collectivization of rural life and the socialist promise of welfare for all, Maoist policy privileged the cities in the distribution of resources, leaving the peasant family to continue playing central roles in the provision of old-age support and in production on private plots (Parish and Whyte 1978). The reforms of the early 1980s dismantled the collectives, privatized health care, and virtually abolished the minimal provision for old-age social security, making the family once again the core unit of production and welfare.

Children have long played crucial roles in the peasant family social and moral economy. Those roles were specified by an implicit intergenerational "contract," or set of social, economic, and moral exchanges between the generations. In these understandings, parents provided for the economic welfare of their children: support in childhood and adolescence; training for productive or reproductive work; dowries for daughters and property at the time of family division for sons. Children reciprocated by demonstrating filiality, contributing to the family economy and, for sons, supporting the parents in old age. As part of their filial duties, sons also had a moral obligation to pay respect to the ancestors and perpetuate the family line. Because of the patriarchal, patrilineal, and patrilocal nature of the Chinese family, personhood in Chinese society has long been gendered in such a way that boys were the children who counted.[5] Only a son could fulfill the duty to carry on the male-centered family line. Because sons would remain with their parents after marriage, parents invested more heavily in their upbringing and education with the expectation that they would support their parents well in old age. For girls, who would join their husbands' families at marriage, the intergenerational contract called for lower educational investments, for anything more would be "wasted" when they married out. Yet girls had important roles to play, especially in helping with housework and childcare. Girls were "small happinesses," as the documentary film with that title put it, but they were happinesses nonetheless.[6]

It was these cultural understandings and socioeconomic arrangements that lay behind the strong son preference expressed by Chinese villagers in the 1980s. In that decade, parents reported strong desires for sons to provide old-age support and, to a lesser extent, labor on the family farm and continuity of the family line (Cheng 1982; Wolf 1985; Whyte and Gu 1987). In some places, parents wanted sons to help defend the family against village bullies and other new predatory forces (Peng and Dai eds.1996; Zhang 2002). Although son preference dominated villagers' reproductive desires in the 1980s, ethnographers also discovered a persistent if less intense desire for a daughter to help with housework and farmwork, especially in parents' later years (Zhao and Zhu 1983; Wolf 1985; Greenhalgh 1993; Zhang 2002). The Shaanxi villagers with whom Greenhalgh worked cherished the image of later life in which their married daughter comes home to do the cooking, wash the laundry, and keep them company with stories of village affairs. It was the daughter who would ease the pain of old age by providing emotional comfort and bodily care.

The values of children to parents also reflected the costs of raising them imposed by the "discipline" of a rapidly developing market. Unlike the 1970s, when the arrival of a new child was rewarded by the state with extra rations and land (Parish and Whyte 1978), in the marketizing economy of the 1980s those incentives disappeared, while the costs of raising children climbed rapidly. Rural parents now faced rising costs not only of bare essentials, such as food and clothing, but also of schooling, health care, and weddings, whose costs had exploded in the reform years. The escalating costs of child care gave rise to a radically new discourse on children. Far from the longstanding view that "many children bring much wealth" (*duozi duofu*), children were now deemed heavy economic burdens (*fudan zhong*). As the 1980s wore on, desires for three children waned, giving way to a near-universal preference for two children—one son and one daughter (Greenhalgh and Li 1995; Zhang 2002).

Despite the diminishing of the family ideal, for village families much was at stake in ending up with two children, including at least one son. In the absence of public forms of social security and in a rapidly changing environment, sons were the vital and irreplaceable keys to economic security and, indeed, the very survival of the family. As a group of Anhui village women lamented, "There is no place in this world for those without sons. Even if it means death, we will keep trying for a son so that we may hold our heads high" (Weisskopf 1985b, A10). Their petition, evidently for reproductive relief, was published in the party organ *People's Daily*. These life-and-death stakes, coupled with the decimation of rural enforcement structures, set the stage for the confrontational politics of population that would unfold in the 1980s.

THE FORCEFUL IMPOSITION OF STATE NORMS (1979–1983)

In the late 1970s, when rural life was still organized in socialist collectives, birth planning was easy to enforce because brigade and team cadres controlled all the essentials of peasant life. As local cadres in Shaanxi explained, if couples failed to cooperate, officials could simply withhold, or threaten to withhold, essential goods, services, and income. Compliance would invariably follow (SG field research; also Parish and Whyte 1978; Nee 1981; Davin 1985).[7] By the early 1980s, however, that system of near-total control had been decimated, undermined by the rural economic and political reforms of 1979–1984 (White 1991, 1992; Greenhalgh 1993). By eliminating collective accounting, boosting peasant incomes, permitting geographic mobility, and reducing the power and prestige of local officials, the reforms opened up a host of new spaces in which peasants could resist the stringent reproductive demands of the center (Zhang 1982; Saith 1984; Wong 1984; White 1987). Decollectivization also strengthened villagers' beliefs that the rights over not only land but also children belonged to them (Wren 1982). The rural reforms also realigned village cadres' interests and loyalties more closely with local society. Decollectivization thus produced two deep-seated enforcement troubles for program managers at the political center: peasant opposition and peasant-cadre collusion.

In the early 1980s, when the state sought to impose its new one-child-for-all demand on the countryside, couples creatively exploited the new openings in the political environment to fiercely resist that demand. Resistance took a myriad forms, from forging documents to concealing pregnancies, bribing officials and doctors, refusing to pay fines, publicly cursing birth cadres, hiding with relatives, finding foster parents for unauthorized children, fleeing in advance of campaigns, migrating to carry a pregnancy to term and, later, joining communities of "birth planning guerrillas" who had escaped to the geographic margins to have babies (e.g., Zhang 1982; Wasserstrom 1984; Zhongguo Tongxun She 1989a; Tyler 1995; Zhou 1996; Ku 2003). In many areas, individual acts of defiance were supported by a larger culture of resistance in which whole villages would keep mum about the presence of a pregnant woman who had sought refuge there during a harsh campaign (Ku 2003). Among China's huge "floating population" of rural-to-urban migrants were not a few who moved in order to give birth to more children. Unrestricted by urban work units or residence officials, peasant communities in the cities sometimes served as "safe havens" where couples could have births without fear of being fined—to the great frustration of local birth planning officials. All these resistances bore the deep imprint of that urgent need for a son. Indeed, one of the most robust findings of the large literature on peasant childbearing is that those with a son largely complied with the birth policy, while those without resisted with a ferocity and sometimes savagery that no leader in Beijing seems to have anticipated.[8]

With successful enforcement defined as fulfillment of targets for births and birth control procedures, women's bodies became the central arena of reproductive struggle. Although women's bodies had been the targets of state efforts in the past, the early 1980s marked the first time the female reproductive body became the site of political struggle on a massive, society-wide scale.[9] Given the stakes involved for rural couples and the central state, the struggle would sometimes be ferocious. Assigned tough targets, village-level cadres focused their energies on the corporeal tasks that would prevent more babies from being born: aborting unauthorized pregnancies, getting women with one child to undergo IUD insertion, and sterilizing one member of couples (invariably the wife) with two or more children. Women resisted these pressures at the corporeal level—illegally removing their IUDs, undergoing fake sterilizations, and so on—giving rise to a new politics of the body that would have serious consequences for their health. Often the women themselves were the main agents in these negotiations. In a story that unfolded in countless villages across the country, a woman would negotiate with her friends and neighbors to conceal an unauthorized pregnancy, only to have it discovered late in the gestational term, a discovery invariably followed by a late-term abortion. The bodily struggles sometimes involved husbands as well. In one case in Guangdong's Longchuan County, a woman whose husband tried to remove her IUD hemorrhaged so badly that she had to be rushed to the hospital. Local officials gave wide publicity to this incident to discourage others from trying the same thing (Wren 1982).

To overcome such difficulties and "reach breakthroughs in population control," in 1983 national political and program leaders launched the first of what would be many nationwide crackdowns on births (Chapter 4). In this Maoist mobilization, local cadres were assigned impossible targets and quietly authorized to use any means necessary, including force and late-term abortions, to achieve them (Qian 1989, 132). The campaign was particularly vicious in Guangdong. In the best of the province's localities, targets were reached by ideological mobilization that could involve ten to twenty visits to the homes of recalcitrant couples by teams of officials (Wren 1982). In the worst of places, such as Dongguan County, where officials were instructed that "all actions that control population are correct," pregnant women were treated like the enemy. According to a Hong Kong reporter, big-bellied women were put in cowpens, handcuffed, and escorted to operating areas by armed personnel (Lo 1981). Another reporter observed women locked in detention cells or hauled before mass rallies and harangued into agreeing to abortions (Wren 1982). When officials in some places insisted on aborting and even sterilizing women with no sons, peasant couples, fearing the end of their families, responded by physically attacking the birth cadres. In one grisly case, a Guangdong peasant with two children pulled out his wife's IUD and got her pregnant. When the commune party secretary pressured the woman to get an abortion, her husband hacked him to death with a meat cleaver. The husband was executed (Weisskopf 1985a). Peasants desperate for another chance for a son also abandoned their baby girls, leaving them in cardboard boxes for others to find or, when a final solution seemed preferable, suffocating them or throwing their bodies into village wells (Yan 1983; Croll 2000). The situation was so serious that *People's Daily*, seeking to stop the violence, warned in early 1983 that "at present, the phenomena of butchering, drowning, and leaving to die female infants . . . have been very serious" (Li and Zhang 1983). With such grim developments, the infant body too became a new site of political struggle. In this first phase of the one-child policy, the state imposition of its putatively scientific but culturally blind norm produced a politics of population that turned out to be gendered, corporeal, and even deadly.

THE PEASANTIZATION OF STATE NORMS (1984–1988)

Facing damaged party-mass relations and fearing serious instability in the countryside, in early 1984 the party Center effectively acceded to peasant demands and authorized the addition of more exceptions to the one-child rule, while encouraging less harsh and coercive methods of birth work (Chapter 4). The relaxation at the Center allowed the emergence of a more negotiational style of politics at the village level. With a mandate from the center to loosen up and few tools with which to enforce a tough policy in any case, local cadres around the country struck reproductive bargains with village couples, resulting in the evolution of new, more lenient, informal community policies. Because villagers' demands for children included the demand for a son, those local policies were invariably male-gendered. In three closely observed Shaanxi villages, for example, all couples were allowed to have two children, including one son, in exchange for women's agreement not to press for more. Women who followed the local rules were exempted from the harsh contraceptive requirements of the center, an exemption that disappeared once they "caused trouble" by getting pregnant outside the plan (SG fieldwork). Similar kinds of cadre-peasant negotiations occurred elsewhere as well (Huang 1998; Potter and Potter 1990; Wasserstrom 1984).

Seeking to "perfect" the formal policy to improve compliance, policymakers in the provinces reacted to these local policy innovations and political pressures by formally expanding the conditions for second children to include the gender of the first. The result was an engenderment of formal policy, in which the majority of provinces and, in 1988, the political center modified the formal reproductive norms so that rural couples whose first child was a girl could have a second (Chapter 4; Zeng 1989). To legitimate that policy change, son preference was reformulated in official population discourse. No longer a "feudal remnant" to be eradicated, now, under the Dengist banner of "proceeding from reality," son preference became part of "peasant reality," to be accommodated until development took care of the problem (Greenhalgh 2001b). Through this mass-line process, the deadly politics of population had allowed peasants to press their most urgent reproductive need—for a son—on the state, leading to a peasantization of national population policy. Far from a minor rule change, the official adoption of this slightly relaxed "daughter-only" (dunuhu) policy, which remains the official policy in the early 2000s, would have broad political consequences. The new policy not only differentiated between urban and rural, creating different rules for each, it also distinguished between male and female, giving formal, indeed, legal recognition to the unequal value of sons and daughters.

Unfortunately, the relaxation of policy and enforcement in the mid-1980s, combined with shifts in age structure that bought huge numbers of women into childbearing age, led fertility to climb sharply in the late 1980s, prompting a tough re-enforcement of birth planning and reimposition of the now "stabilized" one-to-two-child policy in the early 1990s. Despite the slightly looser state fertility norm, strong pressure from the top, coupled with the adoption of uncompromising new enforcement measures, directed this time primarily at cadres, led to a severe tightening of central state control and intense pressures on local enforcers to demonstrate compliance (Chapter 4).

Local studies portray the early 1990s as a tense and terrible time in the history of birth planning. In Shandong and Henan, a rural sociologist saw campaign posters that virtually incited the use of force with such mottos as: "Treat birth planning [offenders] as landlords were treated during the Land Reform" and "Deng Xiaoping says that any method that reduces fertility is a good method" (SG 16Dec03 BJ). In the best of places, where state control over local society was tight and fertility low, the innovations of the early 1990s left villagers and local cadres caught in a tight net of control, able to respond only by silently acquiescing to state demands (Greenhalgh, Zhu, and Li 1994). In other places, where control from above was weak and fertility high, local cadres launched the requisite campaigns but engaged in widespread collusion with peasants to resist state authority and cheat their superiors with false numbers (Zhang 2002). In yet other places, where state authority was uncertain and fertility high, local officials instituted brutally coercive campaigns—involving beating husbands, confiscating property, and demolishing houses—that drove people to violent extremes. In one Henan village, a peasant whose neighbor had informed local officials about his wife's fourth pregnancy crippled the neighbor's wife and young child before beating the man to death (WuDunn 1991c; also WuDunn 1991d). In a Yunnan township, a compulsory sterilization campaign provoked collective protests that injured bodies, upended lives, and destroyed local government institutions (Mueggler 2001).

Whether real or partly doctored from below, the statistics from the early 1990s showed that fertility fell markedly, suggesting that national program leaders had found a winning formula at last. The campaigns of the early 1990s marked the beginning of the end of the decade-long era of strongarmed state imposition of its norms and violent confrontation over rural childbearing. By 1993 measured fertility had fallen to about 1.8, and program leaders, victorious in the battle over numbers, began to shift gears.

Village Transformations: The 1990s and Early 2000s

Despite an unbending policy and the inescapability of birth planning, in the late 1990s and early 2000s both local officials and ordinary peasants in some closely studied villages have reported that tensions over birth planning have eased. A closer look at the rural politics of population reveals two changes that have softened the public conflicts over births. First, rural couples have found a cleaner, more "modern" way to stay within state limits on child numbers while achieving their gender preferences. Second, popular desires for children have declined, the end product of the decimation of the patriarchal peasant family brought on by a half century of socialist construction and marketizing reform. Although it is impossible to know how general these changes are—certainly, conflicts persist in some areas—they deserve close attention because they may well be harbingers of the future.

ENGINEERING GENDERED FAMILIES

The gendered state norm that was forcefully reimposed in the early 1990s did not solve the gender problem. In a rural society in which most couples wanted one son and one daughter, the new policy instead created new gender problems, with formidable consequences. The new, nationally uniform policy was more restrictive than the local policies that had preceded it, requiring villagers with a son to stop childbearing and allowing those with a daughter to have only one more even if it too was a girl. The new policy was enforced by tight administrative means—frequent gynecological exams for women, steep fines for couples, mandatory sterilization for those with two children, tough responsibility systems for cadres—that left local society few options but to comply. Rural couples coped with the new, rigidified policy by intensifying the engineering of their families. With coercive campaigns fading and women's health slowly gaining more program attention, in the 1990s the core struggles over reproduction shifted to the bodies of infant girls and, even more so, of fetuses.

As noted above, the first wave of such gender struggles had centered on infant girls. From the early 1980s, peasant couples had reluctantly begun disposing of their second and third daughters in a desperate attempt to get a son. Although outright infanticide seems to have declined during the 1980s (Croll 2000), Kay Johnson's important research on infant abandonment shows that that practice persisted and even flourished, especially during the forceful campaigns of the early 1980s and late 1980s to early 1990s. In Hubei and Hunan, where the "custom of throwing away [girl] babies" was especially entrenched, those campaigns led to the disposal of vast numbers of infants (Johnson 2004, 10; also Johansson and Nygren 1991; WuDunn 1991b). The abandoned children have been overwhelmingly healthy girls with no brothers, or with one or two sisters, indicating parents' efforts to work the rules to end up with a son.[10] In notes pinned to tiny bodies, villagers have excoriated the regime's birth policy for forcing them to resort to this extreme measure in order to get a son. In the tougher enforcement environment of the 1990s parents began abandoning their infant daughters for a new reason: to avoid newly steep fines (Johnson 2004; also AP 1999). In the 1990s and early 2000s, the decline in the number of girls born has also created a growing black market in newborn female bodies. Poor farmers desperate for a son or unable to afford the crippling fines for excess childbearing have sold their daughters to traffickers, who have marketed them to a society newly hungry for girls—to fill the longings of the childless, to make "complete families" of one boy and one girl, and to serve as child brides for poor village men (Rosenthal 2003). Local cadres, sympathetic to the villagers' plight and financially penalized for exceeding birth targets, have looked the other way.

By the 1990s, if not earlier, a second wave of struggles, this one centered on the unformed body of the fetus, began to overwhelm the first. From the mid-1980s, the spread of ultrasound-B machines into every corner of rural China introduced a new and improved way to ease the conflict between state and family fertility norms. For growing numbers of Chinese couples, prenatal sex determination followed by sex-selective abortion has become an attractive, indeed, a "modern" high-tech alternative to the crude and morally fraught disposal of already-living infants (Kristof 1993b). A path-breaking study by the Chinese scholar Chu Junhong (2001) suggests that, in parts of central China—and probably elsewhere as well—by the turn of the millennium feticide had become an everyday part of the culture of family formation. Over half the 820 women interviewed had used it on their most recent pregnancy, with as many as two-fifths scanning their first pregnancy and two-thirds scanning their last pregnancy. Almost 75 percent of women whose first child was a girl checked the sex of their second fetus, and virtually all (92 percent) aborted the second female fetus. While families ended up with the children they wanted, the sex ratio at birth soared—to 126 boys per 100 girls, even higher than the national average for rural areas of 120 (in 1999).

A MARKETIZATION OF VILLAGE FAMILY NORMS

Beginning in the 1980s and accelerating through the 1990s and early 2000s, the insistent promotion of birth planning, combined with far-reaching transformations in the economy and family, have been fostering profound changes in cultural desires for children in China's villages. Already in the mid-1980s, farm couples were expressing strong preferences for small families of one son and one daughter. With growing marketization and urban migration, how-

TABLE 3
Childbearing preferences, 2001

Ideal number of children	China (%)	Rural (%)	Urban (%)
0	1.1	0.4	3.2
1	35.8	30.1	52.4
2	57.2	62.1	43.1
3+	5.9	7.5	1.4
Mean	1.70	1.79	1.43

PERCENTAGE NAMING ONE CHILD AS IDEAL, BY AGE

Age	China	Rural	Urban
15–19	50.1	47.0	60.1
20–24	51.9	48.7	61.4
25–29	41.7	35.4	60.8
30–34	33.1	27.0	51.2
35–39	29.8	23.2	48.7
40–44	29.1	20.2	50.0
45–49	24.7	19.8	40.3
All groups	35.8	30.1	52.4

SOURCE: 2001 Reproductive Health Survey, based on responses from 39,140 women aged 15–49 to question about ideal family size. Data made available by Zhang Guangyu.

ever, villagers' desires for children continued to shrink and sharpen. In 2001, a national survey suggests, the rural ideal was 1.79 children, well below the ideal of the 1980s (see Table 3).[11] Although these data should be viewed with some caution, provincial data reveal a similar trend. In rural Jilin, for example, the ideal dropped from 2.5 children in 1986 to 1.6 in 1995 (Feng and Zheng 2002). Despite some difficulties interpreting answers to questions about family ideals in the context of a strong family size policy, both the consistency of the finding across surveys conducted around the same time and the size of the changes over time suggest that a real decline in family size preferences has been underway since the early 1990s, evident in all but the poorest areas of the country (Feng and Zheng 2002). Ethnographic data support and fill out this picture. Village ethnographies suggest that during the 1990s rural couples grew wary of having three children or two sons but more eager to raise a daughter (Judd 1994; Greenhalgh and Li 1995; Peng and Dai 1996; Zhang 2002). By the late 1990s and early 2000s, some young newlyweds were opting to stop at one, even if that one was a girl (Xie, Gu, and Hardee 2000; Zhang 2003; Yan 2003). In areas of Jiangsu and Hubei, the majority of young couples who qualified for a second birth because their first was a girl returned their quotas (PDSC 2003e; Zhang Hong, personal communication, 19 July

2003). While daughter desire is growing in some areas, in parts of south and central China (such as Anhui, Guangdong, Guizhou, and Jiangxi), son preference remains intense (Feng and Zheng 2002; Ku 2003; Murphy 2003; SG 11,12Dec03 BJ). One Fujianese peasant may have captured the prevailing sentiment in such places when he declared: "There are just two important things in life now, making money and having sons!" (Kristof 1993b, 3). Perhaps the most dramatic change is the growing willingness among the young to raise only one child. In the 2001 survey, an amazing 49 percent of rural women aged 20 to 24 indicated that a one-child family was their ideal (see Table 3). This is a huge and potentially very significant change.

Behind these transformations in reproductive culture lay decades of insistent propaganda and practice that assigned the right to decide the number of children to the state. Young couples marrying from the mid-1990s on had grown up with birth planning as part of the ambient political culture. The whole apparatus of state birth planning—from the crisis rationale to the restrictive rules to the strong carrots and sticks—had become part of the implicit assumptions and explicit calculations they brought to the issue of family formation (for some evidence, see Kristof 1990; Greenhalgh and Li 1995; Zhang 2002; Yan 2003). The state's long-term efforts to instill new norms played an important, if hard to measure, role in changing the culture of family formation.[12]

Just as culturally transformative, however, were the profound changes in family life brought about by China's deepening marketization and the spread of urban consumer culture accompanying it. To rural people throughout the country, the issue that loomed largest was that of child economics—the escalating costs and vanishing benefits of children (e.g., Yan 2003). In addition to the rising costs noted earlier and the indirect costs incurred from the loss of a busy mother's income, rural parents now had to budget for a new category of "incidental expenses" (*linghuaqian*) defined as necessary to enhance the bodies and minds of their youngsters: nutritional supplements, purchased snacks, educational toys, extra lessons, and more. Reflecting the heavy costs of childrearing, as well as the steep fines meted out to "excess" childbearers, families with several children were among the poorest in their villages, living proof that the old saying about many sons bringing much wealth made sense no more. Instead, more sons brought more worries (*duozi duochou*). Meanwhile, the youngest generation, having grown up in a media-saturated culture and in many cases having experienced city life firsthand, were living in imagined worlds that were urban rather than rural. Carrying modern urban culture, these returned migrants, now roughly one-third of all rural-to-urban migrants, are major forces for reproductive change in the villages (Murphy 2002). More interested in personal happiness than in family obligation, in the 1990s and early 2000s this more individualistic younger generation was pursuing dreams of a consumer-oriented urban lifestyle, complete with fancy clothes, modern appliances, popular youth culture products, nice homes, and nonfarm jobs. Several children were not part of this dream of a newly privatized family life (Murphy 2002; Xie, Gu, and Hardee 2000; PDSC 2003b, 2003e; on the rise of the private family, see Yan 2003). Nor even, it seems, was a son: Chinese social scientists report that young upwardly mobile rural couples are now growing less concerned about their child's gender than about its prospects for social mobility (SG 23Dec03 BJ).

Even as the costs of rearing children were rising, the economic and emotional advantages of having several were shrinking. Although children continued to contribute to the family economy, changes in the rural economy (declining plot sizes, a growing labor surplus) coupled with declining parental control over young people's incomes (a result in part of earlier family division and urban migration of youth) greatly reduced that contribution (Yan 2003; SG 23Dec03 BJ). For parents, however, the biggest and most frightening concern was the growing unwillingness of sons to honor their most fundamental obligation: to support them in old age (Yan 2003; Zhang 2004).

Behind that widespread decline in filiality lay the erosion of the male-centered intergenerational contract, the foundation and cement of Chinese peasant family life. Indeed, the values of children, and hence the desires for them, have dwindled precisely because the patriarchal family itself has been increasingly undermined by decades of socialist construction and marketizing reform. The socialization of the means of production during the collective era had already weakened the reciprocal bond between parents and sons by depriving parents of their major economic contribution to their sons, the family's landed estate. Marketizing reform greatly accelerated the process by handing resources and power to the young, including to young daughters-in-law, who succeeded in precipitating ever-earlier family division (Selden 1993; Judd 1994; Yan 2003; Wang 2004). In the 1980s the newly emerging unfiliality of sons was evident in bitter and very public family disputes between married brothers over which had to support the elderly parents (Greenhalgh 1994b; Zhang Hong 2001). In some areas, the 1990s brought the veritable collapse of the tradition of filial piety and the refusal of even only sons to respect their time-honored obligations. As time passed, growing numbers of rural parents found themselves virtually abandoned by their sons and fearful for their futures in an environment with neither social security nor health insurance (Yan 2003; Zhang Hong 2004; Pang, de Braun, and Rozelle 2004). Increasingly in the 2000s, the rural elderly are preferring to eke out a meager living on their own rather than suffer the conflict and abuse that often comes with co-residence with sons. Unable to afford medical care, when serious illness strikes, growing numbers are taking their own lives, contributing to a rising trend of elder suicide in the villages.

The growing unfiliality of sons, however, had one positive outcome: a newfound appreciation for the value of daughters. Already in the 1980s parents were expressing definite desires for daughters, seeing them as more emotionally caring than sons and gaining value in the labor market of the reform economy. By the late 1990s and early 2000s, village parents in some places were actively cultivating their daughters as emotional and even economic caregivers in old age (Murphy 2002; Zhang 2003; Yan 2003; also Miller 2004). Although still incipient, in at least some areas the desire for a daughter may be slowly becoming a preference for a daughter.

After years of violent struggle, in which peasants successfully impressed their son preferences into state fertility norms, the period of rapid marketization that began around 1993–1994 has seen a remarkable, if still partial, convergence in norms, in which couples in some areas have begun to embrace the official one-to-two-child norm as their own. Virtually unremarked in the Western literature on China's population politics, these changes in peasant fertility culture are politically significant. Together with other changes in the political and legal culture, including the spread of the notion of an individual's right to be free from official abuse, they have quietly enabled the routinizing reforms introduced to date. These cultural changes are also promoting a less conflictual politics of population in many villages today. In some localities, ethnographers and journalists report, birth planning is becoming more genuinely voluntary, and people's wishes are shaping their contraceptive and fertility practices in ways not seen since the 1960s (Chang 2001; Zhang 2002; PDSC 2003e; Yan 2003; Merli, Qian, and Smith 2004).[13] In those areas, the production of one high-quality child has become little short of a "popular social vogue" (PDSC 2003e, 20).

After 20 years of ferocious struggle over the planning of births, both China's rural people and observers of Chinese population politics can breathe a sigh of relief. Yet welcome though these changes are, they deserve at most ambivalent celebration, for the easing of tensions among the living has been achieved at the cost of spreading violence against the not-yet-born and a growing masculinization of Chinese society. We return to these consequences of the rural politics of population numbers in the next chapter.

Creating One-Child Families in the Cities: The 1980s

The conditions of urban life gave rise to a much less confrontational politics of population numbers. In the cities the combination of low childbearing desires and urbanites' structural dependence on their workplaces enabled birth cadres to enforce the one-child policy in the way long considered ideal by program leaders: with propaganda and education as the mainstay. A close look at the micropolitics of policy enforcement reveals urban birth work to be a classic case of the political production of "voluntarism" (Vogel 1967). Through tight institutional control over the essentials of life and intense ideological indoctrination in the necessity of individual sacrifice in the face of national crisis, urban birth cadres succeeded in producing both reproductively disciplined female bodies and what women themselves described as "voluntary" (*ziyuan*) compliance with the one-child policy. This politically "conscientious" (*zijue*) voluntarism was not voluntarism in the sense of free choice. In the Chinese enforcement repertoire, however, it was the best of outcomes, the antithesis of the coerced compliance the party had to settle for in the villages.

URBAN REPRODUCTIVE DESIRES

Like their rural counterparts, in the 1980s the majority of urbanites considered the two-child family to be ideal, though city residents expressed no interest in having three children (Whyte and Gu 1987; Scharping 2003; Feng and Zheng 2002). Son preference, while still conspicuous, was also weaker in the cities. Indeed, among some groups, the 1980s saw the beginning of not merely an acceptance of but even a genuine preference for daughters, who were seen as emotionally closer to their parents and thus more likely to provide personal care in old age (Wolf 1985; Milwertz 1997).

These lower childbearing desires were rooted in a different constellation of child costs and benefits in the urban areas. Whereas in the villages sons were vital sources of labor and old-age security, in the cities parents supported themselves through wage-labor jobs that also provided pensions, the economic foundation of a secure old age. While the social and economic values of children were lower, the direct and indirect (or time) costs of raising children were much steeper in the cities.[14] Those costs rose rapidly in the 1980s, as prices of basic necessities climbed, the state and work unit cut back on social supports, and cultural expectations about the ingredients of proper childrearing grew ever more demanding. By the end of the decade, growing numbers of women were saying that they had the time, money, and energy to raise but one child (Milwertz 1997, 127; also Gates 1993). In the cities, the desire to have more than one child remained deep, but the realities of urban life limited the number of children parents were able to raise well and made sons less vital to family welfare and survival. These features of urban family life would make it easier to enforce the one-child norm.

THE PRODUCTION OF DISCIPLINED BODIES
AND REPRODUCTIVE "VOLUNTARISM"

Enforcement was also eased by the tight networks of control through which the regime managed the urban population. Even after the introduction of a private sector, the great majority of urban people remained employed in state-controlled organizations (Tang and Parish 2000). Couples' structural dependence on their workplaces, which provided not only jobs but also housing, health care, pensions, and other essentials, made active resistance to the one-child rule, if not impossible, then prohibitively costly, for violation of the policy might well bring loss of job and all that went with it. These mechanisms of control permitted birth cadres to enforce the policy through institutionally and ideologically produced "voluntarism," the Maoist ideal. Producing reproductive voluntarism involved the creation of disciplined bodies and accepting minds.

Tight institutional controls enabled birth cadres in the workplace and neighborhood to cooperate in the creation of maternal bodies highly disciplined according to the contraceptive and fertility norms of state policy. At their workplaces, women were subject to tight surveillance and control of their reproductive lives, with everything from their premarital health to their marital status, monthly periods, contraceptive practices, and pregnancies subject to close monitoring and mandatory management (e.g., Rofel 1999). Supplementing the vertical control of the workplace was the daily, horizontal surveillance achieved by the street or residential neighborhood, whose "granny police" of voluntary enforcers kept an eagle eye out for anomalous behaviors and tracked down the noncompliant (Burns 1985; WuDunn 1991c). Together the two formed a tight network of reproductive surveillance and control. Symbolic protests against the relentless control were possible—a woman might, for example, refuse to fill out the proper forms, skip mandated gynecological exams, or even manufacture a physiological excuse for not using an IUD. But there were few avenues for real escape (Croll 1985; Milwertz 1997; Rofel 1999).

Despite the gap between the popular two-child ideal and the state's one-child norm, Cecelia Milwertz's in-depth research in Beijing and Shenyang suggests that, after an initial period of hostility to the new norm, over the 1980s women came to the politically "conscientious acceptance" (*zijue jieshou*) of the state planning of one-child families (Milwertz 1997; on the early 1980s, see Croll 1985; Wolf 1985). Women's tolerant attitude toward cadres' micromanagement of their bodies stemmed in part from their acceptance of the official line that China faced a crisis of human numbers that was sabotaging its development, necessitating a policy of one child for all

(Milwertz 1997; Nie 1999, 131–139). Individuals must voluntarily submit to "the requirement of the nation," the women Milwertz studied felt, because the needs of the nation overrode their own. Despite the deep intrusions birth cadres made in their bodies and lives, women did not find those interventions offensive because they felt that the cadres were only doing the job assigned by their superiors, and they were exercising control in "concerned" (*guanxin*) and "caring" (*zhaogu*) ways. Caring policy enforcement was enforcement that took account of the needs and interests of the women—within the limits set by the policy. In a classic example of politically produced "voluntarism," the women Milwertz studied felt that their cooperation with the intrusive demands of the birth cadres was quite voluntary.

The urban and rural politics of population numbers that unfolded during the 1980s thus differed in systematic ways. Both forms of politics were corporeal and gendered, centering intensely on the control of the female reproductive body. However, in the cities, because meaningful resistance was virtually impossible, enforcement could rely on ideology rather than coercion. Although urban women were subject to structural or institutional coercion applied persistently over their reproductive lives, they escaped the violent crackdowns imposed on the peasantry. The urban politics of population also had a different temporality. Unlike rural policy enforcement, which grew severe and lax with cycles of coercion and resistance, the urban pattern of meticulous control and "voluntary" compliance was more stable. These two patterns of politics also produced differences in birth policy—a one-to-two-child (or daughter-only) policy in the villages and an ungendered one-child-for-all rule in the cities. Although these locational differences were sharp during the long 1980s, since the mid-1990s a combination of forces—massive rural-to-urban migration, the spread of urban consumer culture, the decline in rural childbearing desires, and important shifts in the birth program itself—has led to some blurring of the rural-urban distinction.

Producing the "Quality" Singleton in the Cities: The 1990s and Early 2000s

From the beginning, the state's effort to restrict population numbers was intimately linked to another initiative, that of guaranteeing the "quality" of the next generation. Launched in the late 1970s, the eugenics campaign—*yousheng youyu*, literally superior birth and childrearing—embraced a broad and eclectic array of scientific research programs, state policies, and social activities promoting top-quality health care and education for the young (Champagne 1992; Bakken 2000). (The slogan now has a third component, *youjiao*, for superior education.) Genetic improvement of future generations was certainly part of this. Yet far from mere genetic engineering, the PRC approach to producing quality citizens was based on the philosophy that people are formed by a wide range of genetic, environmental, and educational factors, most of which can be shaped so that that human potential is molded to meet national needs (Champagne 1992, 135–136). For the birth planning establishment, promoting the quality child simultaneously justified its widely unpopular big push for low quantity, and legitimated its claim to be a scientific modernizer capable of transforming China's people into a modern populace equipped to compete in the more global marketplace of the future. As a popular text on the education of the single child has put it, under conditions of economic and political competition in the twenty-first century, China's entry into the world requires a large pool of superior talents (*youxiu rencai*) with world-class educations based on modern science and technology and up to international standards (Wu ed. 2003, 86–88). The emphasis on quality also put a benign face on the one-child policy, presenting the party-state as a caring parent whose heart lay first and foremost with the young. State concerns both tapped into and further provoked parents' anxieties about whether their one (or, in the villages, two) offspring would not only survive but also grow into healthy, well-educated, competitive young adults able to succeed in a rapidly changing society and provide for them in old age.

Because the one-child family spread more rapidly in the cities, and because the scientific and political resources for population upgrading were concentrated in the urban areas, the quality project developed earlier in the cities than in the villages. In the urban areas, state and parental investments in the bodies and minds of the young began to grow rapidly in the 1980s, when the single child became the "sun" around which all planets revolved (Wren 1982). Investments in the young exploded in the 1990s, when China's consumer economy intensified and the quest for the perfect child became a veritable national obsession (WuDunn 1991a; Tyler 1996; Anagnost 1997b). Growing preferences for one-child families contributed to the intensified focus on creating perfect offspring. During the 1990s, the majority of urban women came to view one child as the ideal number. In 2001, 52.4 percent of all urban women and 61.1 percent of those in their twenties named the one-child family the ideal (Table 3). Most urbanites expressed no preference regarding the gender of their child. Indeed, in some studies, more respondents preferred daughters than sons (Feng and Zheng 2002). In the early 2000s, childbearing norms seem to have fallen even further. Young couples wanting no children (dubbed DINKS, for double income no kids) were a growing social presence, exceeding 10 percent of all reproductive-age couples in major cities, such as Shanghai and Beijing (*China Today* 2003). Quite a few urbanites who had

had one child in the 1980s said they would have remained childless had they known how much raising just one would cost (Fong 2004, 74–75).

By contrast, in the late 1980s and early 1990s, the rural population was more likely to be labeled "low in quality" and targeted for heavy-handed eugenic improvement and numerical control through the sterilization of those designated "unfit" and "drains on society" for "genetic" reasons (Chapter 4; Pearson 1995; Johnson 1997; Dikotter 1998).[15] Although the eugenic impulse has remained strong, the prevention of "defective" births has absorbed much less energy than the promotion of "quality" births. By the 1990s, state and parental efforts to upgrade child quality through the enrichment of child nutrition and education had become increasingly prominent features of village life as well (see, esp., Jing 2000b; Murphy 2004; see also Greenhalgh, Zhu, and Li 1994; Zhang 2003).

Judged by the amount of energy and other resources expended by a broad range of social forces, in the post-Deng era quality appears to be replacing quantity as the central arena of population politics. This shift marks a profound transformation in the nature of population power and politics in China. At the most general level, this was a metamorphosis from Leninist to neoliberal biopolitics. This reordering has involved three crucial developments. First, the shift to quality has introduced a new type of norm and, in turn, a new form of population regulation. The quantity norm has been fundamentally repressive, requiring continued, often coercive, regulatory efforts by the state to ensure enforcement. The quality norm, however, is seductive, coinciding with already sky-high popular aspirations for the next generation. State regulation has been accompanied by growing self-regulation emphasizing individual imperatives for parents to raise their children according to the new norms. Second, the shift to quality has given rise to two newly defined and central objects of societal investment and control: the "good mother," who disciplines her body and embraces scientific mothering practices, and the "quality child," who fosters his own bodily and mental capacities. These are neoliberal subjects par excellence.

Third, the emphasis on quality has brought an expansion in the number and range of authorities promulgating child ideals and, in turn, the rapid development of professional/disciplinary power over population and the emergence of the market as a major force disciplining individual desire. The birth commission and its science advisors have been virtually the sole authorities on population quantity. The authorities on child health and education are many and diverse, however, ranging from traditional Chinese medical and religious authorities to other agencies of the state (especially the medical and educational bureaucracies), to international organizations (such as WHO and agencies of the U.N.), to Chinese and transnational corporations. Each seeks to define the norms guiding health and education and to convince parents (and children themselves) to adopt their norms and related practices and products. As population quality is becoming the object of attention of growing numbers of social forces, the state's birth planning establishment is losing the power to directly shape the norms and practices guiding the cultivation of Chinese life to other entities, including, importantly, capitalist corporations. The growing role of transnational corporations, and of market logics of consumer desire and global fantasy more generally, is part of a larger globalization—and neoliberalization—of Chinese population politics charted in this book. This section illustrates some of these broad shifts, focusing on urban areas, where the politics of population quality is more developed and more systematically studied. It traces three aspects or phases of this politics: the production of a newly important subject, the "good mother;" the creation of scientific mothering practices and the disciplined maternal body; and the production of the ultimate goal, the disciplined "quality child."

PRODUCING THE "GOOD (SELF-SACRIFICING, SCIENTIFIC) MOTHER"

At the outset of the reform era, a broad array of social and cultural forces worked to define the quality project as a woman's—that is, a mother's—project. Together these forces created a newly salient subject, the "good mother," and defined her as one who would sacrifice her own interests for her child and use scientific methods to raise a "quality" youngster. The first agent shaping this maternal subject was the state bureaucracy. From the initiation of the one-child policy, the birth program targeted mothers as the key creators of the superior child. Focusing initially on newlyweds, birth planning workers and other agents of the state actively promoted "eugenic" (healthy) births to encourage adherence to the one-child rule (Evans 1997). Through premarital and prenatal testing, medical workers sought to prevent genetically problematic marriages and eliminate "poor quality" embryos, ensuring the genetic soundness of every child (Song 1985). The eugenic campaign gained momentum in the mid-1980s, when the educational efforts were broadened to include the health and education of the only child. In mandatory parenting classes, in propaganda disseminated through the media, and in contests on child-rearing knowledge, the birth program instructed mothers in scientific methods of bodily improvement (feeding, illness prevention, and so on) and intelligence enhancement, all directed at developing the child into a well-bodied, well-educated talent for the nation. These efforts were supported by a burgeoning and avidly consumed popular literature of books, magazines, and newspapers instructing parents, and especially mothers, on techniques for the production of "superior" children (Champagne 1992).[16]

Broader currents in the culture and economy actively supported the state's efforts to turn mothers into dedicated and skilled nurturers of their single children. The early 1980s was a time of renewed political and cultural emphasis on women's domestic roles—and corresponding deemphasis on their work roles (Robinson 1985; Jacka 1990). The state's efforts to upgrade population both benefited from these new notions of femininity and, in turn, contributed to them. In the Maoist years, state propaganda had stressed gender equality, promoting the ideal of the "iron girl" (*tie guniang*) who could compete successfully in the public sphere long dominated by men, while continuing to shoulder primary responsibility for domestic work. As part of the broader scientization and biologization of politics and society, in the early reform years the emphasis on gender similarity and equality gave way to a stress on gender difference and inequality located in the body (Woo 1994; Evans 1997; Yang 1999a, 1999b). Differences in reproductive physiology were now said to dictate a new division of labor, grounded in "nature," in which women's roles and identities were based largely on their activities in the domestic domain. In the early 1980s, when a tight labor market led to widespread calls for women to "return to the kitchen," the traditional notion of the "virtuous wife and good mother" (*xianqi liangmu*) was officially revived and reinforced to encourage women to take those domestic roles seriously (Honig and Hershatter 1988; Weeks 1989; Rosen 1991; Hooper 1998). Being a virtuous wife and good mother took on new meanings in the reform era, however. Instead of being blindly obedient to her husband, the modern woman was expected to become an active and skillful manager of family life—and cocreator, with the state, of the perfect single child.

With modern parenting defined as scientific parenting—where "scientific" denoted authoritative more than based on scientific research (Champagne 1992, 41–43)—and parenting largely a maternal affair, the mothering of a single child expanded into a demanding and complicated, yet important endeavor. Warning anxious new parents to rely on modern expertise rather than traditional wisdom purveyed by "backward" grandparents, the pedagogical materials divided child intelligence into some ten-odd specific abilities, listed parenting activities that promoted each, and presented developmental milestones and tests that parents could use to determine where their child ranked on the scale from "backward" to "prodigy." With every parent urged to create a genius, and those who shirked their duties labeled "sick in thought" (*sixiang bing*), the pressures on parents were intense (Champagne 1992). By the early 2000s, if not before, parents were expected to teach their youngsters not only arithmetic, Chinese characters, the arts, and emotional intelligence, but also English, a crucial skill for the twenty-first century. Popular books introduced children and their parents to such Western favorites as the songs "Old MacDonald Had a Farm" and "London Bridge Is Falling Down" and the fairy tales "Snow White" and "Cinderella" (Qu ed. 2001). With all these responsibilities on their shoulders, it is not surprising that, during the 1980s and 1990s, mothers of single children reported devoting more time, energy, and money to perfecting their one child than their own mothers had spent nurturing several youngsters (Milwertz 1997).

Despite the heavy demands of this new, intensive form of mothering and despite a recent history of apparently close identification with work outside the home, many women actively embraced their new roles as family nurturers who sacrificed their own needs for the sake of their children. They did so not only because the economy now devalued their paid labor while the culture tied women's worth to those reproductive and caregiving roles; the new emphases on mothering also dovetailed with their own intensified needs to ensure support from a child in old age. Although most city couples could expect pensions, those pensions were often inadequate (Unger 1993). Pensions for women were especially limited. Pension or not, a child was irreplaceable as a source of emotional support and, even more so, practical help, especially when illness or physical disability set in (Ikels 1996; Milwertz 1997). Sociological research shows that well into the reform era, adult children in urban areas provided extensive assistance to their elderly parents. While both sons and daughters supplied monetary support, daughters were more filial in providing daily assistance and personal care (Whyte and Xu 2003). Far from reducing the need for a child in old age, changes brought about by the reforms—in particular, wage reform, mandatory retirement, the reduction in pensions and state subsidies for health care, and the growing geographical mobility of children—worked to reinforce the importance of family support for the elderly (Ikels 1993; Whyte ed. 2003; Fong 2004). Moreover, with only one child, it became an urgent matter to ensure that the child would be willing to honor his or her filial obligations. Following the logic of the intergenerational contract, mothers dealt with these heightened anxieties by investing ever more heavily in their only child. Their aim was to cultivate gratitude and indebtedness in their child, so that the child would reciprocate with financial support, health care subsidies, and nursing care later on.[17] Anxious mothers went so far as to pay for pianos and piano lessons for their youngsters, not because they hoped the child would become a good pianist but to nurture in the child a sense of heavy obligation that would be fulfilled in later years (Milwertz 1997; Iritani 2003). In the 1980s, then, women's own worries about their future worked together with broader cultural shifts in the meaning of femininity and with birth planning's new emphasis on population quality to produce a generation of young mothers deeply committed to nurturing perfect children.

Creating healthy babies required healthy mothers embracing health-promoting maternal practices. To this end, the population and medical establishments have undertaken concerted efforts to encourage women to give up traditional practices surrounding pregnancy and infant feeding and to adopt the Western scientific, or biomedical, model of motherhood instead. Popular books on fetal education (*taijiao*) and eugenic births have depicted pregnancy and infant care as difficult tasks that could be successfully accomplished only with the help of medical experts and the charts, diagrams, and lists of standards offered in their pages (e.g., Wang ed. 2002; Liu and Zhang eds. 1999).

A centerpiece of these efforts was a large-scale government program, launched in the early 1990s in cooperation with the World Health Organization (WHO) and United Nations Children's Fund (UNICEF), to encourage women to breastfeed their infants. Suzanne Gottschang's anthropological research on the politics of breastfeeding in a Beijing maternity hospital illuminates the micropolitical dynamics surrounding child quality in the 1990s and early 2000s (Gottschang 2000, 2001). Those dynamics involve the struggles between competing—and cooperating—authorities to establish and instill maternal norms, and the growing success of foreign corporations and market logics of consumer desire in influencing health care practices.

Following U.N. and Chinese government guidelines, in the 1990s more than 5,000 urban hospitals were reorganized into "baby friendly hospitals." The dominant authority in restructuring these institutions was the science promoted by the state's birth planning and medical fields. Medical workers used a variety of means to get women to relinquish private judgment to medical experts, accepting scientific ideas and practices as authoritative. For example, hospital space and time were reorganized in ways that regulated women's ideas, practices, and bodies in relation to infant feeding. Mandatory prenatal classes, postpartum exercises, diet regimes, and breastfeeding sessions conveyed the message that medically guided bodily discipline is best to ensure the health of mother and child. Educational materials presented in classes, on posters, and in brochures also promoted the new routines as scientific, modern, and necessary for child health.

Science was not the only voice of authority in the hospital, however. Transnational consumer culture, with its temptations and sensualities, was also competing to establish and instill maternal norms. Exploited by food and pharmaceutical companies eager to sell health-related products, consumerist images of the sexy, slender maternal body were beamed out at young mothers in colorful advertisements and wall posters (Hooper 1998; Andrews and

Shen 2002). Advertising for maternal nutritional supplements and infant formula, while promoting the goods as scientific products that would foster the development of healthy infant brains, also presented images of the sexualized and consumerist mother who breastfed while remaining slim and beautiful. The two forces, state bureaucracy and capitalist corporation, not only competed by presenting differing norms for the maternal body, they also worked in tandem in appealing to science and modernity as bases for making health care decisions. Reflecting growing corporate influence on the state, foreign food corporations have actually participated in the construction of official child nutrition norms (Jing 2000a, 20).[18] In the hospital Gottschang studied, medical professionals distributed brochures prepared by multinational corporations to educate women about healthful practices, dispensing consumer advertising along with advice on health. Meantime, a third, quieter but still influential voice of authority, tradition, was competing for women's loyalties. Although tradition had no formal representation in the hospital, traditional Chinese medical and religious prescriptions for the care of the pregnant and postpartum body and the newborn, taught by mothers and grandmothers, also influenced young mothers' thinking.

In a wider culture that associates knowledge of scientific ideas and the consumption of scientific products with modernity, young mothers found the appeals to science seductive. All the mothers studied in depth wanted to raise healthy children and many indicated that they would consult a biomedical professional if they encountered health problems. The imperatives of producing a healthy infant, however, often conflicted with women's desires to maintain their own femininity in a culture that idealized the slender, sexualized body. Facing such conflicting norms, women followed some of the program's ideas, tried and rejected other recommended practices, and rejected still others outright. Many rebelled against the idea of attending classes, insisting that breastfeeding and mothering were "natural" activities on which their mothers were the main authorities in any case (Gottschang 2000, 175). Only one-third followed the WHO/UNICEF guideline and breastfed their infants the full recommended four months. In this microcosm of the societal politics of quality, the images and products of transnational consumerist culture were clearly gaining force relative to those of state science.

NURTURING THE "QUALITY (DISCIPLINED, CONSUMERIST, GLOBALIST) CHILD"

The ultimate goal of all these efforts was the "quality child," the personification and guarantor of a new and prosperous global future. In the 1980s, the birth program propagandized and promoted health and education, but other forces, each with its own interests, soon began to take over the work of creating that quality child. From the early 1980s, other government agencies, especially the Ministry of Health, working with the Chinese Academy of Preventive Medicine, began actively promoting child health and nutrition through the development of nutrition surveys, the establishment of dietary guidelines, and the formation of the Program for Chinese Children's Development for the 1990s. Still other agencies oversaw the creation of a children's food industry, the formulation of laws protecting children's health, and the establishment of agencies to enforce them (Guldan 2000; Zhao 2000). In the 1980s and 1990s children's health became a major government enterprise.

The 1990s brought a more economically driven mode of producing quality children. As in the West, in China the explosion of the market brought a growing commercialization of childhood and new definitions of child quality in terms of the consumption of consumer goods and services. Foreign firms played an active role in this process. Since the early 1990s, when corporations were permitted to advertise their products on television, big companies, including such prominent transnational firms as McDonalds, Kentucky Fried Chicken, and H. J. Heinz Co., have become some of the biggest promoters—and sellers—of "child quality." These companies have done what business firms do: define the public's needs in terms of the consumption of their products. McDonalds has been especially creative and successful in tapping into parental anxieties in order to create a market for its goods. The company has advertised its food as scientifically designed and nutritionally beneficial, while creating special child-centered events (such as talent and essay contests) orchestrated to entertain and educate the young diners (Yan 1997; on similar efforts by KFC, see Lozada 2000). Parents have responded enthusiastically, seeing opportunities to nurture the bodies and minds of their youngsters while giving them an opportunity to participate in transnational, especially American, culture. Exploiting the burgeoning opportunities in China, food and pharmaceutical companies have introduced an ever-proliferating number of infant, baby, and toddler products, associating their goods with science, modernity, foreignness, and progress. A visit to some of Beijing's stores for children in late 2003 revealed shelf after shelf of foreign goods—formula, food, breastfeeding devices, advice books, educational toys—all colorfully packaged and offered at much higher cost than Chinese goods. In the absence of strict regulation of product claims, scientistic exaggerations have become commonplace (Guo 2000). In the early 1990s, items such as chocolate and potato chips were promoted as "opening up [child] intelligence" (Anagnost 1997b, 217). By the early 2000s, even diapers were being promoted as products scientifically proven to develop the infant brain. Working with, through, and around the state, by the 2000s corporations had come to play an important role in establishing and instilling the norms of "quality" childhood, creating a young generation "deeply engaged with the products and advertising of global capitalism" (Davis and Sensenbrenner 2000, 54; on state-business relations, see Zhao Yang 2000). By the turn of the century, then, the politics of population quality had been deeply infused with the market logics of individual consumer desire and global consumption fantasy—the fantasy that one can participate in global culture and even become a kind of global person through the consumption of foreign, especially Western, products.

The production of the "quality" child has also brought striking shifts in the locus of population regulation. In the 1980s, the state's new norms for child health and education were eagerly, even anxiously, taken up and pursued by parents. With virtually all urban couples having but one child, that child, whether boy or girl, became a precious commodity. Parents and grandparents invested ever more heavily in their "little emperors and empresses," purchasing for them every health- and education-related food, toy, lesson, and experience available, in an effort to ensure their educational and career successes in an ever more competitive environment (Jing ed. 2000; Lozada 2000; Davis and Sensenbrenner 2000; Fong 2004; Rosen 2004). Such investments are fueled by such success stories as that told by the 2001 best seller, *Harvard Girl Liu Ying*, whose parents scientifically prepared their daughter from birth to get into Harvard University (Rosen 2004). Parents have made enormous sacrifices for their children, spending over half their monthly incomes on their youngsters. In the early 1990s, there were urban families who could not afford telephones or running hot water who nevertheless purchased computers and video games for their child (WuDunn 1991a).

These extraordinary efforts have been driven by the deep desires, anxieties, and fears of parents (Anagnost 1997b; Lei 2003; Fong 2004; Rosen 2004). The desire is to compensate for their own deprived Cultural Revolution childhoods by seeing that their child has everything they did not. Larger consumer investments in the young have also been motivated by the class anxiety of urban parents fearful of losing their privileged position in an economy marked by growing economic differentiation. Parents' obsessive focus on their children is also motivated by the fear that their only child might eventually abandon them—financially, socially, and/or emotionally. To counter that dreaded prospect, parents have "drowned their children in love" (*ni ai*) and commodities, in desperate hope that those investments will be reciprocated by filial comfort, economic support, and nursing care in old age.

With parental anxieties, corporate interests, professional and state concerns all converging on the single child, the result has been the production of a highly disciplined childhood, in which few periods and few arenas of the young child's life have been left unprogrammed. Unstructured play has been increasingly squeezed out of urban Chinese childhood. Over the

1980s, 1990s, and early 2000s, urban childhood has been subject to the "scientific" (educational, psychological, dietary, medical) disciplines of the professions and state bureaucracy and the consumer disciplines of the markets, all specifying norms for the quality child. With parents increasingly internalizing these norms and enforcing them as "self-disciplines" of the family, Chinese children growing up in these decades have lived closely monitored, managed, and even regimented lives (e.g., Tyler 1996).

Meantime, parental overindulgence in their singletons has led to further shifts in the locus of regulation and the emergence of the quintessential self-cultivating neoliberal subject. Parents anxious to secure their child's affections have allowed their youngsters to choose the toys, snacks, fast foods, and other items they will buy, turning them into increasingly independent and sophisticated "superconsumers" (WuDunn 1991a). Ethnographers report that children are now making decisions on everything from food to entertainment to large commodity purchases, including numerous items that affect their health, education, and training (Yan 1997; Watson ed. 1997; Chee 2000; Guo 2000; Lozada 2000; Iritani 2003). Companies are targeting children, directing their advertisements to young eyes and ears, in the process turning China's little emperors into what experts call the "single greatest force in determining consumer decisions today" (Tyler 1996, A6).

While the decision-making power of children should not be exaggerated, their growing role in making individual and household consumer decisions amounts to a new kind of self-regulation of population "quality": by the child himself or herself. These trends are noteworthy because in a culture whose glossy advertisements celebrate the foreign—especially the Western (*yang*)—children are increasingly choosing "trendy" products with global cachet, turning themselves into consumerist versions of the global citizens the state has long sought to create. In a process that the regime probably did not envision, certainly does not control, yet may ambivalently endorse—after all, a prosperous middle class is likely to support the regime—market forces have combined with the state's programmatic efforts and societal dynamics to create a new kind of highly independent, market-minded "quality" person who will increasingly make up the citizenry of twenty-first century China. The result is a kind of "autonomous," neoliberal subject whose interests, desires, and choices align with those of a neoliberalizing market and state that have shaped those interests, desires, and choices to their own ends.

CHAPTER 8

Restratifying Chinese Society

THE PREVIOUS CHAPTER charted the rapid governmentalization of population in the post-Mao years and the effects on those enjoined to be key actors in that process—reproductive women, mothers, and children. In this chapter and the next, we turn to the broader and deeper effects of the intensified governance of population on China's society and politics as a whole. In both chapters we deal somewhat with the effects of professional disciplinary power and individual self-cultivation, but our primary focus is on the effects of bureaucratic state power. Throughout most of the post-Mao period, the state was the dominant locus of population governance, and it was one with formidable powers to reorder social and political life. To understand the broad consequences of governmentalization—some predicted, many more unpredicted—we must begin then by understanding the larger capacities and projects of the PRC regime.

Since it came to power in 1949, the Chinese communist regime has sought to remake the Chinese social order through the creation and forceful imposition of new social categories. Such classifications of life have ranged from special categories created during the Cultural Revolution to punish class enemies, to broader classifications of class, residence, ethnicity, and gender designed to organize and regulate the whole population.[1] Yet the effects of these state projects have almost always differed from their lofty goals of creating a socialist modernity featuring a rapidly industrializing economy and egalitarian society. Only too often have these classifying practices replaced old stratifications with new and set some categories of persons back, even as others have been propelled forward. And so it has been with population.

The greatest social engineering venture of the reform era, the state's birth planning project sought to quantitatively trim and qualitatively upgrade the Chinese population in order to speed China's transformation into a global power. State birth planning has been politically very productive, creating new categorizations and kinds of persons (most crucially planned and unplanned children) that became objects of special treatment, for some rewarding, for others punishing. The state planning of births not only produced new lines of inequality, it also made use of existing divisions in society—in particular, between urban and rural, male and female—to facilitate implementation. Those social divides were accompanied by cultural discourses on peasant feudalism and female inferiority, which the birth program in effect harnessed to serve its ends. By making peasants and women the objects of intense reproductive surveillance and control, the birth program contributed to the striking increases in locational and gender inequality that have marked the reform era. (Little is known about the effect on ethnic inequality, a subject we therefore are unable to treat.[2]) By generating new disparities and exacerbating old ones, the post-Mao population project has worked to restratify Chinese society along reproductive lines. By this we mean two things. First, birth planning added a new, reproductive dimension to preexisting male-female and urban-rural inequalities, deepening those disparities in the process. Second, birth planning created new, reproductively defined and politically meaningful phases of the individual life cycle and categories of personhood in society: pre-, post- and reproductive womanhood; planned and unplanned personhood; and fetalhood, early infancy, and young childhood. Some of these phases of the life cycle have of course been socially and culturally marked before, but the birth program gave them sharp new political definition and content. The birth program has thus remade China's society in very fundamental ways.[3]

Throughout the 1980s and 1990s the official discourse on population highlighted the *intended achievements* of birth planning—births averted, contraceptive prevalence attained, and so on—while neglecting both the *human costs* borne by the targets of control and the *unintended problems* that developed when a demographically ambitious, putatively gender-neutral program interacted with a deeply gendered culture and society. To be sure, internal work reports of the government bureaucracy, such as those analyzed in earlier chapters, registered problems of implementation and how they should be overcome. Yet the impact of harsh enforcement methods on the people was rendered only in abstract political formulations, such as "strained party-mass relations," or in idealistic exhortations, such as "improve the quality of reproductive science and technology." Through such language, the human trauma of having one's body forcefully sterilized and one's hopes for a family cut short was removed from the official record of results and, in turn, from public and scholarly understanding of the larger consequences of the birth program. Also erased was the more concrete damage that has been done to many bodies and lives. Until the late 1990s, for example, the harmful effects on women's bodies and health of the obsessive drive to reach demographic targets were not even assessed, let alone addressed.

Since then the regime's attitude toward these matters has changed. As noted in Chapters 5 and 6, in its embrace of Comprehensive Reform for the twenty-first century the birth commission has acknowledged the damage done in the past, noting the "heavy side costs" of its demographic achievements, including the harm done the vital interests of women. With the active support of the Hu Jintao–Wen Jiabao administration, the commission has charted a new direction aimed at bringing genuine benefits to the people. Under the banners of "reproductive health" and "quality of care," many individuals and groups are working hard to undo the damage done in the past. These are promising developments. But for obvious political reasons, the regime cannot be too explicit or long-winded about the social and bodily price the one-child policy has exacted from the Chinese people. Moreover, many of the costs imposed on rural China in the 1980s and early 1990s are now unmeasurable. They cannot be measured because they were not assessed when they occurred and cannot be reconstructed retrospectively, and because the one-child policy has been enveloped in a climate of pervasive but unnameable fear that has forced its victims to suffer largely in silence (Nie 1999). As a result, even now, when those harmful effects are being officially acknowledged, the language remains vague, the costs largely uncatalogued and unmeasured, and the implicit biological constructs and sociopolitical hierarchies underlying the costs unchallenged. A partial assessment of those costs is the task we undertake here.

Even without precise measurement, it is clear that the human and bodily costs of rapid, essentially coerced fertility decline have been enormous, and unevenly distributed in such a way that it has been the most powerless members of Chinese society—rural women, infant girls, the unborn—who have endured the most. Some of these effects have been brought to light by concerned scholars and journalists, who have illuminated particular problems in particular places. When one steps back to examine the overall effects of state birth planning on China's society, however, the extent of social suffering and the scale of the costs incurred in the name of demographic modernization is staggering. Even the birth program's most vociferous Western critics have not added these up. Not only is the *scale* of the human problems imposed on China's people greater than has been appreciated—in China or the West— but the *scope* of those problems is broader as well. In addition to the oft-noted social-structural distortions and rarely mentioned bodily damage, that harm includes the cultural injury to people's subjectivity, or sense of self, and to their moral equanimity. In insistently rearranging bodies and lives, the state imposed a tangle of bioethical dilemmas on China's people, turning them into "moral pioneers" (Rapp 1999) forced to grapple with such life-and-death issues as abortion, sex selection, and infanticide largely in silence.[4] In this chapter we supplement the official record of achievements with an unofficial (and regrettably incomplete) record of the largely hidden costs of the PRC's muscular approach to population work. In other words, we try to count what the state program does not count, in the process tallying up the social costs—and some benefits—of the pursuit of demographic targets at any cost.

Stepping back from the official transcript also allows us to see that the state's historic neglect of these unintended problems and human traumas is not mere oversight but rather is part of a larger, systematic pattern of inattention to the human costs incurred in reaching "higher goals" for the country set by the political leadership. This pattern will be familiar to students of post-1949 China. One need but remember the Great Leap Forward to realize how pervasive—and costly—the regime's neglect of the people's welfare has been. Indeed, the historical record suggests that the state has not so much *neglected* as actively *produced* certain disadvantaged categories, a process that has allowed it to do and claim other things. In the population arena, during the 1980s and early 1990s, national program leaders were able to produce and claim great demographic gains precisely by not acknowledging, let alone addressing, the social suffering on which those gains were contingent. Reducing the stratifications and sufferings of such unwelcome new social categories as unplanned and abandoned children would have entailed losing some control over the birth rate and, in turn, a renewed threat of population "crisis." Indeed, the state's response went beyond apparent neglect to include actively obstructing solutions to some of the problems it inadvertently created. While one can understand the dilemma faced by China's leaders, the regime has worsened the human suffering by not attending to the problems the birth program has spawned. The state's neglect of the havoc it has unwittingly wreaked in people's lives is an important part of the unofficial record.

The state planning of tiny families has created winners as well as losers, and these deserve attention too. Some of the positive effects—especially the emergence of a new generation of "quality" urban single children—were intended. Others, such as rising status of daughters in small families, were unintended, happy by-products of the way the birth program interacted with a rapidly changing society. To capture a wide range of social effects, the chapter moves roughly historically, beginning with the stratifications and traumas produced in the 1980s and early 1990s, and ending with the more welcome effects that have appeared in the late 1990s and early 2000s. It will argue that the post-Mao birth project helped to create a hard-edged, competitive Chinese modernity in which the new generation of "quality," cosmopolitan, and consumerist singletons exists in a larger cultural sea of peasant suffering and female sacrifice.

Widening the Rural-Urban Divide: Social Suffering in the Villages

Never equal under Mao, urban and rural have remained highly unequal under Deng and his successors.[5] The birth program has built on and, in turn, furthered that stratification of Chinese society along locational lines. Because the bulk of the population problem seemed to lie in the countryside—the peasants made up most of the population and desired larger families—the population policies and practices of the post-Mao state have sharply distinguished between rural and urban. Of course, city and village couples have long had somewhat different reproductive agendas. Yet birth planning has both deepened and widened that reproductive divide through the official constitution and continuous elaboration of urban-rural difference. Urban-rural difference has been constituted through the formulation of varying policies and enforcement techniques. The policy rules, while appearing to privilege the peasants by allowing more exceptions for second children, in fact have favored urbanites because the gap between state policy and societal desire has been smaller in the cities. Enforcement too has been kinder to city people. While urban women have been subject to firm but "caring control," the peasant population, tagged "large in quantity and low in quality," has been identified as the major cause of China's population problems and targeted for coercive control. The result has been a largely unremarked but highly troubling gap in human trauma and social suffering. Although the situation in the villages has eased since the mid-1990s, we dwell briefly on the social suffering meted out to the peasants in the 1980s and early 1990s, for it has had lasting effects on people's bodies and lives and on China's reputation in the eyes of the world.

DEMONIZING DISCOURSES AND VICIOUS PRACTICES

If to Mao the peasants were the ostensible leaders of the revolution, to his modernizing successors they were the cause of China's developmental woes. The Deng-era discourse of modernity posited an essential rural-urban divide in which the countryside was positioned as "behind" in the nation's advance toward progress. Lacking the moral and cultural quality of citizens deemed capable of promoting socialist modernity, China's villagers became the object of florid discourses on rural feudalism, backwardness, and small-mindedness

(Cohen 1993; Kelliher 1994; Feuerwerker 1998; Gaetano and Jacka ed. 2004).[6] In making the peasants the primary target of the effort to limit population growth, the creators of the birth program drew on and vividly elaborated these broader political and cultural discourses. Especially at times of heightened concern about population growth, the peasants were the subject of demeaning and dehumanizing discourses and, in turn, harsh, campaign-like measures of reproductive control. In the early 1980s, when the rural reforms freed villagers from tight cadre control, causing fertility to rise, rural people were denigrated as small-minded, feudal peasants in need of firm and rapid reproductive modernization. Holdovers from the feudal era, the peasants in this new discourse clung to "outmoded reproductive beliefs," remained "ignorant and superstitious," and lived in "primitive economic conditions" that fostered high fertility. The peasants' smallholder economy, revived by the rural reforms, created a "smallholder mentality" marked by narrow-mindedness, selfish acquisitiveness, and family values that were pronatalist and misogynist. In the late 1980s and early 1990s, when fertility began to climb again, the peasants were demonized as "backward elements" whose excess childbearing and low quality were preventing the whole nation from attaining its place of glory in the world. In some of the more lurid accounts, the rural people were represented as the uncivilized Other: dirty, almost bestial beings whose "low spiritual, cultural, and physical quality" threatened to infect the whole nation, reducing its caliber and undermining its modernization (Ai 1988; Ai 1989; Fan and Huang 1989; Wu 1989).

These images of the feudal, backward, and subhuman peasant living on the fringes of the political and human communities helped to justify the use of dehumanizing, at times almost barbaric methods to bring rural population growth under control. Despite the official prohibition on the use of coercion, in the 1983 sterilization campaign coercion was officially condoned by the party committee of the birth commission, which felt that the urgent end justified any means (SBPC Party Group 1984, 36). In the campaigns of the early 1990s, the use of force against person and property was so common that, once fertility was brought under control, these and other abuses were codified in the Seven Don'ts aimed at eradicating them (Chapter 6). The evidence of widespread resort to physical force during these two extended birth planning campaigns is not just credible, it is overwhelming, and it comes from top officials in the birth commission itself (SBPC Party Group 1984; SG 23Nov99 BJ). At other times, when the application of such methods was strongly discouraged by the political Center, their use appears to have been more localized, confined to particular places and leaders who could reach their assigned targets in no other way.

PIGS TO BE SPAYED, OXEN TO BE YOKED

Although few Western scholars have observed a birth control campaign, anthropological research has uncovered what one might imagine: that the trauma of being targeted for forceful surgery is deep and lasting. From these accounts we know that the terrible campaigns of the early 1980s and early 1990s spread terror and panic in the villages, as those targeted for birth control surgery contemplated the loss to the health of their bodies and families that would soon ensue (Huang 1998; Ku 2003; Yan 2003). Especially intense fears surrounded the prospect of sterilization. That operation brought not only the permanent end to one's reproductive capacity but also, villagers believed, the loss of vital essence, *qi*, and, in turn, the dissipation of sexual vigor and energy to work (Potter and Potter 1990; Mueggler 2001). In sharp contrast to the cities, where the prevalence of one-child families allowed the use of the removable IUD, in the rural areas the irreversible sterilization was the method of choice because it represented a permanent solution, the end to cadres' struggles to stop unauthorized babies from being born.

Despite the greater health risks involved, sterilization was usually performed on women in good part because men objected to the operation. Women acquiesced in the surgery because for a man sterilization was considered catastrophic, leading to the destruction of conjugal relations, the end of his ability to work, and the eventual breakup of his family. For a woman, sterilization was believed to bring fearful yet lesser evils: the loss of sexual pleasure, the end of heavy labor, and varying degrees of chronic illness and physical debility (Mueggler 2001; Murphy 2003).[7] Although the actual effects of sterilization have not been and may never be scientifically studied, the beliefs in these effects, which may well be more prevalent in China than elsewhere given the mass-campaign nature of much birth control surgery there, have the status of cultural truism. One well-traveled Chinese rural sociologist put it pointedly, declaring: "Of course, sterilization affects sexual relations!" (SG 16Dec03 BJ). Exacerbating women's dread of the operation, in the 1980s and early 1990s most sterilizations were performed during rushed campaigns, when outside medical teams spent short periods in local areas conducting surgeries en masse, often without adequate facilities, sanitary equipment, or anesthetic medicine. Western press reports and anthropological case studies suggest that many women—how many we will never know—suffered long-term loss of energy and health (we return to this issue below).

Compounding the bodily trauma was the degradation rural women and their families suffered in the birth planning campaigns. Peasants in Shandong described a crude form of humiliation in which: "They dig a hole in the wall of your house, stick your head through and beat you on the backside"

(WuDunn 1991d, 10). In the worst of the mobilizations, birth planning targets were treated no better than farm animals. Indeed, villagers in some places ignored the official term for sterilization, *jueyu*, insisting on *qiao*, the term for spaying female animals, especially pigs (Mueggler 2001; Yan 2003). In some times and places, the spaying of pigs was no mere metaphor. Rural women were taken by force, placed in cages, and transported to quasi-public operating areas, where one after another they had their tubes tied or IUDs inserted without anesthetic. When beds were in short supply, the ground was used instead (Weisskopf 1985a; SG 22Nov99, 12Dec03 BJ; Mueggler 2001).

Asked how the peasants would tolerate such treatment, a village party secretary in Fujian likened them to oxen who could respond only with resignation and silent suffering:

> The first time [we introduced tough birth control regulations] was the most difficult, just like when you put a yoke on an ox's back for the first time. It will resist and struggle. But once the yoke is accepted by the ox, you can tighten it repeatedly, even to the point of choking it to death. Peasants are like oxen. Once they accept something as inevitable, you can continue to tighten the screw. (Huang 1998, 78; quotation from mid-1980s)

Villagers treated like beasts reacted as one might expect—with anxiety, grief, helplessness, and sometimes outbursts of murderous rage. Though the vicious campaigns are now gone, they live on today in frightening dreams and embodied recollections that only students of historical memory can retrieve.

COMMUNITY CADRES AND MEDICAL WORKERS SUFFER IN SILENCE

It was not only those targeted for reproductive surgery that suffered under the yoke of heavy-handed birth planning. Village cadres charged with enforcing a widely hated policy among their relatives and neighbors had to endure private entreaties, public curses, and violent retaliations, and then live for the rest of their lives with those whose fundamental interests they had forever harmed (e.g., Huang 1998; Ku 2003). Their trauma was expressed in nightmares, resignations, and even, in rare cases, attempted suicides (Mueggler 2001). Though it was their political duty as state and party cadres to follow orders from above, many if not the majority considered the policy illegitimate and, when pressure was relaxed, quietly refused to enforce it or effectively obstructed enforcement by such means as breaching the rules themselves or falsifying the numbers they reported to superiors. Cadres' unhappiness with their burden is reflected in surveys showing that over half wanted to resign their posts (Scharping 2003, 198; data from 1988 and 1995).

Medical workers at township and higher levels suffered as well. A small-scale study suggests that, accepting the official discourse, most of the time most OB/GYN doctors were proud of their contributions to the important cause of slowing population growth and accepted the daily rounds of birth control surgeries as part of their routine medical practice (Nie 1999, 165–200). Yet there were times when that professional calm was disturbed. As employees of the state, China's medical practitioners were sometimes required to violate both professional and human ethics by conducting mass surgeries in substandard conditions, aborting fully developed fetuses, and administering lethal injections to unauthorized newborns (Weisskopf 1985a; Nie 1999). In a 2000 case in Hubei that drew widespread revulsion, a baby boy who was slated for late-term abortion because he was a fourth child nevertheless survived with the help of an elderly doctor. The birth officials, angry at this breach of policy, publicly drowned the infant in a rice field. The doctor was so traumatized that she became chronically ill (McElroy 2000).

With the need to dispose of newborns increasingly reduced since the mid-1980s by the spread of ultrasound machines that detect fetal sex, some of these more heart-rending practices have disappeared from the work agendas of China's medical personnel. Yet now they are drawn into a cleaner but equally morally ambiguous strategem to solve "the gender problem" by getting rid of baby girls before they are born. The demand for prenatal sex determination and sex-selective abortion has now rendered medical specialists party to the discarding of female fetal life, a practice that defines girls as less than boys and boosts the sex ratio to levels that are rising by the year. Though their feelings remain largely hidden from view (but see Mosher 1993; Nie 1999), those emotions must surely be troubled, for the birth policy has confronted them with wrenching moral dilemmas. In the new political climate of the 2000s, some are finding ways to right the moral wrongs of the past. One doctor, distressed that she had "destroyed too many little lives," is now "making it up to them" by running a private shelter for children of prisoners (Ni 2004, A4).

Late twentieth-century China was no stranger to social suffering created by the state in the name of utopian goals. While great traumas like the Great Leap Forward have long been part of the record of the state's assault on rural society, lesser traumas like the great birth planning campaigns, whose damage is measured less in deaths than in physical, social, and moral pain, belong on that list. The harsh enforcement of the birth policy during the 1980s and early 1990s built on the larger antipeasant sentiment of the post-Mao years to create a deep urban–rural divide in bodily pain, family trauma, and social suffering. Birth planning helped to weave peasant suffering into the fabric of post-Mao Chinese modernity. A decade later the Hu-Wen administration is beginning to address the urban bias in the birth program. This brief discussion hints at the size of the challenge it faces.

Deepening and Embodying Gender Inequality: Women's Bodies at Risk

By effectively assigning women the main responsibility for population control, birth planning has fundamentally reshaped gender relations, both deepening the divide between men and women and locating gender difference more firmly in the body. This represented a major departure from late imperial days, when gender difference was located in differential kin linkages. It also reflected a major expansion and institutionalization of earlier CCP "woman-work" (*funu gongzuo*), especially in the area of health care. The party's prenatal and birthing campaigns of the early 1950s had relocated gender difference in reproductive physiology and placed woman within the domain of the state, to be mobilized in the service of its reproductive or productive agendas (Barlow 1994; Goldstein 1998; Chapter 3). With its differentiated policies and enforcement methods, the birth program also divided the category "Chinese woman" according to phase in the reproductive cycle. While paying scant attention, at least in the 1980s and 1990s, to women defined as pre- or postreproductive, the birth program has made the married woman of reproductive age a highly salient political category and the target of intense surveillance, intervention, and control.

As noted earlier, this intensified stratification of genders and of women along reproductive lines was part of the larger scientization and biologization of politics and culture in the reform era (on the larger process, see Hua 1995; Evans 1997; Li 2001). The biologization of "population" and "gender" worked to naturalize and even intensify women's subordination by making it biologically immutable and thus beyond political critique. Biology was said to dictate a hierarchical and unchangeable division of social labor in which women, because of their reproductive functions, were responsible for all matters related to reproduction (Evans 1997). Reduced to their procreative bodies, in both discourse and political practice women would become mere instruments of population control and improvement; any damage that might occur to their bodies or social selves bore no scientific, political, or other significance. Drawing on shifting notions of femininity and cultural views of male superiority, the birth program helped to equate womanhood with motherhood by making women's bodies the target of contraceptive control and by tying their identities ever more closely to their reproductive responsibilities. The birth program interacted with and built on these larger cultural currents to produce "the reproductive woman" as the central object of reproductive control.

In a political culture upholding gender equality, the handling of the woman question has been a sensitive issue for the birth commission. It may be that, for women as a whole, birth planning has brought political recognition and glory. As a former vice minister of the commission put it, birth planning represents "women's great contribution to the Chinese nation" (SG 4July93 BJ-JZH). The birth program, along with improvements in health care, has also contributed to the sharp decline in female mortality at all ages that has occurred since the mid-1970s. Maternal mortality has fallen, due in part to the decline in fertility and in part to improvements in reproductive health care available to the majority of women whose pregnancies are sanctioned by the state (Banister 1998). Yet despite the impressive gains in mortality, especially among adult females, morbidity has been a serious problem, especially for women who have been targeted for coercive control or who have run afoul of the birth program in some way. During the 1980s and early 1990s, demographic control was the overriding objective of the birth program; women's bodies and health suffered accordingly. Although the full scope of the problems will never be known, the evidence available strongly suggests that the demographic target-driven birth planning of the 1980s and early 1990s seriously impaired the physical health and emotional well-being of substantial numbers of Chinese women. Since the mid-1990s, the birth commission has sought to change course and make women's health and overall well-being a more central objective of the birth program (SBPC 8 September 2002; Chapter 5). The enhanced concern about health is reflected in the commission's implementation of two nationwide reproductive health surveys, in 1997 and 2001. Although the quality of reproductive health care is improving, much remains to be done, especially in the areas of contraceptive choice and counseling.

"THE REPRODUCTIVE WOMAN": A CULTURAL AND POLITICAL PRODUCTION

As noted in the last chapter, during the Maoist years official propaganda had emphasized gender equality. In the early reform years gender similarity gave way to gender difference, and that difference was rooted in reproductive physiology. The birth policy and enforcement apparatus effectively built on and contributed to the larger process of deepening and relocalizing gender difference in the procreative body. From the beginning, birth planning has been both understood and institutionalized as a primarily women's issue. At the central level, women have played significant roles in the leadership of the birth commission and its forerunner.[8] At the community level, the birth policy has been enforced almost exclusively by women, in both urban and rural areas. Women have also been the major target of reproductive control. Despite occasional pleas to men to do their part, women have borne the great burden of contraception, and that burden has grown over time.

The statistics are striking (see Table 4). Of the four-fifths of a billion operations (male and female sterilizations, abortions, IUD insertions and removals)
performed from 1971 to 2001, 95 percent were performed on women. That
proportion has increased every half decade, rising from 92 percent in the early
1970s to 98 percent in the late 1990s and early 2000s. Although male sterilization is a simpler procedure that poses fewer complications, 74 percent of the
151 million sterilizations done between 1971 and 2001 have been tubec-
tomies. Women's sterilization burden has grown, from 59 percent in the early
1970s to 84 percent in the late 1990s and early 2000s. The ratio of female to
male sterilizations rose especially dramatically between 1990 and 2001, from
3.6 to 6.1. This feminization of birth control surgery underscores the urgency
of today's efforts to spread the burden of contraception more evenly (e.g.,
SBPC 15 May 2002).

Beneath these gendered numbers lie pervasive cultural attitudes affirming
male superiority, male entitlement to sex, and male prerogative in protecting the body from risk. Such attitudes are reflected in the 1997 reproductive
health survey, in which 32 percent of women said it was difficult or impossible to refuse their husbands' demands for sex (Jiang ed. 2000, 350). They
come through too in the 2001 survey, in which only 40 percent of men reported ever having talked to their wives about contraception (SBPC 4 March
2002; on men's attitudes generally, see Rosen 1991). In a much smaller study,
Beijing women undergoing abortions traced their unplanned pregnancies to
their husbands' demand for sex and refusal to use condoms while having it
(Xiao et al. 1995). Even men who used condoms often did so carelessly (or
used defective condoms), with mishaps experienced by half the users (Cheng
et al. 1997; on condom quality, see Gui 1999). Early 2000s efforts to improve
women's contraceptive choice have been stymied by husbands' unwillingness
to take responsibility for condom use, even when their wives' health is endangered (Holcombe 2003). The larger picture that emerges is one in which
women have been expected to put the health and well-being of their husbands and children before their own (Chu 2000; this point is elaborated just
below). And behind these expectations lie deeply entrenched ideas about the
inevitability of gender inequality and women's biological and thus social
responsibility for reproduction. For both men and women, the costs to
women's reproductive health are just one of these many givens. The birth
program has in effect built on and, in turn, further entrenched these gender
biases in the culture.

Following the official narrative of women's liberation under socialism, the
birth program has historically aimed to "liberate" women from onerous
childbearing and childrearing duties, releasing them to become workers. The
theme of women's emancipation, which was a prominent part of birth

TABLE 4
Sterilizations, 1971–2001
(Total Number, by Gender, and as Percentage of All Birth-Control Operations)

Year	Female sterilizations	Male sterilizations	Total sterilizations	Total operations	Percentage sterilizations	Female/ male ratio
1971	1,744,644	1,223,480	2,968,124	13,051,123	22.7	1.43
1972	2,087,160	1,715,822	3,802,982	18,690,446	20.3	1.22
1973	2,955,617	1,933,210	4,888,827	25,075,557	19.5	1.53
1974	2,275,741	1,445,251	3,720,992	22,638,229	16.4	1.57
1975	3,280,042	2,652,653	5,932,695	29,462,861	20.1	1.24
1976	2,707,849	1,495,540	4,203,389	22,385,435	18.8	1.81
1977	2,776,448	2,616,876	5,393,324	25,539,086	21.1	1.06
1978	2,511,413	767,542	3,278,955	21,720,096	15.1	3.27
1979	5,289,518	1,673,947	6,963,465	30,581,114	22.8	3.16
1980	3,842,006	1,363,508	5,205,514	28,628,437	18.2	2.82
1981	1,555,971	649,476	2,205,447	22,760,305	9.7	2.40
1982	3,925,927	1,230,967	5,156,894	33,702,389	15.3	3.19
1983	16,398,378	4,359,261	20,757,639	58,205,572	35.7	3.76
1984	5,417,163	1,293,286	6,710,449	31,734,864	21.1	4.19
1985	2,283,971	575,564	2,859,535	25,646,972	11.1	3.97
1986	2,914,900	1,030,827	3,945,727	28,475,506	13.9	2.83
1987	4,407,755	1,752,598	6,160,353	34,597,082	17.8	2.51
1988	3,590,469	1,062,161	4,652,630	31,820,664	14.6	3.38
1989	4,221,717	1,509,294	5,731,011	29,031,912	19.7	2.80
1990	5,314,722	1,466,442	6,781,164	34,982,328	19.4	3.62
1991	6,753,338	2,382,670	9,136,008	38,135,578	24.0	2.83
1992	4,500,029	858,675	5,358,704	28,017,605	19.1	5.24
1993	3,580,344	641,705	4,222,049	25,114,685	16.8	5.58
1994	3,726,861	671,890	4,398,751	27,967,575	15.7	5.55
1995	2,315,472	464,387	2,779,859	22,236,012	12.5	4.99
1996	2,736,415	546,425	3,282,840	22,953,599	14.3	5.01
1997	2,340,303	436,656	2,776,959	20,418,688	13.6	5.36
1998	1,993,126	329,080	2,322,206	19,458,072	11.9	6.06
1999	1,827,732	318,858	2,146,590	18,209,721	11.8	5.73
2000	1,680,917	312,538	1,993,455	17,720,620	11.2	5.38
2001	1,549,700	254,229	1,803,929	17,070,650	10.6	6.10
Total	112,505,648	39,034,818	151,540,466	826,032,795	18.3	2.88

SOURCES: 1971–1983 *China Health Yearbook 1984*; 1982–1998 *China Health Yearbook 1999*; 1999–2001 *China Health Yearbook 1999–2002*.

NOTE: Operations included in total are IUD insertions and removals, abortions, and male and female sterilizations.

planning propaganda in the 1970s, was greatly downplayed in the 1980s, when women were called on to sacrifice their personal desires for several children to the needs of the nation. A few groups of women, such as urban intellectuals, appear to have taken advantage of the mandated birth limits to negotiate with their husbands for small families, agreements that allowed them to develop their professional identities (SG 20Nov99 BJ-LXJ). For the majority of women, however, the female-gendered character of birth planning, combined with a larger culture of female domesticity and an economy largely hostile to women workers, may well have worked to tie their identities more closely to their roles as reproducers rather than less. To-day women have fewer children than in the past, but now every aspect of reproduction—from spouse selection to marriage, contraception, childbear-ing, and childrearing—has become the object of intense state concern. The effect has been to further politicize and publicize activities that in precom-munist days belonged to the more private sphere of kinship, making them more salient in the lives of individuals, families, and communities. Moreover, the sheer amount of time, energy, and resources now required to bear and rear children has expanded enormously. Especially in the cities, but increasingly in the villages as well, pressures to be a "good mother" of a "quality child" have turned childrearing into a demanding, time-consuming, and money-intensive prospect (Chapter 7). At the same time, the reform economy has brought active discrimination against women in the labor market. Since the early 1980s, women workers in the cities have faced large-scale layoffs, low wages, and segregation in lower-paying jobs and sectors (Robinson 1985; Jacka 1990; He and Chen 1997–98; Riley 1997a). Given the limited nature of the jobs generally available to women, especially in the cities, many may find the nurturing of a child more rewarding than their jobs and invest more of their energies and selves in it. Despite the sharp decline in fertility, then, dur-ing the reform era, the subjectivities of many women appear to have become more rather than less closely tethered to their reproductive roles and respon-sibilities (e.g., Milwertz 1997; Hooper 1998).

WOMEN'S BODIES AND PSYCHOLOGICAL
WELL-BEING AT RISK

The demographic gains of the 1980s and early 1990s appear to have been won at great cost to the physical and psychological health of women, espe-cially those in the rural areas. In the urban areas, the close attention to women's reproductive affairs may well have led to the detection and treatment of common ailments, and, in turn, an improvement in women's reproductive health. Rural women may have enjoyed some of these benefits, especially af-ter the introduction of mandatory gynecological exams in the early 1990s.

The scholarly literature, however, emphasizes instead the harm caused by the targeting of their bodies for reproductive control. Throughout these years, Chinese reproductive health activists have contended, the health of women was considered less worthy of concern than the health of single children, and both were treated as trivial matters relative to the achievement of population control targets (SG 17,20,22Nov99 BJ; see also Li 1996; HRIC 1995). The meticulous collection of data on population—but not women's health—for so many years would seem to bear them out. Deep shame and fear keep both rural women and medical workers from talking about what one woman sociologist with long experience in the villages calls "a truth too terrible to utter" (SG 16Dec03 BJ). The evidence available suggests that, despite the important improvements in female, including maternal, mortality mentioned earlier, the birth program has left rural women with short- and long-term physical problems and with deep psychological wounds that reflect and worsen their low status in the male-dominated culture of village China.

Among short-term health problems, contraceptive failure has been extensive, experienced by roughly one-quarter to one-third of women, virtually all of whom must undergo an abortion (1997 RH survey, in Jiang ed. 2000, 145; also Xie, Gu, and Hardee 2000). During these years, almost three-quarters of abortions were related to contraceptive failure, many to the notorious cheap stainless steel IUD the program relied on for many years (Kaufman 1993; Cheng Yimin et al. 1997; Luo et al. 1999a, b). That troublesome ring caused people so many worries that it interfered with couples' sex lives (Xie, Gu, and Hardee 2000). Although abortions have greatly declined from their early 1990s peak (Table 5), there are other problems surrounding abortion in China that are not reflected in the overall number of procedures.

One problem is the high incidence of repeat abortions (and IUD insertions), which worsen the risks of infection and perforation (Kaufman 1993; Li Bohua 1999). In Shanghai in the early 1990s, young women could expect to have an average of 2.3 and a maximum of 5 abortions over their reproductive lives (Gui 1999). In parts of rural China, women have had up to 9 abortions before finally conceiving a son (Weisskopf 1985b).[9] Another is the prevalence of late-term abortions, widely used in the campaigns of the 1980s and 1990s to eliminate unauthorized pregnancies. Field research in rural Shaanxi in the late 1980s turned up numerous cases of abortions at the eighth or ninth month. Second- or third-trimester abortions pose elevated health risks even where medical facilities are excellent, a situation that rarely obtained during those mobilizations (Zhou et al. 1999). In the 1990s program leaders took steps to reduce the incidence of late-term abortion through early detection of unauthorized pregnancies. Yet the rising tide of

TABLE 5

Abortions, 1971–2001

(Total Numbers and as Percentage of All Birth-Control Operations)

Year	Abortions	Percentage all birth-control operations
1971	3,910,110	30.0
1972	4,813,542	25.8
1973	5,110,405	20.4
1974	4,984,564	22.0
1975	5,084,260	17.3
1976	4,742,946	21.2
1977	5,229,569	20.5
1978	5,391,204	24.8
1979	7,856,587	25.7
1980	9,527,644	33.3
1981	8,696,945	38.2
1982	12,419,663	36.9
1983	14,371,843	24.7
1984	8,890,140	28.0
1985	10,931,565	42.6
1986	11,578,713	40.7
1987	10,489,412	30.3
1988	12,675,839	39.8
1989	10,379,426	35.8
1990	13,493,926	38.6
1991	14,086,313	36.9
1992	10,416,287	37.2
1993	9,496,119	37.8
1994	9,467,064	33.9
1995	7,476,482	33.6
1996	8,834,195	38.5
1997	6,589,869	32.3
1998	7,384,290	37.9
1999	6,764,357	37.1
2000	6,658,550	37.6
2001	6,284,844	36.8
Total	264,036,640	32.0

SOURCES: 1971–1983 *China Health Yearbook* 1984; 1982–98 *China Health Yearbook* 1999; 1999–2001 *China Health Yearbook* 1999–2002.

sex-selective abortions, often performed at the fourth or fifth month, may reverse any gains made. The 1997 reproductive health survey suggests that a disturbing one-fifth of abortions are done in the fourth month or later (Chu 2000). Finally, abortions in China are generally performed without anesthesia, causing what women describe as pain so unbearable it is like having one's heart cut out (Zhou et al. 1999; SG 12Dec03 BJ; Nie 1999).[10] In several studies conducted in the early 1990s, both women and their doctors described abortions as often physically and psychologically agonizing experiences that leave many deeply anxious about having sex (Gui 1999; Zhou et al. 1999). In the 1997 survey, fully 69 percent of women maintained that abortion affected women's physical and mental health, with one-quarter of those indicating that the effects were very serious (Jiang ed. 2000, 131). Yet because of the political dangers associated with criticizing the birth policy, the subject of abortion has been surrounded by what the medical ethicist Nie Jing-bao has called a "nameless fear." That fear has kept both women and their doctors from speaking out about these traumas (Nie 1999, 235–260).

Beyond these short-term costs are the long-term consequences for women's reproductive and general health of inappropriate, botched, or repeated birth control procedures. The case of Hunan's Li Qiuliang, featured in a 1993 *New York Times* article that shocked the international population community with its news of a fearsome new campaign, underscores the potential seriousness of these problems (Kristof 1993a). Twenty-three-year-old Li had her first pregnancy aborted at seven months because she was supposed to give birth in 1992 rather than 1993. Despite the frailty of her health and over the protests of the attending doctor, she was required to abort the pregnancy. During the procedure she bled severely, fell unconscious, and almost died. The operation left her crippled. As Li's account and those of others suggest, health care services have been provided differentially to those who comply with the policy. The result for noncompliers can be deadly. In one 1989–1991 study, women who violated the policy by carrying unauthorized pregnancies to term were four times more likely to die in childbirth than women with state-permitted pregnancies (Ni and Rossignol 1994). In another study from the mid-1990s, village women in Guangdong likened becoming pregnant with an illegal child to "receiving a death sentence," because of the dangers of giving birth at home (Ku 2003, 199). Poor reproductive health care and complications from careless surgery have also led to disabling conditions that have diminished women's lives. Village ethnographies describe women who were forced to undergo sterilization in rushed campaigns as chronically ill, suffering a nagging pain that has impaired their family rela-tions and quality of life (Mueggler 2001).

Despite the low quality of reproductive health care, women generally tell surveyors that they are satisfied with the services they have received (Chu 2000). Women respond this way, some Chinese scholars believe, because after decades of being treated as mere instruments for the fulfillment of birth targets, they have exceedingly low expectations of birth planning services. In addition, they have been socialized to be polite and conditioned to fear political trouble or even persecution if they criticize the birth policy (Chu 2000). The problems also run deeper than this, reflecting a widespread devaluation of women's health and lives—by women themselves. With the exception of sterilization, women undergoing medical procedures seem to have worried not about whether it would harm their health but about whether it would impair their ability to fulfill their duties to produce a son and satisfy their husbands sexually (Xiao et al. 1995). Far from feeling entitled to good health and health care, women felt that their biology, which rendered them inherently more "sickly," made it their destiny to suffer more than men in the domains of sexuality and reproductive health (Evans 1997; Xiao et al.1995; Chu 2001). In placing women's bodies at risk, the birth program has thus reflected and worsened a pervasive view of women's inferiority.

The psychological problems faced by rural women have remained hidden from view, yet the research of Chinese scholars suggests that these burdens are enormous in a culture in which women's main purpose in life has long been to produce a son. Even as they have been targeted by birth cadres for persuasion and mobilization, young rural women have been blamed by their relatives for having a child of the wrong sex. In the 1990s, sonless women in such areas as Anhui and Shaanxi suffered severe discrimination from their husbands, in-laws, and neighbors. In the words of one Anhui villager: "Women with two daughters . . . live miserable lives, especially if they are sterilized. Then there is no more hope. You terminated your family line" (Xie ed. 2000, 485). The result has been social isolation, depression, anxiety, and despair (Zhu et al. 1997). In one mid-1980s study, two-thirds of rural women whose firstborn was a daughter suffered neurasthenia (*shenjing shuairuo*), while over three-quarters endured severe loss of face (Lee and Kleinman 2000).[11] From the official media we learn of cases such as a Jiangxi woman with only a daughter who suffered a mental breakdown after being sterilized (Weisskopf 1985b).

Compounding the psychological problems is the physical abuse—from beating to, more rarely, poisoning and strangling—that women have suffered at the hands of son-hungry husbands (Anagnost 1988; Honig and Hershatter 1988; Lee and Kleinman 2000). Although the beating and divorce of sonless wives may have received the most media attention in the early 1980s, wife battering remains an entrenched feature of rural Chinese life, accepted even by village leaders as matters of family, not state (Pickowicz and

Wang 2002). The physical and emotional strain has led some village women to take their own lives. Young rural Chinese women have been committing suicide at an alarming rate, 66 percent higher than that of rural men (Pearson et al. 2002; Philips, Li, and Zhang 2002). Some of these suicides have been linked to the limitation on births or the trauma of a premarital abortion (Yu and Sarri 1997; Lee and Kleinman 2000; Bossen 2002). In one case, a transportation worker in Shenyang who failed to produce a son drank seven bottles of DDT after her husband, with her in-laws' encouragement, severely beat her. Another woman whose husband strangled her daughter died in a mental hospital after refusing to eat or speak (Weisskopf 1985b). The product of a stringent birth policy enforced in a male-centered society, these sorts of psychological costs are simply immeasurable.

REPRODUCTIVE HEALTH CARE: IMPROVING
BUT IN NEED OF MORE IMPROVEMENT

Since the mid-1990s, the birth commission has sought to alleviate some of these problems with a new emphasis on reproductive health (Chapter 5; many items at NPFPC website). The launching of two major reproductive health surveys is part of this larger commitment to identify and ameliorate the sorts of health problems just discussed. Those surveys reveal encouraging progress in some areas. During the 1990s, the program achieved dramatic improvements in the use of prenatal exams (from 57 percent to 82 percent of women), delivery at birth planning service centers (from 40 percent to 68 percent), and the use of calcium and iron supplements during pregnancy (from about 10 – 20 percent to 40 percent) (SBPC 4 March 2002; see also Short and Zhang 2004). Yet the surveys also expose the persistence of enormous problems in other areas, in particular, contraceptive choice and counseling.

Since the inauguration of birth planning, and especially since the early 1980s, contraceptive choice has been extremely limited and focused on provider-controlled methods, such as the IUD and sterilization. At the same time, counseling about the nature and side effects of these procedures has been negligible. The figures tell a stark story. As late as 1997, fully 59 percent of rural women (and 55 percent of urban women) were told nothing about the operation they were going to have. Forty-six percent left the clinic with no information on postoperative care or likely side effects, and more than three-quarters received no follow-up home visits (Jiang ed. 2000, 153 – 154). In another large-scale survey conducted in 1998, only one-third of women undergoing sterilization received counseling about the procedure (Li 1999). The situation was clearly worse in earlier years of the program. In the late 1980s, birth workers in four counties did not know the contraindications or side effects of the most common methods, and, even when they knew the side effects, they did not know the clinical protocols for treating them (Kaufman et al. 1992b). Even at the Beijing Maternal Hospital, researchers in the early 1990s found, the emphasis was exclusively on performing birth control operations; counseling was simply not part of the hospital's services (Xiao et al. 1995).

These figures provide powerful testimony to the overwhelming emphasis the program has placed on achieving demographic targets, and to the resultant cost in women's bodily and psychic well being. Although the new stress on reproductive health is to be applauded, the challenges ahead remain substantial. One challenge is to address the problems of past targets who were harmed and now deserve restitution. Another is to better meet the health needs of those who have not been targets of control—unmarried women, older women, and infertile women. Although the situation is now changing, over its lifetime the birth program has largely neglected the health needs of these groups, with often serious effects (Handwerker 1998; Luo et al. 1999b; on the changes, see Grady 2003).

Deepening Gender Disparity at Life's Beginning: Infant Girls and Female Fetuses at Risk

The enforcement of state birth planning has also widened gender disparities at the beginning of life, making this a dangerous period for the less-valued gender. Although population planners did not intend to put infant girls at risk, this was the inevitable consequence of a policy that allowed only one or two children while neglecting the gendered nature of personhood in Chinese society. Enforced in the increasingly masculinist culture and socioeconomy of the reform era, the sharp restrictions on childbearing have had damaging, even lethal consequences for infant girls. One measure of these effects is the growing gender gap in infant mortality. In recent decades, infant mortality has declined overall because of improvements in health care, many introduced by the birth program. Yet mortality has declined much more sharply among boys than girls. Between 1982 and 2000, male infant mortality fell 43 percent (from 36.5 to 20.8 per 1,000) while female infant mortality fell 15.4 percent (from 34.5 to 29.2) (Li and Sun 2003). Thus, while some infant girls have benefited from the birth program, others appear to have been vulnerable to gender discrimination. A starker measure of these consequences is the sex ratio at birth (the number of boys born per 100 girls born). The sex ratio at birth has climbed steadily since the early 1980s, reaching a level that is the highest in the world.

What has happened to the "missing girls"? Because of the extreme sensitivity of the subject among national leaders, and the silence and shame surrounding the reluctant disposal of girls in local society, we will never know the full story. Certainly, some of the girls are alive but simply not reported, and thus absent only from the statistics (Johansson and Nygren 1991; Zeng et al. 1993). But the consensus that has emerged since the mid-1990s is that most are truly missing—that is, that the shortage of Chinese girls is both real and extreme. The history of community population politics traced in Chapter 7 suggests that couples are increasingly shifting their gender-manipulation practices from the disposal of infants to the elimination of fetuses. Both raise the sex ratio at birth (infants that disappear are not reported as births). In this section, we take a closer look at the social practices and consequences of these gender manipulations.[12] We begin with the "old-fashioned" techniques for the disposal of unwanted infants: infanticide, discrimination, abandonment, and sale. While some of these practices spare lives, they often severely compromise the welfare of young girls. We then turn to the "modern" techniques of prenatal sex determination followed by sex-selective abortion. These practices not only contribute to the masculinization of Chinese society, they also provoke deep ethical anxieties that represent a major cultural cost of the birth program in the early 2000s.

In the 1980s and 1990s the state took some steps to discourage these gender manipulation practices. Faced, however, with a stark choice between fertility control and gender balance, it chose control, setting up a dynamic in which the intense pursuit of demographic targets effectively contributed to the rising SRB and deteriorating welfare of China's littlest girls. National political and program leaders have now identified the normalization of the sex ratio as a goal for the twenty-first century and taken steps in that direction (discussed at the end of this section). A brief look back suggests the scale and scope of the problems they now face.

THE MASCULINIZATION OF CHINESE SOCIETY: RISING SEX RATIOS AT BIRTH

Historically, Chinese sex ratios at birth were high, especially at times of resource shortage, when families disposed of female infants they could not care for (Skinner 1997; Lee and Wang 1999). In the early PRC, the sex ratio at birth fell from abnormally high levels in the 1930s and 1940s to relatively low and stable levels from the 1950s to the 1970s (Coale and Banister 1994). Since the early 1980s, however, that ratio has worsened markedly (see Table 6). That deterioration can be directly linked to the birth program. Although the biologically normal ratio falls in the range of 105 to 106, census figures reveal a Chinese sex ratio at birth that has risen continuously—from 109 in 1982 to 111 in 1990, 116 in 1995, and 117 (published) and 120 (actual) in 1999 (Lavely 2001; SG 12Dec03 BJ).

TABLE 6

Sex Ratio at Birth and in Early Childhood, 1953–1999

| Year | Sex ratio at birth | SEX RATIO AT BIRTH BY PARITY | | | Sex ratio of population aged 0–4 |
		1	2	3 and higher	
1953	—	—	—	—	107.0
1964	—	—	—	—	105.7
1982	108.5	—	—	—	107.1
1990	111.4	105.2	121.0	127.0	110.2
1995	115.6	106.4	141.1	154.3	118.4
1999	116.9	107.1	151.9	159.4	119.5

SOURCES: Lavely 2001; data on SRB by parity from State Statistical Bureau 2002 (at www.chinapop.gov.cn).

NOTE: Sex ratio is defined as males per 100 females.

The official discourse on population locates the problem of rising sex ratios in the "feudal" countryside, yet the story told by the statistics is that virtually every corner of Han China is becoming ever more masculine (see Table 7). Sex ratios are certainly higher in the countryside, reaching 118 in 1999, but they are also a highly skewed 113 in China's cities. In 1999 the globalizing cities of Guangdong had a sex ratio of 128, the national capital Beijing 113, and the cosmopolitan Shanghai 111. Within the urban population, the most advanced segments of society—younger, better educated, nonmigrant women in cadre and technical jobs—had some of the highest SRBs (Chen 2003). A growing gender imbalance appears to be an ineluctable feature of a rapidly modernizing, increasingly prosperous, ultralow fertility China. To be sure, China is not alone in this. Elsewhere in East and South Asia (especially Taiwan, South Korea, and India) the combination of strong son preference, low fertility, and the availability of technology to detect fetal sex has led to high sex ratios at birth (Banister 2004). Yet China has two distinctions: it has the highest sex ratio in the region and the world, and its government has played direct roles in lowering fertility, in introducing that technology, and, in the ways that we have described, even in exacerbating son preference. Birth planning, in conjunction with China's male-centered culture and market economy, has masculinized the social order, making a big gender gap in numbers a constitutive feature of Chinese modernity.

As might be expected, regional differences are substantial (Table 7). In 1999, only two of China's thirty-one provincial-level units had normal SRBs, and those (Tibet and Xinjiang) were minority regions. The highest provincial SRBs—ranging from 122 to 136—were recorded in a cluster of

TABLE 7

Sex Ratio at Birth, by Province and Rural/Urban, 1999

Province	Overall	Urban	Rural
Beijing	110.56	112.57	104.89
Tianjin	112.51	108.45	120.16
Hebei	113.43	110.79	114.30
Shanxi	112.52	111.22	113.13
Inner Mongolia	108.45	106.27	110.12
Liaoning	112.83	111.33	114.24
Jilin	111.23	110.90	111.55
Heilongjiang	109.71	109.74	109.69
Shanghai	110.64	110.69	110.30
Jiangsu	116.51	113.83	118.52
Zhejiang	113.86	112.98	114.57
Anhui	127.85	118.80	130.87
Fujian	117.93	115.43	119.54
Jiangxi	114.74	109.87	116.37
Shandong	112.17	109.86	113.61
Henan	118.46	116.47	118.97
Hubei	128.18	122.48	132.36
Hunan	126.16	118.63	128.96
Guangdong	130.30	127.71	132.84
Guangxi	125.55	122.62	126.48
Hainan	135.64	140.04	132.79
Chongqing	115.13	108.56	118.09
Sichuan	116.01	110.01	118.16
Guizhou	107.03	108.93	106.57
Yunnan	108.71	104.55	109.72
Xizang (Tibet)	102.73	103.45	102.61
Shaanxi	122.10	114.68	125.61
Gansu	114.82	115.09	114.75
Qinghai	110.35	105.91	111.86
Ningxia	108.79	104.98	110.07
Xinjiang	106.12	106.38	106.02
China	*116.86*	*114.31*	*118.08*

SOURCE: State Statistical Bureau 2002 (www.chinapop.gov.cn), based on 2000 population census.

NOTE: Province includes provincial-level municipalities and autonomous regions.

central and southern provinces that include, from lower to higher, Guangxi, Hunan, Anhui, Hubei, Guangdong, and Hainan. G. William Skinner's macroregional models show a striking intensification over time of reproductive strategizing to get a boy, with the pattern of gender distortion following the urban-regional hierarchy in predictable ways (Yuan and Skinner 2000).[13] On the county level, sex ratios have soared to highs of 185 to 190 in such places as Anhui's Yisong and Jiangxi's Xingan counties. In the year before the 2000 census, those counties together recorded the births of 640 boys but only 353 girls (2000 Census Tabulations, Anhui and Jianxi volumes).

Clearly, these high and rising sex ratios at birth reflect couples' urgent efforts to have a son in a policy context sharply limiting them to one or two children. Such strategies of gender engineering emerge strikingly from statistics on male-female disparities by birth order (see Table 6). In 1999, the SRB was only slightly above normal (107) for first births, but climbed to frightfully high levels of 152 for second births and 159 for the dwindling number of third and higher-order births. The rising SRBs are clearly related to the tightening of population control efforts over time. In one closely studied Shaanxi village, the SRB rose from 105 in the years before 1970 to 121 in the policy tightening of 1979–1983, fell to 109 in the policy relaxation of 1984–1987, and then rose again to 153 in the re-enforcement of 1988–1993 (Greenhalgh and Li 1995). At the national level, the sex ratio at second and third parities saw a huge rise during the intensification of birth planning during the early 1990s, followed by steady but smaller increases in the late 1990s era of policy reform. In the cities the sex ratio is now rising even among first-parity births![14] What all these numbers say is that girls—especially later-born rural daughters, but increasingly also first-born urban daughters—are disappearing from Chinese society, and their disappearance is tied directly if partly to the population control policy.

DEATH BY INFANTICIDE, ABANDONMENT,
AND DISCRIMINATION

The introduction of the one-child policy led to a sharp rise in infant deaths, as parents desperate for sons revived older practices of drowning or otherwise disposing of their infant daughters (Yan 1983; Hom 1991–92). This grisly practice has certainly waned, but it has not disappeared. As late as 2003, infant girls in parts of rural Anhui were still being suffocated by grandmothers who seemed to view life as unbearable without a grandson (SG 11Dec03 BJ; see also Hutchings 1997). In the mid-1990s some villagers in Shaanxi resorted to female infanticide because it was cheaper and less fallible than the process of sex determination followed by abortion. By not giving the infant a name, parents were able to think of it as a fetus and consider its death a form of delayed abortion (Li and Zhu 2000, 384–385; for historical precedents, see Furth 1999).

Since the early 1980s infant girls have also faced high risks of death from abandonment. Abandoned babies have been found on street corners, in hospitals, on piers, in markets—any place they might be found and taken in by new caregivers. The Ministry of Civil Affairs puts the number of children abandoned in the mid-1990s at around 160,000, but specialists believe the real figure is much higher (Johnson 2004, 72). Whatever the absolute numbers, research in the 1990s suggests that a huge proportion of children who have been abandoned—perhaps up to 50 percent—have died before being found. Those who have found their way into state-run orphanages or hospitals may not survive either. Because the children often arrive in fragile condition, and state-run welfare homes have generally been understaffed and underfunded, mortality rates in these institutions appear to be extremely high, averaging perhaps 40 to 50 percent of children and soaring to 90 percent in more remote areas (Johnson 2004, 38, data from early 1990s). In the early 2000s, abandonment appears to be declining and conditions in many welfare homes are improving. These are encouraging developments. (On child mortality in hospitals, see Zhongguo Tongxun She 1989b; Hutchings 1997 and Li and Zhu 2000 suggest that abandonment persists in some places in the early 2000s.)

The untimely death of infant girls has also been tied to discriminatory care in the family. In parts of rural Shaanxi in the mid-1990s, Chinese field researchers found that more than 25 percent of deaths among young girls were beyond expected levels—and the percentage was rising (Li, Zhu, and Feldman 2004). Girls were dying in greater numbers because of unevenness in the distribution of medical care: sick sons were taken to the doctor while sick daughters, particularly those with no brothers, were not. The most vulnerable were infants in the first days of life. The pressure on the Shaanxi village women to have a son was almost unbearable. Having a girl brought shame, humiliation, social ostracism, and bullying charges of "unethical behavior in past life." One unfortunate mother of two girls described her plight thus: "I dare not go outside. I just sit in my house, and carry my daughter with tears" (Li and Zhu 2000, 427).

These practices have combined to produce worrying levels of "excess female mortality"—levels above those normally expected—among young Chinese girls nationwide. Although mortality among young girls was high during the early twentieth century, it had fallen during the early years of the PRC before rising again in recent decades. Careful analysis of the 2000 census suggests that excess child mortality (up to age 5) for girls exists throughout China, though it is much worse in the rural areas. Excess infant mortality (up to age 1) for girls has been worsening since the late 1980s, again, especially in the countryside (Li and Sun 2003). The cumulative result is a serious dearth of girls. Of the cohorts born between 1980 and 2000, an estimated 8.5 million girls, or about 4 percent of the total, are truly missing (Cai and Lavely 2003).

THE TROUBLED ADOPTION OF ABANDONED INFANTS

In an ideal world, the abandoned children who survive their ordeal would all be adopted into welcoming families. But the state's complicated relationship to these infants—who are considered unplanned and thus illegitimate children—makes adoption difficult at best. Kay Johnson's field research in central China suggests that there is an abundance of couples wanting to adopt girls. Both couples who are childless because of poor health and, increasingly in the 1990s, parents with only a son have been eager to adopt the abandoned girls, in the latter case to create "complete" families of one child of each sex (Johnson 2004; see also Song 2000). In this part of China, and undoubtedly elsewhere as well, an informal culture of adoption has developed in which abandoning parents are seeking to "place" their children with suitable families by leaving them at carefully chosen doorsteps, while villagers are taking unrelated infants into their homes and treating them like birth children. Such informal adoptions are not restricted to the countryside. In one well-publicized case, a poor slum-dwelling couple in Beijing who survived by scrounging for things in the garbage picked five infant girls, all slightly disfigured, out of a rubbish bin. Finding the prospect of their death intolerable, the couple took them home to raise (McElroy and Craig 2000). In a happy development, Chinese society has been quietly evolving a cluster of attitudes and cultural practices that help to alleviate the human problems that have emerged in the wake of the one-child policy.

Yet state laws and policies, far from helping to improve the welfare of children, have worked to discourage adoption (Johnson 2004). Introduced in 1991, the PRC's first adoption law was designed to close loopholes in birth planning, not solve the problem of crowded orphanages. Treating adoption as part of birth legislation, the adoption law sharply restricted the pool of adoptive parents to couples who are childless and older (over 35 and, since 1999, over 30). Since few couples wanting to adopt children fit those narrow categories, the vast majority of adoptions—an estimated 80 percent—have been forced underground. Birth planning policies have also impeded the matching of children and families by treating both abandoned and adopted children as punishable over-quota births. Because local cadres prefer to turn a blind eye, few parents who abandon or informally adopt children have had to pay birth planning fines. Yet adoptive parents have been unable to get household registration for their child, leaving the youngster in legal limbo and facing a host of other problems (discussed in the following section).

In these and other ways, state birth planning policies—which, interacting with a male-oriented culture, created the problem of abandoned children—have worked to discourage its solution and harm the welfare of innocent children. Women's rights activists have had difficulty pressing openly for the rights of these children, because such politics is seen as an implicit criticism of the state's birth work (Johnson 2004, 66). Although the international adoption that began in the early 1990s has helped by placing some children abroad and by alleviating the resource shortage in China's orphanages, foreigners can adopt only a small fraction of the children needing homes (on foreign adoption, see Riley 1997b; Evans 2000). With the help of Chinese and international charitable organizations, since the mid-1990s the state has taken important steps to improve the conditions in at least the largest of China's orphanages (Johnson 2004). While these are encouraging developments, as long as adoption remains entangled with birth planning, the domestic adoption of Chinese children—the ideal solution for many—is likely to remain difficult.

TRAFFICKING IN INFANT GIRLS

One of the ugliest practices from old China revived by the imposition of strict birth planning in a patriarchal culture is the trafficking in infant life.[15] The sale and smuggling of babies—the vast majority girls—first drew wide public attention in China in the late 1980s and early 1990s. Despite legal efforts to discourage it, the marketing of babies seems to have increased with the tightening of birth restrictions and the rising value of babies in the late 1990s and early 2000s. Like all commodities, babies have marketable values based on their characteristics. In the early 1990s boys in eastern China were valued at 1000 to 4000 *yuan* (U.S. $125–500), girls at 500 to 1000 *yuan* (U.S. $62.50–125), with the good looking and healthy commanding higher prices (Sun 1990). How many babies have been caught up in the underground smuggling networks that market young life will never be known, but the sale of infants is reportedly widespread in rural areas such as Guangxi and Guizhou, where poverty combines with tough enforcement of birth planning to create a dangerous mix (Rosenthal 2003). The practice flourishes in part because the baby trade is lucrative—for parents, some of whom become "baby making and selling machines," and for middlemen, who join the nouveau riche with their new tractors and houses (Sun 1990). But birth planning also plays an indubitable role. Parents explain their actions as despairing attempts to avoid crippling fines or to get another birth permit that might yield a desperately needed son.

While baby selling provides a way out for dirt-poor, sonless parents, the risks to the babies are fearsome. Unlike parents who abandon their infants, often in strategic places, parents who sell their babies lose all control over their children's fate to traffickers, for whom the tiny bodies are nothing but commodities. Babies are collected from distributors in poor areas and then trucked to buyers all over the country (Rosenthal 2003). Although the lucky ones might end up in good homes, the dangers en route are enormous. In a case that drew national attention in early 2003, 28 baby girls were discovered in the back of a bus—drugged, wrapped in quilts and stuffed, two or three together, into nylon tote bags. One had suffocated to death, the others were barely breathing. In a sign of the determination of the Hu-Wen administration to do something about the rampant discrimination against infant girls, sixteen months later 52 members of a Guangxi-based baby trafficking gang were convicted of the crime. The gang's leaders were sentenced to death (Associated Press 2004).

FETAL INEQUALITY, ETHICAL PERIL

Since the mid-1980s, the spread of ultrasound-B machines into every corner of rural China has introduced a modern, high-tech way to ease the conflict between state fertility norms and peasant desires for sons (Chapter 7). Today, the practice of prenatal sex detection followed by sex-selective abortion is certainly the single greatest contributor to the growing dearth of girls. By the turn of the millennium, field research in central China suggests, the abortion of female fetuses had become a thoroughly normalized practice in the villages (Chu 2001; see also Xie, Gu, and Hardee 2000). While solving an old gender problem, it has created at least two new ones, one bodily, the other ethical.

Because fetal sex cannot be detected with accuracy until the fourth or, more generally, the fifth month of gestation, women undergoing sex-selection abortion must have the procedure late in pregnancy, when health risks are high. One sympathetic official described the bodily dangers as serious but less so than they might be, since so many Chinese hospitals are experienced in conducting late-term abortions (SG 11Dec03 BJ)! Reflecting the wider devaluation of women's health noted earlier, however, to some women these risks seemed trivial relative to the advantages of having a culturally requisite son. Chu Junhong writes of one woman who felt that two sex-selective abortions, one with life-threatening complications, were small prices to pay for the joy and pride she felt in producing a son (2001, 274). Chu's informants strongly preferred sex-selective abortion to infanticide, abandonment, and even adoption out—practices that, they feared, would produce guilty consciences at best and divine punishment at worst. Aborting their fetuses avoided these problems because the fetus was not yet a person. Yet sex-selective abortion produced moral qualms of its own. The vast majority felt that aborting unborn girls was wrong because it "destroys life" and "treats girls unfairly" (2001, 274). In another rural study, roughly 50 to 60 percent of informants in three central China villages believed that life starts before birth, while 25 percent felt that to abort was "equal to killing a human being" (Nie 1999, 118, 124). Practices of infanticide are even more ethically vexed. In the latter study about 60 percent of villagers agreed that "causing the death of a newborn is equal to killing an adult" (Nie 1999, 143; also Li and Zhu 2000). Enveloped in public and private silence, this moral disquiet is another of the uncharted costs of enforcing a tight population policy in a still-patriarchal society.

REGIME PRIORITIES AND THEIR CONSEQUENCES

The fundamental conflict between the goals of fertility decline and gender equality has put the regime in an awkward position. The result has been an official response to the rises in sex-selective abortion and the sex ratio at birth that has been later and weaker than one might expect. Throughout the 1980s, the possibility that the one-child policy would harm infant girls and raise the SRB was a taboo topic, even among the state's demographic policy advisors (SG Nov85, 86 BJ). Top political leaders, such as Zhao Ziyang, issued stern warnings against killing baby girls, but their solution was exhortation, not the introduction of effective countermeasures (Zhao 1982; Greenhalgh 2001b). Since the late 1980s, the central government and, in turn, many provinces, have issued countless notices and legal provisions forbidding the use of ultrasound for sex determination (Chu 2001). Yet with governmental control over the population declining, such bans have proven impossible to enforce at the local level, where bribes and personal connections have more force than law. With the proliferation of private clinics offering sex-detection services, and ultrasound technicians exhibiting as much bias as parents, the situation seems to be beyond government control.

In addition to the regulation of ultrasound devices, government policymakers have sought to arrest the rise in the SRB more generally by introducing major initiatives to improve women's status, ensure old-age security, and connect birth planning with poverty alleviation (Chapter 6; Li and Peng 2000; Keith 1997 on legal measures).[16] In its March 2000 decision, the Central Committee and State Council set the normalization of the sex ratio as a goal for 2010 (article 5). Since then, with new political leaders in charge and new awareness that the culprit is not only the birth program but also the larger culture, the government's commitment to addressing the problem has intensified (Chapter 6). In January 2003, Premier Hu Jintao told the birth planning establishment in a closed meeting that it must arrest the rise in the sex ratio. In a 2004 speech he reiterated this demand, breaking the public silence on this issue among top PRC leaders. To this end, the birth commission has launched an important new program, the Action to Foster Girls (*guan'ai nuhai xingdong*), in a small number of unfortunate counties with extremely high SRBs (SG 22Dec03 BJ). In March 2004, the Ministry of Finance announced a major new pension program for couples with daughters that represented, in the words of one long-time birth official, a "huge commitment of political will" (SG 22Dec03 BJ; *China Daily* 5 August 2004). In early 2005 birth minister Zhang Weiqing announced the government's intention to amend the criminal law to outlaw fetal sex-identification and sex-selective abortion, allowing those practices only for legitimate medical purposes (*China Daily* 2005).

These are extremely encouraging developments. Yet the challenges are daunting. Short of immediate society-wide improvements in women's status—a goal difficult to achieve, given the masculinizing trends in the larger reform environment—seriously to arrest the practice of sex-selective abortion and the rise in the SRB might well require vigorous public condemnation by top PRC leaders, coupled with relaxation of the tight restrictions on childbearing. Although some researchers in the early 2000s are lobbying to move to a two-child policy, in good part to lessen the gender imbalance, policymakers have been reluctant to take these forceful and potentially partly effective steps because they might disturb the low birth rate. Yet the ignoble record of the past and the formidable problems bequeathed the future might persuade them to relent.

Despite the PRC's constitutional commitment to the equality of men and women, in the 1980s and 1990s the birth planning establishment, with the support of the political leadership, in effect used the actually existing gender inequality for its own purposes, reducing population rates on the backs of reproductive women and infant girls, born and unborn. More charitably, it deemed the damage to women and girls the "unfortunate costs" of achieving a "higher goal." This is the way the hardline advocates of the one-child policy justified these gendered practices. However they are represented, the unintended result was a perpetuation of the idea of girls' lesser value, the widespread loss of fetal life, and extremely distorted sex ratios that constitute, in the words of one prominent Chinese demographer, "the crime of the twentieth century against the twenty-first" (SG 28Nov01 US).

If the effects on gender valuations and the population structure are worrying, the larger societal consequences of the loss of female bodies and lives are formidable. The first wave of such effects has cropped up in the shortage of marriageable women. By around 2010, demographers estimate, the marriage market for first marriages will be seriously imbalanced and by 2020 about 8 percent of men, or roughly 1 million individuals, will be unable to find brides (Tuljapurkar, Li, and Feldman 1995; also Das Gupta and Li 1999; Yuan 2000; for historical precedents, see Lee and Wang 1999). The impact is greatest on poor, illiterate men. During the 1980s, the proportion of illiterate and semiliterate men not married at age 40 grew to 19 percent (from 15 percent a decade earlier) (Lee and Wang 1999, 80–81). In 2000, 3.8 percent of men aged 40 had never married, but fully 26.6 percent of those with the lowest level of schooling were not married (Wang and Mason 2004).

The image of armies of bachelors fomenting violence at home and abroad is overwrought and ahistorical (Hudson and Den Boer 2004). Yet the gender gap in marriage is already creating major social problems for poor men—and women. In border provinces, the shortage of brides has been met by importing women from Vietnam and Korea. In a disturbing if understandable development, in poor interior provinces the shortage of marriageable women has given rise to cases of informal polyandrous unions (*yiqi duofu*) in which the wife of one man informally services several others (SG 12Dec03 BJ).

Increasingly since the mid-1980s, the urgent need of poor peasant men for brides has been met by the development of clandestine smuggling networks similar to those described earlier but involved now in the long-distance buying and selling of women and adolescent girls (*maimai hunyin*) (*FEER* 1989; Zhuang 1993; Han and Eades 1995; Demick 2003). While forcible abduction occurs, more commonly, girls are lured or purchased from their families in poverty-stricken areas of the southwest, promised jobs in prosperous regions, and then transported long distances to villages in the northeast, where they are bought by poor villagers desperate for a wife and family. In a notorious case that drew public attention to the problem, in February 1988 a Shanghai research student fell into the hands of a gang who sold her to a Shandong peasant for 2480 yuan (U.S. $667). Raped repeatedly, she made several suicide attempts before being rescued by the Shanghai public security offices in May. This case was unusual because the woman was a well-educated urbanite, she was rescued, and her purchaser was sentenced to 5 years in prison for rape (*FEER* 1989). Escape from these often abusive situations is difficult, despite the work of Chinese women's advocates—including the well-known magazine *Rural Women Knowing All*, which helps rescue readers from violent husbands. The "outside brides" are cut off from their families, while village society often supports the husband, who is seen as having legitimate rights over his purchased bride (Rennie 1999). In one study in Anhui, one in six outside wives reported mistreatment that included being locked up at night by husbands fearing their escape (Han and Eades 1995). For their part, the men often end up cheated or abandoned.

Despite central and provincial government efforts to stop the trafficking in women—most notably by adopting the 1992 Law on the Protection of Women and Infants—county, township, and village officials have often turned a blind eye. At least in some areas, local officials in sending areas have considered large outflows of women beneficial to birth planning, while officials in receiving areas have seen such inflows as a solution to the local marriage problem created not by criminals but by "long-distance matchmakers" (*FEER* 1989, 42; Zhuang 1993). For the traffickers the profits have been enormous, the risk of criminal penalty slight. Given the persistence of pockets of deep poverty in rural China, the abduction and sale of marriageable women may well worsen as the high and rising sex ratios of the 1990s translate into even more serious shortages of brides in the future.

Even if it increases no further, the highly skewed sex ratio of today will have huge and distorting effects on China's culture, society, and polity that are scarcely imaginable today (Hudson and den Boer 2004; D. Yang 2004). Since its introduction, the one-child policy has been promoted as a policy requiring sacrifice today for the benefit of "generations to come." Yet the legacy that the PRC's birth planners will leave to those future generations is mixed at best. That legacy includes a widespread devaluation of the feminine, the tight attachment of women to a broad array of reproductive tasks, and large distortions in the population structure that will haunt planners, policymakers, and ordinary people for decades to come.

Political Exclusions: Unplanned Births, "Low Quality" Persons

Previous sections have shown how the birth program has powerfully stratified Chinese females along reproductive lines, creating different treatments for women in their pre-, post-, and prime reproductive years, and making infancy and fetalhood into politically (and, in turn, socially) salient categories of gendered personhood. The period between infancy and adulthood—childhood and adolescence—has also been profoundly shaped by the birth program. Just as, through labeling, the Maoist regime created good and bad classes, through categorizing all births as planned or unplanned, the post-Mao birth system has bureaucratically produced two types of children and two worlds of childhood.

One world, populated by boys and girls, is the bright new world of planned children, largely singletons. Showered with state and parental support, these youngsters have been shaped into the well-bodied, well-educated "quality" children equipped to lead China into a shiny new, globalized future. Embodying the "low quantity, high quality" norm propagated for so long, these single children have been the very raison d'être of the birth planning program, both proof of its success and justification for all the hardship meted out to so many in the name of lofty goals. Embodying significances far beyond their individual lives, these quality singletons have lived lives of enormous privilege and public visibility.

The other world, inhabited mostly by girls, is the dimmer, publicly invisible but well-populated space of the unplanned child. Usually second- or third-born offspring, these children were born outside the birth planning regime and so are not supposed to exist. Although literally created by the birth program, these unplanned children represent its dark underside, living evidence not only of the gaps in its network of control but also of the continued human problems spawned by that program of population modernization. Deprived of state support and located outside the community of legitimate citizens, these children have endured multiple forms of discrimination, becoming the "low quality" young people the birth program has tried so hard to eliminate. A look at these radically different worlds of childhood, cocreated by the same program, reveals the remarkable political productivity of birth planning, whose central discursive and bureaucratic category has created new forms of Chinese personhood and new lines of political, social, and economic exclusion.

CATEGORIZING BIRTHS: THE STATE PRODUCTION OF UNPLANNED PERSONS

The construct state "birth planning," articulated by Mao in 1956–1957 (Chapter 3), placed the categorical distinction between planned and unplanned births at the heart of China's population control efforts. Since birth planning became a nationwide political and institutional reality in the 1970s, every pregnancy in China has been designated as either planned and legal (*jihuanei shengyu*) or unplanned and illegal (*jihuawai shengyu*). With the introduction of the one-child policy in 1979–1980, planned, especially single children and their parents have been showered with material benefits and political rewards. Higher-order unplanned children and their parents have been subject to punishments ranging from steep fines and confiscation of family property to deprivation of jobs and party membership for parents to the imposition of extra school fees and withholding of textbooks from the "illegal" child (for the latter, see Ku 2003, 205–207). The central government has long forbidden the use of "local policies" permitting cadres to punish the family by excluding the child from the household register (G. Zhang 2004, 37–38). Yet local cadres have often ignored central directives on this issue, for the denial of registration has been one of the few weapons in their arsenal with some power to, if not deter unplanned childbearing, then at least encourage compliance with penalties. The use of this mechanism has given rise to a complicated politics of registration, in which parents have bargained and bribed cadres to obtain registration, while cadres have used the carrot of registration as a bargaining tool with which to convince parents to pay fines and adopt permanent contraception (Zhou 1996; SG field research). Although some, perhaps even many, couples have managed eventually to purchase or otherwise arrange for registration for their unauthorized child, many illegitimate children have remained outside the registration system for years, becoming not just unplanned children, but also unplanned adolescents and even young adults, statuses fraught with difficulties.

A LESSER LIFE FOR LARGE NUMBERS

This complicated politics around the treatment of unplanned births has resulted in diminished lives for large numbers. In China, inclusion in the household register has been a powerful determinant of one's life chances, for participation in the registration system confers membership in the political community of citizens. Those outside the registration regime have remained "black children" (*hei haizi*) or "black persons, black households" (*heiren, heihu*), illegal persons denied access to the social benefits of citizenship. Available statistics suggest that most of the unplanned persons have probably been peasants living in the rural areas or rural migrants in the cities. The vast majority have been girls, although some over-quota boys also end up as black children, a status they shed at school age (Kay Johnson, personal communication, 17 September 2003). For those in the countryside, the household register is a much less important mediator of state services, such as education and health care, than it was in the past (e.g., Zhang Li 1999), although registration appears necessary for childhood inoculations, participation in land distributions, and army enlistment. In the cities, however, registration has provided access to the full range of state services and welfare benefits. The result is that unregistered persons—in particular, rural members of the floating population—have enjoyed much less than full citizenship rights (Solinger 1999; Zhang Li 2001; PDSC 2003d). In the rapidly marketizing economy of the 1990s, some were able to bypass the state's provisioning system and obtain services, such as schooling, from the market. Yet the cost has been high, the quality poor, the struggles difficult and unending (Eckholm 1999; Kwong 2004).[17] Some youngsters, unable to obtain an education or find work, have turned to petty crime, spurring fears among some Chinese observers that the "me-first" generation, unable to distinguish right from wrong, will set off a big wave of juvenile violence (McElroy 1998; Ni 2000).

Beyond the welfare consequences is the much more fundamental problem of subjectivity, or sense of self. Individual stories culled from the press suggest that from an early age, unplanned children tend to feel unwanted, unimportant compared to their siblings, and a burden to their parents, who have often had to endure nightmarish bureaucratic travails in their efforts to obtain registration for such children (Greenhalgh 2003a; Johnson 2004). Parents describe a "black child personality"—withdrawn and self-deprecating ("looking down on themselves;" Kay Johnson, personal communication, 17 September 2003). The legal exclusion of black children from schools and other mainstream institutions only deepens their sense of deprivation. For such persons, creating a positive sense of personhood is likely to be difficult.

How many unplanned children are there? Once again, the numbers are elusive, for the state has not counted its unplanned noncitizens. Yet those numbers may be vast. As of around 2000, as much as 11 percent of China's population (135 million born between 1979 and 1999) may have come into the world unplanned. Given the disarray in China's statistics, it is impossible to estimate how many of those remained in that status.[18] But even if only a small proportion of that estimated 100 million-plus population of unplanned infants failed to obtain official registration, the absolute numbers of illegitimate young persons would be very large. The welfare and human consequences are potentially enormous.

INVISIBILIZING THE UNPLANNED, PRODUCING THE "LOW QUALITY" POPULATION: THE OFFICIAL RESPONSE

Despite the large numbers of unplanned persons effectively created by the birth planning program and despite the severity of the life problems they face, the central government's response has been to look the other way. One reason, surely, is work overload. As one sympathetic official explained, the commission faces too many pressing population problems; this one is serious but less so than many others (SG 25Nov99 BJ).[19] Yet the reasons may lie deeper than this, for large numbers of unplanned children represent awkward evidence of the small gaps in the birth planning system and the difficulties it has faced fulfilling its overarching mission of creating a well-managed, high quality population. With its optimistic rhetoric of planning and progress, the official discourse has worked to invisibilize unplanned persons in the official and public eye, deflecting attention from the problems they face. At least until recently, the discourse has been matched by an official attitude that appears neglectful at best, punitive at worst. The attitude has been that unplanned persons are not the result of a poorly conceived policy that neglected deep-seated cultural desires. Instead, they are the result of ideologically regressive citizens failing to heed the clearly stated law. Yet innocent children and now young people have been punished by exclusion from the political community and deprivation of the basic social supports needed to live in a modernizing society.

Throughout the 1980s and 1990s, this large category of youngsters constituted the deprived "other" of the indulged singleton, a pointed reminder of the continued power of the PRC regime to unwittingly create great suffering and vast privilege in the same bureaucratic act. In the early 2000s, when the birth program is more effective and childbearing desires are declining, the number of unplanned births appears to be falling. The treatment of unauthorized children also appears to be in some flux. New regulations adopted by the Public Security Bureau in 2003 require the registration of all children, regardless of birth status. For its part, the birth commission continues to distinguish sharply between compliers and noncompliers. While it is increasingly rewarding the former, there seems to be little consensus about how to treat the children of those who violate the policy. With an administration that is attentive to social problems, the time may finally be ripe to address this major unintended consequence of the politics of birth planning in years past.

Political Achievements: Planned Children, "Quality Persons"

The ultimate aim of the gargantuan birth project charted in this book was not only to lower fertility; it was to create a new generation of planned, "quality," largely single children equipped to participate in the globalized economy, society, politics, and culture of China's future. Since the birth of its first members around 1980, this new generation of singletons has been the beneficiary of unprecedented state and familial largess. Identified as the hope of the nation's global future, these youngsters have been catapulted into that brave new world with global commodities, global technologies, global experiences, and more. Their lives endlessly celebrated and obsessively charted, China's first generation of singletons is one of the best-known outcomes of the one-child policy, not only in China but around the world, which participates in the fascination with this exotic new creature: the cosmopolitan Chinese.

Less well known outside China are the improvements the birth program has helped to bring about in the well being and opportunities of surviving daughters. In both urban and rural areas, changes in family structure and sentiment—these changes *not* planned by the state—combined with the sharp drop in the number of children to produce a dramatic reevaluation by parents of the worth of sons and daughters. Girls who survived the treacherous waters of fetalhood and infancy could expect not only better care than in the past, but also a rise in status relative to their brothers (if any). We end this chapter with these happier, more long-term effects of the restratification of Chinese society, tracing their development first in the cities, where they appeared as early as the 1980s, and then in the countryside, where they have been emerging since the late 1990s.

THE "QUALITY" GENERATION: CHINA'S SINGLETONS

In sharp contrast to the unfortunate youngsters just described, planned children, especially singletons, have been made central to the political community and showered with support. Massive state and parental efforts to nurture the bodies and minds of this new generation have combined with a booming commodity culture to produce the most materially and educationally privileged generation of young people in Chinese history. The leading edge of today's singleton generation is entering the world with advanced degrees and professional jobs, cell phones and computers, condos and cars (Iritani 2003; Tomba 2004). Indeed, the extraordinary attention they have received in the foreign media seems to attest to the success of the birth program and the other child nurturers in turning this generation of Chinese youngsters into truly global young people, able to compete successfully for attention in the media capitals of the world.

Certainly, the experts and the public at large are right to worry about the psychological and social problems attending the creation of these little emperors and empresses (Fong 2004, 127–177). The focus of intense societal and familial attention, today's single children face pressures to succeed that are almost too great to meet and owe a debt of love to their parents that is almost too vast to repay (Jing 2000a; Iritani 2003). Overwhelmed by the strict discipline and demands, in some extreme cases children have ended their own lives. In one tragic case from the 1980s, a 5-year-old girl forced to practice the piano far more than she could tolerate ended her suffering by ingesting a bottle of DDT (Champagne 1992, 160). In a fit of pique, a 14-year-old Guangdong boy grabbed a meat cleaver and killed his mother and then himself when a power failure prevented her from making his dinner (Tyler 1996). Such cases are rare, but they suggest the extremes to which parent-child relations have been strained. The rash of student breakdowns and suicides and family murders has prompted China's leaders, such as former premier Zhu Rongji, to urge that the nation's overstressed children should be given less homework and more time for sport (Rennie 2000).

The larger society too must pay a price for what it has created. Chinese society must now find a place for what by most accounts is a materialistic, consumeristic, narcissistic generation of young people whose material riches seem matched by their incivility and moral poverty (Yan 2003; Rosen 2004). Feeling entitled to their privileges and empowered by their parents' dependence on them for future support, some members of this generation have taken youth rebellion to extremes. In one late 1990s incident, a boy whose father struck him for refusing to pay attention to his English lessons retorted: "Beat me now and . . . when you're old and weak, I'll beat you till you can't move" (Fong 2004, 147). Yet the new ethos is actively heralded by some. In a veritable celebration of the neoliberal spirit that some of these youngsters seem to embody, in 2002 the publisher of the Chinese edition of *Seventeen* magazine suggested that a healthy dose of materialism and selfishness will help change the thinking of future generations (Rosen 2004, 34).

Lang Lang, the world-renowned piano prodigy, provides a poignant example of the parental sacrifices made for the one-child generation and the extraordinary talent and egotism it can produce in the young (Zhao 2003). Raised by Cultural Revolution parents whose dreams for making their son a globally prominent artist were borne of their own frustrated ambitions, Lang Lang had a piano before he was two and at nine was admitted to the nation's top music conservatory. His parents made enormous sacrifices to nurture their young genius. Lang Lang's father quit his job in Shenyang and moved to Beijing, where he rented a tiny, unheated studio, serving as his son's caretaker and promoter for twelve years while his wife remained in Shenyang. Now in his 20s and based in the United States, Lang Lang is a highly sought-after celebrity, playing 150 concerts around the world each year. He has played solo in New York's Mostly Mozart Festival and appeared numerous times on national television in the United States. While all agree on the pianist's musical talent, music critics in the United States see him as more style than substance. The *New York Times*'s music critic calls his exuberant style exaggerated and tasteless: "He is a sensation and it has gone to his head" (Zhao 2003).

Despite some very real psychosocial problems, today's young generation of highly educated, culturally sophisticated, globally savvy persons will surely facilitate China's entry into the world as a force to contend with. Perhaps just as important, they will change what it means to be Chinese, forcing revision of a host of long-held stereotypes of the mainland Chinese as culturally and economically backward.[20] And the birth planning establishment can claim some credit. By working relentlessly to lower fertility and foster child quality, the birth system has made a major contribution to the production of this new kind of globally savvy person. Indeed, the quality singleton must count as one of its crowning achievements.

CITY GIRLS: TREASURES AT LEAST EQUAL TO BOYS

Perhaps the biggest beneficiaries of the one-child policy have been urban singleton daughters. Their parents' only treasure, since the 1980s single daughters in China's cities have enjoyed privileged childhoods little different from those of their male counterparts (Jing 2000a; Milwertz 1997). The anthropological research of Vanessa Fong, conducted in Dalian during 1997–2000, reveals the advantages teenage girls born under the one-child policy have now reaped (Fong 2001, 2004). With no brothers to compete for their parents' attention and resources, and with parents expecting reciprocation in the form of extensive old-age support, these teens have been socialized to value educational and career success and provided the resources with which to achieve it. Fong argues that this generation of urban singleton girls has been empowered to challenge some of the masculinist gender norms that have long dominated Chinese life. These girls and their parents have successfully defied norms that harm their interests (those presenting girls as unfilial and less worthy of parental investment), even as they have conformed to others (such as norms portraying women as more patient, meticulous, responsible, and obedient) that further their interests in a labor market that offers young women jobs primarily in the service sector and light industry. In a reversal of gender fortunes, in cities such as Shanghai and Dalian young women today enjoy a marriage market that favors brides and a job market with attractive opportunities earmarked for "feminine" applicants. Indeed, some of the hottest and best paying jobs in today's globalizing service economy (bilingual secretaries, public relations girls, fashion models) are open exclusively to young women with good looks and sex appeal, giving rise to a newly self-confident and visible group of misses (*xiaojie*) enjoying social mobility based on youth and beauty (Zhang Zhen 2001). Although the steep gender and class inequalities of the reform era narrow their occupational choices, with the support of their parents and the state they may well be more prepared than Chinese women have ever been for the jobs that are available. And, though their youth will fade and marriage will likely bring pressures to conform to the traditional role of "virtuous wife and good mother," for the time being many of these young women possess the self-confidence that comes from being valued members of their families and the larger society. For them, the one-child policy seems to have been a real blessing.

VILLAGE GIRLS: BETTER UPBRINGING FOR NEW CAREGIVERS

One of the happiest and least expected long-term effects of the one-child policy is a nascent rise in the status of rural girls. In the 1980s, field studies suggest, rural girls, soon to marry out, were treated like "goods on which one loses," allocated a smaller share of family resources and discriminated against in schooling and other areas (Wolf 1985; Zhang 2002). Although peasant couples expressed desires for complete families of one son and one daughter, the boy was seen as an essential source of labor and old-age support, while the girl was merely desirable. Beneath this familiar pattern of son preference and daughter discrimination, however, tectonic shifts were taking place in generational and gender relations within the peasant family

(Chapter 7). As the bond between parents and sons frayed, and filial respect gave way to filial fights and abandonment of the old, parents began to take a fresh interest in their daughters, who were seen as emotionally closer and more reliable than their sons—in short, prospective providers of personal care and even economic assistance in old age. By the end of the 1980s, villagers in many parts of the country were expressing a growing interest in raising a daughter (Greenhalgh and Li 1995; Zhang 2002). Married women's growing economic power, freedom from the demands of in-laws, and closer ties to their natal families have helped make female filiality practically more feasible and culturally more acceptable (Judd 1994; Han and Eades 1995; Xie, Gu, and Hardee 2000; Miller 2004).

By the late 1990s, some field studies suggest, this interest in raising daughters had turned to active efforts to nurture them as future caregivers. In rural Hubei, anthropologist Zhang Hong found, the widespread refusal of sons to provide old-age support has led parents to begin cultivating their daughters as future economic providers by investing heavily in their upbringing and educations (Zhang 2003; see also Yan 2003). In a surprising development, since the late 1990s some parents have become as committed to the well-being of their daughters as of their sons (Zhang 2003). Articulating a new discourse on "giving daughters a fair chance" and "not disappointing their daughters," the Hubei villagers have begun to make substantial financial commitments to the higher education of their girls, even reducing their contributions to their sons' education to support an academically promising daughter. In a context in which the growing geographical mobility and economic selfishness of the young has made filial support increasingly uncertain, rural parents are also accepting new, more bilateral marriage forms in which young couples can live with either set of parents but must provide economic support for both. Although the Hubei village is atypical in some ways, the fundamental dynamics underlying the growing equality in the treatment of sons and daughters include the shrinkage in the number of children and the abrogation of filial duties by sons.[21] These two trends, which are rooted in the larger economic currents of socialist construction and reform, appear to be widespread. If these trends are indeed general, village parents' growing investment in their daughters marks a big and important change. The birth program can claim partial credit for helping improve the status of rural girls by limiting the number of children parents are able to have.

CHAPTER 9

Remaking China's Politics and Global Position

IN WAYS BOTH INTENDED and not, the PRC's post-Mao project on population has had an enormous impact on Chinese politics, rebuilding state power, remaking state-society relations, and reestablishing China's global position in complex and contradictory ways. Almost none of these larger political consequences has been brought to light in the existing literature.[1] In this chapter we widen our exploration of the effects of the PRC's rapid governmentalization of population by canvassing these broad political consequences of the birth project. In each section we first set out what the makers of that project hoped to achieve, before spelling out what they actually achieved and, in main outline, why. In this final chapter before our conclusion, we draw on material introduced earlier and paint with a broad brush.

Strengthening the Socialist Party-State

In population, post-Mao leaders found an ideal arena in which to strengthen a socialist state weakened by the depredations of late Maoism.[2] The opportunities in population lay in its political history and in its conventional definition. Politically, as we have seen, Mao's successors regarded his failure to control population growth one of his major mistakes. By taking decisive charge of this domain, Deng-era leaders could both "rectify an historical error" and demonstrate the ability of a new reform-minded regime to solve one of the most fundamental problems in China's development—and produce modernity at long last. Population was also an attractive domain for the reform regime because "population"—unlike, say, "culture,"—was conventionally defined as a biological entity dictating an approach to governance guided by science. The centrality of science to managing the population problem allowed the state to promote the development of a host of new sciences surrounding population and to present itself as a scientific modernizer committed to using modern science and technology to solve China's developmental problems. Finally, population was an appealing arena for the rebuilding of the socialist state because population processes unfolded over long periods of time and were intimately related to social and economic development. Good population planning and policymaking thus required the sorts of comprehensive, short- and long-term planning capabilities that were the hallmark of the socialist state. Over the next 25 years, the makers of the post-Mao population project took full advantage of these opportunities. With population as their object, they constructed an enormous edifice of knowledge and state bureaucratic power that sought, and largely managed, to take charge of the production and, to a lesser extent, the "quality" of life itself. The results were impressive. The population project has strengthened the socialist party-state, helping to transform it into a powerful, scientific, globally ambitious modernizer whose new powers extend to taking charge of the production and enhancement of life itself. Although science was fundamental to this new project, in part because of the sensitivity of the population question, the population science that created the one-child policy was highly politicized. That left the population field to enforce an overly restrictive policy whose basis was more scientistic than scientific. State birth planning has also extended state power over human numbers into a place it has not gone before—the womb, deemed the source of generativity—while gradually shifting power over human "quality" away from the state to other social and economic entities. Over the last quarter century, the state has both gained and given up power over Chinese life.

POPULATION AND STATE STRENGTHENING

In the reform decades, population has been the site for a remarkable buildup of institutional and discursive power centered in the state. Although that power is specific to the social sector, social issues (including migration, social security, and women's "quality," in addition to the management of population quantity and quality) have come to occupy an ever-larger place on the state's agenda. Behind that expansion of state power lay a particular formulation of the population problem. Drawing on Western science, the makers of the PRC's post-Mao project defined the population problem as a crisis of modernization, in which excessively rapid population growth was sabotaging economic growth and ruining the environment, keeping China forever backward in the global order of things (Chapter 7). The "crisis-of-modernization" formulation was crucial, not only because it demanded tight norms and tough enforcement, significances discussed earlier. It was also crucial in a broader sense, for this crisis required the existence of a strong regime with the political will and might to "save" the nation from backwardness and restore its global greatness, through the firm and uncompromising control of population growth. More specifically, resolving this crisis of the nation required a governmental authority that was *strong*, that is, willing and able to impose a drastic solution despite the domestic political costs; *scientific*, able to understand and manage population in all its dynamic, numerical complexity; and *global-minded*, prepared to scour the world for useful scientific resources and to seek every opportunity to use population work to China's global advantage. Constantly referring to this crisis rationale, and frequently updating the crisis story with new demographic facts and figures, China's population establishment proceeded to build precisely that kind of state.

As a result of these efforts, during the last 25 years population has become the site for the production of a remarkable degree of regime power in the realm of the social. Solving the problem of population has been politically highly productive, entailing the creation of a vast multilevel network of organizations and institutions and a new terrain of socialist legality made up of documents of every sort, from opinions to decisions, regulations, laws, and technical enforcement rules. This organizational and regulatory "sprawl," in Vivienne Shue's (1995) apt description, is not especially surprising, for the placement of a new policy issue on the political agenda often results in the creation of new institutions and laws. Yet population was no ordinary policy issue. The extraordinary difficulty of enforcing the one-child policy—widely known throughout the 1980s and 1990s as the "number-one difficulty" (*diyinan*)—has forced those responsible for population work to be constantly holding work meetings, assessing the dimensions of the new problems that were endlessly cropping up, and creating more rules, plans, measures, and slogans to counter those difficulties. No matter how negative the reaction from ordinary peasants or grassroots cadres, the official response has never been to abandon the effort. Instead, each new wave of opposition has become the occasion for another wave of state- and party-building and the recruitment of ever more collateral sectors of the party, government, and society into population work. The sheer amount of economic resources (time, money, energy, brainpower), to say nothing of political capital, expended in managing the population "crisis" has been striking. The ever greater number and bulk of yearbooks, encyclopedias, chronologies, and other compendia put out by the birth commission and its subsidiary organizations to document their activities attest to this build-up of state capacity around the issue of population. The 1,454-page *Encyclopedia of Birth Planning* (EBP 1997) is but the most extreme example.

The expansion of state power in the domain of population can also be charted in the discursive field, which has witnessed the proliferation of ever more categories of enforcement—planned and unplanned births, compliant and resistant couples, energetic and lax cadres, late and early births, well- and ill-timed marriages, and so on. As life has been sorted into ever more and more finely graded classifications, growing numbers of people and practices have been turned into objects of state surveillance, regulation, and control, with profound effects not just on people's reproductive lives but on their subjectivities and material well-being as well.

The urgent project of "resolving the population crisis" has thus allowed post-Mao leaders to rebuild and expand their regime's institutional, legal, regulatory, and discursive power around a new and important domain: the people themselves. Under the guidance of the party and state, population has mushroomed into a monumental project, involving concerted efforts on the part of virtually every sector of state and society. The political success or failure of the regime's efforts should be measured not in the widespread rural resistance to the one-child rule but in the remarkable popular legitimacy of the larger project. This legitimacy is evident in the virtually universal acceptance of the state's population crisis rationale, of its right to decide the number of children couples will have, and of its right to intervene deeply in people's bodies to enforce its birth limits. A top birth planning official was exaggerating only slightly when he remarked: "All Chinese agree on the necessity of population control. It is no longer [just] a policy, it is a habit" (SG 18Dec03 BJ).[3]

The build-up of regime capacity around population has extended state power into new domains. In the literature on China's population program, the 825 million IUD insertions, IUD removals, abortions, and sterilizations that by 2001 had been conducted on women's (and, to a lesser extent, men's) bodies over the last three decades have been treated as matters of contraceptive prevalence and reproductive health (Table 4). The larger political implications of this surgical effort have scarcely been considered. Yet the power relations that are being created bear close reflection, for every one of these state-mandated surgeries is also a serious political act that has extended the reach of the state to a place it had never gone during Mao's lifetime. State power now reaches not only into the bedroom, intervening in reproductive deliberations and sexual intimacies that had long belonged to the sphere of the patriarchal family. It also reaches into the womb, considered the source of generativity for the woman, her kin, and her community. The intense, life-and-death resistances that have been mounted against sterilization, which in the Chinese cultural scheme dissipates vital essence (*qi*) and stops new life forever, reveal the enormity of the stakes involved in this contest to control the production of new life. With its intervention in population, the state has penetrated to the biological and symbolic core of Chinese society, taking unto itself awesome new powers that go beyond the remaking of the family to the making of human life itself. Although the state's hegemony is far from complete, through population the regime has taken charge of the production and enhancement of life itself.

THE SCIENTIFIC STATE: POPULATION
SCIENCE AND SCIENTISM

Because of the importance of science to the post-Mao regime, an importance that was as much political as instrumental, science—and scientism—were fundamental to the post-Mao population project. In population, as in other fields, the modern scientism of the post-Mao era built on and largely supplanted the Marxist scientism of the Mao era. As noted in Chapter 3, as early as 1965, the first birth commission's director Yang Zhenya described the state's incipient birth planning policy as a scientific application of Mao Zedong Thought to the problem of population. Fifteen years later, the rise of population on the political agenda was accompanied by the emergence of a large array of new sciences of population quantity and quality, all closely linked to the state. Introduced by newly elevated professionals, modern science and its associated technologies have played key roles in the formulation, management, and implementation of the PRC's birth policy. As described in previous chapters, policy formulation has been guided by cybernetic and demographic science; program management has been carried out by scientific (data-based) techniques; and policy implementation has made use of scientific (numerical and biomedical) propaganda and education, as well as modern contraceptive technology. Through both their legitimating functions and their instrumental effects, these modern sciences and technologies of population have strengthened population control and the state. At the mass level, persistent efforts to convey "scientific knowledge" of reproduction to the people have given them quantitative understandings of the population problem and biomedical understandings of reproduction. More generally, state pedagogies have taught ordinary Chinese to reason with numbers and to act in accordance with the knowledge of modern science. Such efforts have brought practical benefits—"empowering" the people with scientific knowledge and improving their health—even as they have reinforced the expert authority of the regime. As Foucault said of modern power generally, the spread of scientific logics is certainly not pernicious, but it is dangerous because it brings other effects in its train.

The story of population science in the PRC is more complicated, however. Because the sciences of population were brought to life by the state and located within it, there was little separation between science and the state, science and politics.[4] With the population issue so politicized (for reasons illuminated in Chapters 3 and 4), scientists working on population had difficulty defining and defending a politically independent realm of science that was in full accord with international scientific norms. Instead, political leaders had the final say over everything, with political criteria often taking precedence over scientific ones. Because modern science was the new reform-era ideology, science became the authority in whose name everything had to be done. As a result, use of the term "science" began to lose its moorings in science-like activities and attach itself to ever more ideas and practices.

In the control of population quantity virtually all policy initiatives—from the original one-child-for-all policy to its later revisions—have been described as the scientific (and thus "correct" or *zhengque*) solutions to the scientifically defined problem of a population-economy-environment crisis. In the promotion of quality too, the term "science" has proliferated out of control, with everything from nutritional supplements to diapers now promoted as scientifically guaranteed to enhance the infant body and brain. In the population domain, "science" seems to have become one of those broad and hence largely meaningless, if powerful and efficacious, terms like "feudalism." Whereas "feudal" appears to mean anything old, bad, and indigenously Chinese, "scientific" has come to mean anything new, good, and foreign. Although population is by no means the only arena in which the meanings attached to "science" have grown diffuse, the domain of population has lent itself especially readily to this tendency. Population has been wide open to scientism because it is a social field and therefore intrinsically fuzzy, because population studies is the most scientific or quantitative of the social sciences, and because population control has involved extremely high political stakes. Yet the consequences of the politicization of science are serious. They were perhaps most serious in the arena of policymaking in the early Deng era.

In the late 1970s and early 1980s, when the one-child policy was being made, science was deeply intermeshed with regime politics, making it difficult to judge what was scientific and what was not. China's leaders certainly had no independent "truly scientific" source of advice; China's people were even less able to differentiate the scientific from the scientistic. Even the scientists may have had difficulty negotiating the border between science and politics, for to be politically influential one had to keep political considerations always in mind, practicing a kind of science that allowed political factors often to enter in (SG 1986–89 BJ, interviews with leading natural and social scientists). This sieve-like boundary between science and politics is important, because what was done in the name of science was often more scientistic than scientific. Although this is not the place for an extended discussion of Chinese population science, a few pointed examples can make the point (for fuller treatment, see Greenhalgh 2003b, 2005b). For instance, the year 2080 population target that underlay the one-child policy was rooted in little more than educated guesswork. Although population is a social realm, as noted in the introduction to this part, the one-child policy was created from a physical science (cybernetics) that excluded cultural and social factors by definition. The larger body of work that produced the one-child policy was based on Club-of-Rome concepts that were widely derided by many in the international population studies community and on an empirical foundation that was shaky by any standard. Of course, in any country much that goes by the name of science (and especially social science) is based on contested concepts and limited data. Yet this was an extreme case, and one whose consequences were especially severe. While the use of "science" as a set of analytical tools and a legitimating rationale has certainly strengthened the state in the ways just described, the politicized nature of Chinese population science has meant that the state has been vigorously enforcing a policy that was neither meaningfully scientific nor realistic. The consequences for China's society need no repetition.

Fortunately, that early triumph of cybernetic science, enduring though its effects have been, represented only the first skirmish in a battle of population sciences that has continued to this day. In the intervening decades, many people have promoted many different agendas on population under the banner of modern science and social science. As we saw in Chapter 6, in the early 2000s science has become the authority for some remarkably people-oriented projects on population. This development suggests that various assemblages labeled "science" may hold the potential to transform China's population project in quite fundamental—and positive—ways. We consider this possibility in the next chapter.

Transforming State-Society Relations

Because it sought to radically remake Chinese society, the birth planning project inevitably transformed relations between state and society. Following the machine-like model of the engineer, beginning in the early 1980s program designers created a giant social-systems-engineering apparatus aimed at facilitating the meticulous control of individual reproduction and the production of particular subjects charged with population limitation and perfection. This apparatus instilled top-down authority relations that, though aspiring to engineer subjects who would make the right demographic decisions, instead subjected people to relentless control by cadres of the state. The result was predictable: intense resistance from the peasants and the necessity of yet stronger controls. Demographic engineering created as many problems as it solved. The project of ideologically producing "voluntarism," crucial to the CCP's identity as a party that does not coerce the people, was also fraught with problems. Although the "conscientious acceptance" of the one-child norm spread rapidly among urban couples, it spread slowly among the rural majority, making the production of voluntarism the always-unfinished project of the birth program.

In the early 2000s, official worries about reproductive decision making and voluntarism are deepening. With Chinese society undergoing rapid change, program leaders feel a sense of impending crisis, for a rights-oriented, market-minded populace will not tolerate the sorts of administrative measures that have been required to keep rural fertility down in the past (Chapter 6). Concerned about sustaining their work, since the mid-1990s, and especially since 2000, reformers have introduced new techniques of governance based on new scientific logics. These still partial shifts—from direct control by the state to indirect regulation of "autonomous, self-regulating" subjects; from natural science rationales to social science logics espousing a "human-centered" approach; and from top-down governance to village self-government—are part of a larger state-to-society shift in modes of regulation that is occurring in the PRC in the early twenty-first century. How much these reforms will change things remains to be seen. Although some of the changes make a real difference to individuals, in the early 2000s "individual autonomy," "people as the core," and "democracy" remain limited and closely managed by the central state.

Meanwhile, ethnographies suggest, profound changes are underway in rural Chinese society. While the state remains preoccupied with figuring out how to manage fertility decline from above, in the villages farm families caught up in the capitalist market are experiencing deep disruptions that are fostering the very self-regulation and voluntarism the state has long sought to induce. More evident in wealthier and more urbanized areas and groups, these changes, which are the product less of the birth program than of the disciplining of desire by the market, the professions, and other forces within modern society, might eventually lead to the better harmonized state-society relations the birth program has always sought to create.

ENGINEERING SOCIAL CHANGE: FROM SUBJECTION
TO SUBJECT-IFICATION

Since the beginning of the reform period, the PRC has taken an unusual social engineering approach to population work that has significantly rearranged the relations between state and society. The principal architects of the one-child policy were systems engineers who laid out a vision of population control as a giant social-systems-engineering project (e.g., Song, Tuan, and Yu 1985, 29–32). Aided by an increasingly technocratic culture and a government increasingly headed by engineers, their vision caught on to become the official model for the quantitative aspect of birth work. Reaffirmed again and again in the 1980s and 1990s, the systems-engineering model now occupies a central place in Comprehensive Reform for the early 2000s (Chapter 6). (On the larger trends in culture and politics, see Suttmeier 1989; Hua Shiping 1995; Li Cheng 2001; on the social engineering of human "quality," see Bakken 2000, 50–81.)

The notion of population engineering was no mere metaphor. Quite the contrary. Over the last few decades China's birth system has created a giant apparatus that seeks—and to a surprising extent achieves—meticulous surveillance, management, and control of practically every aspect of the reproductive lives of 1.3 billion Chinese. China's demographic "engineers" (scientists, planners, administrators, and so on) created this institutional, legal, political, and discursive apparatus by applying a kind of macro-to-micro systems thinking rarely applied with such rigor to a field of social policy. Certainly, the *dream* of engineering social change has been widely shared by social planners throughout the world (Scott 1998). Yet rarely has that dream been so well implemented as in the PRC's birth program. Following standard organizational schemes in the PRC bureaucracy, the makers of the Chinese program divided the work into vertical-functional systems (policy-and-legislation, planning-statistics-finance, propaganda-and-education, science-and-technology, personnel, and so on), and horizontal-territorial systems (center, province, prefecture, county, township, village). They then systematically connected the birth system to other systems (the health ministry, the economic ministries, the public security system, the mass organizations, and so forth), creating a giant super-system embracing China's population-economy-society. Today, the engineers of China's population continue to technically perfect the program apparatus through informatization and computerization, processes aimed at improving the gathering, processing, and delivery of data so that accurate information will flow rapidly within and between the subsystems making up the whole. The results have been remarkable. Even with all the resistances, slippages, holes, and patches in the network of control, China's population planners have achieved a degree of totalistic control over a society's demographic affairs that may be unique in human history. For individuals, and especially women, who have been positioned as key agents of birth limitation and child perfection, population engineering has brought the subjection of ever more aspects of reproductive thought and practice to the regulatory power of a (selectively) control-obsessed state. The degree of regulation has been quite stunning. Simply to give birth to a first child, for example, in the early 1990s a woman had to fill out twelve different forms (Scharping 2003, 94–96).

This detailed control of the levers of demographic change might well appeal to the tinkering imagination of the engineer. The social scientist, however, is likely to be troubled by the machinelike character of the model underlying the larger project, the values it embodies, and the power relations it specifies. Underlying and organizing this engineering project is a mechanistic model in which the human as human has no place. Radically materialistic, this model removes the messy stuff of culture, social structure, and politics, treating people—that is, women—like biological entities whose "vital rates" can be manipulated up or down with no attention to the cultural, social, and political causes or consequences of those manipulations. The engineering model also specifies a top-down set of power relations that leaves ordinary people subject to the will of the engineer-administrator in the state. This culture-blind, top-down model of population transformation has been the dominant, indeed, hegemonic approach to birth planning since its inception. Selected social and cultural factors have come to inform the policy rules and their implementation through the efforts of China's social scientists and through the workings of the mass line (Chapters 3 and 7). Yet throughout the 1980s and 1990s there was no significant change in the top-down state-centric structure of decision making and authority relations.

The reforms underway in the early 2000s seek to reduce the red tape by abolishing some of the micromanagerial practices in which reproduction has become enmeshed. While a cursory inspection might suggest that little has changed, in fact these reforms are part of a profound shift in the underlying strategy of reproductive regulation that was detailed in Chapter 6. Under "birth according to plan" the regime charged its agents with directly controlling every aspect of reproduction. It was a costly approach that was resisted by rural cadres and masses alike. The new "birth according to law" being promoted in the 2000s seeks a more indirect form of control that works through individual desires and interests. Birth according to law assumes an "autonomous, self-regulating individual" and seeks to construct that kind of individual. The social-systems apparatus is being reengineered to produce a more "active" subject who can "autonomously" regulate herself in the way the state wishes. With this shift from Leninist to neoliberal biopolitics, a critical shift is underway from individual *subjection* to individual *subject-ification*. The aim of these neoliberalizing reforms is not less control, it is better control—that is, better effects at lower administrative and political cost to the state. Yet it matters greatly to individuals whether they are being subjected to direct state control, shaped into revolutionary-socialist subjects planning their births "voluntarily," or fashioned into market-socialist subjects regulating their reproduction "autonomously." We return to this issue in the book's Conclusion.

These shifts have been accompanied and partly guided by new scientific reasoning about reproductive regulation. Since the late 1970s, when "population" was brought into being as an object of science and governance, Chinese scientists and officials have realized that population had its own intrinsic regularities and laws (age structure dynamics, population momentum, and so on) that had to be respected in order for state regulation to be effective. In the 1980s and early 1990s Leninists tried to run birth planning on a natural science model, reducing people to biological objects of control and neglecting the cultural and social context that shaped those biological processes. The results fell short of expectation. Since the mid-1990s, program and political leaders have come to believe that for regulation to be effective, intervention must be indirect and treat its objects as cultural subjects rather than simply biological bodies. Guided by social science understandings, reformers have introduced new "client-centered" approaches that "make people the core" in order to promote "all-round human development." While this shift is promising, the mechanistic systems-engineering apparatus that guides birth work poses formidable obstacles to change, for the top-down relationships it specifies are the very opposite of the relationships the human-centered reforms seek to promote. Chinese reformers have faced an uphill battle trying to upend an entrenched authority structure (SG 22Nov99 BJ). Foreign organizations assisting them have found the challenges of flattening the organizational structure of management and evaluation to be daunting (Holcombe 2003). Although a modified engineering apparatus may well permit the creation of the kinds of self-regulating reproductive subjects desired by the state, that entrenched apparatus may work to ensure that the state continues to play a much larger role than the market in shaping the interests, needs, and desires of those "autonomous" reproductive subjects. What may evolve is a distinctly Chinese "Leninist neoliberalism" in which the party-state plays a significant role in defining human-centered reproductive management and in assembling the necessary rationalities and techniques to carry it out.

MANAGED DEMOCRACY: THE SOLUTION TO THE EARLY 2000S PROGRAM CRISIS?

In their search for ways out of the perceived crisis of disliked methods and dissatisfied publics, the Comprehensive Reformers have also introduced a form of "managed democracy" in birth planning. Yet the limitations of "democracy" in the Chinese context constrain the potential of this new solution. As described in Chapter 6, reproductive democracy involves not the introduction of "family planning" by individuals but rather the integration of state birth planning into the ongoing experiment in village self-government.

Will village self-administration of birth planning improve methods and ease public discontent? The answer is "yes, but." On the positive side, even though the procedural changes are small, incremental improvements are likely to mean a lot to villagers, especially given the way the program has treated women in the past (Chapter 8). By making it next to impossible for cadres to violate the rules or engage in financial malfeasance, the changes may make village leaders more accountable and the exercise of authority less arbitrary, giving ordinary villagers a sense of empowerment in relation to their immediate leaders. Yet, as in other domains of rural governance, the evidence for the effectiveness of village democracy in solving fundamental problems suggests skepticism (Bernstein and Lu 2003). Although villagers will surely welcome having more say in how their lives are administered, the village administration of birth planning leaves many of the tough enforcement measures in place. These measures include compulsory sterilization and steep fines for couples, and stringent responsibility systems for cadres. Field studies suggest that birth planning is still treated like "official" state business, although that business must now be conducted in legally prescribed ways (Alpermann 2001; also O'Brien 1996). Moreover, village adherence to state law is now more closely monitored by township officials, and birth planning remains one of the policy areas in which pressure from higher levels of the government is consistently strong (Alpermann 2001). Like revenue collection, birth planning has "hard targets" that cadres subject to tight responsibility systems cannot, and generally do not, ignore (O'Brien and Li 1999). And, aside from these issues of enforcement, the highly restrictive policy, far from being relaxed, is now embedded in national law. That policy is contributing to the widespread abortion of female fetuses and, in turn, a general if muffled distress about the ethical violations and skewed gender ratios. This sense of distress may not be expressed in the formal political arena, but it is likely to leave villagers feeling that Comprehensive Reform does not address the core problems associated with the birth program.

The major reason village self-administration is unlikely to solve the fundamental problems of the birth program is that it represents top-down democracy that is managed from above and designed to advance primarily regime interests. Both the procedures and the substance of birth planning are dictated by national program leaders (with, of course, structured input from localities through provincial and national work conferences). Although individual couples do have somewhat more room for maneuver under managed democracy, their circle of freedom remains small and confined to minor matters; they do not engage with the core issues of population policy. As O'Brien and Li (1999) remind us, the center trusts the masses only so far. In birth planning, local desires regarding the core issues—the number of children allowed and the necessity of using "long-term, effective" contraception—are largely structured out of the political process. Yet realistically, change can take place only one step at a time. Lest we sound too pessimistic, we want to underscore the existence of a large middle ground in which the PRC can mitigate all sorts of problems—of both state and society—by improvements that stop short of all-out democratization. Despite its limitations, for the time being partial democratization represents an advance.

AN INCREASINGLY SELF-REGULATED AND SELF-DISCIPLINED POPULATION

While the central state remains preoccupied with figuring out how to produce "self-regulating" subjects and "democratic" villages, the view from the community and family levels suggests that the concerns of the central government are quietly being obviated by massive change in family structure and sentiment. Encouraged by the professions and the market, which have shaped people's needs and desires to their own ends, these transformations in domestic life have been working to promote self-regulation to the "modern norms" of low quantity and, even more so, high quality.

Self-correction to the state norm has long been the dominant mode of regulating population "quality." As argued in Chapter 7, because the state norm of the healthy, well-educated child has been seductive, serving parental security needs and social mobility aspirations, parents have taken the quality project as their own, investing enormous amounts of time, money, and energy in enhancing the bodies and minds of their children. As more and more societal forces have entered the scene, the whole society now seems to be in the business of producing the quality child. Self-regulation is not a problem in this sphere. Even in the sphere of quantity, whose norm has been repressive, self-regulation appears to be spreading. As discussed in Chapter 7, profound changes in rural family life and child economics— initiated by the socialist transformations of the 1950s, quickened by the marketizing reforms of the 1980s, and further deepened by the economic rush and transnationalization of the 1990s and early 2000s—have led to striking changes in childbearing preferences. In some areas, son preferences have been waning, daughters have been gaining value, and family size ideals have been shrinking. Already evident in the 1980s, these changes have accelerated in the late 1990s and early 2000s, as the first generation of young people born under the one-child policy comes of marital and reproductive age. Though prompted largely by broader economic and political transformations rather than by the efforts of the regime's birth program, these changes in reproductive culture have led to a growing convergence between state and farmer fertility norms.[5] Although these changes are still very partial and are more evident in "modern" (urbanized, educated, wealthy) areas and groups, they suggest that, if economic development continues to spread, self-regulation and eventually even one-childization may well be the wave of the rural future. In the quantity dimension too, the state's role has begun to shrink and will likely continue to do so.

When we consider both dimensions of population policy, it becomes clear that Chinese society has become increasingly self-regulatory, especially since the early 1990s. If this analysis is correct and people are embracing the official norms for reasons only partly of the state's making, then the real crisis facing the birth program may be not that people are not self-correcting to the official norm but that people are accepting that norm too enthusiastically. The result of this increasingly market-driven "normalization" of Chinese society is fertility that is extremely low and likely to fall further. Rapid decline in childbearing to such minimal levels is bringing serious social problems, including a sharpening gender imbalance and an imminent crisis of social security (discussed more just below). The 2003 renaming of the birth commission as the National Population and Birth Planning Commission is a timely change, for the commission will now have to devote growing attention to managing the problems created by the earlier excessive success of the birth planning project.

Globalizing China

The makers of the post-Mao population project had truly global ambitions. Chapters 5 and 6 have highlighted the globalizing impetus behind the reforms launched since the mid-1990s. Although less evident, the birth project had important international and internationalizing features from the late 1970s (Chapters 3 and 4). The transnational has figured in both the means and the ultimate ends of state birth planning. In devising solutions to China's population problems, PRC policymakers and program leaders drew extensively, and increasingly, on concepts and techniques circulating in the international environment, sinifying and incorporating them wherever useful. Even more important, their aims were transnational, seeking to make signal contributions to China's transformation into a global power. More specifically, in the early post-Mao era, the makers of the population project sought through population control to create a modern society whose internal characteristics would match the global norm, whose low growth rate would speed the achievement of world-class per capita income levels, and whose physical and mental quality would constitute a labor force able to successfully compete in the global capitalist economy. Population was thus crucial to the social and economic projects of a globalizing regime. Birth planning was also motivated by ethical objectives. The makers of the one-child policy fervently hoped that birth planning would demonstrate China's advance beyond the isolationism of the Maoist era and its emergence as a responsible and ethical member of the world community of nations.

The results of these diverse globalizing initiatives were mixed. Efforts to utilize transnational resources have multiplied China's links to global science and policy networks. Global media attention, while embarrassing, has also made PRC leaders more savvy about, and responsive to, the power of the media in world politics. Population control also helped China create a society more fitting to its aspirations as a modern, global power. By the turn of the millennium, China's society had been normalized to the global standard in some respects, though it had grown severely distorted in others. Economic goals—in particular, boosting per capita income—provided a major rationale for the adoption of the drastic one-child policy. China's rapid fertility decline may have contributed to the spectacular economic growth of recent decades by producing a "demographic bonus" of a large number of working-age people at a crucial time. By the same token, however, the resulting burden of a rapidly aging population may well jeopardize economic growth in the future. To the extent that the birth program accelerated the fertility decline—an extent that is probably significant but unmeasurable—the birth program deserves some credit for both economic boom and prospective slowdown. Finally, in the arena of ethics, drastic control of Chinese population growth has contributed handsomely to the decline in worldwide population growth rates, enhancing China's reputation as a responsible member of the world community. At the same time, however, the means used to achieve these ends have provoked ethical concerns around the world. Despite the fervent hopes of its makers, the population project has left the PRC with a moral stigma that it will be difficult to remove. Today's reforms are designed in part to restore China's image as a nation that treats its people well.

NEW CONNECTIONS TO THE WORLD

From the beginning, the makers of the PRC's post-Mao population program have drawn heavily on the global stock of scientific techniques, policy ideas, and contraceptive technologies. This search for foreign tools has been a deliberate and basic strategy of program building. As a recent birth commission report puts it, "China has always fully recognized the role and cherishe[d] the positive effects of international exchanges and cooperation" (SBPC 2001b). The result has been a large influx of foreign, largely Western, concepts and methods, growing connections to the world—and a policy and program quite deeply if selectively influenced by external ideas.

In policy formulation, the PRC has drawn extensively on foreign scientific ideas and techniques. As noted earlier, the one-child-for-all policy created in

1979–1980 was based on cybernetic methods borrowed from Europe, while its crisis rationale was modeled on notions popularized by the U.S.-based Club of Rome in the early to mid-1970s. The late 1980s decision to "stabilize" that policy in its one-to-two-child guise was based on the results of a decomposition analysis that showed that the fertility rise of the late 1980s was primarily a result of changes in the age structure and age-related behaviors (as well as administrative decentralization), not the policy relaxation of the mid-1980s (Zeng Yi 1989). The underlying techniques were drawn from international demography, whose methods Chinese scholars began to absorb only from the early 1980s.

In policy implementation, the package of normative, remunerative, and coercive methods used during the Deng era drew largely on Chinese ideas and precedents. Since the early 1990s, however, enforcement methods have been significantly internationalized. As discussed in Chapter 5, the reforms introduced in the mid-1990s were based almost exclusively on transnational ideas and ideals, suitably sinified to fit the local context. The new emphases on quality of care, reproductive health, informed choice, client rights, and women's empowerment, for example, all derived from initiatives emanating from the United Nations conference in Cairo in 1994. The Comprehensive Reform launched in the early 2000s borrowed extensively from the Western literature on organizational leadership and public administration. Major innovations in project management and program evaluation—including "scientific management," "democracy," "human-centered" service delivery, and "management by objectives"—have been modeled on best practice in the West (Chapter 6). In rhetoric and to a growing extent also in reality, the PRC is bringing its program into line with international thinking on policy enforcement and program administration. Contraceptive technology has also become increasingly internationalized. Since the early 1990s, for example, the original Chinese-made steel ring IUDs have been gradually replaced by the safer, internationally standard copper-T IUDs, and the subdermal implant Norplant has taken its place among the contraceptive options available to some categories of couples.

Solving China's population problems has also integrated China's population professionals into global scientific, family planning, and social policy networks (Chapter 5). Central to this process has been the United Nations Population Fund (UNFPA), which opened an office in Beijing in 1979. As part of its many educational, technological, contraceptive, and programmatic projects in China, the UNFPA has sent perhaps hundreds of Chinese professionals abroad for short- and long-term training, while bringing fewer but significant numbers of foreign specialists to China. Since the mid-1980s and especially since the mid-1990s, when the Fourth World Conference on

Women held in Beijing helped revitalize the Chinese women's movement, foreign foundations and nongovernmental organizations working on women's issues have been increasingly active in China (Wang Zheng 1997; Hsiung, Jaschok, and Milwertz eds. 2001). In the still restrictive political climate of the PRC, these growing links to transnational organizations have been crucial, providing Chinese activists and reformers inside and outside the population establishment with concepts, political support, and external resources to promote new agendas on women's health and empowerment (Greenhalgh 2001a; Kaufman 2003).

The global media have also helped to transnationalize Chinese perspectives by fostering an acute sensitivity to world public opinion. While PRC population affairs have long attracted the interest of foreign journalists, the heavy-handed methods used to enforce the one-child policy attracted enormous and highly critical media attention, attention for which the PRC appears to have been completely unprepared (SG 12March02 CB). Beginning in the early to mid-1980s, and continuing until around the mid-1990s, the Western media beamed a steady stream of grisly images into living rooms around the world. Through these images and the disturbing stories associated with them, Westerners, and perhaps especially Americans, came to associate the PRC's birth program with such inhumanities as pregnant women being locked in birth planning jails, unauthorized babies being killed at birth, and peasants feeling pressured to abandon or kill their infant daughters. This media treatment has generated highly negative—and lasting—public opinion toward China, especially in the West. In the early 2000s, Greenhalgh's students at the University of California, when asked the first thing that comes to mind when they think of China's birth program, most often replied "the terrible consequences for baby girls."

At the same time, however, the media treatment has made PRC program and political leaders acutely self-conscious about how their population work is represented abroad and especially sensitive to representations of the program as coercive or brutal (SG 4Nov98, 15April, 24June, and 14Oct99 NJ, top population officials). Although it took them many years to learn how to respond constructively, by around the mid-1990s program leaders had absorbed some important lessons. The desire to change world opinion by creating a more positive image of the birth program is certainly one of the major impetuses behind the reforms initiated in the mid- to late 1990s. Although PRC officialdom did not invite or welcome the critical attention of the foreign media, as a result of that attention national program and political leaders have become both more media savvy—that is, aware of the impact of media-shaped public opinion on political leaders around the world—and more responsive to the political effects of the global media in world affairs. Official denials notwithstanding, informal discussions with national and provincial birth officials make clear that the sensationalistic Western media accounts have also helped them see the human rights problems in the harsh approach of the Deng era. Meantime, more scholarly critiques, especially those presented as constructive suggestions rather than hostile reproaches, have provided intellectual support to internal critics of the one-child policy—of which there are many. Discussions over many years suggest that, although the media accounts have sometimes provoked a hardline response, over the long-run those accounts, together with the scholarly critiques, have become quiet forces for reform.

A MODERN, GLOBAL SOCIETY?
SEX AND AGE DISTORTIONS

The makers of the post-Mao population project have also sought to create a modern society that fit the social and economic profile of a global power. The modernity project has had three parts, the first two examined here, the third in the next section. First, using the Western industrialized countries as their model and guide, the creators of the one-child policy sought to eliminate demographic anomalies in the Chinese social body—in particular, the bumps in the age structure caused by the post-Great Leap and Cultural Revolution baby booms—in order to create a society that was normalized to the Western standard (e.g., Tian 1981). As a 2003 article by a top population specialist indicates, that effort has succeeded in important ways (Table 8). Comparing China with the world, the more developed countries, the less developed countries, and Asia, the author shows that by 2000, China's ultralow crude birth and total fertility rates were remarkably close to those of the more developed countries. China's net increase rate had fallen below the world level, although it remained far above that of the developed countries. Life expectancy was also close to the Western standard. In some ways, China has gone a remarkable way toward achieving a "global, modern" population.

But the excessively rapid smoothing out of these anomalies created two other anomalies that are not shared, or not shared to the same extent, by the model countries: a severely distorted and, as of 2000, still rising sex ratio and an imminent crisis of aging and social security. These two trends carry ominous implications for China's future socioeconomic development and even political stability. At 120 boys per 100 girls (in 1999), China's highly imbalanced sex ratio at birth far outstrips the international average of 105 to 106. The social consequences of this trend—including huge numbers of poor rural men with no marriage prospects and huge numbers of poor rural women kidnapped and sold as brides—were laid out in Chapter 8. With few effective solutions in sight (though many experiments are underway) this problem

TABLE 8
China 2000: An Increasingly Modern, Global Society

Region	CBR (per 1,000 pop.)	NIR (per 1,000 pop.)	IMR (per 1,000 pop.)	TFR	LE (years)	Percentage urban
World	22	1.3	56	2.8	67	46
MDCs	11	.1	8	1.6	75	75
LDCs	25	1.6	61	3.2	64	40
Asia	22	1.4	55	2.7	67	37
China	15	.9	31	1.8	71	36

SOURCE: Gu 2003b.

NOTE: CBR = crude birth rate; NIR = natural increase rate; IMR = infant mortality rate; TFR = total fertility rate; LE = life expectancy; MDCs = more-developed countries; LDCs = less-developed countries.

will grow ever more severe as the one-child generation comes into marriageable age.

The PRC also faces an imminent future of rapid aging due both to the speed of its fertility decline and a notable rise in life expectancy. In 2004 a manageable 11 percent of China's people were 60 and older. But that figure is projected to rise to 15 percent by 2015, when the baby-boom generation begins to reach old age, and 28 percent by 2040, when the number of Chinese elderly will reach 397 million. (In 2040 a slightly lower 25 percent of Americans will be in that age group; Jackson and Howe 2004; also Zeng et al. 2002.) The rising numbers of Chinese elderly are worrying because the PRC's public pension system is far from prepared to handle the increase and because the time to create an effective retirement system is fast running out.

The bleak prospect is that, unlike Western countries, which grew rich before they grew old, China may grow old before it grows rich (Jackson and Howe 2004). In the early 2000s a mere 25 percent of the workforce—55 percent of urban workers and a paltry 11 percent of rural workers—had a pension of any sort. Health insurance is equally limited. Meanwhile, the shrinkage of the state-owned sector, in which public pensions are concentrated, is making the existing pension system unaffordable, even before the age bulge begins to strain resources. For a variety of reasons, the retirement reforms initiated by the state in the 1990s are not working (Frazier 2004). The pension for sonless elderly introduced in 2004 by the birth program is helpful, but it can solve only a small part of the problem because coverage is restricted to particular and relatively small categories of couples. Without an effective public retirement system, the majority of China's elders must rely on their families to provide protection from destitution. But with fertility falling, migration rising, and a dearth of daughters and daughters-in-law to provide care, the family support network for the elderly is under extraordinary strain.

Experts warn that, unless the PRC acts soon and decisively to seriously strengthen its retirement system, beginning in 2015 and accelerating thereafter, the country will face an old-age support crisis of immense proportions. Unless it is handled well, they contend, the aging problem could undermine China's ability to achieve a prosperous and peaceful long-term future and prevent its emergence as a great power. These are sobering prospects.

A second socioeconomic goal was associated with the quality project in population. By upgrading the bodies and minds of the new generation, China's population planners, working with officials in other sectors of the government, intended to produce a quality citizenry and a quality labor force able to compete successfully in the capitalist global economy China was entering. Those efforts appear to have paid off in rising overall levels of child health and education. For example, the 2000 census documents dramatic increases in secondary and higher education and reductions in illiteracy (Lavely 2001). Although the improvements have been unevenly spread, with the urban population benefiting more than the rural, and the coastal areas more than the hinterlands, overall they have been impressive. In conjunction with other efforts, birth planning has helped upgrade the quality of Chinese labor, making it increasingly competitive in the global economy—perhaps too competitive, those worried about the outsourcing of American jobs might say.

A MODERN ECONOMY? DEMOGRAPHIC BONUSES AND ONUSES

A third major reason for slowing population growth was to speed the rise in per capita living standards. Indeed, in line with international thinking at the time, "resolving the population-economy crisis" was the single most important rationale for the drastic limitation of population growth undertaken in the 1980s and 1990s. In 1980 the regime announced that it would achieve a "comfortable" standard of living by the turn of the century, concretized as US$800–1,000 per capita domestic product. By shrinking the denominator of the income-over-population fraction, population control would ensure the attainment of this goal. In the 1980s and 1990s China's economy spurted, growing at an average annual rate of 9 percent. By the end of 2000, the per capita GDP had topped US$800 (based on the official exchange rate), meaning that "overall, China had reached a 'well-off' state of socioeconomic development" (SBPC 20 April 2003). Although the income goal was handily achieved, it is not clear how much population restriction contributed to it. (Nor is it clear how much the birth program contributed to population change.) The decline in Chinese population growth rates certainly lessened pressure on economic and ecological resources, but the impact on living standards and economic growth rates appears to have been dwarfed by the unexpected speed of economic growth.

Complicating matters, in the 1980s the international demographic community revised its views of the impact of rapid population growth on economic growth. The orthodox position that population growth hinders economic development was replaced by a view in which population is a more neutral factor (Working Group 1986). In China, for almost two decades, this view, which challenged the CCP line, could have no public support. By the turn of the millennium, however, a third position had gained prominence in the Western literature, returning to an insistence that "population matters" for economic development. This position provided a new and more precise explanation of how it matters: through a potential "demographic dividend" to economic development from demographic transition, if timing and policies are right (Bloom, Canning, and Sevilla 2003). The argument of the "dividend" school is that, because of changes in age structure, demographic transition provides a temporary surplus of potentially productive adults over dependent children and retirees. Appropriate social policies can translate the temporary surplus of workers into a bonus for economic development. This then feeds back to reinforce demographic transition, establishing a "virtuous circle" that can shift a country from low-level to high-level social and economic equilibrium within little more than a generation.

The completion of demographic transition ends the bonus and begins a demographic onus. The surplus productive adults retire and the country then has to provide for them. In the best case, by then the country has become rich enough to afford to do so. In the worst case, during demographic transition the appropriate social and economic policies are not in place, so the additional adult workers do not reach their productive potential, reinforcing a "vicious cycle" of poverty and underdevelopment and further miring the country in the "poverty trap" at a low-level socioeconomic equilibrium. This literature finds that, in the "miracle economies" of East Asia (other than the PRC) the demographic dividend accounts for an astonishingly high proportion of growth—20 to 40 percent (Bloom, Canning, and Sevilla 2003).

China provides a dramatic case of both the bonus and onus of the demographic dividend perspective. In this analysis, the rapid fertility decline of the late Mao and Deng eras helped provide not just a demographic bonus that propelled economic development, it also helped China jump through a once-in-history window of developmental opportunity that under Mao it had gone a long way toward missing (Bloom, Canning, and Sevilla 2003; Yu 2003). The demographers Wang Feng and Andrew Mason (2004) have calculated that 15 percent of China's economic growth between 1982 and 2000 can be attributed to that demographic dividend. By around 2000 the age-structure gains began to slow. Over the three decades 1982 to 2013, the dividend accounts for a much smaller 4 percent of the increase in output per capita. The gains from the demographic dividend, they argue, can be of much longer duration if they are re-invested in capital, human capital, or institutional development. Yet if the demographic benefits of a large working-age population accelerated economic growth in the past, the demographic burden of a rapidly aging population may well slow China's growth in the future. Depending on the mechanism(s) by which resources are reallocated—family, market, and/or state—the rapid aging of China's population may lead to a rapid growth in the capital stock, a major expansion of intergenerational transfer programs (state or family), or, more soberly, a serious decline in the economic well-being of the elderly (Wang and Mason 2004). To the extent that the birth program accelerated the demographic transition—an extent that was certainly substantial, though it cannot be precisely calculated—the program deserves credit for both recent boom and potential bust.

A GLOBAL GOOD CITIZEN? ETHICAL QUESTIONS AND QUESTION MARKS

The makers of the post-Mao population project also saw in population an opportunity to build China's reputation as an ethical member of the community of nations. In the late 1970s and early 1980s, the newly formed population field was keenly aware that the world was watching to see how they would handle the population question. A broad reading of official statements and scholarly writings from the time suggests that, to this group, population control offered rare opportunities to demonstrate China's civilized ethics and advanced sense of responsibility toward the world at large and toward its own people (a key source is Liu, Song, and others 1981). With an inordinately large and rapidly growing population, in the late 1970s the PRC faced the world's most serious population problem. If it could successfully limit its own population growth, the planners thought, China would help slow the growth of the whole world's population—and demonstrate the People's Republic to be a responsible member of the world community. If it could contribute substantially to lowering global growth rates, the PRC would show the world that it possessed a global ethics meriting worldwide respect.[6]

Population control also presented a special opportunity for the PRC to prove to the world the superiority of socialism.[7] Though classic Marxism did not anticipate the need for population control, in an 1881 letter to Karl Kautsky, Friedrich Engels had said: "If communist society should one day be compelled to regulate the production of human beings, as it regulates the production of goods, then it and it alone will do this without any difficulty" (quoted in Song 1981, 26). China's population field seized on this statement, elaborating its implications for late twentieth-century China. To population writers, the socialist advantage lay in the efficacy of socialist institutions and in the communist party's superior treatment of the masses. The PRC's extensive experience with population control in the 1970s had thrown up a distinctively Chinese and apparently highly humane way to control population growth: through reliance first and foremost on propaganda and education. By relying primarily on educational methods in the post-Mao period as well, the PRC would show the world that its new regime would not resort to coercion, as its predecessor sometimes had in other matters, but would rely instead on "state guidance and mass voluntarism." By achieving low fertility through persuasion rather than force, the PRC would earn a reputation as a regime that treated its people in an ethical way, despite the enormity of the task. These were the expectations of those creating and publicly promoting the new birth planning project of the post-Mao era.

Things did not turn out as planned, however. Despite apparently good intentions, when faced with intense resistance to the one-child policy, birth planners quickly resorted to using physical force, attempting to save face domestically and internationally by calling the target-driven campaigns of the early 1980s and early 1990s "propaganda-and-education months" (*xuanquan yue*). In the early 1980s, before word about these heavy-handed methods leaked out, the PRC was widely praised by foreign observers for reversing the demographic foot-dragging of the Maoist years and taking serious measures to arrest the growth of its huge population. In 1982, the international demographic community applauded China's success in carrying out its first modern census. In 1983, the United Nations awarded Qian Xinzhong, the PRC birth minister (along with Indian Prime Minister Indira Gandhi), the first United Nations Population Award for success in tackling the problem of rapid population growth (Li ed. 1987; *PDR* 1983). This is the kind of reaction the Chinese had hoped for and expected.

Within two years, however, the tide of world opinion had decisively turned. By the mid-1980s, the foreign media had begun to vividly document widespread human rights abuses in the program. Equally important, the issue of coercion in the PRC program got caught up in the abortion debates in the United States, becoming the cause celebre of social conservatives with antiabortion agendas (Winckler 2005). In 1985 the U.S. government defunded the United Nations Population Fund because of its "participation in the management of a program of forced abortion and involuntary sterilization" (Crane and Finkle 1989). Every year for the next six years the issue of coercion in the PRC birth program resurfaced in noisy debates in Washington, D.C., giving China a black face again and again. Although President Bill Clinton restored the U. N. agency's funding in 1992, in the summer of 2002 the administration of President George W. Bush again withheld the U.S. contribution to UNFPA (some $34 million) because of its work in China

(Kaufman 2003; Winckler 2005).[8] In early 2005 Secretary of State Condoleezza Rice affirmed the administration's commitment to keeping the pressure on Beijing to improve its human rights record in this and other areas. Meantime, some outspoken human rights organizations have continued their longstanding attacks on China with blanket condemnations of the birth program as unflaggingly coercive.

For China, the negative press and punitive responses have been difficult to deal with, though for different reasons at different times. In the 1980s and early 1990s, the criticisms were hard to manage in part because some of the charges were substantially true, even if overgeneralized and sensationalized. In the early 2000s, the categorical condemnations may be even harder to accept, not because all abuses have ended—they have not. The all-out attacks may be harder to accept because they neglect all the work that program managers have done during the past decade to remove those abusive practices and gradually bring the program into line with accepted international practice. Officially, the PRC reaction to foreign criticism has most often been to deny the charges or, when they were substantiated by a Chinese investigation, blame the coercion on overzealous local officials. Yet, one senses, the charges of coercion have been a source of national humiliation and shame, both because they have exposed the brutal practices sometimes used, especially in the earlier years, to the outside world and because they conflict with the party's and program's images of themselves as institutions that do *not* use force to lower birth rates. The energies being poured in the early 2000s into reforming the birth program and doing other good works, such as fostering south-to-south cooperation in family planning, must be understood as part of a larger, self-conscious effort to restore face and pride for the birth program in the international arena (Winckler 2005). For Westerners concerned to reduce the coerciveness of the Chinese program, the most productive response to these developments would be to avoid categorical denunciations and develop instead a more differentiated critique that acknowledges and encourages the progress to date, while pointing to areas that still need work and suggesting how those problems might be addressed.

In the early 2000s, the PRC is widely considered an internationally responsible regime whose successful efforts to lower its own population growth rates have made an important contribution to the world at large. During the period between 1960–65 and 2000–05, China's efforts at population control boosted the global fertility decline from 39 to 46 percent, while increasing the worldwide decline in population growth from 30 to 38 percent.[9] On this score the birth program has achieved what its creators had hoped for. Yet praise from the international community has been subdued, for in the minds of many the *how* of fertility control has been as important as the *how much*. To be sure, the prohealth, prowoman, anticoercion reforms initiated in the late 1990s have been cautiously praised by family planning specialists as steps in the right direction. As the reforms continue to develop and deepen, the program's international image certainly should improve. Yet memories of the coercion once used against the Chinese people have faded slowly. Given the way the coercion issue has played out in the United States, the persistent resort to coercive practices in the PRC program over many years has had the untoward effect of complicating if not jeopardizing the work of the UNFPA in providing reproductive health services to poor women in Asia, Africa, and Latin America. This is not what PRC program leaders had intended.

Despite the efforts of reformers to remove the moral stigma, an ethical question mark hangs over the Chinese program to this day. And when the issue of coercion is finally put to rest, its place will be taken by another legacy of the program: the rising sex ratio at birth and the disappearance from Chinese society of millions of baby girls. This problem, which, unlike coercion, has been stubbornly resistant to the measures adopted so far to combat it, will certainly leave another ethical question mark over the program, a mark that will grow bigger if that sex ratio continues to rise. And down the road, the second harmful social structural legacy of the birth program—the rapid aging of the population—will present ethical problems of yet another sort. Generations of Chinese without old-age support would mar China's image and self-image as a nation that, unlike the heartless West, respects and cares for its elderly. Despite the high hopes of its creators, the population program has been at best a problematic site for the construction of an ethical China. While creating some positive new images, it has also led to the revival of older images of China as a nation with a coercive state and misogynist culture.

In today's reform environment, opportunities exist to change that. The most significant step the government could take would be to relax the one-child policy. Although abandoning the policy would not stop the rise in the sex ratio at birth, it would be a constructive step because it would discourage some couples from eliminating their female fetuses, and it would remove the conflict between the official goals of gender equality and fertility reduction by eliminating a fertility policy that constrains or encourages large numbers of couples to abort their unborn daughters. By making this difficult choice, and by speaking out forcefully and publicly against the practice of sex-selective abortion, the PRC's leaders could make good on their promise to care for *all* the Chinese people. Those steps would also signal to the world that the PRC has accepted the international norms that reproductive programs should be gender-equitable and people-centered.

CHAPTER 10

Conclusion: Lenin, Foucault, and the Governance of Population in China

LENINISM HAS BEEN an extreme example of a top-down "statist" approach to power. That is the approach on which the PRC has mainly relied, lingeringly so in the early twenty-first century in its insistence that the CCP must remain the "ruling party." Foucault has provided a more comprehensive analysis of modern power, one that recognizes the continued relevance of the state but emphasizes the rising importance of other forms of governance: discipline through professional institutions and self-regulation by individuals. That is the combination toward which, by the turn of the millennium, the PRC had begun to evolve. We conclude by elaborating on the relevance to Chinese population politics of Lenin and Foucault and the contrasting processes they emphasize. A final section suggests the implications of the striking recent changes in Chinese population politics for U.S. policy.

Reforming Regime Capacity: Maoism, Stalinism, Reformism

In the late 1980s, in a perceptive metaphor, Zbigniew Brzezinski characterized the reform of communism as a process of peeling back successive layers to reveal an enduring core of Leninism (Brzezinski 1989, 41). In the Gorbachev era in the Soviet Union those layers were, from outside to inside, Brezhnevism, Stalinism, and Leninism. In Deng's China we can say that they were Maoism, Stalinism, and Reformism. As Brzezinski was writing, the Maoist-Stalinist version of PRC birth planning was still under construction. Nevertheless, his image of peeling back layers provides a useful summary of the reform of PRC birth planning since then. By the turn of the millennium the program had largely put the revolutionary mobilization of Maoism behind it and had begun to shift the balance within Stalinism from bureaucratism toward professionalism. In the early twenty-first century that left the program's Leninist core pursuing Reformism through socialist marketization, initiating a shift within it from sheer marketization toward more provision of socialist social programs. We will proceed from the inside out.

Thus, at its core, the PRC's population project has been Leninist and remains significantly so at the beginning of the twenty-first century. Under classic Leninism, at the macro level, a tightly organized revolutionary party acts as the vanguard of the proletariat and justifies its actions by its superior understanding of historical processes, based on Marxism. It thereby denies "the masses" any say in the definition of "the situation" and therefore of the nation's and their own interests. At the micro level, in principle Leninism claims to respect individuals but believes that their interests can be aligned with party policy. Members of the "right" classes will have the right interests; errant individuals can be reminded of their correct interests through indoctrination; members of the "wrong" classes should be destroyed. In practice, in its determination to use its scientific diagnoses to transform society, Leninism has ended up using terror to enforce its prescriptions on everyone, including the proletariat and even the regime apparatus itself. In the population-and-reproduction domain, PRC leaders claimed, and perhaps believed, that through the application of Leninist-Maoist work methods, in the long run couples could be made to understand that limiting their childbearing was in their own best interests. As top party leaders said at each crucial juncture, the regime could control population growth "if we just do our work well" (e.g., ME 820901, Hu Yaobang at the Twelfth Party Congress). In the meantime, in practice, the regime used manifold forms of coercion—from the high-pressure mobilization of Maoist campaigns to the sheer physical terror of compulsory sterilization to the steep economic penalties of crippling fines—to impose its understanding of national and family demographic interests on everyone. PRC birth planning has been Leninism in action.

The PRC population project has also been Stalinist and, at the beginning of the twenty-first century, partially remains so. The early PRC, lacking access to the capitalist West, copied Stalinism as a mode of postrevolutionary economic organization and social administration. Stalinism took Lenin's aspiration to socialist planning and embodied it in an elaborate bureaucratic-professional state. In the case of PRC birth planning this meant technocratic policies and paraprofessional implementation, constructed during the 1980s, strengthened in the early 1990s, and somewhat adapted to marketization starting in the middle 1990s. The PRC has since abandoned literal planning of births, but whether the Comprehensive Reform of the first decade of the twenty-first century will eventually dismantle demographic Stalinism or simply further rationalize it remains to be seen. Recent literature on how

Stalinist planning actually worked suggests why it misdirected development in the PRC, including in birth planning. The reason was not only that China could not equal Russia in planning because it was more agricultural and less modernized. The reason was also that Soviet planning itself was largely an inspirational fiction: not based on facts, not operationally detailed, and not the actual basis for decisions on resource allocation and production mix (Gregory ed. 2001; Gregory 2004). Small wonder that central planning could not work acceptably on the most intimate behaviors of the world's largest population.

The PRC population project was also Maoist, but it had largely ceased to be so by the turn of the millennium. On the one hand, Mao intensified many Stalinist techniques, particularly late 1940s mobilization of urban factory workers to maximum effort (Kaple 1994; Filtzer 2002). Unfortunately, these were techniques that did not work very well and that the Soviet Union soon abandoned. On the other hand, Mao made many genuine innovations, particularly the "mass line" for constructing a working relationship with peasants in largely rural China. Rather consequentially for the relationship between population and power in China, there were both similarities and differences between Mao and Foucault. Both emphasized the need for institutions to impose discipline and to teach individuals to regulate their own behavior. However, whereas Foucault assumed some autonomy for both professions and individuals, Mao aspired to an unmediated relationship between himself and the masses. He suppressed professional discourses, including those about reproduction and population (Evans 1997). The result was that he forfeited the much more pervasive control that modern neoliberal societies achieve through autonomous professional disciplines and individual self-regulation (Winckler 1998). To give him credit, Mao was extremely cautious about what, without coercion, the PRC regime could accomplish toward regulating reproduction, until China became more developed. Deng overrode that judgment and pressed forward using a largely Maoist approach.

In the mid-1980s Brzezinski observed the intactness of the PRC's core Leninism quite concretely, in a long private dinner conversation with Hu Yaobang (Brzezinski 1989 , 160−162). At the time, Hu was the PRC's leading advocate of political reform, but as party general secretary he remained confident that such reform must be "top down." In population, as in other domains, successive PRC reforms of regime capacity have all been initiated from above, even in the early twenty-first century. "What is to be done" is being decided by party technocrats and implemented by leading the public to understand the correctness of their decisions. At the same time, the Hu Jintao era is shifting toward neoliberal policy instruments, devolving functions to local society and strengthening indirect state regulation. Continuing its

Leninist vanguard role, the party has chosen to lead the establishment of neo-liberalism in China, by promoting institutions for disciplining society and by instilling attitudes of personal responsibility. In the early 2000s China's biopolitics is in transition from Leninism to neoliberalism. From the regime's point of view, the making of policy remains largely Leninist; from society's point of view, life is becoming increasingly neoliberal.

China's Leninist Population Project: Triumph or Tragedy?

Since the fall of the Berlin Wall, students of communism in the former Soviet Union and Eastern Europe have pronounced it a "grand failure" and a "great tragedy" (Brzezinski 1989; Malia 1994). In China, the regime's pursuit of a gradual transition from communism suggests that, overall, it failed there as well. Did the specifically population part of the CCP's Leninist project produce triumph or tragedy?

In terms of the PRC's own goal of limiting population, on the surface state birth planning appears to have been a phenomenal success—if we start the clock in the 1970s. Between the early 1970s and the early 2000s, fertility plummeted—from just under 6 to well under 2 children per woman—enabling China to achieve near-parity with the West and to claim membership in the club of socially advanced nations. If regime policies had caused this rapid demographic transition, that would be the single most spectacular success of any would-be totalitarian state, in particular because the achievement has been one not just of relatively successful ongoing enforcement but also of helping to change popular norms to reduce enforcement costs. However, even if we credit the regime with producing the decline, if we start the clock around 1980 when the one-child policy was launched, the program's success in reaching its quantity goals appears more modest. After 20 years and 617 million more birth control operations (conducted between 1980 and 2001), fertility fell by about one birth, from 2.54 (in 1979–1981) to an estimated 1.55 births per woman, a substantial decline, though still above the one-child-per-couple level envisioned by some of the policy's makers (for the details, see Table 1).

However, regime policy was not the sole cause—or possibly even the main cause—of the decline in births, as the PRC birth program itself would eventually admit. Macrosocioeconomic change and microfamily change produced much of the reduction (Chapter 7). In the 1950s socialist collectivization produced major changes in the family that eventually reduced childbearing desires. By the time the birth program was seriously introduced in the countryside in the mid-1970s, fertility was already falling from five past four and three toward two. In the 1970s, the state program may simply have provided the means to fulfill the growing desire of families to limit their own size. Since then, fertility aspirations have been low and falling still further (by 2000 to below two). According to couples themselves, much of the reason is the disciplines of marketization, which rapidly spread consumer culture while quickly reversing the economics of children, whose costs have skyrocketed even as their values to parents have plummeted. The postponement of marriage and childbearing have also contributed to the decline in fertility over these decades (on the 1990s, see Zhang Guangyu 2004, 189–212).

Unfortunately, it is difficult statistically to separate the role of the program in reducing fertility from that of socioeconomic development, for the program closely tracked socioeconomic change, being most effective in times and places where social change was most rapid and advanced. Roughly speaking, the shares may have been about fifty-fifty in the 1970s and 1980s, with the program contribution greatly declining in the 1990s and 2000s (e.g., Feeney and Wang 1993). The program itself drew on a range of experience, including that of other developing countries, to suggest that it may have accounted for 54 percent of the 338 million births "averted" between the early 1970s and the late 1990s (*YB00*, 184–197, a report from the birth program to PRC leaders). Even if we could accept that figure, probably most of the birth program's contribution resulted from the sorts of things that population programs were doing in those other developing countries: educating the public and facilitating contraception. Thus the birth program's contribution was undeniably important—in introducing a new small-family norm, in making it culturally acceptable, and in providing the contraceptive means by which people could realize that new ideal. Probably relatively little of the birth program's share of fertility decline resulted from making the small family mandatory and from using heavy-handed techniques to enforce it. At least in the early 1990s, state coercion probably did produce a sudden sharp drop in fertility, but at that time that drop could be maintained only through the continued application of "administrative constraints," as the PRC birth program itself insisted. Fertility decline became self-sustaining and self-stabilizing only in the mid-to-late 1990s, when dramatic changes in the wider economy—and, in turn, in the family—helped produce low and stable fertility for the first time. This brief discussion is meant to be only suggestive. But if much of the decline in fertility can be traced to social and economic change and to the more conventional parts of the birth program, then the coercive part may have been largely unnecessary. That is a sobering thought.

These uncertainties about the extent to which the Leninist component of the PRC's birth program succeeded in limiting births make it difficult to assess Leninism's contribution to some of the birth program's other objectives, such as facilitating economic growth, creating a "coordinated" and "sustainable" relationship between "population, resources, and environment," and even promoting women's reproductive health. All three of these domains display some of the same strengths of a Leninist approach to regime capacity: decisiveness in setting priorities, tightness of cadre organization, and effectiveness at mass education. They also reveal some of the same limitations: too simple and too direct intervention in complex social processes, too much involvement in the activities that need regulating to regulate them effectively, and too exclusive reliance on ideological indoctrination and political mobilization.

PRC leaders' main perception of the relationship between population growth and economic growth was as a race of rates: agriculture could not grow faster than 2 percent and a 2 percent rate of population growth would eat up any progress, including in industry, at least to the extent that industry relied on agriculture. In those terms, limiting births probably did prevent population growth from slowing economic growth, if not actually accelerating it. However, to the extent that the birth program contributed to economic development, it is likely that the main contribution was not that envisaged by this static accounting approach, through "reducing the denominator" in long-run calculations of per capita resources and income. Instead, the main contribution may well have been to help China seize a "strategic opportunity" to reap a "demographic bonus" from a rapid transition from high to low fertility, accompanied by strongly prodevelopment economic policies (Bloom, Canning and Sevilla 2003; *YB03*, 362–366; Yu 2003; Chapter 9). Something of such a concept may have been implicit in the sense of urgency that post-Mao leaders felt about the need to accelerate China's economic development and to prevent the 1980–1995 "peak" of new young couples from having many children. However, PRC leaders were not sophisticated enough demographically to imagine a bonus theory. In any case, the fundamental problem was not that China's population was too large but that PRC leaders did not understand how to promote economic development.

PRC leaders were perspicacious in institutionalizing a policy domain that attempts to relate population, resources, and environment. This is a domain in which limiting the growth of population might help, since China is demonstrably running out of some key resources (water, energy) and conspicuously overloading its environment (air and water pollution). But again the real problem is not so much population growth as constructing a regulatory regime adequate to limit the waste of resources and the destruction of the environment. The PRC has not been good at that, because for most of its history the regime itself has been the main agent of that waste and destruction, and it has yet to achieve much distance from the agencies that are continuing it. Moreover, if the PRC has been more successful at limiting population than it has been at limiting waste and pollution, the reason is probably that it was easier to try to address the problem of resources and environment by imposing reproductive costs on the Chinese family than it was to try to rein in either the state's own economically failing industrial giants or the local collective and private industries that were actually generating most of the economic growth.

In reproductive health, PRC leaders deplored the high rates of mortality among mothers and infants in early twentieth century China and did something about it, mostly through improving general living standards and access to basic medical care but also through the health system's promotion of more modern methods of childbearing. Between 1950 and 1980 maternal and infant mortality declined by a factor of ten (Institute for Health Science 2003; Chapter 8). It may have helped that during that period MCH services and birth control were delivered together. This exhausted the easy gains from early development. Nevertheless, the health system made further reduction a priority objective. It better trained more village doctors to promote sanitary methods of child delivery, to increase the proportion of deliveries in hospitals, and to refer problematic pregnancies to appropriate levels of care. Between 1980 and roughly 2000, those rates, though declining more slowly, still have roughly halved. It probably did not help that MCH work and birth work were now separated. Still, the contribution of reduced childbearing, though indirect, was probably substantial: fewer births exposed mothers to fewer risks and limited resources concentrated on fewer children. Despite these important improvements in mortality, however, problems of reproductive morbidity remained serious, especially in the 1980s and 1990s (Chapter 8). Some were created by the coercive campaigns of those decades. Since the mid-1990s, program leaders have been shifting their attention to these problems.

The enormous, relatively well-funded, and increasingly well-trained birth system significantly increases regime health capacity, as the birth system demonstrated with alacrity during the 2003 SARS epidemic and as it promises to do for HIV/AIDS. On more ordinary matters of reproductive and child health the birth system can make three kinds of contributions: first by continuing to upgrade its birth workers to avoid doing harm, second by adding some elementary services for identifying problems and referring them to the health system (e.g., reproductive tract infections), and third perhaps by delivering some elementary forms of treatment (Kaufman, Zhang and Fang 1997; Winckler 2005). An issue is how this asset can be used most effectively—formally outside or inside the health system? If the birth system remains separate from the health system, it can exercise its "can do" attitude. If it is merged once again with the health system, it could help correct that system's "can't do" reputation.

Clearly, then, the birth program has made some contributions to progress toward PRC leaders' other main goal for it, raising the quality of China's population. A direct contribution has been fostering child health through mandatory prenatal and early childhood interventions. A less direct but larger contribution may have been that falling fertility created rising desire for the "quality child" on the part of parents, grandparents, educators, and society. In an ever more competitive world, guaranteeing the success of one's only child required investing heavily in its physical and mental well-being. At least in urban areas, the program was outstandingly successful in helping to produce a generation of healthy, well-educated, highly cosmopolitan singletons equipped to lead China into a globalized future.

In rural areas the record on quality appears to be more mixed. A Chinese observer has posited that, to avert 300 million births, over thirty years the birth program spent 300 billion Chinese yuan. He wondered what those resources might have accomplished if spent not on lowering the quantity of births but on raising the quality of education, particularly for rural women (PI 031125, Wu Gongsen). The observer estimated that the three billion yuan would have been enough to put all of China's 180 million illiterate and semi-illiterate population through primary school, plus put another 100 million rural women through high school. In China the number of children borne by rural women with high school education is only 1.2! This is a striking suggestion. During the same period, local governments considered themselves strapped for funds to support education, and in many poor areas girls did not attend school (UNDP 1999, 44). Yet by the early twenty-first century the international development community believes that improvements in women's basic education produce high payoffs, including both voluntary reduction in childbearing and increased investment in childrearing. Aside from this educational opportunity cost, there are also other cultural costs to the quality project: women more closely tied to their mothering roles and youngsters showered with all that money can buy but bereft of collective values. These cultural costs are steep and are likely to rise as those single children become the adults who form the core of Chinese society.

To what extent can we briefly peer into the future of China's population program? A comprehensive answer exceeds the expertise of the authors and the remaining space available in the book. Nevertheless, we can outline the matter, at least as it is being explored by officials and demographers in China in the Hu era. Many have become preoccupied with a particularly demanding form of forward population projection, in which the point is not to forecast final totals and an endpoint in time but instead to map out the timing of changes in population composition that are likely to occur along the way — including the likely relationship of those changes to surrounding economic and environmental developments. Essentially this over-time perspective is an extension of the "demographic dividend" literature that looked back on the past relationship between the timing of fertility decline and the timing of economic takeoff and looked forward at the future relationship between the timing of aging and the timing of economic maturity. Such matters were the object of the large "strategic planning" exercise presented to PRC leaders at the beginning of 2005 as part of the basis for the population component of the Eleventh Five-Year Plan (2006–2010) and for longer-range plans (Chapter 6). Let us briefly sketch the topic in terms of the basic dimensions of population set out at the beginning of this book—quantity, quality, and location—at both the micro- and macrolevels. The discussion draws largely on a speech by Zhang Weiqing treating these dimensions as problems of "population security" (PI 040325, to one of the symposia launching strategic planning, mentioned in Chapter 6). In those terms, the guesses and worries about the future most frequently expressed by PRC officials in the middle of the first decade of the twenty-first century ran somewhat as follows.

On *quantity*, the microcomponent is individual fertility behavior. Allegedly that remained above the policy rate and, even so, remained "unstable," so the government must continue to regulate it. The macrocomponent of quantity is ultimate total population size. Estimates of when that would peak ranged from 2030 to around 2050—obviously the lower the better but whether sooner or later was better remained unclear. On *quality*, the microcomponent that drew particular concern was a rise in "defective" births (Chapter 6). The macrocomponent of quality is population structure, where analysts found problems not only of sex and age but also of employment. The sex ratio was already at an all-time high and PRC leaders hoped to prevent any further rise (Chapters 6 and 8). Aging was expected to peak about 2050 and PRC leaders were increasingly addressing how to provide those seniors with retirement security. The proportion of working-age population was expected to peak about 2040. The rise would create problems of employment, the fall would make it harder to support all those seniors. On *location*, the microcomponent is migration, or rather the constant movement of job seekers from place to place. That movement was expected to continue—and to continue to pose a challenge to surveillance and service. The macrocomponent of location is distribution of population between rural and urban. Estimates varied of the eventual proportion urban (perhaps 60 percent) and when that would be reached (perhaps 2050). Obviously, that much urbanization would strain city resources, but it would also facilitate giving a much larger proportion of the population access to urban benefits.

As some demographers pointed out, in the face of so many dimensions and interactions, policymakers should take care that "emergency" action along one dimension does not create problems along the others, including the economic and social environment—as the one-child policy had done, one might add. Of course, all of these matters were subject to political "spin," usually in the direction of stressing "problems" that the population-and-birth program was needed to solve. (The timing of peaks follows remarks by senior demographer Tian Xueyuan in PI 040412. See also Dali Yang 2004.)

In any case, in evaluating the contribution that the PRC's Leninist population project has made to China's future socioeconomic development, one must face the question of at what cost any demographic gains were made. In human terms, China's grand experiment in state birth planning was a colossal tragedy. To be sure, there were beneficiaries, in particular, the urban singletons who were showered with state and familial support. Yet the human suffering inflicted in the name of demographic modernization is staggering. Were we able to tally up the damage to women's bodies and psyches, the trauma experienced by millions of peasants coercively sterilized as though they were "pigs being spayed," and the number of young female lives lost through abandonment and neglect (for which we do have some measures), the vicious campaigns of the 1980s and early 1990s would require a place alongside the great human tragedies of the Maoist era in the "black book of communism" (Courtois et al. 1999). Why this social suffering produced by the birth program is not part of the record of communism's traumas warrants consideration. Perhaps it is missing because unlike, say, the Great Leap, whose trauma can be measured in lives lost, here the suffering was felt in less easily measured forms of psychic and bodily damage. Perhaps it is missing because the state did not measure the costs to women's health at the time, rendering them forever unmeasurable. (One figure it did collect, though—826 million birth control operations conducted during 1971–2001—hints at the magnitude of the possible problems.) Finally, perhaps the human costs of state birth planning are not on the list of communism's traumas because the targets of the birth program were female gendered—reproductive women and infant girls—making the costs "culturally appropriate" and thus less noteworthy.

Today's sponsors of Comprehensive Reform have expressed the belief that, earlier in the program's history, the Chinese people were willing to forgive its forceful intervention in their lives. Perhaps they were. Villagers in some areas are now openly "thankful" to the state for having forced them to limit their births, because the costs of raising children have climbed so rapidly. But the human costs of the program do not all lie in the past. The forced fertility decline of past years has led to distortions in the age and sex structure today that are leading to a second wave of problems that includes a marriage crisis for men, the risk of kidnapping and sale for women, and a social security crisis for hundreds of millions of rural couples. The birth program, originated to reduce "the state's burden," has created burdens on the state that have been and will be enormous. These burdens include not only the economic resources required to enforce such an unpopular policy for so long, but also the political costs the state has incurred in damage to "party-cadre-mass relations" (ranging from coercion to corruption). Even the regime must wonder whether the demographic gains were worth all these costs.

Foucault in China: Population, Modern Power, and "Reproductive Freedom"

The governmentalization of population charted in this book has entailed the rapid development of biopower—power over the production and cultivation of life itself. As noted in our Problematique (Chapter 2), in his writings on the West Foucault depicted this power over life as a new and distinctively modern form of power, one that arose in the eighteenth century in conjunction with the emergence of the capitalist economy (Foucault 1978). Positive rather than negative or repressive, modern power has increasingly focused on the population (at the macrolevel) and the body (at the microlevel), taking these as objects of a new kind of governance whose knowledges and practices are rooted in modern science.

China's twentieth-century population project, launched at the very moment that China sought to reenter the capitalist world economy, would seem to provide an especially striking case of the rapid emergence of this new form of power. Although earlier Chinese states in principle possessed the power to shape what some have called "bare life," that power remained potential only (Agamben 1998). In practice, efforts to shape the quantity and quality of the Chinese population did not gain institutional expression under either the late imperial (1644–1911) or the Republican (1911–1949) state. Since the founding of the PRC, however, and especially since the death of Mao, the governmentalization of population has proceeded apace. Indeed, because it was essentially coerced, at least initially, the biopoliticization of society and politics in China may have proceeded more rapidly than anywhere else in the world.

The adoption of population as a central object of political management and transformation represents a rupture in China's century-long project of national modernization. As the historian Susan L. Glosser (2003) has shown, beginning in the late 1800s successive groups of Chinese reformers linked national salvation to family reform. Between the 1910s and the early 1950s, influential figures in the New Culture movement, the Nationalist party,

Shanghai entrepreneurial circles, and the Communist party argued that the traditional Chinese family had to be reformed for China to become a strong, wealthy, modern nation. In the 1970s the PRC reframed that object of modernizing efforts, effecting an historic shift from *the family* to *the population* as the key entity that had to be modernized for China to regain its historic greatness and become a force to contend with on the world stage. Efforts to reform the family were not eliminated, but they were embedded in the larger population project and transformed in the process. The significance of this development bears underlining. As described in Part 2, the late twentieth-century emergence of this new power over not just the family, a social institution, but biological life itself, has been highly productive—in ways that have not been fully appreciated. The rise of biopolitics has created new or reconfigured sites of power (the reproductive woman, the quality child), types of bodies (the contraceptively controlled woman, the obsessively managed child), and types of neoliberal selves ("quality," consumerist, self-governing) readied for participation in the global marketplace and engagement with a gradually neoliberalizing state (Chapter 6). The population project has succeeded where successive family projects failed, helping to make the dream of the twentieth century—making China great again—a reality in the twenty-first.

From a Foucauldian perspective, the late twentieth-century emergence of population as a sustained and central object of Chinese science and governance carries great significance, for it signals China's entry into a modern political era in which population has become not merely a target of government but an end in itself, indeed, a central raison d'être of government. In China, shaping the population—its size, its internal structure and characteristics, its movement, its social security—has certainly become a central end of government, at times an end as important as growing the economy. This is a notable development in a Marxist country in which political life is econocentric. The governmentalization of population is also significant from a more conventional political science perspective, for it has expanded the social domain of government activity. Indeed, the emergence of "the population problem" has carried extraordinary benefits for the regime. Whatever its demographic limitations, the birth planning project was an outstanding success in creating a new political reality—"the population crisis"—a problematic reality so serious that only a strong party and state would be able to handle it. In an era of Marxist ideological decline, the scientific management of population became a compelling new rationale for a massive buildup of the institutional and regulatory capacities of the state and an extension of the state's reach into the womb. Population also benefited the CCP, giving the party and party-related mass associations a new arena in which to demonstrate their self-sacrificing spirit and their continued usefulness in a rapidly changing society. This biopolitical project thus helped to perpetuate and strengthen the power and capacity of the PRC regime. Although the state's firm control over population size has made this power over life in China significantly more state-centered than in the more familiar West European cases, in the area of population quality the power to define and instill norms has shifted to other social forces, including professional institutions, some closely affiliated with the state, others becoming more independent; capitalist corporations; international agencies; and, increasingly, individuals. The Chinese state continues to set and promote norms on health and education, but in creating a "quality" modern population China is coming to resemble other modern societies in which the state is one governing agent among others.

In biopolitical regimes, life and death are closely related. Foucault distinguished two types of relationship between power and biological life and death. Old-fashioned sovereign power is based on the sovereign's right to "make die," with its implicit corollary, the power to "let live" (2003, 25–26, 240). Modern biopower, preoccupied with promoting human life, characteristically involves the power to "make live" and, for those cases where that is deemed inappropriate, its corollary power to "let die" (ibid., 241). Although biopower is newer, sovereign power does not disappear, and in modern societies the two intertwine. In his limited remarks on the subject, Foucault commented in effect that socialism, with its intent to forcefully promote human flourishing in all its aspects, may tend to create particularly extensive and complex overlaps between sovereign power and biopower (ibid., 261). In his critique of Foucault, Agamben (1998) emphasizes the dark underside of biopower, suggesting that all power, including biopower, rests ultimately on the ability to take life. Despite their differing emphases, for both theorists power over life is intimately related to power over death. Overall, the PRC case confirms these conjectures. However, the proportions of sovereign power and biopower differ by policy dimension, time period, and local circumstance.

In China it is the quantity dimension that has involved the most complex and consequential politics of death. In principle the CCP would like to have persuaded all PRC citizens voluntarily to limit their childbearing and to have provided all couples with the contraceptive means to do so, thereby avoiding unauthorized pregnancies and births and thus the need to "remedy" them after they occurred. In practice, the policy of limiting couples to one or two children, introduced in a pro-natal and male-centered reproductive culture, has contributed to the deaths of large numbers of infants and to the end of life for even larger numbers of fetuses (in both cases disproportionately females). The politics of these deaths has unfolded in two stages, each involving different mixes of sovereignty and biopower. In the initial years of stringent limits and severe enforcement (roughly 1979–1983), the proportion of the direct sovereign power to make die was significant. The party-state covertly sanctioned the killing of infants by medical workers, birth cadres, and even parents, through its insistence that no third children—and few second children—see the light of day. Later, enforcement shifted toward indirect biopower, letting die. The regime allowed the ending of the lives of millions of infants and fetuses by such acts as holding fast to the one-child policy; taking only limited measures to prevent the spread of ultrasound machines and their use in sex-determination; enforcing an adoption policy that supported rigid birth limitation rather than child welfare; and closing its eyes to the triaging of abandoned children taken to state orphanages.

One major way in which these Chinese developments differ from the European cases of aberrant biopolitics concerns the groups officially targeted for limitation or improvement. The Holocaust is a key case for both Foucault and Abamben, and Foucault generalizes it, suggesting that racism may always be essential to biopower. Here the more obvious argument is that, once biopolitics becomes a dominant preoccupation, the state requires what might be called a "negative racism" to identify inferior minorities that must be eliminated in order to strengthen the majority (ibid., 2003, 256–259). That was the main preoccupation in Nazi Germany, but definitely not in the PRC, which long allowed non-Han minorities greater latitude to reproduce than the Han majority. However, one can read a less obvious argument into Foucault—or at least into Nazi Germany—that preoccupation with biopolitics also implies a "positive racism" which requires the majority to purify themselves of their own weak elements, at least by preventing them from reproducing (ibid., 257–258; Spektorowski 2004). This power to "make not live" (our term) was marginal to the Nazis but more central to the CCP, which has strongly discouraged reproduction by the genetically "defective." That eugenic policy was applied to both the Han majority and the ethnic minorities.

Another major way in which China differs from Europe is that, because the PRC's main focus of limitation and improvement was the majority Han Chinese population itself, overall, the PRC's purposes and methods were more positive. Regime policies did cause couples to resort to sex-selective infanticide and abortion, but the regime did not intend that. Official policy did not condone these practices of death but instead declared them illegal. The regime's actual goal was to enhance life by allowing only an environmentally sustainable number of high quality births. Overall, the PRC's population project has been guided by a logic not of mortality but of vitality. The ethical implications of the two logics are quite different. Just as the PRC's economic policy was guided by the slogan "Let some get rich first to lead all to common wealth," one might say that its population policy was guided by the implicit slogan: "Allow only some births to lead all to common health."

A final major way in which China differs from Europe concerns the greater role of gender in Chinese biopolitics. In the West, cultural definitions of gender difference compete with biological ones, whereas in China gender has been defined in terms of difference in reproductive biology (Chapter 8). CCP commitments to Marxism and humanism have allowed official policy to hold that the genders, though equal, are biologically and thus socioculturally different. These gendered differentiations have been most evident in the quantity part of the population project, in which the party-state allowed women to bear the great burden of contraception and permitted practices of death in which the bodies of female infants and fetuses were targeted for elimination. As in the West, biopower seems to require some means of biological differentiation and elimination to enhance the biological fitness of the whole. However, in China and some other Asian countries, racism has been supplemented with or replaced by sexism as the primary if unofficial means of distinguishing good from bad biologies. Yet this solution is problematic because it results in a population that is biologically flawed by an imbalance between sexes that threatens to undermine the very perfection that both regime and couples sought to achieve. However this problem is resolved in the PRC, the China case makes clear that Foucault's analysis is Eurocentric and needs to be amended to include alternative modes of biopolitical differentiation and "improvement."

Because of distinctive features of China's administrative and political setup, in particular, the existence of mesoinstitutions connecting levels of the administrative system, in that country the two poles of modern power over life are especially densely connected. This issue—how and how tightly the political center is connected to the community—is also of interest from the institutional perspectives of political science. The answers turn out to be very interesting. In China's multilevel structure for the administration of birth planning, the center is relatively tightly connected to the province, and so on down the line, with local cadres in urban enterprises and rural villages working to ensure that the regulations of the population emanating from the center are translated into the appropriate disciplines of the individual body (health exams, contraceptive practices, and so on) at the local level. How the regime achieves this top-to-bottom connectedness is far from straightforward, however, for in principle the national level simply sets standards. In practice, though, in the area of birth planning, national political leaders manage to achieve considerable control over their subnational counterparts because birth policies are highly demanding and intrusive and because birth work is now central to the routine evaluation of all party and state personnel. The state's intense and unremitting concern about population and its prodigious efforts to manage not just quantity but also quality have led to the construction of dense networks of power relations that extend vertically and horizontally throughout the political system. China thus links these two poles—macro and micro, social body and individual body—into a tightly interlocked network of power relations that undoubtedly leave individuals more bound by the reproductive regulations of a central governing authority than anywhere else in the world.

The PRC also stands out for the immensity and noxiousness of the effects of its biopolitical project of population control on (particular) women and girls, especially during the long 1980s era of hard birth planning. Building on a deeply gendered traditional culture, the PRC's population enhancement project combined a stridently scientistic and nationalistic rationalization for population control with a potent mix of Leninist interventions to produce a brutal form of reproductive management that imposed steep bodily, social, and ethical costs on rural women while snuffing out the lives of girl babies and female fetuses. Imposed in the increasingly masculinist culture, economy, and politics of the reform era by a regime that allowed no independent women's movement and brooked no dissent from its "basic national policy" on population, this biopolitical project as a whole remained unchallenged.

The loss of female life and the devaluation of the feminine matter not just to the female half of China's population. In the twenty-first century the costs are being borne by the whole society as the increasingly male-heavy population structure worsens emerging crises of marriage, aging, and social security. The PRC case underscores the need for feminist research not only on the disciplines of the reproductive body, but also on the regulations of the population-as-a-whole. Governmental projects of population optimization affect the bodies, lives, and selves of a substantial majority of women in Asia, Africa, and Latin America. The Chinese case highlights the intimate connections between science, the bio, and gendered bodies. Students of biopower should pay more attention to the gendered character of biopolitics and to the new gender and other stratifications of bodies and selves that are produced in the name of optimizing collective health, welfare, and vitality. The PRC case bears witnessing not only for the practical reasons that China is home to 20 percent of the world's women and its globalizing economy and society are increasingly affecting the shape of the world to come. The PRC case is also critical theoretically because it allows us to observe what happens when a Marxist-Engelsian solution to the woman question is abandoned for a Leninist-Stalinist one, which in turn is abandoned for a neoliberalmarketist one. Viewed through the lens of biopolitics, the answer would seem to be that the forms and agents of gender subordination change, but the woman question is never—or has not yet been—resolved.

In the area of population quality, the rapid development of market forces since the early 1990s has introduced new and seductive logics of individual consumer desire and global consumer fantasy that easily compete with the state's earlier logics of collectivist socialist virtue and Chinese nationalist fervor. The disciplines of the Leninist state have been vying with—and collaborating with—Foucauldian forces and the disciplines of the capitalist marketplace, bringing broad shifts in the power to shape population norms and practices from the state to transnational corporations. In the early twenty-first century, state discipline is becoming capitalist discipline, and external discipline is becoming self-discipline. As in the advanced liberal societies of the West, in China the governance of population increasingly works through the autonomy and agency—and ultimately through the desires, needs, rights, interests, and choices—of individuals (cf. Dean 1999, 149–175). But various governing authorities, seeking to create subjects capable of exercising their freedom responsibly, have already shaped those desires, needs, and choices, and have deployed indirect means for their surveillance and regulation (documented in Chapters 5 and 6). The reproductive self-discipline of the contemporary Chinese, then, is not freedom in the sense of autonomy or "natural liberty." Instead, it is an artifact of numerous "practices of liberty" embedded in systems of domination. Instilled in individuals by multiple authorities—the birth bureaucracy, the disciplinary institutions of such fields as medicine, psychology, and education, and the capitalist market—this self-discipline is a kind of regulated freedom that is guided by powerful logics of science, technology, the market, and transnational consumer culture. Just as reproductive "voluntarism" and "self-consciousness" were (and still are) politically produced by the state, today's reproductive self-discipline is produced by forces seeking to shape individual desires and behaviors to their own ends.

The Chinese people remain intensely governed, but the mode of governance is changing. In place of the crude and occasional intervention of the state, China's people now face a much more subtle yet insidious form of power that is continuous and dispersed throughout the institutions of modern society and within their own selves, and masked by the language of truth and power. Like the First World people they have long aimed to emulate, China's people are now "free" to make reproductive "choices" that leave them essentially entrapped. Chinese parents are "free" to "desire" to produce and cultivate "few, quality children," while young people are "free" to "choose" to devote their childhoods to perfecting their bodies and minds in an intense competition for status in which, as teenagers in Dalian put it, "people eat people" and "there's just one road [to mobility in the world system that] everyone is trying to squeeze onto" (Fong 2004, 29, 179). Of course, it makes a big difference to China's people whether they are being shaped into "revolutionary-socialist" subjects "voluntarily" complying with state policy or "market-socialist" subjects regulating their own reproduction in accord with state norms. In the market socialism of the 2000s, reproductive subjects are largely free from physical coercion. They benefit from the population quality and welfare projects of the state, and they enjoy the seductive pleasures of the market. Moreover, the compulsions of the market are hidden. Given a choice, most Chinese would undoubtedly take the market. From the vantage point of China's population project, a project that touched and transformed virtually every Chinese, the ongoing process of neoliberalization may be, if not good, then at least no worse than ambiguous for China's people.

Science, Democracy, and Chinese Modernity

By taking charge of population quantity and quality, the state promised to modernize Chinese society and normalize it to the global standard. But what kind of modernity did that birth project help create? In the 1980s and 1990s, birth planning reinvigorated many of China's least humane social and cultural traditions, contributing to a modernity of great inequality in which a privileged urban elite existed in a larger cultural sea of peasant suffering and maternal sacrifice (Chapter 8). The birth program fostered a modernity in which peasants and women, the objects of modernizing efforts in the past, were again blamed for China's backwardness and made to bear the burden of forced demographic modernization. In its haste to accelerate demographic transition, the birth program created a masculinizing and aging social structure in which large gaps in the numbers of males and females and an imbalance between old and young have become constitutive features of Chinese modernity. The birth project sought to eliminate an economic crisis, but it created the equally if not more serious social and cultural crises of child hunger, bride deprivation, the sale of human life, and geriatric distress in the form of lonely elders bereft of both sons and social security. In the 2000s the regime is trying earnestly and energetically to undo some of the damage. The challenges ahead are daunting.

Widely promoted in the May Fourth movement for modernization a century ago, "science" and "democracy" are terms laden with hope for a better Chinese future. Science and democracy were fundamental to the population project as well, taking different forms as the larger Leninist project into which birth planning fit shifted. Yet the promise of these constructs to enhance human well-being remains very partially fulfilled, or fulfilled in complex and contradictory ways. In the area of science, for example, the application of modern statistics and reproductive science has helped make population control targets more reasonable and contraceptive technologies more effective and less damaging to women's health. Yet in the policy arena, the early influence of physical science left China with an urgent crisis rationale and an impossible policy that in our view did far more harm than good. In enforcement, the spreading influence of engineers and engineering logics left the birth program with a social-systems-engineering approach that positioned people as objects of control of demographic engineers in the state (Chapter 9). Now a central feature of Comprehensive Reform, this top-down mechanistic model for social change is likely to discourage the kinds of people-centered innovations today's reformers are trying to introduce (Chapter 6). Until the regime allows a more independent science to develop, or until a critique of the role of science in society emerges, the promise of "science" to enhance human welfare (as opposed to simply facilitating statist control) is likely to remain limited.

Yet when we move beyond the notion of science as a universal field with fixed rules of practice and look at what "science" means in the Chinese context, a more hopeful and open-ended picture emerges. For in the PRC, as elsewhere, the meaning of "science" is up for grabs. In the post-Mao political context, in which modern science and technology have been defined as the motive forces for progress and modernization, nothing can be authoritative unless it bears the label "science." But, in the population arena, as in other domains of policy, the meanings of science and scientist have changed as different people have claimed the labels and used them to press for different projects. The defense cyberneticists who claimed the label "population scientist" in the late 1970s and early 1980s have been succeeded by a host of social scientists of varying disciplines promoting more socially oriented and culturally sensitive projects. In a whispered battle of population sciences, some younger social scientists now confide that, in their view, it is ridiculous, "a joke" (that is, a national embarrassment), that China's population policy of the last twenty-five years was created by a group of rocket scientists (SG 24Dec03 BJ). Not surprisingly, those physical scientists continue to assert (not whisper) that their work was forward-looking and correct (SG 23Dec03 BJ). In the early 2000s, the label "science" is attached to some proposals that shift population work further in the direction of societal self-regulation. Scholars recommending a shift to a two-child policy have framed their work in these terms. In his speech to the 2004 annual summit on population, resources, and environment, top leader Hu Jintao stated emphatically that China's concept of development (including its population development) must be "scientific," and that "scientific" means "human-centered" (Chapter 6). Clearly, in the coming years science will continue to be a major site for struggles over population policy. In observing these contests, the questions we should ask will be not "is this science?" but "who is doing the science? for what ends? by what logics? and with what techniques?" As science projects contend and new assemblages of "scientific" logics, techniques, and practices emerge, the promise of science in the population arena may be fulfilled after all—though in ways we cannot predict.

Today's democracy project in birth planning is an important step forward, reducing the number of regulatory mechanisms and making the power of birth cadres less arbitrary and abusive. Although village self-government and other reforms have enabled the birth program to shed many of its most objectionable practices, especially in more developed localities, the village self-administration of birth planning has limits. Like the larger experiments in village self-government, it gives people more say over small matters without disturbing the policy and political fundamentals. Just as much of the science in birth planning is scientism—the trappings more than the reality—so too is much of the democracy in birth planning actually democratism—the people's voice in name only. Without serious political reform, the kinds of freedoms embodied in such international concepts as "reproductive choice" will remain largely slogans in China.

Lack of genuine democracy impedes full reform of reproductive policy at the elite level as well. The stringent birth limits of the one-child era were imposed by a small cohort of about-to-retire former revolutionary leaders, imposed not only on society but also on younger national political and program leaders. Many younger program leaders said from the beginning that a strict one-child policy would not work and have been working quietly ever since to relax the policy, first by increasing the number of exceptions that allow two children, and then by striving to make the two-child option available to all. As of the early 2000s, reformers have renewed their efforts to demonstrate that a two-child policy is sufficiently attractive, socially and politically, that national program leaders can afford to recommend it to national political leaders, and that national political leaders can afford to adopt it. But as of the early 2000s, national political leaders continue to hesitate. One reason is their worry that fertility might rebound. However, another is that, in the intense competition of elite Chinese politics, advocating change of this "basic national policy" involves political risks that, so far, no national political leaders—or not enough of them—feel in a position to take. In a democratic political system, it would have been very difficult to adopt stringent birth limits. Without a democratic political system, it may remain very difficult to abolish them.

Nevertheless, the conventional Western conclusion that, in the final analysis, nothing will work in China without democratization needs qualification. A new variant of Chinese Leninism—particularly Leninist neoliberalism—may somewhat succeed at combining democracy and centralism, development and redistribution. It is certainly important that China democratize. Still, the question for the future goes beyond how soon China will adopt any particular Western institution for democracy. The governmentalization framework allows one to pose a larger question with a longer history, a question that applies equally to China and to the West. What are the possible viable arrangements of the relationships between state power, disciplining social institutions, and individual self-regulation? China, like the West, has a long history of creative answers to earlier versions of this question. In the future, China, like the West, is likely to pioneer its own answers to the early twenty-first century version of the question, which requires an answer that serves human development and allows popular democracy. In that advance, the population-and-reproduction domain has been in the vanguard, absorbing new human-centered international ideals of quality care and client autonomy.

How mutually compatible are Chinese Leninism, human development, and neoliberal practices? On the one hand, trying to be "late Leninist," "human centered," and "advanced liberal" at the same time will involve some grinding contradictions. Policymaking that does not publicly air all political views and represent all social interests is both developmentally unwise and democratically unjust. Policy implementation that does not allow autonomous initiatives from civil society—professional institutions, nongovernmental organizations, and private individuals—is not as effective or efficient as it could be. On the other hand, there may be some constructive complementaries between Leninism and liberalism for promoting "all-round human development." For addressing traditional legacies of gender inequality, the PRC can mobilize its formidable socialist propaganda capacity to accelerate any equalization that in the long run marketizing modernization may contribute. For addressing future challenges to "population security," the PRC can simultaneously deploy socialist redistributive welfare programs to assist the disadvantaged while employing marketizing social insurance schemes for the more fortunate rest of the population. For sustaining long-term development, the PRC's remaining socialism may help provide some coordination for overcoming China's all too real contradictions between population, resources, and environment, while the PRC struggles toward some environmentally friendly neoliberal regulation of resource-exhausting marketization.

If they have read them at all, outsiders have tended to regard past PRC leaders' statements of elaborate "guiding ideologies" as so much communist jargon. By the beginning of the twenty-first century, however, the PRC's policy process became increasingly adept at defining viable visions and methodically turning them into realities. Outsiders would be well advised to pay attention, and to consider the possibility that what they are witnessing is a process of rethinking that is gradually positioning China to become truly modern: more scientific and participatory, more uniformly prosperous and—although populous—more powerful.

From Confrontation to Constructive Engagement: Implications for U.S. Policy

China's birth program has long been a hot-button issue for American politicians and a source of tension in U.S.-China relations. It has also been a troubling issue for ordinary Americans. In the 1980s, a handful of politicians and their advisors created an emotionally gripping narrative about coercion in the Chinese program. Based on ad hoc information—local reports of use of strong-armed methods and individual testimonies of couples harmed by them—this narrative holds that the program is highly and unchangingly coercive and implies that coercion is virtually the only thing worth paying attention to in the program. With the exception of the Clinton presidency, successive administrations have used this narrative as grounds for withholding U.S. funds from the UNFPA because of its work in China. For the last 20-odd years the dominant American response to China's population program has been this punitive one focused single-mindedly on the issue of coercion.

In the Deng and Jiang eras, the coercion narrative was helpful in drawing attention to the egregious violation of human rights in the Chinese program. Today, however, that old approach is limiting both our understandings of and our responses to the important changes that have been taking place in China since the mid-1990s. This book's more systematic and scholarly review of China's policy and program indicates that, although Hu era leaders remain determined to slow population growth through mandatory birth limits, they appear equally determined to eliminate implementation abuses and deliver real social benefits, particularly to the most disadvantaged. Our main conclusion is that there has been a major shift in both regime approach and public attitudes. Although the policy remains legally mandatory, societal preferences are approaching policy limits, so that clumsy practices are becoming less necessary and less likely. At the same time, larger trends in

Chinese politics and legal culture are now encouraging greater respect for citizen rights. Ignoring this crucial context, some American politicians have used individual cases of harm from the early 2000s to claim that nothing has changed. Such a claim is misleading at best, for it neglects major transformations in the larger politics and program that are working to reduce the incidence of objectionable practices overall.

That does not mean that abuses no longer occur. Quite the contrary. In an effort to meet national policy demands, some provinces continue to enforce birth limits strictly while some localities persist in using clumsy methods. The problems appear to be more serious in the most populous provinces with the fastest growing populations (e.g., Guangdong, swamped with in-migrants) and in the least developed areas where fertility aspirations remain above legal limits (e.g., in central and western China). Individuals caught in these enforcements continue to suffer. Realistically, the elimination of strong-armed methods will take time, since use of such methods had become standard practice in some areas for almost two decades. Until such practices disappear, continued critique of coercive enforcement is important. Today growing numbers of Chinese—population professionals, intellectuals, politicians, and ordinary Chinese—would join in that critique. To be effective in encouraging positive change, however, criticism of the bad must be paired with acknowledgment of and support for the good.

Though it embodies important moral values, the punitive approach to China is based on problematic ethical premises. That approach implicitly assumes that rights to reproductive freedom are absolute. If that assumption were valid and couples had an absolute right to produce any number of children whenever they pleased, then early twenty-first century PRC birth policy remains retrograde and unacceptable, because PRC birth limits remain mandatory and backed by substantial fines. However, most contemporary ethical theories concede that rights are never absolute. Some tradeoff is likely between libertarian rights of freedom from state interference and social-democratic rights to social services that require some state intervention. Both PRC policies and American responses to them involve tradeoffs between competing rights and objectives. Both sides face difficult practical and ethical choices. The PRC is deliberately limiting the reproductive freedom of current generations in order to preserve the sustainability of development and the quality of life of future generations. In the name of reproductive freedom, the United States is protesting this restriction, but at the cost of the UNFPA's capacity to deliver reproductive health services desperately needed by millions of women in countries less developed than China. U.S. policy toward China also involves a tradeoff between promoting improved economic and security relations with the PRC and asserting the reproductive values of some Americans in the international arena. In this complex moral world, each side should endeavor to understand the values that are privileged by the other and the values that are sacrificed by its own choices. For Americans the challenge is to understand China on its own terms. This book has made clear that the problem is not that the PRC program lacks ethical grounding. To the contrary, from the inception of that project China's leaders have grappled with specifically Chinese ethical concerns regarding the regime's treatment of the masses and China's responsibility to the world. Today the PRC regime also largely accepts the international ideals for population policies and reproductive rights set forth in the mid-1990s. Then, as now, the unresolved issues have concerned how to apply those ideals under Chinese circumstances.

Given these political and ethical complexities, how should American policymakers and concerned citizens respond? (For more extensive answers see Greenhalgh 2002; Winckler 2002b.) Perhaps the least productive approach is the current one in which the administration and a few like-minded organizations refuse to recognize and reward progress in China when it occurs; vilify non-Chinese scholars and professionals who are trying to report the facts and promote reforms, discouraging such efforts; and penalize the whole world by denying support to global governmental and nongovernmental organizations that constructively engage the PRC. The times call for fresh thinking and new responses. Condemning China for ethical transgressions makes less sense now because the problem is not so much persuading the PRC to adopt Western ideals—the PRC now largely accepts those ideals. The problem now is finding ways to implement those jointly held ideals in a context that is changing rapidly but continues to contain traces of older Leninist structures that allow abuses to persist. According to the "developmental" approach to rights taken by China's leaders, the main question is one of feasibility. Demographic feasibility dictates that implementation measures not allow fertility to rebound. Economic feasibility requires that local resources be available to fund better administration and more benefits. Political feasibility demands that particular measures win credit for individual leaders within the elite and win legitimacy for the regime within society. For Americans, effective intervention requires both understanding the feasibility constraints facing the regime and helping to alleviate them through bilateral and multilateral assistance to the Chinese birth program in such matters as employing voluntary methods, raising technical standards, and combating HIV/AIDS.

Effective response also requires a subtle grasp of the dynamic politics of population in the PRC. Reflecting a cold war view, the coercion story treats China's political system as monolithic and unchanging. Our work shows that this image of the regime was far from accurate in the past and is even less accurate today. Since the early 1990s, China's rapid entry into global networks has engendered a new, more fluid and transnationalized politics of population in which reformers have been gaining voice relative to hardliners, power has been devolving from center to locality and state to society, and a new, civil society-like space has been emerging in which activists and NGOs have begun working to improve women's reproductive health and rights. These changes present promising opportunities for Americans to help the program translate its new ideals into reality. Politically, the most constructive approach foreigners can take is to strengthen the reform movements that are developing with conceptual, technical, and financial support. By identifying and working with reform-minded forces in China, Americans can promote goals widely shared by Americans and growing numbers of Chinese.

China is changing—and fast. It is high time for the American response to China's population policy to change as well. While continuing to criticize the human rights violations that will likely continue to occur, if decreasingly, for some time, we need to move beyond condemnation and punishment to constructive engagement. This book has provided a political roadmap that could be used to create a more productive approach that respects China's ethical and political realities, works with rather than against concerned Chinese, and engages China as a partner on the world stage.

Notes

1. Among reviews of historical approaches to Chinese population matters, the classic is Ho 1959. More recent accounts include Dikotter 1995, 1998; Lee and Campbell 1997; Lee and Wang 1999.

2. Major studies of demographic trends and dynamics include Coale 1984; Banister 1987; Peng 1991; Poston and Yaukey eds. 1992; Goldstein and Wang eds. 1996; Peng and Guo eds. 2000. Scharping 2003 provides an excellent review of the broad findings.

3. Book-length treatments include Orleans 1972; Tien 1973, 1991; Aird 1972, 1990; Chen and Kols 1982; Banister 1987; Wang and Hull eds. 1991; Scharping 2003. Scharping 2003, 13–25, provides an extended characterization of these two demographic literatures.

4. See, for example, Croll, Davin, and Kane eds. 1985; Wolf 1985; Kane 1987; Greenhalgh 1994, 2003a; Greenhalgh and Li 1995; Milwertz 1997; Croll 2000; Mueggler 2001; Zhang Weiguo 2002; Yan 2003, 190–215; Johnson 2004.

5. See especially White 1990, 1991, 1994a, 1994b; Winckler 1999, 2002.

6. Among political science topics on agenda setting, in general the book makes clear when and why PRC leaders considered population important. Space limits preclude a more detailed account for each episode of policy formulation. On implementation, see White 1987; Hardee-Cleaveland and Banister 1988; Banister and Harbaugh 1994; Smith et al. 1997; Merli, Qian, and Smith 2004. On the process of defining a population policy domain, space limits also preclude treating the interface between population and reproduction and topics that the PRC has defined as part of the same policy domain (resources and environment) or as closely related (such as employment, antipoverty, and social security). On resources and environment see Ross 1988; Qu and Li 1994; Schapiro 2001; Economy 2004.

7. On the politics of the PRC's population statistics, see Zhang Weiguo 2002; Scharping 2003; on the work of numbers in the development of governmental reasoning, Greenhalgh 2004b.

CHAPTER 7   THE SHIFTING LOCAL POLITICS OF POPULATION

1. The socialist planning rationale was, of course, "scientific" in another way: it was based on the scientific socialism of Marxism-Leninism, understood as a comprehensive philosophy uniting human and natural worlds (for more, see Miller 1996, 5).

2. Long-term population projections carried out by Chinese researchers showed that China's human numbers would grow ceaselessly unless fertility levels were drastically reduced. The "backwardness" of China's people was established by comparing selected "qualities" of China's population, especially its educational level, with levels attained in the West. Cybernetic models were also used to define the solution to the population problem. The Club of Rome was an international group of largely natural scientists who in the early 1970s developed a global systems model in which population growth acted to destroy the environment and, for that reason, required strong, even drastic, control (Meadows et al. 1972).

3. Issues of family size and composition, including infant survival, have long been domains of family and kin politics in China. In the post-Mao era the state entered this political domain, reshaping it in the process. Citations to these historical precedents can be found in Chapter 8.

4. There is little work in English on the politics of migrant fertility. The topic is treated in passing in Scharping 2003, 281–283. There are numerous books and articles on the problem—though not the politics—of migrant fertility in Chinese.

5. Such views were very much alive in the 1980s. In her 1980 interviews in five provinces, Margery Wolf encountered many rural women who would agree with the Shaanxi informant who told her: "Country people only *count* boys" (Wolf 1985, 256). In many parts of China girls were not even given names (Watson 1986).

6. In the 1984 film on sexual politics, "One Village in China: Small Happiness," peasants described the birth of a son as a "big happiness," that of a daughter a "small happiness."

7. Village cadres could also reduce fertility by eliminating the positive incentives for childbearing (such as extra plots and rations) built into the structure of collective life. The later-longer-fewer policy was also relatively easy to enforce because fertility desires were quite moderate, with men in some areas wanting three to four children and women desiring only two (Parish and Whyte 1978).

8. Useful entries into the demographic and anthropological literatures on resistance are Li 1995; Scharping 2003, 261–263; and Croll 2000.

9. In the PRC, the early 1950s campaign to modernize childbirth through the training of midwives was the first time women's bodies had been subject to state intervention on a wide scale (Chapter 3; Davin 1976; Goldstein 1998).

10. In Johnson's (2004) research in central China, boys made up about 10 percent of abandoned children, and they were mostly disabled or extremely ill.

11. The best data from the 1980s come from the World Fertility Survey's In-Depth Fertility Survey. In seven provinces studied in 1985 and 1987, the mean ideal family size, assuming the existence of the birth program, averaged 2.5 children and ranged from 1.9 in Liaoning to 3.1 in Guizhou (Scharping 2003, 215). The ideal without the birth control program ranged from 2.2 in Liaoning to 3.6 in Gansu (Zhang Guangyu, personal communication, 1/30/04). The 2001 survey, which was

conducted by the State Birth Planning Commission, assumes the existence of the birth program. Although these data should be interpreted with some caution, they are consistent with other data and with larger changes in Chinese society and population politics. A detailed analysis of the 2001 data can be found in Zhang 2004, 162–188.

12. One small-scale study conducted by an independent Chinese researcher in 1997 seems to suggest high levels of acceptance of the official rationale among the rural people. More than 80 percent of respondents in three villages agreed that rapid population growth was obstructing China's development, while more than 90 percent agreed that China must strictly carry out birth planning policy and that the one-child policy is beneficial not only to the country but to individuals and families as well (Nie 1999, 131–139).

13. In some places, however, state quotas and crackdowns still seem to be in force (Murphy 2003).

14. On the eve of the reforms, Chinese demographers estimated that the costs of raising a child to age 16 were 1,600 yuan in the villages, 4,800 in towns, and 6,900 in the cities (Liu, Wu, and Zha 1980).

15. The narrowly eugenic element of Chinese population policy began to take shape in the mid-1980s. In 1988 Gansu Province issued a set of regulations calling for the compulsory sterilization of the intellectually impaired. In 1993 the government circulated a draft law on eugenics and health protection that drew widespread international criticism from human rights groups. The law, which was modified and passed in 1994 under the name Maternal and Infant Health Care Law, contains provisions promoting the use of prenatal diagnosis of hereditary diseases and premarital check-ups to detect hereditary and certain mental disorders. It authorizes sterilization for those considered unfit to reproduce. Such eugenic efforts to "improve" the population by preventing the reproduction of those deemed genetically inferior have a long history in Republican China and direct precedents in Chinese communist marriage laws of the 1930s, 1950, and 1980 (Johnson 1997; Dikotter 1995, 1998; Sigley 1996; Bakken 2001).

16. In her early 1990s research in Beijing and Shenyang, Milwertz (1997) found that as many as 80 percent of the mothers and 61 percent of the fathers in her study had read books and magazines on child education.

17. Research in the Hebei city of Baoding in the mid-1990s showed the efficacy of those investments. Parents who invested more in their children at an earlier time received more assistance from them in old age (Chen Jieming 2003).

18. The American food giant Heinz has developed nutrition education programs to influence Chinese child care officials and professionals. Some of the food recommendations for Chinese babies promoted by the Heinz Institute of Nutrition Science were incorporated into the Chinese National Nutritional Development Plan for the 1990s (Jing 2000a).

CHAPTER 8   RESTRATIFYING CHINESE SOCIETY

1. On "class status" categories and their effects, see Billeter 1985. For the *hukou* classification of peasant/nonpeasant household, see Potter 1983 for the Maoist era,

and see Cheng and Selden 1994; Chan and Zhang 1999; Solinger 1999; Zhang 2001 for the reform years. The effects of the state's categorizations of ethnicity and gender are examined in Gladney 1991; Schein 2000; Litzinger 2000 (ethnicity); and Barlow 1994; Evans 1997; Rofel 1999 (gender). Thoughtful overviews of the categorizing practices of Chinese statecraft are Yang 1989; Barlow 1994.

2. Treatments of birth planning among China's 55 ethnic minorities include Goldstein et al. 2002; Scharping 2003, 150–155.

3. Large-scale state interventions in women's reproductive health began in the early 1950s, with the campaigns to improve sanitation, spread knowledge of reproductive physiology, and create modern midwifery practices. The birth program that began in earnest in the early 1970s represented both a continuation of these efforts and an extension of them to a new domain: that of family size. For the earlier efforts and their significance, see, Davin 1976, 131–134; Barlow 1994; Evans 1997; Goldstein 1998.

4. Since the mid-1990s, Chinese medical ethicists have been able to quietly examine issues such as patients' rights, informed consent, and patient privacy in the birth program. Some of this important discussion is taking place in the pages of the journals *Chinese Medical Ethics* and *Medicine and Philosophy*.

5. Maoism produced an enormous income gap between city and countryside by fixing people in their place of birth, promoting self-reliance, controlling prices and wages, and subsidizing urbanites through the state monopoly over the grain trade. The 1980s and 1990s brought significant worsening of income disparities between provinces, between east and west, within urban and rural areas, and between male and female. Economic assessments of these trends can be found in Riskin, Zhao, and Li 2001; Khan and Riskin 2001.

6. Rural migrants to the cities have been depicted in similar ways (Davin 1999; Lei 2001; Zhang Li 2001).

7. In the 1997 RH survey, 74 percent of village women and 59 percent of city women said that the wife should undergo sterilization. Only 11 percent of villagers and 13 percent of urbanites believed that the husband should be sterilized (Jiang ed. 2000, 145).

8. A woman headed the State Birth Planning Commission and its forerunner between 1978 and 1981 and from 1988 to 1998. Women have also been important at the level of vice minister, holding four out of fifteen such positions between 1981 and 1994 (EBP 1997, 460).

9. In the 1997 RH survey, 17.2 percent of women had had two or more IUD insertions, while 2.9 percent had had three or more. Ten (9.8) percent had undergone two or more abortions, while 2.6 percent had endured three or more (Jiang ed. 2000, 151).

10. Chinese health researchers estimate that only about 10 percent of abortions are performed with painkiller. The reasoning is that those who have violated state policy should not be entitled to pain relief subsidized by the state (SG 12Dec03 BJ).

11. Neurasthenia is a common name for illnesses combining physical symptoms with depression and/or anxiety. In the PRC, this condition has served to express in somatic terms critiques of a political system that could not be spoken.

12. For evidence of the proactive nature of such reproductive strategizing in con-

temporary China, the intimate connection to family system norms, and variations in these strategies across space, time, and ethnicity, see Skinner, Henderson, and Yuan 2000; Yuan and Skinner 2000, Skinner 2003, and, on family systems and demographic behavior, see Skinner 1997.

13. Lavely and Cai (2004) show dramatic increases in regional differences in juvenile sex ratios (ages 0–4) in the last two decades of the twentieth century that do not correspond to provincial boundaries. Their work suggests that high sex ratios are prominent on some macroregional peripheries and appear related to conservative family system norms.

14. In the urban areas, Chinese researchers explain, unmarried couples are cohabiting and getting pregnant. If the fetus is male, the couple marries and has the child. If it is female, it is aborted (SG 12Dec03 BJ).

15. Before the establishment of the PRC, China had one of the world's largest and most complex markets in human life, especially child life. Particularly in times of destitution, poor peasants often sold their sons and, even more, daughters, who, as outsiders to the patrilineal kinship system, could be bought and sold at will. Hard times also brought to life gangs of bandits who survived by kidnapping and selling children. The market in people effectively ended with the communist victory (Watson 1980).

16. Since the mid-1990s the Chinese government has launched major initiatives to improve the well-being of women, who have been hurt by the reforms. Many of these initiatives have been introduced under the auspices of the State Council's Outlines for Women's Development (1995–2000 and 2001–2010), which have been aimed at improving women's economic, legal, political, educational, and health status. In birth planning, a wide range of initiatives launched in the mid-1990s—poverty-alleviation programs, such as Project Happiness, experiments in expanding men's roles in birth planning, and the new client- and health-centered reorientation of the program more generally—all seek to improve women's overall well-being. See SBPC 15 October 2001; 2001; 15 May 2002; 8 September 2002.

17. In the early 2000s, some regular schools in such places as Beijing, facing a dearth of registered children, have opened their doors to the unregistered. Yet the proportion of "black children" able to gain admission to and afford state schools is low (Kwong 2004).

18. Official figures on unplanned births indicate that, between 1979 and 1999, as many as 82 million children were born into illegality. Those numbers declined sharply over time (from about 32 percent of all births in the early 1980s to 7 percent in the late 1990s). Yet this figure excludes unreported births, estimated at 32 percent of births in the late 1980s and 27 percent in the 1990s and early 2000s (SG interviews, 2, 4 July 1993, Beijing; Zhang Guangyu 2004). Estimates that include unreported births suggest that from 1979 to 1999, roughly 135 million unplanned births may have taken place. If all those infants lived, that works out to 11 percent of China's 1999 population of 1.259 billion who came into the world unplanned (for details, see Greenhalgh 2004). Unfortunately, there is no way to estimate how many of these infants remained outside the registration system to become unplanned children and, by the early 2000s, young adults. These persons remain uncounted and, given the general disarray of population statistics, uncountable. Certainly, some, maybe a great

many, registered in the "clean-ups" and "amnesties" offered birth offenders in the 1982, 1990, and 2000 censuses (Zhang 2004). But many did not, and there is no way to know how large those numbers are.

19. In the crucial area of education for illegal migrant children in the cities, a belated directive issued by the education ministry and pubic security bureau in 1998 did not recognize the right of such children as citizens to an education, but suggested that local governments should provide school facilities for them nonetheless. Some local governments have responded sympathetically, but most have been unwilling to commit their resources to schooling a group they consider troublemakers. In this vacuum, entrepreneurs have mobilized resources from civil society and various government agencies to set up migrant children schools, which other government entities have then shut down. For this fascinating story, see Kwong 2004.

20. The classic critique is Isaacs 1958; more recently, Zhang 1998; on other redefinitions of "Chineseness," see Ong 1999.

21. Uxorilocal marriages (in which the groom marries into the bride's family) are relatively common in this area. Although this practice, which seems to lessen son preference, makes this area unusual, elsewhere uxorilocal marriages have become more prevalent since the advent of the one-child policy (Xie, Gu, and Hardee 2000).

CHAPTER 9   REMAKING CHINA'S POLITICS AND GLOBAL POSITION

1. An exception is Yang and Zheng 2004, who argue that birth planning illustrates and may well encourage strong central-provincial relations. The anthropological writings of Anagnost (1997a) and Mueggler (2001) tease out some of the implications of the birth project for state power and party hegemony.

2. This discussion of state strengthening draws inspiration from the work of Ann Anagnost (esp. 1997a), whose writings illuminate the discursive power of "population"; Eric Mueggler (2001), whose ethnography highlights the ways in which birth planning serves as the raison d'être of party and state in rural China; and Lisa Rofel (1999), whose work sheds light on the significance of birth work to the construction of a particular kind of gendered Chinese modernity.

3. In the new political climate of the early 2000s, popular acceptance of the state's right to manage childbearing may be slightly eroding, however. In some places a tiny minority of people is daring to claim that childbearing is a "personal freedom" and that excess childbearing will not burden the nation (PDSC 2003d). Whether these views will become more prevalent remains to be seen.

4. This discussion draws heavily on Greenhalgh's interviews with Chinese population specialists, especially in 1985, 1986, 1988, 1999, and 2003

5. Actually, program leaders have long anticipated such changes, explaining that "development will eventually solve the problem." But they may not have anticipated the sorts of family dynamics through which "development" would work its demographic magic.

6. A U.S.-based professor who grew up in Shanghai in the 1970s remembers state propaganda exhorting people to plan their births because "we don't want to burden the world with too many Chinese" (Mei Zhan, personal communication, 8 January 2004).

7. The following draws on interviews with Liu Zheng and Wu Cangping in November 1985 and 1986. Writings by both those scholars develop similar points.

8. In addition to the long-lived critique of coercion, over the years the program has been criticized for numerous other violations of international human rights. Among the bigger issues of contention have been the treatment of abandoned children in state orphanages and the eugenic intent and practices of a law drafted in the early 1990s that was aimed at keeping the genetically "unfit" from reproducing. At times the charges have been valid; at other times they have been exaggerated. China has responded to such complaints with internal investigations and, in some cases, changes designed to address the critics' concerns. The eugenics law, for example, was renamed and somewhat modified in response to the international outcry. For some of these politics, see L. Johnson 1997; K. Johnson 2004.

9. Between 1960–65 and 2000–05, world fertility fell from 5.0 to 2.7; that is, by 2.3 births, or 46 percent. China's fertility dropped from 5.7 to 1.8; that is, by 3.9 births, or 68 percent. Fertility in the world apart from China dropped from 4.76 to 2.92; that is, by 1.84 births, or 39 percent. China's contribution to the global fertility decline, then, was to raise the decline from 39 to 46 percent. Similarly, over the same period, world population growth fell 38 percent from 1.97 percent per year to 1.22 percent per year, while China's fell 65 percent, from 2.07 percent to 0.73 percent. In the world except for China population growth fell 30 percent, from 1.94 percent to 1.35 percent. China thus changed the world's growth-rate decline from 30 percent to 38 percent.

Abbreviations

AFP	Agence-France Presse
ALP	Advanced Leadership Program. From 1998 to 2002, through foreign travel and seminars, introduced PRC national and provincial birth planning officials to recent international developments in family planning policy and practice.
BJ	Beijing
BPA	Birth Planning Association. The birth program's mass association for promoting birth control and related activities.
CB	Canberra, Australia
CCP	Chinese Communist Party
Chen	Chen Li. From 2003, the director of the population-and-birth commission's new population planning department.
CPIRC	China Population Information and Research Center. Under many name changes, the birth commission arm for policy research and information dissemination
CPPCC	Chinese People's Political Consultative Conference. The second of the PRC's main national representative bodies; includes some noncommunist parties and delegates.
CTBP	China Today Birth Planning. The 1992 volume on birth planning in the China Today series.
Cui	Cui Li. In the late 1990s and early 2000s, director of the birth commission's personnel department.
DXP	Deng Xiaoping. A key PRC party and government leader from the early 1950s who ran China from the late 1980s through the early 1990s, greatly intensifying birth planning.
EBP	*Encyclopedia of Birth Planning*. The PRC birth program's major compilation of past policy documents, assembled in the 1990s and published in 1997. A major source for the policy history in this book.

FBIS-CHI   Foreign Broadcast Information Service, China Daily Report. FBIS performs monitoring and translation for the U.S. government. Since the late 1990s, included in the electronic database World News Connection (WNC), accessible in many university libraries.

FEER   Far Eastern Economic Review

GV   Geneva, Switzerland

JZH   Jiang Zhenghua. Mathematical demographer, in the 1980s professor and director of population studies at Xi'an Jiaotong University; in the 1990s vice minister of the birth commission; by the 2000s, vice chairman and deputy speaker of the National People's Congress.

LP   Li Peng. Government premier from 1987 to 1998, then head of the NPC until 2003. A technocratic central planner who strongly favored "hard" birth planning.

LXJ   Li Xiaojiang. Leading PRC women studies scholar, with varied institutional affiliations.

LXZ   Li Xiuzhen. Administered maternal and child health work in the health ministry from 1962 until 1981, and most national-level birth planning leading groups and offices.

MDJ   Mudanjiang, Heilongjiang. National model for Comprehensive Reform, particularly during 2002.

ME   Main Events. Chronology of PRC birth planning cited in References under Yang Kuixue, Liang Jimin, and Zhang Fan 2001.

NC   North Carolina

NPC   National People's Congress. Highest legislative body of the PRC government (as opposed to the party).

NPFPC   National Population and Family Planning Commission of China. The PRC's official English translation of the name of its birth commission, since 2003 when "population" was added to the commission's name. Its new Web address is www.npfpc.gov.cn, in English, with Chinese also available from the home page. See also SBPC, SFPC, and SPBPC.

NJ   New Jersey. ALP sessions for PRC birth leaders were held near Princeton 1998–2002.

NS   Nafis Sadik. Long-term head of the United Nations Population Fund (UNFPA) who in the 1990s urged the PRC birth program to reform.

PBSC   Politburo Standing Committee. In practice, the most authoritative decision-making body in the PRC party-state.

PI	Popinfo. Shanghai-based website posting materials on PRC population and birth planning at www.popinfo.gov.cn.
PPY	Peng Peiyun. Birth minister from 1988 to 1998 who astutely balanced the need to placate national political leaders by reducing fertility with the need to initiate program reform.
PRC	People's Republic of China
QH	Qinghai
SBPC	State Birth Planning Commission. The English translation used in this book of the name of the PRC birth commission, from its founding in 1981 until 2003 when "population" was added to its name. See also NPFPC, SPBPC, SFPC.
SFPC	State Family Planning Commission. The PRC's official English translation of the name of its birth commission, from its establishment in 1981 until its name change in 2003. Its old Web address www.sfpc.gov.cn has been discontinued. See also NPFPC, SBPC, and SPBPC.
SPBPC	State Population and Birth Planning Commission. The English translation used in this book of the name of the PRC birth commission since 2003 when "population" was added to its name. See also NPFPC, SBPC, and SFPC.
SRB	Sex ratio at birth. Normally about 106 males to 100 females, much higher in China—and rising—in part because of state birth planning.
SSB	State Statistical Bureau. Top agency for national data for planning purposes, including in population affairs. Title later changed to National Bureau of Statistics.
TFR	Total Fertility Rate. Roughly speaking, within a given cohort of women, the average total number of children that a woman is likely to have during her lifetime.
TY	Taiyuan, Shanxi
UNFPA	Originally United Nations Fund for Population Activities. Later renamed United Nations Population Fund but retained its original acronym.
WGQ	Wang Guoqiang. Career administrator in the birth system, long high in the program's administration department. By the early 2000s promoted to vice minister. A firm but centrist implementor of reform.
WHO	World Health Organization. Has conducted many programs and projects in China. Some have been related to birth-control, often promoting reform of PRC birth planning.

WJC — Wu Jingchun. Birth vice minister from 1988–1994 overseeing technology, propaganda, and eventually party discipline.

WTO — World Trade Organization, which the PRC joined in 2002.

WZY — Wang Zhongyu. From the early 1990s to the early 2000s, a top national reformer of the PRC's management of economy and society. From 1998 to 2003 as secretary general of the State Council personally oversaw reorientation of birth policy and renovation of birth work.

YB — *Yearbook.* Since 1986, the birth program's annual compendium of its new policies and ongoing activities. Until the early 2000s the official English title was *China Family Planning Yearbook*; in Chinese, *Zhongguo Jihua Shengyu Nianjian*. Probably has been changed to *China Population and Family Planning Yearbook.*

YXJ — Yu Xuejun. Long head of the birth commission's research arm CPIRC, from 2004 head of the commission's policy-and-law department.

ZBG — Zhao Baige. Dynamic career science-and-technology administrator in the birth system—in Shanghai, New York, and Beijing. In the 1990s headed the S&T department, in the 2000s promoted to vice minister. A major proponent of reform.

ZEL — Zhang Erli. Engineering professor, headed birth commission planning and statistics department, helped design evaluation systems and, later, launch experiments at Quality of Care.

ZJX — Zhao Jiuxiang. Birth director in Mudanjiang, Heilongjiang in the late 1990s and early 2000s who turned that regional city's birth work into a national model of Comprehensive Reform.

ZMC — Zhang Mincai. From the early 1980s helped pioneer birth work in the Chinese military, later secretary general of the China Population Studies Association.

ZWQ — Zhang Weiqing. Former philosophy graduate and governor of Shanxi, birth vice minister from 1995 and minister from 1998 (until 2007).

Agamben, Giorgio. 1998. *Homo Sacer: Sovereign Power and Bare Life*. Stanford, CA: Stanford University Press.

Ai Xiao. 1988. "Worries about population," *People's Daily* (14 January): 1, 3. In FBIS-CHI-88-012, 44–47.

———. 1989. "I hope that everyone will conscientiously carry out family planning—An interview with Peng Peiyun, Minister of the SBPC," *People's Daily* (14 April): 5. [In Chinese]

Aird, John S. 1972. "Population policy and demographic prospects in the People's Republic of China," in *People's Republic of China: An Economic Assessment*, pp. 220–331. Washington, DC: U.S. Government Printing Office. [A Compendium of Papers Submitted to the Joint Economic Committee, Congress of the United States.]

———. 1990. *Slaughter of the Innocents: Coercive Birth Control in China*. Washington, DC: AEI Press.

Ali, Kamran Asdar. 2002. *Planning the Family in Egypt: New Bodies, New Selves*. Austin, TX: University of Texas Press.

Allison, Graham T. 1971. *Essence of Decision: Explaining the Cuban Missile Crisis*. Boston, MA: Little, Brown.

ALP [Advanced Leadership Program]. 2000. *Mid-Term Assessment*. San Francisco: Public MediaCenter. Program of SBPC, Public Media Center, and Center for Health and Social Policy.

Alpermann, Bjorn. 2001. "The post-election administration of Chinese villages," *China Journal* 46 (July): 45–67. [Case study 1: Birth planning, 54–59.]

Anagnost, Ann. 1988. "Family violence and magical violence: The woman as victim in China's one-child policy," *Women and Language* 11,2 (Winter): 16–22.

———. 1997a. *National Past-times: Narrative, Representation, and Power in Modern China*. Durham, NC: Duke University Press.

———. 1997b. "Children and national transcendence in China," in Kenneth G. Lieberthal, Shuen-fu Lin, and Ernest P. Young (eds.), *Constructing China: The Interaction of Culture and Economics*. Ann Arbor, MI: Center for Chinese Studies, University of Michigan, pp. 195–222.

Andrews, Julia F., and Kuiyi Shen. 2002. "The new Chinese woman and lifestyle magazines in the late 1990s," in Link, Madsen, and Pickowicz (eds.), pp. 137–162.

AP [Associated Press]. 1999. "More than ever, Chinese abandon baby girls," *New York Times* (22 April): A10.

———. 2004. "Court convicts 52 of baby-trafficking in China," *New York Times*, 24 July: A3.

Apter, David E., and Tony Saich. 1994. *Revolutionary Discourse in Mao's Republic.* Cambridge, MA: Harvard University Press.

Bachman, David. 1985. *Chen Yun and the Chinese Political System.* Berkeley: Center for Chinese Studies, Institute of East Asian Studies, University of California, Berkeley.

———. 1991. *Bureaucracy, Economy and Leadership in China: The Institutional Origins of the Great Leap Forward.* New York, NY: Cambridge University Press.

Bakken, Borge. 2000. *The Exemplary Society: Human Improvement, Social Control, and the Dangers of Modernity in China.* Oxford, UK: Oxford University Press.

Banister, Judith. 1984. "Population policy and trends in China, 1978–83," *China Quarterly* 100 (December): 717–741.

———. 1987. *China's Changing Population.* Stanford, CA: Stanford University Press.

———. 1998. "Population, public health and the environment in China," *China Quarterly* 156 (December): 986–1015.

———. 2004. "Shortage of girls in China today," *Journal of Population Research* 21,1 (May): 19–45.

Banister, Judith, and Christina Wu Harbaugh. 1994. *China's Family Planning Program: Inputs and Outcomes.* Washington, DC: U.S. Bureau of the Census.

Barlow, Tani E. 1994. "Theorizing woman: Funu, guojia, jiating (Chinese woman, Chinese state, Chinese family)," in Angela Zito and Tani E. Barlow (eds.), *Body, Subject, and Power in China.* Chicago: University of Chicago Press, pp. 253–289.

Baum, Richard. 1993. "The road to Tiananmen: Chinese politics in the 1980s," in MacFarquhar (ed.), pp. 340–471. [Also in 1997 edition.]

———. 1994. *Burying Mao: Chinese Politics in the Age of Deng Xiaoping.* Princeton, NJ: Princeton University Press.

———. 2000. "Jiang takes command: The fifteenth national party congress and beyond," in Hung-mao Tian and Yun-han Chu (eds.), *China under Jiang Zemin.* Boulder: Lynne Rienner, pp. 15–31.

Bernstein, Thomas P., and Xiaobo Lu. 2003. *Taxation without Representation in Contemporary Rural China.* New York: Cambridge University Press.

Billiter, Jean-Francois. 1985. "The system of 'class status,'" in Stuart R. Schram (ed.), *The Scope of State Power in China.* London: School of Oriental and African Studies, pp. 127–169.

Blecher, Marc, and Vivienne Shue. 1996. *Tethered Deer: Government and Economy in a Chinese County.* Stanford, CA: Stanford University Press.

Bloom, David E., David Canning, and Jaypee Sevilla. 2003. *The Demographic Dividend: A New Perspective on the Economic Consequences of Population Change.* Santa Monica, CA: RAND. [Population Matters series.]

Bongaarts, John, and Susan Greenhalgh. 1985. "An alternative to the one-child policy in China," *Population and Development Review* 11,4 (December): 585–617.

Bossen, Laurel. 2002. *Chinese Women and Rural Development: Sixty Years of Change in Lu Village, Yunnan.* Lanham, MD: Rowman and Littlefield.

Bowie, Robert R., and John K. Fairbank (eds.). 1965. *Communist China 1955–1959: Policy Documents with Analysis.* Cambridge: Harvard University Press.

BPA [Birth Planning Association]. 1999. *Update.* Beijing: BPA. [Spring 1999 issue of periodic English briefing.]

Brehm, John, and Scott Gates. 1997. *Working, Shirking, and Sabotage: Bureaucratic Response to a Democratic Public.* Ann Arbor: University of Michigan Press.

Bruce, Judith. 1990. "Fundamental elements of the quality of care: A simple framework," *Studies in Family Planning* 21,2 (March–April): 61–91.

Burchell, Graham, Colin Gordon, and Peter Miller (eds.). 1991. *The Foucault Effect: Studies in Governmentality.* Chicago: University of Chicago Press.

Brzezinski, Zbigniev. 1989. *The Grand Failure: The Birth and Death of Communism in the Twentieth Century.* New York: Scribners.

Burns, John F. 1985. "In China these days, an only child is the only way," *New York Times* (5 May): sec. 4, 24.

Burns, John P. 2003. "Governance and public sector reform in the People's Republic of China," in Anthony B. L. Cheung and Ian Scott (eds.), *Governance and Public Sector Reform in Asia: Paradigm Shifts or Business as Usual?* London: Routledgecurzon, pp. 67–89.

Cai Yong, and William Lavely. 2003. "China's missing girls: Numerical estimates and effects on population growth," *China Review* 3,2 (Fall): 13–29.

CECC [Congressional-Executive Commission on China]. 2002. *Women's Rights and China's New Family Planning Law: Roundtable before the Congressional-Executive Commission on China, One Hundred Seventh Congress, Second Session, September 23, 2002.* Washington, DC: U.S. Government Printing Office.

Champagne, Susan. 1992. *Producing the Intelligent Child: Intelligence and the Child Rearing Discourse in the People's Republic of China.* Ph.D. diss., Stanford University.

Chan, Kam Wing, and Li Zhang. 1999. "The *hukou* system and rural-urban migration in China: Processes and changes," *China Quarterly* 160 (December): 818–855.

Chang, Leslie. 2001. "China tries easing its approach to brutal family-planning policy," *Wall Street Journal* (2 February).

Chao, Chien-min, and Bruce J. Dickson (eds.). 2001. *Remaking the Chinese State: Strategies, Society, and Security.* London: Routledge.

Chatterjee, Nilanjana, and Nancy E. Riley. 2001. "Planning an Indian modernity: The gendered politics of fertility control," *Signs: Journal of Women in Culture and Society* 26,3 (Spring): 811–846.

Chee, Bernadine W. L. 2000. "Eating snacks and biting pressure: Only children in Beijing," in Jing Jun (ed.), 48–70.

Chen Jieming. 2003. "The effect of parental investment on old-age support in urban China," in Whyte (ed.), pp. 197–224.

Chen, Haifeng (ed.). 1984. *Chinese Health Care: A Comprehensive Review of the Health Services of the People's Republic of China.* Lancaster: MTP Press. [Modern Chinese medicine, Volume 3. Published in association with the People's Medical Publishing House, Beijing]

Chen, Pi-chao, and Adrienne Kols. 1982. "Population and birth planning in the People's Republic of China," *Population Reports* 25 (January-February), Series J: J577-J618.

Chen Wei. 2003. *Induced Abortion in China: Trends, Patterns and Determinants.* Ph.D. diss., Dept. Demography, Australian National University.

Cheng Du. 1982. "Fertility survey in the rural areas of Hubei Province," *Population Research* 5 (September): 36–38, 31.[In Chinese]

Cheng, Tiejun, and Mark Selden. 1994. "The origins and social consequences of China's hukou system," *China Quarterly* 139 (September): 644–668.

Cheng Yimin, Zhu Wei, Li Zhimin, Zhang Yang, and Wang Aiying. 1997. "Contraceptive practices of women requesting termination of pregnancy: A study from China," *Contraception* 55,1 (January): 15–17.

China Daily. 2004. "China's reverse baby bonus," *China Daily* (5 August), www .chinadaily.com.cn.

China Daily. 2005. "China to outlaw sex-selective abortion," *China Daily* (7 January).

China Journal. 1995. *Elite Politics in China,* Special issue, *China Journal* 34 (July).

China Journal. 2001. *The Nature of Chinese Politics Today,* Forum discussion, *China Journal* 45 (January): 21–158.

China Quarterly. 2004. *China's campaign to 'open up the West': National, provincial and local perspectives,* Special issue, *China Quarterly* 178 (June).

China Strategy. 30 January 2004. *Decision-Making Under the New Leadership,* 1. Washington, DC: International Security Program, Center for Strategic and International Studies.

China Today. 2003. "Shanghai's DINK households hit 12.4 percent," *China Today* 52,2 (February): 6.

Chu, Junhong. 2000. "Study on the quality of the family planning program in China." Paper presented at the Annual Meeting of the Population Association of America, Los Angeles, CA.

———. 2001. "Prenatal sex determination and sex-selective abortion in rural central China," *Population and Development Review* 27,2 (June): 259–281.

Clarke, Adele E. 1998. *Disciplining Reproduction: Modernity, American Life Sciences, and the Problems of Sex.* Berkeley: University of California Press.

CLM [China Leadership Monitor]. www.chinaleadershipmonitor.org.

Coale, Ansley J. 1984. *Rapid Population Change in China, 1952–1982.* Washington, DC: National Academy Press.

Coale, Ansley J., and Judith Banister. 1994. "Five decades of missing females in China," *Demography* 31,3 (August): 459–479.

Cohen, Myron L. 1993. "Cultural and political inventions in modern China: The case of the Chinese 'peasant,'" *Daedalus* 122,2 (Spring): 151–170.

Courtois, Stephane, et al. 1999. *The Black Book of Communism: Crimes, Terror, Repression.* Cambridge, MA: Harvard University Press.

Crane, Barbara B., and Jason L. Finkle. 1989. "The United States, China, and the United Nations Population Fund: Dynamics of U.S. policymaking," *Population and Development Review* 15,1 (March): 23–59.

Croll, Elisabeth. 1985. "The single-child family in Beijing: A first-hand report," in Croll, Davin, and Kane (eds.), pp. 190–232.

———. 2000. *Endangered Daughters: Discrimination and Development in Asia.* London: Routledge.

Croll, Elisabeth, Delia Davin, and Penny Kane (eds.). 1985. *China's One-Child Family Policy*. London: Macmillan.

CTBP [China Today Birth Planning]. China Today. 1992. *China Today: The family planning cause*. Beijing: China Today. [In Chinese. Birth planning volume of China Today series]

CTHW2 [China Today Health Work, Volume 2]. China Today. 1986. *China Today: Health Work*. Beijing: China Today. [In Chinese. Public health volume of China Today series]

Dahl, Robert, and Charles Lindblom. 1953. *Politics, Economics and Welfare: Planning and Politico-Economic Systems Resolved into Basic Social Processes*. New York: Harper.

Das Gupta, Monica, and Li Shuzhuo. 1999. "Gender bias in China, South Korea and India, 1920–1990: Effects of war, famine and fertility decline," *Development and Change* 30,3 (July): 619–652.

Davin, Delia. 1976. *Woman-Work: Women and the Party in Revolutionary China*. Oxford: Clarendon.

———. 1985. "The single-child family policy in the cities," in Croll, Davin, and Kane (eds.), pp. 83–114.

———. 1999. *Internal Migration in Contemporary China*. New York: St. Martin's.

Davis, Deborah, and Stevan Harrell (eds.). 1993. *Chinese Families in the Post-Mao Era*. Berkeley: University of California Press.

Davis, Deborah S., and Julia S. Sensenbrenner. 2000. "Commercializing childhood: Parental purchases for Shanghai's only child," in Deborah S. Davis (ed.), *The Consumer Revolution in Urban China*. Berkeley: University of California Press, pp. 54–79.

Dean, Mitchell. 1999. *Governmentality: Power and Rule in Modern Society*. London: Sage.

Demick, Barbara. 2003. "N. Korea's brides of despair," *Los Angeles Times* (18 August): A1, 5.

Diamant, Neil J. 2000. *Revolutionizing the Family: Politics, Love, and Divorce in Urban and Rural China, 1949–1968*. Berkeley: University of California Press.

Dikotter, Frank. 1995. *Sex, Culture and Modernity in China*. Honolulu: University of Hawaii Press.

———. 1998. *Imperfect Conceptions: Medical Knowledge, Birth Defects, and Eugenics in China*. New York: Columbia University Press.

Dorris, Carl E. 1976. "Peasant mobilization in North China and the origins of Yan'an communism," *China Quarterly* 68 (December): 697–719.

Dreyfus, Hubert L., and Paul Rabinow. 1982. *Michel Foucault: Beyond Structuralism and Hermeneutics*. 2nd ed. Chicago: University of Chicago Press.

Du, Peng. 2000. "The ethnic minority population in China," in Peng and Guo (eds.), pp. 207–215.

Du, Peng, and Tu Ping. 2000. "Population ageing and old age security," in Peng and Guo (eds.), pp. 77–90.

Dutton, Michael R. 1992. *Policing and Punishment in China: From Patriarchy to the People*. New York: Oxford University Press.

EBP [Encyclopedia of Birth Planning]. Peng, Peiyun (ed.). 1997. *Encyclopedia of Birth Planning*. Beijing: China Population Press.

Eckholm, Erik. 1999. "For China's rural migrants, an education wall," *New York Times* (23 December): 1, 8.

Economy, Elizabeth. 2004. *The River Runs Black: The Environmental Challenge to China's Future*. Ithaca, NY: Cornell University Press.

Edin, Maria. 2003. "State capacity and local agent control in China: CCP cadre management from a township perspective," *China Quarterly* 173 (March): 35–52.

Eggerstsson, Thrain. 1990. *Economic Behavior and Institutions*. New York: Cambridge University Press.

Etzioni, Amitai. 1961. *A Comparative Analysis of Complex Organizations*. New York: Free Press of Glencoe.

Evans, Harriet. 1997. *Women and Sexuality in China: Dominant Discourses of Female Sexuality and Gender Since 1949*. Cambridge, UK: Polity.

Evans, Karin. 2000. *The Lost Daughters of China: Abandoned Girls, Their Journey to America, and the Search for a Missing Past*. New York: Putnam.

Fan Xiangguo, and Huang Yuan. 1989. "China's illegal population," *New Observer* 4,25 (February): 28–32. [In Chinese]

Feeney, Griffith, and Wang Feng. 1993. "Parity progression and birth intervals in China: The influence of policy in hastening fertility decline," *Population and Development Review* 19,1 (March): 61–101.

FEER. 1989. "People pedlars," *Far Eastern Economic Review* (23 February): 41–42.

Feng Xiaotian, and Zheng Qingsong. 2002. "Study of transition in fertility desire among rural and urban residents over the last twenty years," *Market and Population Analysis* 9,5 (September): 21–31. [In Chinese]

Ferguson, James. 1990. *The Anti-Politics Machine: "Development," Depoliticization, and Bureaucratic Power in Lesotho*. Cambridge, UK: Cambridge University Press.

Feuerwerker, Yi-tsi Mei. 1998. *Ideology, Power, Text: Self-Representation and the Peasant "Other" in Modern Chinese Literature*. Stanford, CA: Stanford University Press.

Fewsmith, Joseph. 1994. *Dilemmas of Reform in China: Political Conflict and Economic Debate*. Armonk, NY: M. E. Sharpe.

———. 1997. "Reaction, resurgence, and succession: Chinese politics since Tiananmen," in Roderick MacFarquhar (ed.), *The Politics of China: The Eras of Mao and Deng* (2nd ed.). New York: Cambridge University Press, pp. 472–531.

———. 2001. *China Since Tiananmen: The Politics of Transition*. New York: Cambridge University Press.

———. 2004. "Promoting the scientific development concept," *China Leadership Monitor* 11 (Summer), www.chinaleadershipmonitor.org.

Filtzer, Donald. 2002. *Soviet Workers and Late Stalinism: Labour and the Restoration of the Stalinist System after World War II*. Cambridge, UK: Cambridge University Press.

Fong, Vanessa L. 2001. "China's one-child policy and the empowerment of urban daughters," *American Anthropologist* 104,4 (December): 1098–1109.

———. 2004. *Only Hope: Coming of Age Under China's One-Child Policy*. Stanford, CA: Stanford University Press.

Foucault, Michel. 1978. *History of Sexuality. Vol. 1: An Introduction*. New York: Random House.

————. 1980. "The politics of health in the eighteenth century," in Colin Gordon (ed.), *Power/Knowledge: Selected Interviews and Other Writings, 1972–1977, Michel Foucault.* New York: Pantheon, pp. 166–182.

————. 1991. "Governmentality," in Burchell, Gordon, and Miller (eds.), pp. 87–104.

————. 1997a. "Security, territory, and population," in Rabinow (ed.), pp. 67–71.

————. 1997b. "The birth of biopolitics," in Rabinow (ed.), pp. 73–79.

————. 1997c. "On the government of the living," in Rabinow (ed.), pp. 81–85.

————. 2003. *"Society Must Be Defended" : Lectures at the College de France, 1975–76.* New York: Picador.

Frazier, Mark W. 2004. "China's pension reform and its discontents," *China Journal* 50 (January): 97–114.

Fukuyama, Francis. 2004. *State-building: Governance and World Order in the 21st Century.* Ithaca: Cornell University Press.

Furth, Charlotte. 1999. *A Flourishing Yin: Gender in China's Medical History, 960–1665.* Berkeley: University of California Press.

Gates, Hill. 1993. "Cultural support for birth limitation among urban capital-owning women," in Davis and Harrell (eds.), pp. 251–276.

Gaetano, Arianne M., and Tamara Jacka (eds.). 2004. *On the Move: Women and Rural-to-Urban Migration in Contemporary China.* New York: Columbia University Press.

Gilley, Bruce. 1998. *Tiger on the Brink: Jiang Zemin and China's New Elite.* Berkeley: University of California Press.

————. 2004. *China's Democratic Future: How It Will Happen and Where It Will Lead.* New York: Columbia University Press.

Ginsburg, Faye D., and Rayna Rapp (eds.). 1995. *Conceiving the New World Order: The Global Politics of Reproduction.* Berkeley: University of California Press.

Gladney, Dru C. 1991. *Muslim Chinese: Ethnic Nationalism in the People's Republic.* Cambridge, MA: Council on East Asian Studies, Harvard University.

Glosser, Susan L. 2003. *Chinese Visions of Family and State, 1915–1953.* Berkeley: University of California Press.

Goldstein, Alice, and Wang Feng (eds.). 1996. *China: The Many Facets of Demographic Change.* Boulder: Westview.

Goldstein, Joshua. 1998. "Scissors, surveys, and psycho-prophylactics: Prenatal health care campaigns and state building in China, 1940–1954," *Journal of Historical Sociology* 11,2 (June): 153–184.

Goldstein, Melvyn C., Ben Jiao (Benjor), Cynthia M. Beall, and Phuntsog Tsering. 2002. "Fertility and family planning in rural Tibet," *China Journal* 47 (January): 19–39.

Gordon, Colin. 1991. "Governmental rationality: An introduction," in Burchell, Gordon, and Miller (eds.), pp. 1–51.

Gottschang, Suzanne K. 2000. "A baby-friendly hospital and the science of infant feeding," in Jing Jun (ed.), 160–184.

————. 2001. "The consuming mother: Infant feeding and the feminine body in urban China," in Nancy N. Chen, Constance D. Clark, Suzanne Z. Gottschang, and Lyn Jeffery (eds.), *China Urban: Ethnographies of Contemporary Culture.* Durham, N.C.: Duke University Press, pp. 89–103.

Grady, Denise. 2003. "Pregnancy created using egg nucleus of infertile woman," *New York Times* (14 October): 1, 18.

Greenhalgh, Susan. 1986. "Shifts in China's population policy, 1984–1986: Views from the central, provincial and local levels," *Population and Development Review* 12,3 (September): 491–515.

———. 1990a. "The evolution of the one-child policy in Shaanxi, 1979–1988," *China Quarterly* 122 (June): 191–229.

———. 1990b. "Population studies in China: Privileged past, anxious future," *Australian Journal of Chinese Affairs* 24 (July): 357–384.

———. 1993. "The peasantization of the one-child policy in Shaanxi," in Davis and Harrell (eds.), pp. 219–250.

———. 1994a. "Controlling births and bodies in village China," *American Ethnologist* 21,1 (February): 3–30.

———. 1994b. "The peasant household in the transition from socialism: State intervention and its consequences in China," in Elizabeth M. Brumfiel (ed.), *The Economic Anthropology of the State*. Lanham, MD: University Press of America, pp. 43–64.

———. 1996. "The social construction of population science: An intellectual, institutional, and political history of 20th century demography," *Comparative Studies in Society and History*, 38,1 (January): 26–66.

———. 2001a. "Fresh winds in Beijing: Chinese feminists speak out on the one-child policy and women's lives," *Signs: Journal of Women in Culture and Society* 26,3 (Spring): 847–886.

———. 2001b. "Managing 'the missing girls' in Chinese population discourse," in Carla Maklouf Obermeyer (ed.), *Cultural Perspectives on Reproductive Health*. Oxford: Oxford University Press, pp. 131–152.

———. 2002. "Women's rights and birth planning in China: New spaces of political action, new opportunities for American engagement," in CECC, pp. 11–14, 53–56.

———. 2003a. "Planned births, unplanned persons: 'Population' in the making of Chinese modernity," *American Ethnologist* 30,2 (May): 196–215.

———. 2003b. "Science, modernity, and the making of China's one-child policy," *Population and Development Review* 29,2 (June): 163–196.

———. 2004. "Making up China's 'black population,'" in Simon Szreter, Hania Sholkamy, and A. Dharmalingam (eds.), *Categories and Contexts: Anthropological and Historical Studies in Critical Demography*. Oxford: Oxford University Press, pp. 148–172.

———. 2005a. "Globalization and population governance in China," in Aihwa Ong and Stephen J. Collier (eds.), *Global Assemblages: Technology, Governmentality, Ethics*. Malden, MA: Blackwell, pp. 354–372.

———. 2005b. "Missile science, population science: The origins of China's one-child policy," *China Quarterly* 182 (June): 253–276.

Greenhalgh, Susan, and Li Jiali. 1995. "Engendering reproductive policy and practice in peasant China: For a feminist demography of reproduction," *Signs: Journal of Women in Culture and Society* 20,3 (Spring): 601–641.

Greenhalgh, Susan, Zhu Chuzhu, and Li Nan. 1994. "Restraining population growth in three Chinese villages," *Population and Development Review* 20,2 (June): 365–395.

Gregory, Paul R. 2004. *The Political Economy of Stalinism: Evidence from the Soviet Secret Archives.* New York: Cambridge University Press.

———(ed.). 2001. *Behind the Facade of Stalin's Command Economy: Evidence from the Soviet State and Party Archives.* Stanford, CA: Hoover Institution Press.

Gu, Baochang. 1996. *A Comprehensive Discussion of the Situation of Population in China.* Shanghai: Shanghai Academy of Social Sciences Press. [In Chinese]

———. 1998. "Toward a quality of care approach: Reorientation of the family planning program in China." New York: The Population Council.

———. 2000. "Promotion of the quality of care program in family planning: An important way to realize the 'two transitions,'" *YB 2000*, pp. 214–218. [In Chinese]

———. 2003a. "Strategy of the IPPF and development of the China family planning association," *YB 2003*, pp. 374–378.

———. 2003b. "Population, reproductive health and poverty alleviation in China." Paper prepared for UNFPA Consultation on Population, Reproductive Health, Gender, and Poverty Reduction, Princeton, New Jersey.

———(ed.). 1996. *Reproductive Health and Planned Birth: International Perspectives and Trends.* Beijing: China Population Press. [In Chinese]

Gu, Baochang, Ruth Simmons, and Diana Szatkowski. 2002. "Offering a choice of contraceptive methods in Deqing County, China: Changing practice in the family planning program since 1995," in Nicole Haberland and Diana Measham (eds.), *Responding to Cairo: Case Studies of Changing Practice in Reproductive Health and Family Planning.* New York: Population Council, pp. 58–73.

Gui Shi-xun. 1999. "Factors affecting induced abortion behavior among married women in Shanghai, China," in Mundigo and Indriso (eds.), pp. 78–97.

Guldan, Georgia S. 2000. "Paradoxes of plenty: China's infant- and child-feeding transition," in Jing Jun (ed.), pp. 27–47.

Guo, Yuhua. 2000. "Family relations: The generation gap at the table," in Jing Jun (ed.), pp. 94–113.

Guo Zhigang, Zhang Erli, Gu Baochang, and Wang Feng. 2003. "Diversity of China's fertility policy by policy fertility," *Population Research* 5 (September): 1–10. [In Chinese]

Hamrin, Carol Lee. 1990. *China and the Challenge of the Future: Changing Political Patterns.* Boulder: Westview.

Hamrin, Carol Lee, and Suisheng Zhao (eds.). 1995. *Decision-making in Deng's China: Perspectives from Insiders.* Armonk, NY: M. E. Sharpe.

Han, Min, and J. S. Eades. 1995. "Brides, bachelors and brokers: The marriage market in rural Anhui in an era of economic reform," *Modern Asian Studies* 29,4 (October): 841–869.

Handwerker, Lisa. 1998. "The consequences of modernity for childless women in China: Medicalization and resistance," in Lock and Kaufert (eds.), pp.178–205.

Hardee-Cleaveland, Karen, and Judith Banister. 1988. "Fertility policy and implementation in China, 1986–1988," *Population and Development Review* 14,2 (June): 245–286.

Harding, Harry. 1981. *Organizing China: The Problem of Bureaucracy, 1949–1976*. Stanford, CA: Stanford University Press.

———. 1987. *China's Second Revolution: Reform after Mao*. Washington, DC: The Brookings Institution.

———. 1993. "The Chinese state in crisis, 1966–9," in MacFarquhar (ed.), pp. 148–247. [Also in 1997 edition]

He Zhiyong, and Chen Xin. 1997–98. "Women's lament: A perspective on the flagrant violation of the legal rights of women workers," *Chinese Sociology and Anthropology* 30,2 (Winter): 76–84.

Hedstrom, Peter, and Richard Swedberg (eds.). 1998. *Social Mechanisms: An Analytical Approach to Social Theory*. New York: Cambridge University Press.

Ho Ping-ti. 1959. *Studies on the Population of China, 1368–1953*. Cambridge, MA: Harvard University Press.

Hobsbawn, Eric, and Terence Ranger (eds.). 1982. *The Invention of Tradition*. Cambridge, UK: Cambridge University Press.

Holcombe, Susan. 2003. "Learning from experience, accelerating implementation, deepening quality: Assessment report on the 2001–2003 phase of implementing the SFPC's pilot project in quality of care," report to the Ford Foundation, Beijing Office. (unpublished manuscript, Ford Foundation)

Hom, Sharon K. 1991–92. "Female infanticide in China: The human rights specter and thoughts toward (an)other vision," *Columbia Human Rights Law Review* 23: 249–314.

Honig, Emily, and Gail Hershatter. 1988. *Personal Voices: Chinese Women in the 1980s*. Stanford, CA: Stanford University Press.

Hooper, Beverley. 1998. "'Flower Vase and Housewife': Women and consumerism in post-Mao China," in Krishna Sen and Maila Stevens (eds.), *Gender and Power in Affluent Asia*. London: Routledge, pp. 167–193.

Hope, Nicholas C., Dennis Tao Yang, and Mu Yang Li (eds.). 2003. *How Far Across the River? Chinese Policy Reform at the Millennium*. Stanford, CA: Stanford University Press.

Horn, David G. 1994. *Social Bodies: Science, Reproduction, and Italian Modernity*. Princeton, NJ: Princeton University Press.

HRIC [Human Rights in China]. 1995. *Caught between Tradition and the State: Violations of the Human Rights of Chinese Women*. New York: HRIC.

Hsiung, Ping-chun, Maria Jaschok, and Cecelia Milwertz (eds.). 2001. *Chinese Women Organizing: Cadres, Feminists, Muslims, Queers*. Oxford: Berg.

Hua, Shiping. 1995. *Scientism and Humanism: Two Cultures in Post-Mao China (1978–1989)*. Albany, NY: State University of New York Press.

Huang, Jing. 2000. *Factionalism in Chinese Communist Politics*. New York: Cambridge University Press.

Huang, Shu-ming. 1998. *The Spiral Road: Change in a Chinese Village Through the Eyes of a Communist Party Leader* (2nd ed.). Boulder: Westview.

Huang, Yanzhong. 2004. "Bringing the local state back in: The political economy of public health in rural China," *Journal of Contemporary China* 13,3 (May): 367–390.

Huang, Yanzhong, and Dali L. Yang. 2004. "Population control and state coercion in China," in Naughton and Yang (eds.), pp. 193–225.

Hudson, Valerie M., and Andrea Den Boer. 2002. "A surplus of men, a deficit of peace," *International Security* 26,4 (Spring): 5–38.

Hudson, Valerie M., and Andrea M. Den Boer. 2004. *Bare Branches: The Security Implications of Asia's Surplus Male Population.* Cambridge, MA: MIT Press.

Hughes, Owen E. 2003. *Public Management and Administration: An Introduction.* New York: Palgrave MacMillan.

Hutchings, Graham. 1997. "Female infanticide 'will lead to army of bachelors,'" *Daily Telegraph* (11 April).

Institute for Health Science. 2003. "Yunnan, China, 1980–1999," in Marjorie A. Koblinsky (ed.). *Reducing Maternal Mortality: Learning from Bolivia, China, Egypt, Honduras, Indonesia, Jamaica, and Zimbabwe.* Washington, DC: The World Bank, pp. 41–50.

Ikels, Charlotte. 1993. "Settling accounts: The intergenerational contract in an age of reform," in Davis and Harrell (eds.), pp. 307–333.

———. 1996. *The Return of the God of Wealth: The Transition to a Market Economy in Urban China.* Stanford, CA: Stanford University Press.

———(ed.). 2004. *Filial Piety: Practice and Discourse in Contemporary East Asia.* Stanford: Stanford University Press.

Iritani, Evelyn. 2003. "Loving the little emperor," *Los Angeles Times* (2 August): A1, A5.

Isaacs, Harold R. 1958. *Images of Asia: American Views of China and India.* New York: Harper & Row.

Jacka, Tamara. 1990. "Back to the wok: Women and employment in Chinese industry in the 1980s," *Australian Journal of Chinese Affairs* 24 (July): 1–23.

Jackman, Robert W. 1993. *Politics without Force: The Political Capacity of Nation States.* Ann Arbor: University of Michigan.

Jackson, Richard, and Neil Howe. 2004. *The Graying of the Middle Kingdom: The Demographics and Economics of Retirement Policy in China.* Washington, DC: Center for Strategic and International Studies, and Newark, NJ: Prudential Foundation.

Ji, Fengyuan. 2004. *Linguistic Engineering: Language and Politics in Mao's China.* Honolulu: University of Hawaii Press.

Jiang, Zhenghua (ed.). 2000. *Collection of Data from the 1997 National Population and Reproductive Health Survey.* Beijing: China Population Publishing House. [In Chinese and English. *See also* SBPC and CPIRC (eds.) 1997.]

Jing Jun. 2000a. "Introduction: Food, children, and social change in contemporary China," in Jing Jun (ed.), pp. 1–26.

———. 2000b. "Food, nutrition, and cultural authority in a Gansu village," in Jing Jun (ed.), pp. 135–159.

———(ed.). 2000. *Feeding China's Little Emperors: Food, Children, and Social Change.* Stanford, CA: Stanford University Press.

JOD [Journal of Democracy]. 2003. *China's Changing of the Guard,* Special issue, *Journal of Democracy* 14,1 (January 2003): 5–74.

Johannsson, Sten, and Ola Nygren. 1991. "The missing girls of China: A new demographic account," *Population and Development Review* 17,1 (March): 35–51.

Johnson, Kay Ann. 1983. *Women, the Family, and Peasant Revolution in China.* Chicago: University of Chicago Press.

————. 2004. *Wanting a Daughter, Needing a Son.* St. Paul, MN: Yeong and Yeong Book Co.

Johnson, Linda. 1997. "Expanding eugenics or improving health care in China: Commentary on the Provisions of the Standing Committee of the Gansu People's Congress Concerning the Prohibition of Reproduction by Intellectually Impaired Persons," *Journal of Law and Society* 24,2 (June): 199–234.

JOICFP [Japanese Organization for International Cooperating in Family Planning]. 1994. *A Grassroots Movement to Improve the Quality of Life: Integrating Family Planning with Health Care and Community Development Activities: 10-year Experience of the Integrated Project in China 1983–1993.* Tokyo: Nihon Keishoku.

Judd, Ellen R. 1994. *Gender and Power in Rural North China.* Stanford, CA: Stanford University Press.

Kane, Penny. 1987. *The Second Billion: Population and Family Planning in China.* Ringwood, Australia: Penguin.

Kaple, Deborah. 1994. *Dream of a Red Factory: The Legacy of High Stalinism in China.* New York: Oxford University Press.

Kaufman, Joan. 1993. "The cost of IUD failure in China," *Studies in Family Planning* 24,3 (May/June): 94–196.

————. 2003. "Myths and realities of China's population program," *Harvard Asia Quarterly* 7,1 (Winter): 21–25.

Kaufman, Joan, Kaining Zhang, and Jing Fang. 1997. "Rural Chinese women's unmet need for reproductive health services," in *23rd IUSSP General Population Conference, Symposium on Demography of China.* Beijing: China Population Association, October 1997, pp. 485–490.

Kaufman, Joan, Zhang Erli, and Xie Zhenming. Forthcoming. "Quality of care in China: Scaling up a pilot project into a national reform program," in Ruth Simmons, Peter Fajans, and Laura Ghiron (eds.), *From Pilot Projects to Policies and Programs: Strategies for Scaling Up Innovations in Health Service Delivery.* Geneva: WHO.

Kaufman, Joan, Zhang Zhirong, Qiao Xinjian, and Zhang Yang. 1989. "Family planning policy and practice in China: A study of four rural counties," *Population and Development Review* 15,4 (December): 707–729.

————. 1992a. "The creation of family planning service stations in China," *International Family Planning Perspectives* 18,1 (March): 18–23.

————. 1992b. "The quality of family planning services in rural China," *Studies in Family Planning* 23,2 (March/April): 73–84.

Keith, Ronald C. 1997. "Legislating women's and children's rights and interests in the PRC," *China Quarterly* 149 (March): 29–55.

Keller, Evelyn Fox. 1995. "Gender and science: Origin, history and politics," *Osiris* 10: 27–38.

Kelliher, Daniel. 1994. "Chinese Communist political theory and the rediscovery of the peasantry," *Modern China* 20,4 (October): 387–415.

Khan, Azizur Rahman, and Carl Riskin. 2001. *Inequality and Poverty in China in the Age of Globalization.* New York: Oxford University Press.

Kluver, Alan R. 1996. *Legitimating the Chinese Economic Reforms: A Rhetoric of Myth and Orthodoxy.* Albany, NY: State University of New York Press.

Krause, Elizabeth L. 2005. *A Crisis of Births: Population Politics and Family-Making in Italy*. Belmont, CA: Wadsworth / Thomson.

Kristof, Nicholas D. 1990. "More in China willingly rear just one child," *New York Times* (9 May): 1, 8.

———. 1993a. "China's crackdown on births: A stunning, and harsh, success," *New York Times* (25 April): 1, 12.

———. 1993b. "Peasants of China discover new ways to weed out girls," *New York Times* (21 July): A1, 6.

Ku, Hok Bun. 2003. *Moral Politics in a South Chinese Village: Responsibility, Reciprocity, and Resistance*. Lanham, MD: Rowman and Littlefield.

Kwong, Julia. 2004. "Educating migrant children: Negotiations between the state and civil society," *China Quarterly* 180 (December): 1073–1088.

Lam, Willy Wo-lap. 1995. *China after Deng Xiaoping*. New York: Wiley & Sons.

———. 1999. *The Era of Jiang Zemin*. New York: Prentice-Hall.

Lampton, David M. 1977. *The Politics of Medicine in China: The Policy Process, 1949–1977*. Boulder: Westview Press.

——— (ed.). 1987. *Policy Implementation in Post-Mao China*. Berkeley: University of California Press.

——— (ed.). 2001. *The Making of Chinese Foreign and Security Policy in the Era of Reform, 1978–2000*. Stanford, CA: Stanford University Press.

Lardy, Nicholas R. 1987a. "Economic recovery and the 1st Five-Year Plan," in MacFarquhar and Fairbank (eds.), pp. 144–184.

———. 1987b. "The Chinese economy under stress, 1958–1965," in MacFarquhar and Fairbank (eds.), pp. 360–397.

———. 1998. *China's Unfinished Economic Revolution*. Washington, DC: Brookings Institution.

———. 2002. *Integrating China into the Global Economy*. Washington, DC: Brookings Institution.

Lardy, Nicholas, and Kenneth Lieberthal (eds.). 1983. *Chen Yun's Strategy for China's Development: A Non-Maoist Alternative*. Armonk, NY: M. E. Sharpe.

Lavely, William. 2001. "First impressions from the 2000 census of China," *Population and Development Review* 27,4 (December): 755–769.

Lavely, William, and Cai Yong. 2004. "Spatial variation in juvenile sex ratios in the 2000 census of China." Paper presented at the annual meeting of Population Association of America, Boston, 1–3 April.

Lee, James, and Cameron Campbell. 1997. *Fate and Fortune in Rural China: Social Organization and Population Behavior in Liaoning, 1774–1873*. Cambridge, UK: Cambridge University Press.

Lee, James Z., and Wang Feng. 1999. *One Quarter of Humanity: Malthusian Mythology and Chinese Realities*. Cambridge, MA: Harvard University Press.

Lee, Peter Nan-Shong, and Carlos Wing-Hung Lo (eds.). 2001. *Remaking China's Public Management*. Westport, CT: Quorum Books.

Lee, Sing, and Arthur Kleinman. 2000. "Suicide as resistance in Chinese society," in Elizabeth J. Perry and Mark Selden (eds.), *Chinese Society: Change, Conflict and Resistance*. London: Routledge, pp. 221–240.

Lei, Guang. 2003. "Rural taste, urban fashions: The cultural politics of rural/urban difference in contemporary China," *positions* 11,3 (Winter): 613–640.

Lemke, Thomas. 2001 " 'The birth of bio-politics': Michel Foucault's lecture at the College de France on neo-liberal governmentality," *Economy and Society* 30,2 (May): 190–207.

Li Bohua. 1999. "Report on reproductive health survey," *China Population Today* 16,3 (June): 2–9.

Li Cheng. 2001. *China's Leaders: The New Generation*. Lanham, MD: Rowman and Littlefield.

Li Chengrui (ed.). 1987. *A Census of One Billion People: Papers for International Seminar on China's 1982 Population Census*. Beijing: State Statistical Bureau.

Li, Jiali. 1995. "China's family planning program: How and how well has it worked? A case study of Hebei Province, 1979–1988," *Population and Development Review* 21,3 (September): 563–585.

Li Jianguo, and Zhang Xiaoying. 1983. "Infanticide in China," *New York Times* (11 April): 25.

Li Shuzhuo, and Sun Fubin. 2003. "Mortality analysis of China's 2000 population census data: A preliminary examination," *China Review* 3,2 (Fall): 31–48.

Li Shuzhuo, and Zhu Chuzhu. 2000. *Research and Community Practice on Gender Difference in Child Survival in China*. Beijing: China Population Publishing House. [In English and Chinese]

Li Shuzhuo, Zhu Chuzhu, and Marcus W. Feldman. 2004. "Gender differences in child survival in contemporary rural China: A county study," *Journal of Biosocial Science* 36 (January): 83–109.

Li, Xiaorong. 1996. "License to coerce: Violence against women, state responsibility, and legal failures in China's family-planning program," *Yale Journal of Law and Feminism* 8, 119 (Summer): 145–191.

Li Yongping, and Peng Xizhe. 2000. "Age and sex structures," in Peng and Guo (eds.), pp. 64–76.

Lieberthal, Kenneth. 1993. "The Great Leap Forward and the split in the Yan'an leadership, 1958–65," in MacFarquhar (ed.), 87–147.

———. 1995. *Governing China: From Revolution Through Reform*. New York: W.W. Norton.

Lieberthal, Kenneth, and Michel Oksenberg. 1988. *Policy Making in China: Leaders, Structures and Processes*. Princeton, NJ: Princeton University Press.

Lieberthal, Kenneth, and Michael Lampton (eds.). 1992. *Bureaucracy, Politics and Decision-Making in Post-Mao China*. Berkeley: University of California Press.

Link, Perry, Richard P. Madsen, and Paul G. Pickowicz (eds). 2002. *Popular China: Unofficial Culture in a Globalizaing Society*. Lanham, MD: Rowman and Littlefield.

Liu Longyan, and Zhang Jianhua (eds.). 1999. *Quality Births and Fetal Education Work*. Beijing: China Population Press. [In Chinese]

Liu Zheng, Song Jian, and others. 1981. *China's Population: Problems and Prospects*. Beijing: New World Press.

Liu Zheng, Wu Cangping, and Zha Ruichuan. 1980. "Five recommendations for controlling China's population growth," *Population Research* 3 (October): 1–5. [In Chinese]

Litzinger, Ralph. 2000. *Other Chinas: The Yao and the Politics of National Belonging.* Durham, NC: Duke University Press.

Lo Ming. 1981. "'Leftism' has not changed, and pregnancy is a crime." *Cheng Ming Jih Pao* JPRS 78,709 (10 August): 88–92.

Lock, Margaret, and Patricia A. Kaufert (eds.). 1998. *Pragmatic Women and Body Politics.* Cambridge, UK: Cambridge University Press.

Lozada, Eriberto P., Jr. 2000. "Globalized childhood? Kentucky Fried Chicken in Beijing," in Jing Jun (ed.), pp. 114–134.

Lu, Xiaobo. 2000. *Cadres and Corruption: The Organizational Involution of the Chinese Communist Party.* Stanford, CA: Stanford University Press.

Luo Lin, Wu Shi-zhong, Chen Xiao-qing, and Li Min-xiang. 1999a. "First-trimester induced abortion: A study of Sichuan Province," in Mundigo and Indriso (eds.), pp. 98–116.

———. 1999b. "Induced abortion among unmarried women in Sichuan Province, China: A survey," in Mundigo and Indriso (eds.), pp. 337–345.

Lupia, Arthur, and Mathew D. McCubbins. 1994. "Learning from oversight: Fire alarms and police patrols reconstructed," *Journal of Law, Economics & Organization* 10,1 (April): 96–125.

Ma, Yinchu. 1997. "New population theory," in *Ma Yinchu's Collected Papers on Population.* Hangzhou: People's Press, pp. 67–107.

MacFarquhar, Roderick. 1974. *The Origins of the Cultural Revolution: Volume One: Contradictions among the People, 1956–1957.* New York: Columbia University Press.

———. 1983. *The Origins of the Cultural Revolution: Volume Two: The Great Leap Forward, 1958–1960.* New York: Columbia University Press.

———. 1993. "The succession to Mao and the end of Maoism, 1969–82," in MacFarquhar (ed.), pp. 248–339.

———. 1997. *The Origins of the Cultural Revolution: Volume Three: The Coming of the Cataclysm, 1961–1966.* New York: Columbia University Press.

MacFarquhar, Roderick (ed.). 1993. *The Politics of China, 1949–1989.* Cambridge, UK: Cambridge University Press.

———(ed.). 1997. *The Politics of China: The Eras of Mao and Deng.* New York: Cambridge University Press.

MacFarquhar, Roderick, and John K. Fairbank (eds). 1987. *The Cambridge History of China: Volume 14, The People's Republic, Part I: The Emergence of Revolutionary China, 1949–1965.* Cambridge, UK: Cambridge University Press.

———. 1991. *The Cambridge History of China: Volume 15, The People's Republic of China, Part 2: Revolutions within the Chinese Revolution, 1966–1982.* Cambridge, UK: Cambridge University Press.

Madsen, Richard. 1995. *China and the American Dream: A Moral Inquiry.* Berkeley: University of California Press.

Malia, Martin E. 1994. *The Soviet Tragedy: A History of Socialism in Russia, 1917–1991.* New York: Free Press.

Manion, Melanie. 1993. *Retirement of Revolutionaries in China: Public Policies, Social Norms, Private Interests.* Princeton, NJ: Princeton University Press.

———. 1998. "Why use campaigns to control corruption?" Paper for workshop on cadre monitoring and reward: Personnel management and policy implementation in the PRC, San Diego, California.

Martin, Emily. 1987. *The Woman in the Body: A Cultural Analysis of Reproduction.* Boston: Beacon.

McElroy, Damien. 1998. "China fears crime wave of one-child generation," *Daily Telegraph* (7 May).

———. 2000. "Anger sweeps China over baby-killers," *Sunday Telegraph* (27 August).

McElroy, Damien, and Olga Craig. 2000. "Victims of China's one-child policy find hope," *Daily Telegraph* (30 July).

ME [Main Events]. See Yang, Liang, and Zhang 2001.

Meadows, Donella H., Dennis L. Meadows, Jorgen Randers, and William W. Behrens III. 1972. *The Limits to Growth: A Report for the Club of Rome's Project on the Predicament of Mankind.* New York: Universe.

Merli, M. Giovanna, Zhenchao Qian, and Herbert F. Smith. 2004. "Adaptation of a political bureaucracy to economic and institutional change under socialism: The Chinese state family planning system," *Politics and Society* 32,2 (June): 231–256.

Miller, Eric T. 2004. "Filial daughters, filial sons: Comparisons from rural north China," in Ikels (ed.), pp. 34–52.

Miller, H. Lyman. 1996. *Science and Dissent in Post-Mao China: The Politics of Knowledge.* Seattle: University of Washington Press.

———. 2003. "The Hu-Wen leadership at six months," *China Leadership Monitor* 8 (Fall), www.chinaleadershipmonitor.org.

———. 2004. "Party Politburo processes under Hu Jintao," *China Leadership Monitor* 11 (Summer), www.chinaleadershipmonitor.org.

Milwertz, Cecilia Nathansen. 1997. *Accepting Population Control: Urban Chinese Women and the One-Child Family Policy.* Richmond, Surrey, UK: Curzon Press.

Ming, Siu Yat. 1999. "The evolution of family planning policies," in David C. B. Teather and Herbert S. Yee (eds.), *China in Transition: Issue and Policies.* New York: St. Martin's, pp. 221–241.

Mosher, Steven W. 1993. *A Mother's Ordeal: One Woman's Fight against China's One-Child Policy.* New York: Harcourt Brace.

Mudanjiang. 2002. *Collection of Materials on Comprehensive Reform of Population and Birth Planning in Mudanjiang City.* Mudanjiang: Mudanjiang City Government.

Mueggler, Eric. 2001. *The Age of Wild Ghosts: Memory, Violence, and Place in Southwest China.* Berkeley: University of California Press.

Mundigo, Axel I., and Cynthia Indriso (eds.). 1999. *Abortion in the Developing World.* London: Zed.

Murphy, Rachel. 2002. *How Migrant Labor is Changing China.* Cambridge, UK: Cambridge University Press.

———. 2003. "Fertility and distorted sex ratios in a rural Chinese county: Culture, state, and policy," *Population and Development Review* 29,4 (December): 595–626.

———. 2004. "Turning Chinese peasants into model citizens: Population quality discourse, demographic transition and primary schools," *China Quarterly* 177 (March): 1–20.

Nathan, Andrew J., and Bruce Gilley. 2002. *China's New Rulers: The Secret Files.* New York: New York Review of Books.

Naughton, Barry. 1988. "The Third Front: Defense industrialization in the Chinese interior," *China Quarterly* 115 (September): 351–386.

———. 1995. *Growing Out of the Plan: Chinese Economic Reform 1978–1993*. New York: Cambridge University Press.

———. 2004a. "The western development program," in Naughton and Yang (eds.), pp. 253–295.

———. 2004b. "Financial reconstruction: Methodical policymaking moves into the spotlight," *China Leadership Monitor* 10 (Spring), www.chinaleadershipmonitor.org.

Naughton, Barry J., and Dali L. Yang (eds.). 2004. *Holding China Together: Diversity and National Integration in the Post-Deng Era*. New York: Cambridge University Press.

Nee, Victor. 1981. "Post-Mao changes in a South China production brigade," *Bulletin of Concerned Asian Scholars* 13,2 (April-June): 32–40.

Ni, Ching-ching. 2000. "Two families—but no place to call home," *Los Angeles Times* (29 March): A1, 10.

———. 2004. "Freeing children of convicts," *Los Angeles Times* (1 March): A1, 4.

Ni, Hanyu, and Annette MacKay Rossignol. 1994. "Maternal deaths among women with pregnancies outside of family planning in Sichuan, China," *Epidemiology* 5,5 (September): 490–494.

Nie, Jing-Bao. 1999. *Voices Behind the Silence: Chinese Moral Beliefs and Experiences of Abortion in Cultural Context*. Ph.D. diss., Institute for the Medical Humanities, University of Texas Medical Branch.

NPFPC [National Population and Family Planning Commission]. The PRC's official English translation of the name of its birth commission, since 2003 when "population" was added to the commission's name. See also SBPC, SFPC, and SPBPC.

O'Brien, Kevin. 1996. "Rightful resistance," *World Politics* 49,1 (October): 31–55.

O'Brien, Kevin J., and Lianjiang Li. 1999. "Selective policy implementation in rural China," *Comparative Politics* 31,2 (January): 167–186.

Ong, Aihwa. 1999. *Flexible Citizenship: The Cultural Logics of Transnationalism*. Durham, NC: Duke University Press.

Orleans, Leo A. 1972. *Every Fifth Child*. Stanford, CA: Stanford University Press.

———. 1974. *China's Experience in Population Control: The Elusive Model*. Washington, DC: U.S. Government Printing Office.

———(ed.). 1979. *Chinese Approaches to Family Planning*. White Plains, NY: M. E. Sharpe.

Orren, Karen, and Stephen Skowronek. 1995. "Order and time in institutional study: A brief for the historical approach," in James Farr, John S. Druzek, and Stephen T. Leonard (eds.), *Political Science in History*. New York: Cambridge University Press, pp. 296–317.

Oudshoorn, Nelly. 1994. *Beyond the Natural Body: An Archaeology of Sex Hormones*. London: Routledge.

Pang, Lihua, Alan de Brauw, and Scott Rozelle. 2004. "Working until you drop: The elderly of rural China," *China Journal* 52 (July): 73–94.

Parish, William L., and Martin King Whyte. 1978. *Village and Family in Contemporary China*. Chicago: University of Chicago Press.

Paxson, Heather. 2004. *Making Modern Mothers: Ethics and Family Planning in Urban Greece.* Berkeley: University of California Press.

PCO [State Council, Population Census Office and State Statistical Bureau, Population Statistics Department comps.] July 1991. *10 Percent Sampling Tabulation on the 1990 Population Census of the People's Republic of China (Computer tabulation).* Beijing: China Statistical Publishing House. [In Chinese]

PDR [Population and Development Review]. 1983. "United Nations Population Award to Indira Ghandi and Qian Xinzhong," *Population and Development Review* 9,4 (December): 747–753.

PDSC [Population and Development Studies Center]. 2003a. "Investigation project on social compensation fee (background introduction)." (unpublished report, People's University of China, Beijing) [Accompanied by adjunct reports below]

———. 2003b. "Investigation report of Huoshan County of Anhui Province," adjunct to PDSCa.

———. 2003c. "Investigation report of Yuzhong County of Gansu Province," adjunct to PDSCa.

———. 2003d. "Investigation report of Qianjiang City of Hubei Province," adjunct to PDSCa.

———. 2003e. "Investigation report on Taicang City of Jiangsu Province," adjunct to PDSCa.

Pearson, Veronica. 1995. "Population policy and eugenics in China," *British Journal of Psychiatry* 167,1 (July): 1–4.

———. 1996. "Women and health in China: Anatomy, destiny and politics," *Journal of Social Politics* 25,4: 529–543.

Pearson, Veronica, Michael R. Phillips, He Fengsheng, and Ji Huiyi. 2002. "Attempted suicide among young rural women in the People's Republic of China: Possibilities for prevention," *Suicide and Life-Threatening Behavior* 32,4: 359–369.

Peerenboom, Randall. 2002. *China's Long March toward the Rule of Law.* New York: Cambridge University Press.

Peng Xizhe. 1991. *Demographic Transition in China: Fertility Trends Since the 1950s.* Oxford: Clarendon.

Peng Xizhe, and Dai Xingyi (eds.). 1996. *The Fertility Culture of Chinese Village Communities.* Shanghai: Fudan University Press. [In Chinese]

Peng Xizhe, and Guo Zhigang. (eds.). 2000. *The Changing Population of China.* Oxford: Blackwell.

Peng, Zhiliang. 2000. "Thoroughly implementing the mass line is a basic guarantee of doing a good job of the work of the birth planning associations," in *2000 YB,* pp. 218–221. [In Chinese]

Perkins, Dwight H. 1991. "China's economic policy and performance," in MacFarquhar and Fairbank (eds), pp. 475–539.

Perkins, Dwight, and Shahid Yusuf. 1984. *Rural Development in China.* Baltimore, MD: Johns Hopkins University Press. [For the World Bank]

Perry, Elizabeth J., and Mark Selden (eds.). 2000. *Chinese Society: Change, Conflict and Resistance.* London: Routledge.

Phillips, Michael R., Li Xianyun, and Zhang Yanping. 2002. "Suicide rates in China, 1995–1999," *Lancet* 359,9309: 835–840.

PI [Popinfo]. Shanghai-based website posting materials on PRC population and birth planning, www.popinfo.gov.cn.

Pickowicz, Paul G., and Liping Wang. 2002. "Village voices, urban activists: Women, violence, and gender inequality in rural China," in Link, Madsen, and Pickowicz (eds.), pp. 57–88.

Poston, Dudley L., and David Yaukey (eds.). 1992. *The Population of Modern China*. New York: Plenum.

Potter, Sulamith. 1983. "The position of peasants in modern China's social order," *Modern China* 9,4 (October): 465–499.

Potter, Sulamith, and Jack Potter. 1990. *China's Peasants: The Anthropology of a Revolution*. Cambridge, UK: Cambridge University Press.

Qian Xinzhong. 1989. *New Articles on Population*. Chengdu: Sichuan People's Press. [In Chinese]

Qian Xuelin. 1987. *The Scientific and Systems Engineering of Socialist Modernization Construction*. Beijing: Central Party School Press. [In Chinese: *Shehui zhuyi . . .*]

Qu Geping, and Li Linchang. 1994. *Population and the Environment in China*. Boulder: Lynne Rienner.

Qu Mujie (ed.). 2001. *Doing Ability Games: Games to Enhance Intelligence, Ages 0–6*. Beijing: China Women's Press. [In Chinese]

Rabinow, Paul. 1989. *French Modern: Norms and Forms of the Social Environment*. Cambridge, MA: MIT Press.

———(ed.). 1997. *Michel Foucault, Ethics: Subjectivity and Truth*. New York: New Press.

Rapp, Rayna. 1999. *Testing Women, Testing the Fetus: The Social Impact of Amniocentesis in America*. New York: Routledge.

Rennie, David. 1999. "26,000 arrests over trade in women and children," *Daily Telegraph* (9 June).

———. 2000. "'Spare the child' plea by Chinese leader," *Daily Telegraph* (6 March).

Retherford, Robert D., Minja Kim Choe, Jiajian Chen, Li Xiru, and Cui Hongyan. 2005. "How far has fertility in China really declined?" *Population and Development Review* 31,1 (March): 57–84.

Riley, Nancy E. 1997a. "Gender equality in China: Two steps forward, one step back," in William A. Joseph (ed.), *China Briefing: The Contradictions of Change*. Armonk, NY: M. E. Sharpe, pp. 79–108.

———. 1997b. "American adoptions of Chinese girls: The sociopolitical matrices of individual decisions," *Women's Studies International Forum* 20,1 (January-February): 87–102.

Riskin, Carl, Zhao Renwei, and Li Shi (eds.). 2001. *China's Retreat from Equality*. Armonk, NY: M. E. Sharpe.

Robinson, Jean C. 1985. "Of women and washing machines: Employment, housework, and the reproduction of motherhood in socialist China," *China Quarterly* 101 (March): 32–57.

Rofel, Lisa 1999. *Other Modernities: Gendered Yearnings in China after Socialism*. Berkeley: University of California Press.

Rose, Nikolas. 1999. *Powers of Freedom: Reframing Political Thought*. Cambridge, UK: Cambridge University Press.

Rosen, Stanley. 1991. "Chinese women in the 1990s: Images and roles in contention," in Maurice Brosseau and Lo Chu Ken (eds.), *China Review 1991*. Hong Kong: Chinese University of Hong Kong, pp. 17.1–17.28.

———. 2004. "The victory of materialism: Aspirations to join China's urban moneyed classes and the commercialization of education," *China Journal* 51 (January): 27–51.

Rosenthal, Elizabeth. 2003. "Bias for boys leads to sale of baby girls in China," *New York Times* (20 July): 6.

Ross, Lester. 1988. *Environment Policy in China*. Bloomington: Indiana University Press.

Sabatier, Paul A. (ed.). 1999. *Theories of the Policy Process*. Boulder: Westview Press.

Saich, Tony, and Xuedong Yang. 2003. "Innovation in China's local governance: Open recommendation and selection," *Pacific Affairs* 76,2 (Summer): 185–208.

Saith, Ashwani. 1984. "China's new population policies: Rationale and some implications," *Development and Change* 15,3 (June): 321–358.

Sawicki, Jana. 1991. *Disciplining Foucault: Feminism, Power, and the Body*. New York: Routledge.

SBPC [State Birth Planning Commission]. The English translation used in this book of the name of the PRC birth commission, from its founding in 1981 until 2003 when "population" was added to its name. See also NPFPC, SFPC, and SPBPC.

———. 2001a. "Project initiatives: Gender equity and women's empowerment," www.sfpc.gov.cn/en. [now www.npfpc.gov.cn]

———. 2001b. "International exchanges and cooperation in the field of population and family planning," www.sfpc.gov.cn/en. [now www.npfpc.gov.cn]

———. 19 August 2001. "Statistics bulletin of family planning (No.1, 2001)," on SBPC English website under Data, www.sfpc.gov.cn/en. [now www.npfpc .gov.cn]

———. 15 October 2001. "Outline of Women's Development," www.sfpc.gov.cn. [In Chinese] [now www.npfpc.gov.cn]

———. 4 March 2002. "National family planning & reproductive health survey (2001)," on SBPC English website under Fresh News, www.sfpc.gov.cn/en. [now www.npfpc.gov.cn]

———. 15 May 2002. "Male participation heralds gender equality," www.sfpc.gov .cn/en. [now www.npfpc.gov.cn]

———. 6 June 2002. "Report of Personnel Department on Mudanjiang work on Comprehensive Reform." [Posted on www.popinfo.gov.cn at the time]

———. September 2002. *Collection of Materials on Comprehensive Reform of Population and Birth Planning (Mudanjiang Conference)*.Beijing: China Population Press. [Various provinces]

———. 8 September 2002. "Project Happiness helps a total of 120,000 mothers living in poverty," www.sfpc.gov.cn/en. [now www.npfpc.gov.cn]

———. 20 April 2003. "Reform brings marked increase in quality of life for Chinese," www.sfpc.gov.cn/en. [now www.npfpc.gov.cn]

——— (ed.). 1996. *The Road of Hope: Collection of Materials from the National Birth Planning Work Conference to Exchange Experience on the "Three Links."* Beijing: China Population Press.

SBPC and CPIRC (eds.) [State Birth Planning Commission and China Population Information and Research Center]. 1997. *Charts for the 1997 National Population and Reproductive Health Survey*. Beijing: China Population Publishing House. [In Chinese and English]

SBPC Party Group. 1984. "Report of the conditions regarding the work of family planning (March 22, 1984)," in White (ed.) 1992, pp. 31–39.

Scarman, Leslie. 1972. *Violence and Civil Disturbance in Northern Ireland in 1969*. Belfast: Her Majesty's Stationery Office.

Scharping, Thomas. 2003. *Birth Control in China, 1949–2000: Population Policy and Demographic Development*. London: Curzon.

Schein, Louisa. 2000. *Minority Rules: The Miao and the Feminine in China's Cultural Politics*. Durham, NC: Duke University Press.

Schoenhals, Michael. 1992. *Doing Things with Words in Chinese Politics: Five Studies*. Berkeley: Institute of East Asian Studies, University of California.

Schurmann, Franz. 1971. *Ideology and Organization in Communist China* (2nd ed.). Berkeley: University of California Press.

Scott, James C. 1990. *Domination and the Arts of Resistance: Hidden Transcripts*. New Haven, CT: Yale University Press.

———. 1998. *Seeing Like a State*. New Haven, CT: Yale University Press.

Selden, Mark. 1971. *The Yenan Way in Revolutionary China*. Cambridge, MA: Harvard University Press.

———. 1993. "Family strategies and structures in rural North China," in Davis and Harrell (eds.), pp. 139–164.

SFPC [State Family Planning Commission]. The PRC's official English translation of the name of its birth commission, from its establishment in 1981 until its name change in 2003, thereafter still used in the commission's website address: www .sfpc.gov.cn. See also NPFPC, SBPC, and SPBPC.

Shambaugh, David L. 1984. *The Making of a Premier: Zhao Ziyang's Provincial Career*. Boulder: Westview.

Shambaugh, David (ed.). 2000. *The Modern Chinese State*. New York: Cambridge University Press.

Shapiro, Judith. 2001. *Mao's War against Nature: Politics and the Environment in Revolutionary China*. Cambridge, UK: Cambridge University Press.

Shen, Juren, et al. 1990. *Achievements of Ten-year China/UNFPA Cooperation (1979– 1989)*. Beijing: Ministry of Foreign Economic Relations and Trade.

Shi, Chengli. 1988. *A History of Birth Planning in China*. Urumqi: Xinjiang People's Press. [In Chinese. Items cited as "Shi" plus date are in the long chronology in this book]

Shirk, Susan L. 1993. *The Political Logic of Economic Reform in China*. Berkeley: University of California Press.

Short, Susan, Ma Linmao, and Yu Wentao. 2000. "Birth planning and sterilization in China," *Population Studies* 54,3 (November): 279–291.

Short, Susan E., and Zhai Fengying. 1998. "Looking locally at China's one-child policy," *Studies in Family Planning* 29,4 (December): 373–387.

Short, Susan, and Zhang Fengyu. 2004. "Use of maternal health services in rural China," *Population Studies* 58,1: 3–19.

Shue, Vivienne. 1995. "State sprawl: The regulatory state and social life in a small Chinese city," in Deborah Davis, Richard Kraus, Barry Naughton, and Elizabeth J. Perry (eds.), *Urban Spaces in Contemporary China*. Washington, DC: Woodrow Wilson Center Press and Cambridge: Cambridge University Press, pp. 90–112.

Sigley, Gary. 1996. "Governing Chinese bodies: The significance of studies in the concept of governmentality for the analysis of government in China" *Economy and Society* 25,4 (November): 457–482.

Skilling, H. Gordon, and Franklyn Griffiths (eds). 1971. *Interest Groups in Soviet Politics*. Princeton, NJ: Princeton University Press.

Skinner, G. William. 1997. "Family systems and demographic processes," in David I. Kertzer and Tom Fricke (eds.), *Anthropological Demography: Toward a New Synthesis*. Chicago: University of Chicago Press, pp. 53–95.

———. 2003. "Family and reproduction in Southeastern China: A comparison of Cantonese, Hakka, and Yao," *Asian Anthropology (2)*: 1–47.

Skinner, G. William, and Edwin A. Winckler. 1969. "Compliance succession in rural communist China: A cyclical theory," in Amitai Etzioni (ed.), *A Sociological Reader on Complex Organizations* (2nd ed.). New York: Holt, Rinehart and Winston, pp. 410–438.

Skinner, G. William, Mark Henderson, and Yuan Jianhua. 2000. "China's fertility transition through regional space," *Social Science History* 24,3 (Fall): 613–652.

Smith, Herbert L., Tu Ping, M. Giovanna Merli, and Mark Hereward. 1997. "Implementation of a demographic and contraceptive surveillance system in four counties in North China," *Population Research and Policy Review* 16,4 (August): 289–314.

Solinger, Dorothy J. 1984. *Chinese Business Under Socialism*. Berkeley: University of California Press.

———. 1993. *China's Transition from Socialism: Statist Legacies and Market Reforms, 1980–1990*. Armonk, NY: M. E. Sharpe.

———. 1999. *Contesting Citizenship in Urban China: Peasant Migrants, the State, and the Logic of the Market*. Berkeley: University of California Press.

———(ed.). 1984. *Three Visions of Chinese Socialism*. Boulder: Westview.

Song Jian. 1981. "Population development—Goals and plans," in Liu, Song, and others, pp. 25–31.

Song Jian. 2000. "Adoption into families with reproductive-age women," in Jiang (ed.), pp. 88–95. [In Chinese]

Song Jian, Chi-Hsien Tuan, and Yu Jing-Yuan. 1985. *Population Control in China: Theory and Applications*. New York: Praeger.

Song Qixia. 1985. "Progress has been made in premarital health examination and prenatal examination," *Birth Planning Edition [Health Daily]* (31 May): 1. In JPRS-CPS-85-080 8 August.

SPBPC [State Population and Birth Planning Commission]. The English translation used in this book of the name of the PRC birth commission since 2003 when "population was added to its name. See also NPFPC, SFPC, and SBPC.

Spektorowski, Alberto. 2004. "The eugenic temptation in socialism: Sweden, Germany, and the Soviet Union," *Comparative Studies in Society and History* 46,1 (January): 84–106.

Stacey, Judith. 1983. *Patriarchy and Socialist Revolution in China*. Berkeley: University of California Press.

Steinmo, Sven, Kathleen Thelen, and Frank Longstreth (eds.). 1992. *Structuring Politics: Historical Institutionalism in Comparative Analysis*. New York: Cambridge University Press.

Sun Qi. 1990. "The tide of baby trading in Shandong, Henan, and Anhui," *The Mirror (Ching pao)* 154 (10 May): 85.

Sun, Muhan. 1987. *A Draft History of Chinese Birth Planning*. Beijing: Women's and Children's Press. [In Chinese]

Sun, Yan. 1995. *The Chinese Reassessment of Socialism, 1976–1992*. Princeton: Princeton University Press.

Suttmeier, Richard P. 1974. *Research and Revolution: Science Policy and Societal Change in China*. New York: Lexington.

———. 1989. "Conclusion: Science, technology, and China's political future— A framework for analysis," in Denis Fred Simon and Merle Goldman (eds.), *Science and Technology in Post-Mao China*. Cambridge: Council on East Asian Studies, Harvard University, pp. 375–396.

Tang Wenfang, and William L. Parish. 2000. *Chinese Urban Life Under Reform: The Changing Social Contract*. Cambridge, UK: Cambridge University Press.

Teiwes, Frederick C. 1993. "The establishment and consolidation of the new regime, 1949–57," in MacFarquhar (ed.), pp. 5–86.

Teiwes, Frederick, and Warren Sun. 1999. *China's Road to Disaster: Mao, Central Politicians, and Provincial Leaders in the Unfolding of the Great Leap Forward*. Armonk, NY: M. E. Sharpe.

Tian Xueyuan.1981. "A survey of population growth since 1949," in Liu, Song, et al., pp. 32–54.

Tien, H. Yuan. 1973. *China's Population Struggle: Demographic Decisions of the People's Republic, 1949–1969*. Columbus: Ohio State University Press.

———. 1991. *China's Strategic Demographic Initiative*. New York: Praeger.

Tuana, Nancy. 1993. *The Less Noble Sex: Scientific, Religious, and Philosophical Conceptions of Woman's Nature*. Bloomington: Indiana University Press.

Tuljapurkar, Shripad, Li Nan, and Marcus W. Feldman. 1995. "High sex ratios in China's future," *Science* 267 (10 February): 874–876.

Twohey, Michael. 1999. *Authority and Welfare in China: Modern Debates in Historical Perspective*. New York: St. Martin's.

Tyler, Patrick E. 1995. "Birth control in China: Coercion and evasion," *New York Times* (25 June): 1, 8.

———. 1996. "As a pampered generation grows up, Chinese worry," *New York Times* (25 June): 1, 6.

Tomba, Luigi. 2004. "Creating an urban middle class: Social engineering in Beijing," *China Journal* 51 (January): 1–26.

UNDP [United Nations Development Program]. 1999. *The China Human Development Report*. New York: Oxford University Press.

Unger, Jonathan. 1993. "Urban families in the eighties: An analysis of Chinese surveys," in Davis and Harrell (eds.), pp. 25–49.

———. 1998. "Cultural revolution conflict in the villages," *China Quarterly* 153 (March): 82–106.

Vogel, Ezra F. 1967. "Voluntarism and social control," in Donald W. Treadgold (ed.), *Soviet and Chinese Communism*. Seattle: University of Washington Press, pp. 168–184.

Walker, Kenneth R. 1964/1998. "Appendix A: A Chinese discussion of planning for balanced growth (A summary of the views of Ma Yinchu and his critics)," in Robert F. Ash (ed.), *Agricultural Development in China, 1949–1989: The Collected Papers of Kenneth R. Walker (1931–1989)*. Oxford: Oxford University Press, pp. 331–355.

Wang, Danyu. 2004. "Ritualistic coresidence and the weakening of filial practice in rural China," in Ikels (ed.), pp. 16–33.

Wang Feng, and Andrew Mason. 2004. "The demographic factor in China's transition." Paper presented at the Conference on China's Economic Transition: Origins, Mechanism, and Consequences, Pittsburgh, 4–7 November.

Wang, Hong. 1991a. "The population policy of China," in Wang and Hull (eds.), pp. 42–67.

———. 1991b. "Population planning in China," in Wang and Hull (eds.), pp. 68–87.

Wang Jingsong. 1995. *People's Republic of China: Politics and Government*. Beijing: Central Party School Press. [In Chinese]

Wang, Jiye, and Terence H. Hull (eds.). 1991. *Population and Development Planning in China*. Sydney, Australia: Allen & Unwin.

Wang Weifeng (ed.). 2002. *Good Fetal Education, High Intelligence*. Beijing: China Population Press. [In Chinese]

Wang Zheng. 1997. "Maoism, feminism, and the UN conference on women: Women's studies research in contemporary China," *Journal of Women's History* 8,4 (Winter): 126–152.

Warwick, Donald P. 1982. *Bitter Pills: Population Policies and their Implementation in Eight Developing Countries*. New York: Cambridge University Press.

———. 1986. "The Indonesian family planning program: Government influence and client choice," *Population and Development Review* 12,3 (September): 453–490.

Wasserstrom, Jeffrey. 1984. "Resistance to the one-child family," *Modern China* 10,3 (July): 345–374.

Watson, James L. 1980. "Transactions in people: The Chinese market in slaves, servants, and heirs," in James L. Watson (ed.), *Asian and African Systems of Slavery*. Berkeley: University of California Press, pp. 223–250.

———(ed.). 1997. *Golden Arches East: McDonald's in East Asia*. Stanford, CA: Stanford University Press.

Watson, Rubie. 1986. "The named and the nameless: Gender and person in Chinese society," *American Ethnologist* 13,4 (November): 619–631.

Weeks, Margaret R. 1989. "Virtuous wives and kind mothers: Concepts of women in urban China," *Women's Studies International Forum* 12,5 (September): 505–518.

Weisskopf, Michael. 1985a. "Abortion policy tears at China's society," *Washington Post* (7 January): A1, 20.

———. 1985b. "China's birth control policy drives some to kill baby girls," *Washington Post* (8 January): A1, 10.

Weston, Timothy B., and Lionel M. Jensen (eds). 2000. *China Beyond the Headlines*. Lanham, MD: Rowman and Littlefield.

White Paper. 2000. [State Council, Information Office]. *China's Population and Development in the 21st Century*. Beijing: State Council. [English on SBPC website at www.sfpc.gov.cn/en/whitepaper.htm. Chinese original in *YB 2001*, pp. 36–41]

White, Tyrene. 1987. "Implementing the 'one-child-per-couple' population program in rural China: National goals and local politics," in Lampton (ed.), pp. 284–317.

———. 1990. "Post-revolutionary mobilization in China: The one-child policy reconsidered," *World Politics* 43,1 (October): 53–76.

———. 1991. "Birth planning between plan and market: The impact of reform on China's one-child policy," in *China's Economic Dilemmas in the 1990s: The Problems of Reforms, Modernization, and Interdependence*, Vol. I. Washington, DC: U.S. Government Printing Office, pp. 252–269. [Study Papers Submitted to the Joint Economic Committee, Congress of the United States]

———. 1992. "The population factor: China's family planning policy in the 1990s," in William A. Joseph (ed.), *China Briefing, 1991*. Boulder: Westview Press, pp. 97–117.

———. 1994a. "The origins of China's birth planning policy," in Christina K. Gilmartin, Gail Hershatter, Lisa Rofel, and Tyrene White (eds.), *Engendering China: Women, Culture, and the State*. Cambridge, MA: Harvard University Press, pp. 250–278.

———. 1994b. "Two kinds of production: The evolution of China's family planning policy in the 1980s," in Jason L. Finkle and C. Alison McIntosh (eds.), *The New Politics of Population: Conflict and Consensus in Family Planning*. Supplement to *Population and Development Review* 20, pp. 137–158.

———. 2000a. "The shape of society: The changing demography of development," in Tyrene White (ed.), *China Briefing 2000: The Continuing Transformation*. Armonk, NY: M. E. Sharpe, pp. 95–121.

———. 2000b. "Domination, resistance and accommodation in China's one-child campaign," in Perry and Selden (eds.), pp. 102–119.

——— (ed.). 1992. *Family Planning in China*. Special issue, *Chinese Sociology and Anthropology* (Spring).

Whiting, Susan H. 2001. *Power and Wealth in Rural China: The Political Economy of Institutional Change*. New York: Cambridge University Press.

———. 2004. "The cadre evaluation system at the grass roots: The paradox of party rule," in Naughton and Yang (eds.), pp. 101–119.

Whyte, Martin King (ed.). 2003. *China's Revolutions and Intergenerational Relations*. Ann Arbor: Center for Chinese Studies, University of Michigan.

Whyte, Martin King, and S. Z. Gu. 1987. "Popular response to China's fertility transition," *Population and Development Review* 13,3 (September): 569–571.

Whyte, Martin King, and Xu Qin. 2003. "Support for aging parents from daughters versus sons," in Whyte (ed.), pp. 169–196.

Williamson, Oliver 1975. *Markets and Hierarchies*. New York: Free Press.

Winckler, Edwin A. 1999. "Re-enforcing state birth planning," in Winckler (ed.), pp. 181–203.

————. 2002a. "Chinese reproductive policy at the turn of the millennium: Dynamic stability," *Population and Development Review* 28,3 (September): 379–418.

————. 2002b. "Positive recent developments in China's reproductive policy," in CECC, pp. 8–11, 46–53.

————. 2005. "Maximizing the impact of Cairo on China," in Wendy Chavkin and Ellen Chesler (eds.), *Where Human Rights Begin: Essays on Health, Sexuality, and Women, Ten Years after Vienna, Cairo and Beijing*. Piscataway, NJ: Rutgers University Press.

———— (ed.). 1999. *Transition from Communism in China*. Boulder: Lynne Rienner.

———— (with Susan Greenhalgh). 1998. "State and Marriage in China." Paper for conference on Gender and the Initiation of Sexual Activity, Center on Poverty, Gender and Social Inequality, University of Maryland, College Park MD, 25–26 June 1998.

Wolf, Margery. 1985. *Revolution Postponed: Women in Contemporary China*. Stanford, CA: Stanford University Press.

Wong Siu-lun. 1984. "Consequences of China's new population policy," *China Quarterly* 98 (June): 220–240.

Woo, Margaret Y. K. 1994. "Chinese women workers: The delicate balance between protection and equality," in Gilmartin et al. (eds.), pp. 279–295.

Working Group on Population Growth and Economic Development, Committee on Population, Commission on Behavioral and Social Sciences and Education, National Research Council. 1986. *Population Growth and Economic Development: Policy Questions*. Washington, DC: National Academy Press.

World Bank. 1985. *China: Long-term Development Issues and Options*. Baltimore, MD: Johns Hopkins University Press.

Wren, Christopher S. 1982. "China's birth goals meet regional resistance," *New York Times* (15 May): 1, 7.

Wu Boyi (ed.). 2003. *Family Education of the Single Child*. Beijing: China Population Press. [In Chinese]

Wu Cangping. 1989. "Quantity and quality of China's rural population in connection with industrial restructuring," *China's Rural Economy* 2: 15–19. [In Chinese]

WuDunn, Sheryl. 1991a. "For China, it's the year of the spoiled child," *New York Times* (17 February): 10.

————. 1991b. "China's castaway babies: Cruel practice lives on," *New York Times* (26 February).

————. 1991c. "Changsha journal: In China's cities, the busybodies are organized," *New York Times* (13 March).

————. 1991d. "China, with ever more to feed, pushes anew for small families," *New York Times* (16 June): 1, 10.

Xiao Yang, Hu Yukun, Bai LiJun, and Jiang Xiuhua. 1995. "Determinants of unwanted pregnancy and abortion in Beijing, China," *Reproductive Health Matters* 5 (May): 95–102.

Xiao, Zhengqin. 1999. *The Think Tank of Premier Zhu Rongji*. N.p.: Pacific Century Press. [In Chinese]

Xie Zhenming. 2000. "Population policy and the family-planning programme," in Peng and Guo (eds.), pp. 51–63.

Xie Zhenming, Gu Baochang, and Karen Hardee. 2000. *Family Planning and Women's Lives in Three Provinces of the People's Republic of China.* Beijing: China Population Information and Research Center and Washington, D.C.: The Futures Group Intntl. [Published in China as Xie Zhenming (ed.). 2000. *Birth Planning and Women's Lives.* Beijing: China Population Press. (In Chinese)]

Yan Zheng. 1983. "Sex ratio of China's newborns normal," *Beijing Review* 26,18 (9 May): 9, 13.

Yan, Yunxiang. 1997. "McDonald's in Beijing: The localization of Americana," in Watson (ed.), pp. 39–76.

———. 2003. *Private Life Under Socialism: Love, Intimacy, and Family Change in a Chinese Village, 1949–1999.* Stanford, CA: Stanford University Press.

Yang, Dali L. 1999. "Economic crisis and market transition in the 1990s," in Winckler (ed.), 151–177.

———. 2004. "Economic transformation and state rebuilding in China," in Naughton and Yang (eds.), pp. 120–145.

Yang Kuixue, Liang Jimin, and Zhang Fan. 2001. *Overview of Main Events in China Population and Birth Planning.* Beijing: China Population Press. [Cited as ME]

Yang, Mayfair Mei-hui. 1989. "The gift economy and state power in China," *Comparative Studies in Society and History* 31,1 (January): 25–54.

———(ed.). 1999a. *Spaces of Their Own: Women's Public Sphere in Transnational China.* Minneapolis: University of Minnesota Press.

———. 1999b. "From gender erasure to gender difference: State feminism, consumer sexuality, and women's public sphere in China," in Yang (ed.), pp. 35–67.

Yang, Zhong. 2003. *Local Government and Politics in China.* Armonk, NY: M. E. Sharpe.

YB [China Birth Planning Yearbook]. State Birth Planning Commission. *China Birth Planning Yearbook.* Beijing: State Birth Planning Commission or China Population Press. [In Chinese. Annual since 1986. Currently compiled for the SPBPC by the CPIRC. Cited in the text as YB plus two numbers giving the year—e.g., YB02 for Yearbook 2002.]

Yu Meiyu, and Rosemary Sarri. 1997. "Women's health status and gender inequality in China," *Social Science and Medicine* 45,12 (December): 1885–1898.

Yu Xuejun. 1999. "The population problem is the crux of sustainable development," in *YB 1999,* pp. 248–252. [In Chinese]

———. 2003. "Demographic transition and strategic opportunity in China," in *YB 2003,* pp. 362–366. [In Chinese]

Yu Xuejun, Lu Jiehua, Li Jianxing, Chen Gong, and Chu Junjiang. 2000a. "Population and birth planning is a prerequisite for the development of western China," in *YB 2000,* pp. 197–202. [In Chinese]

Yu Xuejun, Chen Wei, Li Jianxing, Lu Jiehua, Sheng Lang, and Lin Xiaohong. 2000b. "A study of population problems under low-level fertility in China," in *YB 2000,* pp. 204–211. [In Chinese]

Yu Xuejun, Lu Jiehua, and Liu Hongyan. 2001. "On the theory and practice of comprehensive reform of birth planning," in *YB 2001,* pp. 233–238. [In Chinese]

Yuan, Jianhua, and G. William Skinner. 2000. "Shaping the gender configuration of offspring sets: The spatial patterning of reproductive strategizing in contemporary China." Paper presented at the annual meeting of the Association for Asian Studies. San Diego, 9–12 March.

Yuan Xin. 2000. "Demographic impact of China's high sex ratio at birth," in Jiang (ed.), pp. 73–80. [In Chinese]

Zeng Yi. 1989. "Is the Chinese family planning program 'tightening up'?" *Population and Development Review* 15,2 (June): 333–337.

Zeng Yi, Tu Ping, Gu Baochang, Xu Yi, Li Baohua, and Li Yongping. 1993. "Causes and implications of the recent increase in the reported sex ratio at birth in China," *Population and Development Review* 19,2 (June): 283–302.

Zeng Yi, James W. Vaupel, Xiao Zhenyu, Zhang Chunyuan, and Liu Yuzhi. 2002. "Sociodemographic and health profiles of the oldest old in China," *Population and Development Review* 28,2 (June): 251–274.

Zhang Guangyu. 2004. *China's Far Below Replacement Level Fertility: A Reality or Illusion Arising from Underreporting of Births?* Ph.D. diss., Dept. Demography, Australian National University.

Zhang Hanxiang, Huang Qihai, and Yang Wujun. 1997. "Explore comprehensive solution to China's population problem: New task in China's family planning under socialist market economic conditions," *People's Daily* (12 September), translated in FBIS 97-287 (14 Oct 97).

Zhang Hong. 2001. "Guest editor's introduction: Eldercare issues in contemporary China, Part I," *Chinese Sociology and Anthropology* 34,1 (Fall): 3–25.

———. 2003. "Bracing for an uncertain future: New coping strategies of rural parents under China's one-child policy—A case study from a Hubei village." Paper presented at Fairbank Center for East Asian Studies, 21 February.

———. 2004. "'Living alone' and the rural elderly: Strategy and agency in post-Mao rural China," in Ikels (ed.), pp. 63–87.

Zhang Huaiyu. 1982. "New problems in the control of population in the rural areas brought about by implementation of agricultural production responsibility systems," *Population Research* 1 (January): 31–34. [In Chinese]

Zhang, Li. 2001. *Strangers in the City: Reconfigurations of Space, Power, and Social Networks Within China's Floating Population*. Stanford, CA: Stanford University Press.

Zhang, Longxi. 1998. *Mighty Opposites: From Dichotomies to Differences in the Comparative Study of China*. Stanford, CA: Stanford University Press.

Zhang, Wei-guo. 1999. "Implementation of state family planning programmes in a northern Chinese village," *China Quarterly* 157 (March): 202–230.

Zhang, Weiguo. 2002. *Economic Reforms and Fertility Behavior: A Study of a North China Village*. London, UK: Taylor and Francis.

Zhang Zhen. 2001. "Mediating time: The 'rice bowl of youth' in fin de siecle urban China," in Arjun Appadurai (ed.), *Globalization*. Durham, NC: Duke University Press, pp. 131–154.

Zhao Liren, and Zhu Chuzhu. 1983. "A preliminary inquiry into the problem of second births outside the plan," *Population Research* 3 (May): 36–39. [In Chinese]

Zhao Yang. 2000. "State, children, and the Wahaha Group of Hangzhou," in Jing Jun (ed.), pp. 185–198.

Zhao Yilu. 2003. "A prodigy, a piano, hardship, stardom," *New York Times* (2 September): C1, 5.

Zhao Ziyang. 1982/1992. "The control over the growth of the population is something to which the entire society must pay great attention," in White (ed.), pp. 57–58.

Zheng, Shiping. 1997. *Party vs. State in Post-1949 China: The Institutional Dilemma.* New York: Cambridge University Press.

Zheng, Yongnian. 2004. *Globalization and State Transformation in China.* New York: Cambridge University Press.

Zhongguo Tongxun She. 1989a. "Couples with more than one child seek shelter along borders of Hunan, Hubei, Sichuan, and Guizhou," Hong Kong broadcast (20 January), in JPRS-CAR-89-014 (15 February): 44–45.

———. 1989b. "Phenomenon of discarding baby girls becomes serious in Fujian," Hong Kong broadcast (22 March), in FBIS-CHI-89-056 (24 March): 61.

Zhou, Kate Xiao. 1996. *How the Farmers Changed China: Power of the People.* Boulder: Westview.

Zhou Wei-jin, Gao Er-sheng, Yang Yao-qing, Qin Fei, and Tang Wei. 1999. "Induced abortion and the outcome of subsequent pregnancy in China: Client and provider perspectives," in Mundigo and Indriso (eds.), pp. 228–244.

Zhu, Chuzhu, Li Shuzhuo, Qiu Changrong, Hu Ping, and Jin Anrong. 1997. *The Dual Effects of the Family Planning Program on Chinese Women.* Xi'an: Xi'an Jiaotong University Press. [In English and Chinese]

Zhu Tianyin. 1999. *Chen Yun and Ma Yinchu.* Beijing: Cultural Press. [In Chinese]

Zhuang, Ping. 1993. "On the social phenomenon of trafficking in women in China," *Chinese Education and Society* 26,3: 33–50.